HAVING THOUGHT

HAVING THOUGHT

Essays in the metaphysics of mind

JOHN HAUGELAND

HARVARD UNIVERSITY PRESS

Cambridge, Massachusetts and London, England 1998

Library of Congress Cataloging-in-Publication Data

Haugeland, John, 1945–
    Having thought : essays in the metaphysics of mind / John Haugeland.
        p.   cm.
    Includes bibliographical references and index.
    ISBN 0-674-38233-1 (alk. paper)
    1. Philosophy of mind.   I. Title.
BD418.3.H38   1998
128'.2—dc21   97–44542

Book design and typesetting by John Haugeland;
body set in Adobe Jenson 12 on 13 by 25.

Should ever one see more deeply than others,
it's for being stood on the shoulders by giants.

Contents

Toward a New Existentialism   1

Mind

1 The Nature and Plausibility of Cognitivism   9
2 Understanding Natural Language   47
3 Hume on Personal Identity   63

Matter

4 Analog and Analog   75
5 Weak Supervenience   89
6 Ontological Supervenience   109

Meaning

7 The Intentionality All-Stars   127
8 Representational Genera   171
9 Mind Embodied and Embedded   207

Truth

10 Objective Perception   241
11 Pattern and Being   267
12 Understanding: Dennett and Searle   291
13 Truth and Rule-Following   305

Acknowledgments   363
Bibliography   367
Index   379

Having Thought

Toward a New Existentialism

UNDERSTANDING—MAKING SENSE OF THINGS—is the mark of the mental. This is not to deny that intentionality, rationality, objective knowledge, or self-consciousness might also be marks of the mental, but only to put the emphasis more nearly where it belongs. For, in my view, each of these latter, properly understood, presupposes understanding and is impossible without it. Understanding is always "of" something—objects, in a broad sense—but this of-ness is not the same as that of beliefs and desires. Thus, understanding is not the same as knowledge, a special kind of knowledge, or even a complex structure or totality of knowledge. Rather, understanding is a fundamentally distinct phenomenon, without which there could be no knowledge or mind at all. It needs, therefore, a different discussion— a discussion which, as it seems to me, has been missing in philosophy.

Understanding is the mark of the human. This is a better way to make the point, and for two reasons. On the one hand, understanding is *not* exclusively *mental* but is essentially corporeal and worldly as well; but, on the other, it *is* exclusively (and universally) *human*. Accordingly, intentionality, rationality, objective knowledge, and self-consciousness, properly understood, are likewise exclusively human. By 'human', I don't mean specific to homo sapiens. Humanity is not a zoological classification, but a more recent social and historical phenomenon—one which happens, however, so far as we know, to be limited to homo sapiens.

It is, of course, tendentious to deny intentionality and rationality to other mammals (never mind to prehistoric homo sapiens). That there is a difference in kind, not merely in degree, between the "cognitive" capacities of people and those of other mammals strikes me as so obvious as to need no argument; and I will offer none. No doubt, there are senses in which many animals can be said to "know", "want", and even "understand" things around them; but these are not the same as the senses in which people can be said to know, want, and understand things. Classing these uncritically together is as great an obstacle to insight as was classing whales with fish or the sun with the planets. Disputing the terms in which to express this is pointless.

More interesting is the question of *what* distinguishes people from non-people: what—if anything—is the root or essence of their distinctiveness. Many answers have been offered, from being made in God's image, or having rational or immortal souls, to the capacity for language, culture, and/or free recognition of normative constraints. In my view, the last of these comes closest—indeed, is exactly right, given a certain reading of "free recognition". Again, however, I do not undertake to defend this alternative against others, but at most to begin to articulate it.

Existential commitment is the mark of the human. This is an even better way to make the basic point, for, as it seems to me, human understanding is itself made possible by the distinctive sort of commitment that I call *existential*. It is the capacity for this sort of commitment that I am inclined to think is relatively recent—almost certainly more recent than language, and perhaps more recent than cities and writing. Like city-building and writing, the possibility of existential commitment is part of a cultural heritage (not just a biological or "natural" capacity). But, though and as culturally born and harbored, it is precisely a capacity for *individual* freedom: the freedom, namely, to take responsibility for the norms and skills in terms of which one copes with things. The ability to take such responsibility, to *commit*, is, as I attempt to show, the condition of the possibility of understanding, hence of knowing, objects.

These ideas are not new. They are announced, if not emphasized, in Kuhn (1962/70), and developed further, though rather differently, by Heidegger (1927/62). What I mean by 'existential commitment' is closely related, so I believe, to what Heidegger meant by 'authentic care', and also (albeit less closely) to what Kierkegaard meant by 'faith' and Nietzsche by 'autonomy'. A philosophy of mind and of science in which these essentially human capacities are restored to center stage is what I mean by "a new existentialism". But the point is not limited to intellectual pursuits. The general form of free human commitment—or care or faith—is love. Thus, best of all:

Love is the mark of the human.

The thirteen essays collected here, spanning some two decades, are all about understanding and intelligibility in one way or another, often several. They are arranged, roughly by topic, under four heads: Mind, Matter, Meaning, and Truth. As it turns out, this arrangement is also roughly chronological.

Under the first head, Mind, stand three essays from the late seventies, two about cognitive science (or artificial intelligence) and one about Hume. "The Nature and Plausibility of Cognitivism" (1978) is concerned with understanding in two complementary ways. How, on the one hand, can the mind itself be understood scientifically—in particular, what is the structure of the scientific understanding sought in cognitive science? And how, on the other hand, could a mind, so understood, itself be an understander? The main conclusions (which I still take to be basically correct, even if, in retrospect, awkwardly developed) are: first, that, though the character of the explanatory grasp sought in cognitive science is scientifically unprecedented, it is nevertheless perfectly legitimate; but, second, that the systems so intelligible are themselves incapable of understanding anything.

"Understanding Natural Language" (1979) pursues the latter theme, arguing that, even in the special case of understanding prose—a case particularly congenial to AI—no system lacking a sense of *itself* as "somebody" with a complete life of its own (and about which it particularly cares) can possibly be adequate as a model of human understanding. I call this cared-about wholeness *existential* holism", and offer a number of examples to illustrate its importance to ordinary language ability.

"Hume on Personal Identity" (~1977), the oldest and shortest essay in the volume, is also about the wholeness (or unity) of the self, but in the limited context of an exegesis of Hume's recantation of his own earlier account in the appendix to the *Treatise*.

The essays under the second head, Matter, address putative constraints on the *intelligibility* of mind in nature—particularly in its relation to the material or physical. "Analog and Analog" (1981) considers and rejects the too-common thesis that any analog system (for instance, a brain) can be digitally simulated to any desired degree of precision. The principal contribution is an analysis of the notions of digital and (especially) analog devices, in terms of which the thesis can so much as be responsibly confronted.

"Weak Supervenience" (1982) challenges that version of supervenience-based materialism that is equivalent to token identity theory, and proposes a substitute "weaker" version (now usually called "global supervenience"). The paper first rebuts Davidson's alleged proof of the token identity of mental with physical events; then shows that weak supervenience does not entail token identities; and, finally, presents some examples meant to suggest that token identity theory is in fact rather implausible.

"Ontological Supervenience" (1984) extends that implausibility argument (in a somewhat irreverent tone) by articulating and undermining a handful of seldom-explicitly-stated "intuitive" considerations that might seem to support a materialist identity theory.

Under the third head, MEANING, the chapters are at first glance more diverse; but they are all concerned with that relationship, whatever it may be, between us and the world, in terms of which we can be said to have minds and be intelligent at all. "The Intentionality All-Stars" (1990) uses the various positions on a baseball team as a whimsical metaphor to sort and relate the most common contemporary approaches to the old problem of intentionality. Three positions are examined and contrasted in particular detail: (i) the idea that intentionality resides primarily in language-like internal representations, in virtue of the processes that use and modify them; (ii) the view that intentionality resides primarily in situated agents, in virtue of the patterns of interactions between such agents and their environments; and (iii) the suggestion that intentionality resides primarily in the social practices of a community, in virtue of the instituted norms sustaining and governing those practices.

At the time of that writing (as late as 1988), I attributed this third suggestion to Heidegger, Dewey, Sellars, and Brandom (among others); and I cautiously endorsed it myself. It now seems to me that the attribution to Heidegger (at least) was quite mistaken; and, what's more, my own view is now significantly changed (though I still think mine and Heidegger's are a lot alike).* There's no denying that social institution and its norms have been critical to the emergence and maintenance of human culture; and, so, to that extent, they have also been prerequisite to what I now regard as essential to genuine intentionality: human understanding and commitment. (There is, to be

---

* In my "Heidegger on Being a Person" (1982), on which the relevant section of the All-Stars was originally based, I attributed to Heidegger and tacitly endorsed the thesis or "slogan": *All constitution is institution.* (18) I now repudiate both the attribution and the endorsement; Brandom, however, still embraces the idea.

sure, an intentionality-*like* phenomenon for which social norms alone are sufficient, much as there is one for which biological-functional norms suffice.) But existential commitment is crucially *not* social; and, as such, it makes possible a kind of normativity that goes beyond anything merely instituted. (See especially chapter 13 below.)

"Representational Genera" (1989), perhaps the most disheveled piece in the volume, undertakes to distinguish qualitatively different *kinds* of representation—not just species, but genera—on the basis of the characteristic structure of what they represent. The motive for the project, at best partially realized, is to ask and determine what might be distinctive of so-called distributed representations (the kind that, apparently, would be easiest to implement in networks of neurons). Along the way, however, a lot of effort is expended in setting up an approach to the problem, and illustrating it in terms of the more familiar cases of symbolic and pictorial representations.

"Mind Embodied and Embedded" (1995) argues, from principles of intelligibility drawn from systems theory, that the customary divisions between mind and body and between mind and world may be misplaced, in a way that more hinders insight than promotes it. The suggestion is that trying to understand the structure and functions underlying intelligence in terms of interactions across mind/world and mind/body "interfaces" might be like trying to understand the operation of an electronic circuit in terms of divisions that arbitrarily cut across its *electronic* components. That is, mind, body, and world might not be the right "components" in terms of which to understand the operations of intelligence. Meaning may be as much a corporeal and worldly phenomenon as it is "mental".

The four essays under the fourth head, TRUTH, have more in common than do those under any of the earlier heads. All four are concerned with the possibility of *objectivity*, and they all approach it in terms of an idea of *constitution* grounded in commitment. "Objective Perception" (1996—though written several years earlier) argues that, in order to specify the object of *human* perception—a kind of objectivity not available to animals—the object itself must be constituted in terms of constitutive standards to which the perceiver is antecedently committed. It is also argued that such commitment does not (at least not in principle) require language.

"Pattern and Being" (1993) brings that same point about constitution to bear on Dennett's "mild realism", as propounded in his "Real Patterns" (1991), arguing that his central discussion of patterns is confused unless a systematic distinction is drawn between two different levels of patterns, both of which are required for the reality (or being) of entities, in the sense he intends. Once that distinction is in place, moreover, his trademark notion of a "stance" can be made considerably clearer, and the intentional stance, in particular, can be divided into two distinct versions: a weaker one for animals and computers, and a stronger one for people—only the latter of which involves understanding, and thus has properly to do with intentionality.

"Understanding: Dennett and Searle" (1994) undertakes the unlikely task of reconciling Dennett and Searle on the prerequisites for genuine intentionality, by agreeing with each on a number of his most cherished views, while disagreeing with each (sometimes both) about a few points that strike me crucial. The pivotal issue is *understanding* (as distinct from mere knowing or believing), which, as I read them, neither Dennett nor Searle seriously addresses, and, without which, neither of their accounts of intentionality can be adequate. In the course of the discussion, I defend a sort of compromise on the disputed cases of animals and AI systems, by assigning them together to a new category—systems with *ersatz* intentionality—thereby preserving the best intuitions on both sides.

"Truth and Rule-Following" (new in this volume) is the longest and most difficult chapter. The aim is to spell out more thoroughly the fundamental ideas of constitution, commitment, and objective understanding introduced in the preceding three chapters, and to show how they enable a new account of truth in terms of beholdenness to objects. The principal innovations are an explicit distinction between norms of proper performance (such as might be socially instituted) and those of objective correctness, and the concept of an excluded zone—which shows for the first time how empirical beholdenness is concretely possible. Interesting corollaries include: (i) a distinctive exposition of the interdependence of objectivity with subjectivity, via the free commitment to standards that grounds objective constraints; (ii) an alternative to coherence theories of truth that are based on the so-called principle of charity; and thus (iii) a potential rehabilitation of the notion of disparate conceptual schemes—or, as it is better to say, of "constituted domains of objects".

The basic Kantian/Heideggerian conclusion can be summed up this way: the constituted objective world and the free constituting subject are intelligible only as two sides of one coin.

Mind

CHAPTER ONE

The Nature and Plausibility of Cognitivism

Cognitivism in psychology and philosophy is roughly the position that intelligent behavior can be explained (only) by appeal to internal "cognitive processes"—that is, rational thought in a broad sense. Sections 1 to 5 attempt to explicate in detail the nature of the scientific enterprise that this intuition has inspired. That enterprise is distinctive in at least three ways: it relies on a style of explanation which is different from that of mathematical physics, in such a way that it is not basically concerned with quantitative equational laws; the states and processes with which it deals are interpreted, in the sense that they are regarded as meaningful or representational; and it is not committed to reductionism, but is open to reduction in a form different from that encountered in other sciences. Spelling these points out makes it clear that the cognitivist study of the mind can be rigorous and empirical, despite its unprecedented theoretical form. The philosophical explication has another advantage as well: it provides a much needed framework for articulating questions about whether the cognitivist approach is right or wrong. The last three sections take that advantage of the account, and address several such questions, pro and con.

1 SYSTEMATIC EXPLANATION

From time to time, the ills of psychology are laid to a misguided effort to emulate physics and chemistry. Whether the study of people is inherently "humanistic" and "soft" (Hudson 1972), or whether states described in terms of their significance necessarily escape the net of physical law (Davidson 1970/80, 1973/80), the implication is that psychology cannot live up to the standards of rigorous science, and perhaps cannot be a science at all. But science itself often leaves behind efforts to say what it can and cannot be. The cognitive approach to psychology offers, I think, a science of a distinctive form, and thereby sidesteps many philosophical objections—including those born of a dazzled preoccupation with physics. In my first five sections I will try to characterize that form.

Science in general is an endeavor to understand what occurs in the world; hence explanation, which is essentially a means to understanding, has a pivotal importance. Scientific explanations differ from common sense explanations at least in being more explicit, more precise, more general, and more deliberately integrated with one another. Without attempting a full analysis, we can notice several broad characteristics which all scientific explanations share. They depend on specifying a range of features which are exhibited in, or definable for, a variety of concrete situations. They depend on knowing or hypothesizing certain regularities or relationships which always obtain in situations exhibiting the specified features. And they depend on our being able to see (understand), for particular cases, that since the specified features are deployed together in way X, the known regularities or relationships guarantee that Y. We then say that Y has been *explained* through an appeal to (or in terms of) the general regularities and the particular deployment of the features. The regularities and deployment appealed to have been presupposed by the explanation, and not themselves explained—though either might be explained, in turn, through appeal to further presuppositions.

Philosophers have coined the term *deductive-nomological* for explanations in which the presupposed regularities are formulated as laws (Greek: *nomos*), and for which the guarantee that Y will occur is formulated as a deductive argument from the laws plus statements describing the deployment X. (Hempel and Oppenheim 1949) It can be maintained that all scientific explanations are deductive-nomological, though in many cases that requires a counterintuitive strain on the notion of "law". So to avoid confusion I will introduce some more restricted terminology, and at the same time illustrate several different ways in which the foregoing schematic remarks get fleshed out.

The most familiar scientific explanations come from classical mechanics. The situational features on which they depend include masses, inertial moments, distances, angles, durations, velocities, energies, and so on—all of which are quantitative, variable magnitudes.

The known regularities or relationships are expressed as equations (algebraic, vectorial, differential, or whatever) relating the values of various variables in any given situation: $F = ma = dp/dt$, for instance. Usually some of the equations are designated laws and the others definitions, but there's a well known trade-off in which are which. Equations are conveniently manipulable and combinable in ways that preserve equality; that is, other equations can be mathematically derived from them. The standard form of an explanation in mechanics is such a derivation, given specified deployments of masses, forces, and what have you. (See Newton's derivations of Kepler's laws.) It is the derived equational relationships which are explained (or sometimes the actual values of some of the variables so related, determined by plugging in the known values of others).

I use *derivational-nomological* for this special case form of deductive-nomological explanation—where the distinction of the special case is that the presupposed regularities are expressed as equational relationships among quantitative variables, and the deduction is a mathematical derivation of other such equations (and then, perhaps, computing some of the values). Besides mechanics, fields as diverse as optics, thermodynamics, and macro-economics commonly involve derivational-nomological explanations.

But what is important here is that there are other forms or styles of explanation, even in advanced sciences. I will delineate (only) two such distinct styles, though I will not claim that the distinctions are sharp. The claim is rather that interesting differences can be characterized among prime examples, despite the fact that intermediate cases blur the boundaries. Only one of these further styles is relevant to cognitive psychology; I delineate them both because they are superficially similar, and easily confused. Thus explicitly distinguishing them permits a closer focus on the one we want. These distinctions are independent of anything peculiar to psychology, and I will draw them that way first, to keep separate issues as clear as possible

Imagine explaining to someone how a fiber-optics bundle can take any image that is projected on one end and transmit it to the other end. I think most people would come to understand the phenomenon, given the following points. (If I am right, then readers unfamiliar with fiber optics should nevertheless be able to follow the example.)

1 The bundles are composed of many long thin fibers, which are closely packed side by side, and arranged in such a way

that each one remains in the same position relative to the others along the whole length of the bundle;

2   each fiber is a leak-proof conduit for light—that is, whatever light goes in one end of a fiber comes out the other end of the same fiber;

3   a projected image can be regarded as an array of closely packed dots of light, differing in brightness and color; and

4   since each end of each fiber is like a dot, projecting an image on one end of the bundle will make the other end light up with dots of the same brightness and color in the same relative positions—thus preserving the image.

Clearly that was not a derivational-nomological explanation. One could, with effort, recast it as a logical deduction, but I think it would lose more perspicuity that it would gain. (Diagrams would help much more.) If we do not try to force it into a preconceived mold of scientific explanations, several distinctive aspects stand out as noteworthy. First, what is explained is a disposition or ability of a kind of object (compare Cummins 1975). Second, the explanation makes appeals (presuppositions) of two basic sorts: that the kind of object in question has a certain form or structure (compare Putnam 1975b, 1973), and that whatever is formed or structured in that way has certain dispositions or abilities. (The object is a bundle of "parallel" fibers, and each fiber is able to conduct light without leaking.) Third, any object structured in the presupposed way, out of things with the presupposed abilities, would have the overall ability being explained. That is, it doesn't matter how or why the fibers are arranged as they are, or how or why they conduct light; these are simply presupposed, and they are sufficient to explain the ability to transmit images.

I call explanations of this style *morphological*, where the distinguishing marks of the style are that an ability is explained through appeal to a specified structure and to specified abilities of whatever is so structured. (These specifications implicitly determine the "kind" of object to which the explanation applies.) In science, morphological explanations are often called "models" (which in this sense amount to specifications of structure), but that term is both too broad and too narrow for our purposes. Logicians have a different use for it, and few would call the fiber-optics account a model.

On the other hand, the account of how DNA can replicate itself *is* called a model—the double-helix model—and it is morphological. Simplistically put, the structure is two adjacent strands of sites, with each site uniquely mated to a complementary one in the other strand. And the sites have the ability to split up with their mates and latch onto an exactly similar new one, selected from a supply which happens to be floating around loose. This process starts at one end of the double strand, and by the time it reaches the other end there are two double strands, each an exact replica of the original. At the opposite extreme of sophistication, an explanation of how cups are able to hold coffee is also morphological. The specified structure is little more than shape, and the specified abilities of what is so structured amount to rigidity, insolubility, and the like.

Now consider a case that is subtly but importantly different: an explanation of how an automobile engine works. As with morphological explanations, this one appeals to a specified structure, and to specified abilities or dispositions of what is so structured. But in addition, and so important as to dominate the account, it requires specification of a complexly organized pattern of interdependent interactions. The various parts of an engine do many different things, so to speak "working together" or "cooperating" in an organized way, to produce an effect quite unlike what any of them could do alone.

I reserve the term *systematic* for explanations of this style, where the distinction from morphological explanation is the additional element of organized cooperative interaction. Strictly, it is again an ability or disposition which gets explained, but the ordinary expression "how it works" often gives a richer feel for what's at stake. A consequence of this definition is that objects with abilities that get systematically explained must be composed of distinct parts, because specifying interactions is crucial to the explanation, and interactions require distinct interactors. Let a *system* be any object with an ability that is explained systematically, and *functional components* be the distinct parts whose interactions are cited in the explanation. In a system, the specified structure is essentially the arrangement of functional components such that they will interact as specified; and the specified abilities of the components are almost entirely the abilities so to interact, in the environment created by their neighboring components. Note that what counts as a system, and as its functional components, is relative to what explanation is being offered. Other examples of systems (relative to the obvious explanations) are radios, common mouse-traps, and (disregarding some messiness) many portions of complex organisms.

Fiber-optics bundles and DNA molecules are deceptively similar to systems, because they have clearly distinct components, each of which contributes to the overall ability by performing its own little assigned "job". But the jobs are not interdependent; it is not through coopera-tive interaction that the image transmission or replication is achieved, but only an orderly summation of the two-cents' worth from each separate fiber or site. In an engine, the carburetor, distributor, spark plugs, and so forth, do not each deliver a portion of the engine's turning, in the way that each site or fiber contributes a portion of the replication or image. The job metaphor can be expanded to further illustrate the difference. In old-fashioned plantation harvesting, each laborer picked a portion of the crop (say one row), and when each was done, it was all done. But at a bureaucratic corporation like General Motors, comparatively few workers actually assemble automobiles; the others make parts, maintain the factories, come up with new designs, write paychecks, and so on. All of these tasks are prerequisite to continued production, but only indirectly, through a complex pat-tern of interdependencies. A system is like a bureaucratic corporation, with components playing many different roles, most contributing to the final outcome only indirectly, via the organized interactions.

I have described three different styles of explanation, each of which can be scientifically rigorous and respectable. They are all abstract or formal, in that they all abstract certain features and regularities from a variety of concrete situations, and then show how the resulting forms make certain properties or events intelligible in all such situations. But they differ notably in the nature of the abstract forms they specify, at least in clear cases. Only the derivational-nomological style puts an explicit emphasis on equations of the sort that we usually associate with scientific laws. But I shall claim that only the systematic style is directly relevant to cognitive psychology. The the charge of slavishly imitating mathematical physics does not apply to cognitivism, and it doesn't matter that quantitative equational laws of behavior seem to be few and far between. Many of the points I have made have been made before,[1] but no one, to my knowledge, has previously distin-guished morphological and systematic explanation. The importance of that distinction will emerge in section 4.

2 SYSTEMATIC REDUCTION

Traditional philosophical concerns for the unity of science and for the metaphysical doctrine of materialism (the doctrine that everything is "ultimately just" matter in motion) customarily lead to questions about scientific reduction. Psychological concepts and theories are prime targets for such questions because they are not, at first glance, materialistic. This is not the place for a full discussion of the problem of reduction, but my position about the nature of cognitivism will have several specific implications which should be pointed out. Some of these derive from the suggestion that cognitivist explanation is systematic, and those can be considered independently of issues peculiar to psychology.

An aspect common to all explanations discussed in the last section (indeed, to all explanations) is that they presuppose some things in the course of explaining others. More particularly, they presuppose certain specified general regularities, which are appealed to, but not themselves explained. But such regularities often can be explained, by appeal to others that are more basic. Such further explanation is *reduction*, though obviously it counts as reduction only relative to the explanations whose presupposed regularities are being explained. This is a fairly broad definition of reduction, and includes cases which aren't very exciting in form. Thus Newton's derivation of Kepler's laws counts as a reduction of Kepler's explanations of planetary positions.

A more famous reduction in classical physics, and one with a more interesting form, was that of thermodynamics to statistical mechanics. In outline, the values of the variables occurring in the equations of thermodynamic theory were found (or hypothesized) to correlate with quantities definable statistically in terms of the mechanical variables for groups of molecules. For example, the absolute temperature of a region was found to be proportional to the average kinetic energy of the molecules in that region. Such correlations are expressed in specific equations called "bridge equations". It then turned out that the laws of thermodynamics could be mathematically derived from the laws of mechanics, some plausible statistical assumptions, and these bridge equations. The effect was to explain the regularities which were presupposed by thermodynamic explanations—in other words, to reduce thermodynamics.

Reductive explanations which explain the equational laws presupposed by derivational-nomological explanations I call *nomological reductions.* Note that the definition refers to the style of explanation being reduced, not to the style of the reducing explanation. The reduction of thermodynamics is often cited as a paradigm of scientific reduction, as if all others should have a similar structure. But a moment's reflection shows that this structure only makes sense if the explanation being reduced in derivational-nomological; otherwise there would be no equational laws to derive, and probably no quantitative variables to occur in bridge equations.

The regularities presupposed by morphological and systematic explanations are mainly the specified dispositions or abilities of whatever is structured in the specified way. Hence, *morphological* and *systematic reductions* (which are pretty similar) are explanations of those abilities. Such reducing explanations can themselves be of various styles. Thus an explanation of how thin glass fibers can be light conduits would be, I think, borderline between morphological and derivational-nomological. But the explanation of how DNA sites can do the things appealed to in the replication explanation is fairly complex and, for all I know, systematic.

In explaining a system, almost all the abilities presupposed are abilities of individual components to interact with certain neighboring components in specified ways. Since intricate, interdependent organization is the hallmark of systems, the abilities demanded of individual components are often enough themselves rather sophisticated and specialized. Conversely, since systems typically have abilities strikingly different from those of any of their separate components, systematic organization is a common source of sophisticated and specialized abilities. These considerations together suggest that very elaborate systems could be expected to have smaller systems as functional components. And frequently they do—sometimes with numerous *levels* of systems within systems. For example, the distributor system of a car is a component in the (larger) ignition system, which, in turn, is a component in the complete engine system. Such a multilevel structure of nested systems is a *systematic hierarchy.* (See Simon 1969/81 for further discussion of hierarchical organization.)

So a systematic reduction of the highest system in a systematic hierarchy would involve systematic explanations of the specified interactive abilities of its functional components; and perhaps likewise for reductions of those, and so on. Only at the lowest level would systematic reductions be a different style of explanation (typically morphological; compare the explanation of a crankshaft or piston to that of a coffee cup). Since any scientific reduction is also a scientific explanation, it will explicitly presuppose certain regularities, which can be enquired after in turn. At any given time, however, some regularities will not be explainable. Modern wisdom has it that in the golden age these will include only the "fundamental" laws of physics, all others being reducible to them (perhaps through many stages of reduction). A sequence of reductions taking the presuppositions of an explanation all the way to physics is a *complete reduction*. A complete reduction of psychology is one of the traditional dreams of unified science.

A common misconception is that reductions supplant the explanations they reduce—that is, render them superfluous. This is not so. Consider the fiber optics reduction. There could be any number of different explanations for why different kinds of fibers can conduct light; thus glass threads, with variable index of refraction versus radius, would call for a different explanation than would hollow silver tubes. But those are irrelevant to the explanation of how the bundle transmits images. The latter takes light conduction in the fibers for granted and goes on to tell us something new. This something new would be lost if we settled exclusively for explanations of light conductivity; and on the other hand, it would not be lost (given the original morphological explanation) even if light conductivity were totally inexplicable. The two explanations are independent, even though one is of the presuppositions of the other (compare Putnam 1973).

The main point of this section has been that reductions, like explanations, are not all alike. Hence, the reduction of thermodynamics cannot serve as a universal paradigm, despite its ubiquitous use as an example. In particular, if I am right that cognitivist explanation is systematic, then any reduction of cognitivism would be systematic reduction (a point to be taken up further in section 5). This means at least that cognitivists are not interested in "psycho-physical bridge" equations (*pace* Fodor 1974/81), nor are they worried if none are possible (*pace* Davidson 1970/80).

3 INTENTIONAL INTERPRETATION

Because the study of the mind presents special scientific difficulties all of its own, I have so far mentioned psychology only incidentally. At the heart of these special difficulties is the problem of "significance" or "meaningfulness". Large portions of human behavior, preeminently linguistic behavior, are meaningful on the face of it, and a larger portion still is "rational" or "intelligent" in a way that involves significance at least indirectly. Yet meaningfulness is a slippery notion to pin down empirically, and there are conceptual difficulties in connecting "meanings" with the physical order of cause and effect. So serious are the problems that some investigators have even tried to study behavior entirely without regard to its significance—but their achievements have been narrow and limited. Cognitivism, on the other hand, gives the meanings of various states and processes a central importance. In this section, I will show how that can be compatible with the rigorous demands of empirical science.

I take my cue from the pioneering work of Quine (1960) and the refinements it has inspired.[2] His original concern was the translation of utterances in totally alien languages; since cognitivism's topic is broader, we generalize "translation" to "intentional interpretation" and "utterance" to "quasilinguistic representation". These must now be explicated.

Suppose we come upon an unfamiliar object—a "black box"—which someone tells us plays chess. What evidence would it take to convince us that the claim was empirically justified? It is neither necessary nor sufficient that it produce tokens of symbols in some standard chess notation (let alone, physically move the pieces of a chess set). It is not sufficient because the object might produce standard symbols but only in random order. And it is not necessary, because the object might play brilliant chess, but represent moves in some oddball notation.

So it is up to the person who claims that it plays chess to tell us how it represents moves. More particularly, we must know what in its behavior is to count as its making a move, and how to tell what move that is. Further, we must know what effects on it count as opponents' moves, and how to tell what moves they count as. Succinctly: we must know what its inputs and outputs are, and how to interpret them. Note that the inputs and outputs must be of some antecedently recognizable or identifiable types, and the interpretations of them must be according to some antecedently specifiable regular scheme; otherwise, we will suspect that the "interpretation" is being made up along the way, so as to make things come out right.

Of course, simply specifying the interpretation does not convince us that the object really plays chess. For that we would need to watch it play a few games—perhaps with several opponents, so we're sure there's no trick. What will count as success in this test? First, each output that the object produces must turn out, under the specified interpretation, to be a legal move for the board position as it stands at that time. Second, depending on how strictly we distinguish blundering from playing, the moves must be to some extent plausible (the hypothesis is only that it plays, not that it plays well). If the object passes this test in a sufficient variety of cases, we will be empirically convinced that it is indeed a chess player.

Further, when the object passes the test, the original interpretation scheme is shown to be not merely gratuitous. This is important because, in themselves, interpretation schemes are a dime a dozen. With a little ingenuity, one can stipulate all kinds of bizarre "meanings" for the behavior of all kinds of objects; and insofar as they are just stipulations, there can be no empirical argument about whether one is any better than another. How would you test, for example, the claims that producing marks shaped like 'Q–B2' represented (meant)

1 one (or another) particular chess move,

2 the solution of a logic problem, or

3 a scurrilous remark about the Queen of England and the Bishop of Canterbury?

Nothing observable about those marks in themselves favors one rendition over another. But one can further observe when and where the marks are produced, in relation to others produced by the same object, and in relation to the object's inputs. If those relationships form a pattern, such that under one interpretation the observed outputs consistently make reasonable sense in the context of the other observed inputs and outputs, while under another interpretation they don't, then the first interpretation scheme as a whole is observably "better" (more convincing) than the second. In our example, the pattern amounts to playing legal and plausible chess games, time after time. None (or at most very few) of the countless other conceivable interpretations of the same marks would make such sense of the observed pattern, so the given interpretation is empirically preferable.

The problem now is to generalize the points made about this specific example. I believe there are principled limits to how precisely such a generalization can be stated; but let us proceed with a few definitions, relying on intuitions and examples to keep them clear.

1 A set of types is *uniquely determinable* relative to a specified range of phenomena iff

   i) for almost every phenomenon in that range one can unequivocally determine whether it is a token (instance) of one of the types, and if so, which one; and

   ii) no phenomenon is ever a token of more than one type.[3]

2 An *articulated typology* (relative to a range of phenomena) is an ordered pair of uniquely determinable sets of types such that

   i) tokens of types in the second set (*complete types*) are composed of one or more tokens of types in the first (*simple types*); and

   ii) no token of a simple type ever actually occurs in the specified range of phenomena except as a component of a complete type.

For example, suppose a sheet of paper has a chess game recorded on it in standard notation (and has no other markings but doodles). Then relative to the marks on that page, the typographic characters used in chess notation are the simple types of an articulated typology, and the sequences of characters that would canonically represent moves (plus odds and ends) are the complete types. Note that definitions of complete types may include specifications of the order in which they are composed of simple types, and that in general this order need not be merely serial.

3 An *intentional interpretation* of an articulated typology is

   i) a regular general scheme for determining what any token of a complete type means or represents such that

   ii) the determination is made entirely in terms of

      (a) how it is composed of tokens of simple types; and

      (b) some stipulations about ("definitions of") the simple types.

4 A *quasilinguistic representation* is a token of a complete type from an intentionally interpreted articulated typology.[4]

Obviously, the identity of a quasilinguistic representation is relative to the specified typology and interpretation, and hence also to a specified range of phenomena. The complete types in the chess notation typology are quasilinguistic representations (of moves), relative to the chess interpretation.

I am unable to define either "mean" or "represent", nor say in general what kinds of stipulations about simple types (3-ii-b, earlier) are appropriate. In practice, however, it is not hard to give clear intentional interpretations; there are two common ways of doing it. The first is translation into some language or notation that we, the interpreters, already understand. Thus a manual might be provided for translating some strange chess notation into the standard one. The second is giving an "intended interpretation", in roughly the logicians' sense. Thus, a function can be defined from a subset of the simple types onto some domain—say, chess pieces and board squares; then the meanings of tokens of complete types (for example, what moves they represent) are specified recursively in terms of this function, plus the roles of other simple types (such as punctuation) characterized implicitly by the recursion.

Definitions 1 to 4 were all preparatory for the following:

5   An object is interpreted as an *intentional black box* (an IBB) just in case

i) an intentionally interpreted articulated typology is specified relative to the causal influences of its environment on it—the resulting quasilinguistic representations being *inputs*;

ii) likewise for *outputs*, relative to its causal influences on its environment; and

iii) it is shown empirically that under the interpretations the actual outputs consistently make reasonable sense in the context (pattern) of actual prior inputs and other actual outputs.

One important complication with this should be spelled out explicitly. Since the inputs and outputs "make sense" in virtue of a *pattern* they exhibit—a pattern that is extended in time—an IBB interpretation can also attribute enduring intentional "states" (and changes therein) to an object. For instance, a blind chess player (person or machine) must keep track of, or "remember" the current position, updating it after each move; and any player will continuously "know" the rules, "desire" to win, and so on. In some cases, an input/output pattern can be so complicated that no sense can be made of it at all without attributing a rich (though slowly varying) "inner life" of beliefs and desires. It is important to realize, however, that this is "inner" only in the sense of an interpolation in the (external) input/output pattern—nothing is being said about the actual innards of the object.

Sometimes it will be convenient to use the term 'IBB' on the assumption that such an interpretation can be given, even though the specifics are not known. The chess-player example with which this section began is an IBB; so are adding machines, logic-problem solvers, automated disease diagnosticians, and (applying the definitions fairly flexibly) normal people.

There are three problems with this definition that need immediate comment. First, "making reasonable sense" under an interpretation is not defined—and I doubt that it can be. Again, however, it is seldom hard to recognize in practice. Often, explicit conditions can be stated for making sense about certain problem domains or subject matters; these I call *cogency conditions*. For the chess player, the cogency condition was outputting legal and plausible moves in the context created by the previous moves. For interpreting an object as an adding machine, the condition is giving correct sums of the inputs; for a medical diagnostician it is giving good diagnoses relative to the symptoms provided. For reasons beyond the scope of this discussion, I don't think any effort to articulate completely general cogency conditions can succeed (though various authors have tried, at least for interpreting creatures as language users[5]). But it doesn't matter much in actual field or laboratory work, because by and large everyone can agree on what does and doesn't make sense.

Second, if one is knee-jerk liberal about what makes reasonable sense, then all kinds of objects can be trivially interpreted as IBBS. Thus a flipped coin might be interpreted as a yes-no decision maker for complex issues tapped on it in Morse code.[6] I will assume that such cases can be ignored.

Third, and most serious, the requirement that inputs and outputs be quasilinguistic representations appears to rule out many perceptions and actions. In at least some cases, this problem can be handled indirectly. Suppose an alleged chess player used no notation at all, but had a TV camera aimed at the board and a mechanical arm which physically moved the pieces. The problem of showing that this device indeed plays chess is essentially the same as before. It must consistently make legal and plausible moves. This succeeds, I think, because we can give quasilinguistic descriptions of what it "looks" at and what it does, such that if they were the inputs and outputs, the object would count as an IBB. In such cases we can enlarge our interpretation and say that the object perceives and acts "under those descriptions" (sees that ..., intends that ..., and so on), and regard the descriptions as inputs and outputs. Where this strategy won't work, my definition won't apply.

In this section I have addressed the question how meaningfulness or significance can be dealt with empirically. In brief, the idea is that although meaningfulness is not an intrinsic property of behavior that can be observed or measured, it is a characteristic that can be attributed in an empirically justified interpretation, if the behavior is part of an overall pattern that makes sense (for instance, by satisfying specified cogency conditions). In effect, the *relationships* among the inputs and outputs are the only relevant observational data; their intrinsic properties are entirely beside the point, so long as the relationships obtain. But the fact that they have some characteristics or other, independent of the interpretation (that is, they are causal interactions with the environment), means that there is no mystery about how states with significance "connect" with the rest of nature (Davidson 1970). The upshot is that a psychological theory need not in principle ignore meaningfulness in order to maintain its credentials as empirical and scientific.

4 INFORMATION PROCESSING SYSTEMS

The last section showed only that there is an empirically legitimate way to talk about significances in scientific theories. It did not say anything about what kind of scientific account might deal with phenomena in terms of their meanings. To put it another way, we saw only how the notion of IBB could have empirical content, not how anything could be *explained*. Yet an IBB always manages to produce reasonable outputs, given its inputs; and that's a fairly remarkable ability, which cries out for explanation. There may be many ways to explain such an ability, but two in particular are relevant to cognitivism. One will be the subject of this section, and the other of the next.

If one can systematically explain how an IBB works, without "de-interpreting" it, it is an *information processing system* (an IPS). By "without de-interpreting", I mean explaining its input/output ability in terms of how it would be characterized under the intentional interpretation, regardless of whatever other descriptions might be available for the same input and output behavior. For example, if our chess player is an IPS, that means there is a systematic explanation of how it manages to come up with legal and plausible moves as such, regardless of how it manages to press certain type bars against paper, light certain lights, or do whatever it does that gets interpreted as those moves.

In a systematic explanation, the ability in question is understood as resulting from the organized, cooperative interactions of various distinct functional components, plus their separate abilities. Further, whatever result it is that the object is able to yield (in this case the IBB outputs), is typically delivered directly by some one or few of the functional components. Now, since we're not de-interpreting, those few components which directly deliver the outputs of the IPS must have among their presupposed abilities the ability to produce the outputs as interpreted. But if attributing this ability to those components is to be empirically defensible, then they must be IBBs themselves. Hence the effects on them by their functional neighbors in the system (the interactions appealed to in the explanation) must be their IBB inputs, which means that they too are dealt with as interpreted. But since these inputs are at the same time the effects delivered by other components, those other components must be able to deliver effects (outputs) under an interpretation. Consequently, they also— and by the same argument, all the functional components of an IPS— must be IBBs.

Moreover, all the interpretations of the component IBBs must be, in a sense, the same as that of the overall IBB (= the IPS). The sense is that they must all pertain to the same subject matter or problem. This actually follows from the preceding argument, but an example will make it obvious. Assuming that the chess playing IBB is an IPS, we would expect its component IBBs to generate possible moves, evaluate board positions, decide which lines of play to investigate further, or some such. These not only all have to do with chess, but in any given case they all have to do with the same partially finished game of chess. By contrast, components interpreted as generating football plays, evaluating jockeys, or deciding to pull trump could have no part in explaining how a chess player works.

Still, the sense in which the interpretations have to be the same is limited. First, of course, the types which get interpreted can vary throughout; they might be keyboard characters in one case, electric pulses in another, and so forth. More important, the internal "discourse" among component IBBS can be in a richer "vocabulary" than that used in the overall inputs and outputs. Thus, chess-player inputs and outputs include little more than announcements of actual moves, but the components might be engaged in setting goals, weighing options, deciding which pieces are especially valuable, and so on. Even so, they all still pertain to the chess game, which is the important point. (The importance will become clearer in section 5).

It is natural in a certain way to seek a systematic explanation of an IBB's input/output ability. Seeing this is to appreciate one of the essential motivations of cognitivism. The relevant ability of an IBB is to produce reasonable outputs relative to whatever inputs it happens to get from within a wide range of possibilities. In a broad sense of the term, we can think of the actual inputs as posing "problems", which the IBB is then able to solve. Now only certain outputs would count as reasonable solutions to any given problem, and those are the ones for which some kind of reasonable argument or rationale can be given. (Cogency conditions are typically spelled out as a relevant rationale for certain outputs as opposed to others, given the inputs.) An argument or rationale for a solution to a problem amounts to a decomposition of the problem into easier subproblems, plus an account of how all the subsolutions combine to yield a solution of the overall problem. (How "easy" the subproblems have to be is, of course, relative to the context in which the rationale is required.) The point is that the separate IBB components of the IPS can be regarded as solving the easier subproblems, and their interactions as providing the combination necessary for coming up with the overall solution. The interactions in general must be organized and "cooperative" (that is, systematic) because rational considerations and relationships generally "combine" in complexly interdependent and interlocking ways. (This is why the systematic/morphological distinction is important.)

So, the interacting components of an IPS "work out", in effect, an explicit rationale for whatever output they collectively produce. And that's the explanation for how they manage to come up with reasonable outputs; they, so to speak, "reason it through". This also is the fundamental ideal of cognitive psychology: intelligent behavior is to be explained by appeal to internal cognitive processes—meaning, essentially, processes interpretable as working out a rationale. Cognitivism, then, can be summed up in a slogan: the mind is to be understood as an information processing system.[7]

This suggestion rests on two innovative cornerstones, compared to older notions about what psychology should look like as a science. The first is that psychological explanation should be systematic, not derivational-nomological; hence, that psychology is not primarily interested in quantitative, equational laws, and that psychological theories will not look much like those in physics. The second is that intentional interpretation gives an empirically legitimate (testable) way of talking and theorizing about phenomena regarded as meaningful; hence, that psychology does not have to choose between the supposedly disreputable method of introspection, and a crippling confinement to purely behavioral description. Together they add up to an exciting and promising new approach to the study of the mind.

5 INTENTIONAL REDUCTION

The abilities of component IBBs are merely presupposed by an IPS explanation. That explanation can be systematically reduced—in the sense of section 2—by turning one's attention to explaining those component abilities. If it happens that the components are themselves IPSs, then reduction can proceed a step by appealing to the organized interactions and abilities of still smaller component IBBs, and so on. An extension of the argument in the last section shows that all the IBB components at all the levels in such a hierarchy must be interpreted as having the same subject matter; for example, all their inputs and outputs pertain to the same game of chess, or whatever.

Obviously, then, a complete reduction to physics (or electronics or physiology) would have to involve some further kind of step; that is, eventually the abilities of component IBBs would have to be explained in some other way than as IPSs. By definition, IPS explanation does not involve de-interpretation. Explanation of an IBB's input/output ability that does involve de-interpretation I call explanation by *instantiation*. We shall see that instantiation has two importantly distinct forms.

An object of the sort computer engineers call an 'and-gate' is a simple IBB. It has two or more input wires, and a complete input type is (for example) a distribution of positive and negative voltages among those wires. It has one output wire, and is constructed electronically to put a positive voltage in this wire if and only if all the input voltages are positive; otherwise it puts out a negative voltage. Now the cogency condition for a proposition conjoiner is that it give the truth-value 'true' if and only if all the conjoined propositions are true; otherwise it gives 'false'. Since this truth function for 'and' is isomorphic to the electrical behavior of the object (taking positive voltage as 'true' and negative as 'false'), the object can be interpreted as an and-gate.

But to explain how the object manages to satisfy the prescribed cogency conditions, one would not look for component IBBS interpretable as "reasoning the problem through". Rather, one would de-interpret and explain the electrical behavior in terms of the electric circuitry and components. The electrical circuit might well be a system, but it would not be an IPS. Since the first step of the explanation is de-interpretation, it is an explanation by instantiation; I call it *physical instantiation* because the remainder of it is expressed in physical terms.

Not all instantiations, however, are physical instantiations. For example, computer-based chess players are generally written in a programming language called LISP, in which the inputs and outputs of program components are interpreted as operations on complex lists. So interpreted, these components are IBBS, but their subject matter is not chess. What happens, however, is that the input/output constraints (cogency conditions) on the lowest level components in the chess related hierarchy are isomorphic to the constraints on IBBS built up in LISP.[8] Thus, the required abilities of bottom-level chess player components can be explained by de-interpreting (or re-interpreting) them as IBBS solving problems about list-structures—IBBS which can then be understood as IPSS working through the rationale for the LISP problem. This, too, is reduction by instantiation, but I call it *intentional instantiation*, because the redescribed ability is still an IBB ability, just about a different subject matter.

Actually, in a complete reduction of a fancy computer program, there can be several stages of intentional instantiation. Thus, LISP languages are generally written (compiled) in still more basic languages—say, ones in which the only IBB abilities are number-crunching and inequality testing (the conditional branch). The last intentional instantiation is in a primitive "machine language", so-called because that is the one which is finally reduced by physical instantiation. The real genius of computer science has been to design ever more sophisticated languages which can be compiled or intentionally instantiated in cruder existing languages. If it weren't for intentional instantiations, machines built of flip-flops and the like would hardly be candidates for artificial intelligence.

It is easy to confuse the maneuver of explaining an IBB by intentional instantiation with that of explaining it as an IPS. The essential difference is the re-interpretation—or, intuitively, the change in subject matter. Since I have already used "change of level" to describe the move from IPS to its separate components, I will use "change of *dimension*" to describe the move of de-/reinterpretation involved in an instantiation. One can think of the many dimensions in a sophisticated system as forming a hierarchy, but dimension hierarchies should not be confused with the earlier level hierarchies. There can be different level hierarchies on different dimensions, but they are orthogonal rather than sequential. That is, it's a mistake to think of the lowest level on one dimension as a higher level than the highest level on a lower dimension. Thus, an and-gate is not a higher level component than a disk memory; they are components on different dimensions, and hence incomparable as to level.

In this section, I have outlined what a reduction of cognitive psychology to the relevant physical dimension theory would look like. I have not argued that cognitivism is committed to such reducibility. It would be theoretically consistent to maintain that, at some bottom level, the presupposed IBB abilities were simply not explainable (much as physics cannot explain its fundamental laws). Nevertheless, I suspect that many investigators would strongly resist such a suggestion, and would feel their work was not done until the reduction was complete.

6 Fallacious supporting arguments

In sections 1 through 5, I have given a general characterization of the cognitivist approach to psychology, and its possible reduction. In so doing, I have shown how it is innovatively different from earlier approaches more captivated by the image of physics, and how it can be unimpeachably rigorous and empirical all the same. However, it seems to me that the eventual success of this program, for all its attractiveness, is still very much in doubt. In the remaining three sections, I hope to make clear my reasons for caution—taking as much advantage as possible from the explicit characterization just completed. I will begin in this section by pointing out the flaws in two seductive general arguments to the effect that some cognitivist theory or other *must* be right.

The first argument is directed more specifically at the systematicity cornerstone, though as we have seen, the two cornerstone innovations go hand in hand (see the end of section 4). It goes like this. We know that the nervous system is composed of numerous distinct and highly organized "functional components"—namely neurons; and (assuming materialism) there is every reason to believe that the human IBB is somehow instantiated in the nervous system. So, all that remains to be found are how the neurons are grouped into higher level components, how the first instantiation proceeds, how the lowest components on that dimension are grouped into higher components, what the next instantiation is, and so on. That is, we need only "build back up" the intentional and systematic reductions described in sections 2 and 5, until we reach the overall IBB. That's an enormous task, of course, but since we know there are organized components at the bottom, we know in principle it can be done.

Formally this argument is circular. The reductions mentioned in describing the "building back up" presuppose the very systematicity that the argument is supposed to prove. But the idea behind the reasoning is so attractive that it is tempting to think that the circularity is an artifact of the formulation, and that a better version could be found. To see that this is not so, we must expose in detail the real basis of the formal circularity.

As we observed in section 1, scientific explanation is essentially a route to understanding; and the understanding is achieved in part through specifying certain features and regularities that are common to the range of situations where that kind of explanation applies. The demands of rigor and explicitness that distinguish some explanations as scientific require that the features and regularities specified "encompass" or "encapsulate" every consideration that is relevant to understanding the phenomenon being explained. In a way, the explanatory insight derives precisely from the realization that these few specific features and regularities are all you need to know, in order to be sure that phenomenon Y will occur; everything else is extraneous. Thus, the beauty of Newton's mechanics is that a few quantitative magnitudes and equational laws encapsulate everything that is relevant to the motions of a great many bodies. For example, the colors, textures, personalities, and so on of the planets can all safely be ignored in predicting and understanding their positions as a function of time.

In a systematic explanation, a comparable encapsulation is achieved in the specification of a few determinate modes of interaction among a few distinct components with particular specified abilities. Indeed, finding interfaces among portions of an object, such that this kind of encapsulation is possible, is the fundamental principle of individuation of functional components—and hence a sine-qua-non of systematic explanation. For example, dividing the interior of a radio (or engine) into adjacent one-millimeter cubes would not be a decomposition into functional components; and the reason is exactly that the resulting "interfaces" would not yield any evidence of encapsulating what's relevant into a few highly specific interactions and abilities. By contrast, a resistor can be a functional component, because (almost) nothing about it matters except the way it resists the flow of electricity from one of its leads to the other. (Compare Simon 1969/81 on "partial decomposability"; and Marr 1977 on type-1 versus type-2 theories.)

So if neurons are to be functional components in a system, some specific few of their countless physical, chemical, and biological interactions must encapsulate all that is relevant to understanding whatever ability of that system is being explained. This is not at all guaranteed by the fact that cell membranes provide an anatomically conspicuous gerrymandering of the brain. More important, however, even if neurons were components in some system, that still would not guarantee the possibility of "building back up". Not every contiguous collection of components constitutes a single component in a higher-level system; consolidation into a single higher component requires a further encapsulation of what's relevant into a few specific abilities and interactions—usually different in kind from those of any of the smaller components. Thus the tuner, pre-amp, and power amp of a radio have very narrowly specified abilities and interactions, compared to those of some arbitrary connected collection of resistors, capacitors, and transistors. The bare existence of functionally organized neurons would not guarantee that such higher-level consolidations were possible. Moreover, this failure of a guarantee would occur again and again at every level on every dimension. There is no way to know whether these explanatory consolidations from below are possible without already knowing whether the corresponding systematic explanations and reductions from above are possible—which is just the original circularity.

The second argument I will refute starts from the top rather than the bottom and is directed primarily at the intentional interpretation cornerstone, with its associated idea of "working out the rationale". Formally this argument amounts to the challenge: What else could it be? But it is much more persuasive than that brazen rendition suggests. If one disregarded the intentional interpretation of any sophisticated IBB, it would be quite incredible to suggest that there was some elegant relation between the particular set of influences from the environment that we call inputs, and the particular set of influences on the environment that we call outputs. The relevant actual pattern can hardly even be described except in some way that is tantamount to specifying the cogency conditions which the object in fact meets. But since what we observe is that the object consistently meets these otherwise quite peculiar conditions, and since the conditions themselves are typically made explicit by spelling out some rationale, what else could explain the observations than that the object works the rationale out? How else would it happen to come upon those particular outputs time after time?

To show that a "what else could it be?" argument is inconclusive, one need only come up with a conceivably viable alternative. One need not make a case that the alternative is in fact more probable, just that it's viable. I will try to construct such an alternative, drawing on recent neurophysiological speculations about holographic arrangements and processes. Fairly detailed hypothetical models have been proposed for how holograms might be realized in neural structures; and there is some empirical evidence that some neurons behave in ways that would fit the models.[9]

Optical holograms are photographs of interference patterns, which look kind of like the surface of a pond that has just had a lot of pebbles thrown in it. But they have some interesting properties. First, they are prepared from the light bouncing off an ordinary object, and can subsequently be used to reconstruct a full three-dimensional image of that object. Second, the whole image can be reconstructed from any large enough portion of the hologram. (That is, there's no saying which portion of the hologram "encodes" which portion of the image.) Third, a number of objects can be separately recorded on the same hologram, and there's no saying which portion records which object. Fourth, if a hologram of an arbitrary scene is suitably illuminated with the light from a reference object, bright spots will appear indicating (virtually instantaneously) the presence and location of any occurrences of the reference object in the scene (and dimmer spots indicate "similar" objects). So some neurophysiological holographic encoding might account for a number of perplexing features of visual recall and recognition, including their speed, some of their invariances, and the fact that they are only slightly impaired by large lesions in relevant areas of the brain.

What matters to us is that a pattern-recognizer based on these principles would not (or need not) be an IPS. There are not distinct functional components whose relevant interactions are confined to intentionally interpreted articulated typologies. That is, there is nothing going on which can be regarded as "working out a rationale" with quasilinguistic representations. By contrast a typical computer-based pattern-recognizer is an IPS. Thus, searching for discontinuities in luminance gradients, proposing that they are edges, checking for connexity among proposed edges, hypothesizing invisible edges so as to complete coherent objects, and so on are all rational procedures relative to the "problem" of identifying objects.[10]

The neurophysiologists cited have rightly confined their speculations to recognition and recall processes, because there one at least has shreds of evidence to work with.[11] We, however, who are answering a "what-else-could-it-be?" argument, needn't be so circumspect.

Another interesting property of optical holograms is that if a hologram of two objects is illuminated with the light from one of them, an image of the other (absent) object appears. Thus such a hologram can be regarded as a kind of "associator" of (not ideas, but) visual patterns. So imagine a set of such associated patterns, in which the first member of each is a common important substructure in chess positions, and the other is one or two moves which are generally powerful or dangerous around such structures. It seems to me that a set-up like that could be a nearly instantaneous "plausible-move generator" for chess positions in general. In fact, it would mesh nicely with some of what is known about how human chess players perceive the board and their options.[12] Implementation of such a device by optical means might well be impossible; but it is worth pointing out how much more general the neural medium (potentially) is. In the first place, transforms other than the Fourier transform could be implemented just as easily—including, perhaps, "custom" transforms for particular problems. Second, n-dimensional transforms are easily possible. Third, since neurons are connected "point-to-point", even the analog of an ordinary hologram wouldn't have to be arrayed as a surface—

physically, the "dots" could be distributed *ad libitum*, making possible all kinds of mingling and interaction among distinct "images". I have no clear idea what difference any of this would make; but it seems likely that the differences could be substantial. And, after all, the capabilities of regular holograms would have been difficult to visualize not so long ago.

Again, the point is that no "plausible-move generator" based on principles anything like this speculation would be an IPS. Nothing in it would "reason through" the move and counter-move alternatives that rationalize any move it proposed. Yet a chess player is a paradigm of what the "what-else-could-it-be" argument should apply to. (It's no accident that chess players are the most common IPS example.) I therefore take that argument to be refuted. I am not envisioning, of course, that humans (chess players included) engage in no cognitive "reasoning a problem through"; introspection, for all its ills, is enough to scotch that. But cognitive psychology is exciting and important for the unobvious thesis that cognitive information processing can explain much more than deliberate cogitation and reasoning; and for that larger thesis, the argument considered is inconclusive.

This last observation should put the whole present section in perspective. All I claim is that a few commonplace assumptions will not suffice to demonstrate that cognitivism is the right approach to psychology. That should offend no one, since it only means that the position is not trivial and obvious—as clearly it isn't.

7 Potentially serious hurdles

In this section, I want to mention three issues which it seems to me may be serious hurdles for cognitivism—serious in the sense of being equally hard to duck or get over. They are: moods, skills, and understanding. I cannot prove that cognitivist accounts of these phenomena are impossible. My aim is rather to show that such accounts are going to be required if cognitivism is to succeed, and that it's dubious whether they will be possible.

7.1 Moods

I will try to illustrate the nature of the difficulty with moods by contrasting it with another, which is superficially similar, but more plausibly duckable. There is a long and tortured tradition in philosophy for distinguishing two kinds of mental phenomena: roughly, cognitive or intellectual states versus felt qualities or the purely sensuous given.[13] Paradigm "felt qualities" would be pains or mere awarenesses of present red (not categorized or conceptualized as such). Several recent articles have argued that such states have some kind of determinate immediate character which is independent of any interpretation and/or any role in a systematic organization.[14] It would follow that they do not accord with the cognitivist notion of a mental state or process.

But without even taking sides on the particular issue, I think we can see that it doesn't matter much to cognitivism—which is, after all, only a theory of cognitive states and processes. In other words, if felt qualities are fundamentally different, so be it; explaining them is somebody else's business. This amounts to a kind of "segregation" of psychological phenomena, along roughly traditional lines. Such segregation can be legitimate (not a fudge) given one important assumption. Segregated noncognitive states can be effective in determining intelligent behavior only insofar as they somehow generate quasilinguistic representations ("red there now", "left foot hurts") which can be accepted as *inputs* by the cognitive IPS. This assumption is plausible enough for felt qualities, and perhaps for some other states as well. I have in mind the much disputed mental images.[15] Since any cognitivist theory must include some mechanism for getting from retinal images to cognitive descriptions of what is seen, I don't see why that same mechanism couldn't also take inputs from some precognitive visual "tape recorder"—perhaps one with adjustments for orientation, size, and location. Then playbacks from the recorder would have whatever nondiscursive, image-y quality perception has, and cognitivism would be unruffled. Finally, it may even be that some emotions (such as gratitude and regret) can be accommodated with a standard elaboration of this same segregation strategy—roughly, by treating them as compound states, with a cognitive (representational, propositional) component, and a separate noncognitive (qualitative, feeling) component.

But I am much less sanguine about a similar segregation for moods. The difference is that moods are pervasive and all-encompassing in a way that felt qualities and images are not. The change from being cheerful to being melancholy is much more thorough and far-reaching than that from having a painless foot to having a foot that hurts. Not only does your foot seem different, but everything you encounter seems different. The whole world and everything in it, past, present, and future, becomes grayer, duller, less livable. Minor irritations and failings are more conspicuous and less remediable; ordinary things are no longer fun, lovely, or pleasing. If melancholy were an input representation ("melancholy here now") it would have to accompany and infect every other input, and transform the meanings of them all. But moods not only affect how things look, they affect how one thinks. What seems reasonable when you're cheerful seems foolish when you're melancholy, and vice versa. Likelihoods and improbabilities invert, as do what seems relevant to an issue and what seems beside the point.

Moods come upon us, but they are neither direct observations nor inferences. Many things affect our moods, but our moods also affect how things affect us; and in neither case is it quasilinguistic or rational. We do not state or believe our moods, or justify them on the basis of evidence or goals; they are just the way things are. In sum: moods permeate and affect all kinds of cognitive states and processes, and yet, on the face of it, they don't seem at all cognitive themselves. That suggests, at least until someone shows otherwise, that moods can neither be segregated from the explanation of cognition nor incorporated in a cognitivist explanation.

7.2 SKILLS

The second hurdle I want to mention concerns skills. I see three prima facie (not conclusive) reasons for doubting that the etiology of skillful behavior is cognitive. First, with rare exceptions, articulateness about a skill, no matter how detailed nor in what specialized quasilinguistic notation, is neither necessary nor sufficient for having it; it always takes practice, and often expert examples and talent ($\neq$ intelligence). Even a Rhodes scholar could not learn to play good ping pong just from listening to thousands of detailed lectures about it; and even a Rhodes scholar ping-pong champion might be hard pressed to give a single detailed lecture on the subject. Second, a person who is acquiring or upgrading a skill may deliberately and thoughtfully try to execute certain maneuvers, but the thought and deliberation cease at just about the time the maneuvers become skillful and "natural"; the expert doesn't have to think about it. Third, skillful activity is faster than thought. Not only do skilled typists and pianists not have to think about what they're doing with their fingers; they *can't*. If they turn their attention to their fingers, as a novice must, their performance slows down and becomes clumsy, rather like a novice's.

A cognitivist can explain these phenomena away by postulating some "unconscious" information processing which is somehow more efficient than, and immiscible with, that conscious thinking which is archetypically cognitive. But Dreyfus (1972/92, 106) asks an interesting pointed question about this ploy, in the special case of chess skills. It is known that intermediate, advanced and great chess players are alike in consciously considering on the order of a hundred plays in thinking out a move. They differ in their "skill in problem conception" (de Groot 1965)—that is, in preselecting which moves to think about. Now the rationales for these good preselections would be enormously long if they were spelled out (many thousands of plays). It's possible that players have some marvelously efficient unconscious information processor which works through these rationales; but if so, then why would anyone with such a splendid unconscious ever bother to deliberate consciously and tediously over a hundred plays? The implication is that the skillful preselection and the tedious cogitation differ not just in efficiency and consciousness, but in kind, and that neither could adequately substitute for the other. I think it would take powerful arguments (or prejudices) to outweigh this natural construal of the evidence—and only slightly less so in the case of skills in general.

But so what? If skillful behavior has to be explained in some non-cognitivist way—call it X (maybe something to do with holograms)—then why not employ the segregation strategy introduced above for felt qualities and images? I think the danger here is not that the segregation strategy wouldn't work, but that it might work too well. "Skill" is such a broad and versatile notion that all kinds of things might fall under it. For example, the ability to act appropriately and adroitly in various social situations is a sort of skill, as is the art of conversation, and even everyday pattern recognition; moreover, these are like our earlier examples in that, to whatever degree one has mastered the skill, one needn't think about it to exercise it. But if very many such things turned out to be explainable in way X, rather than as the abilities of an IPS, then cognitive psychology would narrow dramatically in scope and interest. In the worst case, little would remain to call "cognitive" except conscious deliberation and reasoning—and that's hardly news.

7.3 UNDERSTANDING

The third hurdle I want to raise for cognitivism is understanding; but this needs immediate qualification. In one sense, IPSs undoubtedly can understand, because computers programmed to be IPSs can do it. We could build a chess player for example, that "understands" entered moves in any of three notations. What that means is that it responds appropriately (sensibly) to inputs in any of those forms. This is the same sense in which existing programs "understand" selected English sentences about colored blocks,[16] airline reservations, and what not. Such usage is perfectly legitimate, but it's not all there is to understanding.

There is another notion of understanding, which, for convenience, I will call *insight* into why certain responses make sense, or are reasonable. As any teacher of arithmetic or logic knows, many students can learn the routines for getting the right answers, without the slightest insight into what's going on. And when original scientists struggle to find new and better theories, they grope for new insights into the phenomena, or new accounts that "make sense". Whether or not a new account, perhaps expressed in an unprecedented formulation, makes sense or is intelligible, is something which great scientists (and then their colleagues) can *just tell*. Of course, whether an account is scientifically acceptable also depends on how well it accords with observations; but that does not determine whether it makes sense in the first place—both are necessary in science. The ability to tell when a whole account, a whole way of putting things, makes sense, is what I mean by insight.

The intelligibility of the whole account (or way of talking) then determines which particular utterances make sense, and what sense they make. Thus it is only because quantum mechanics is an intelligible theory that one can make sense of talking about the wavelength of a particular electron (but not about the rest mass of a photon). And this brings us back to the conditions on interpreting something as an IBB. The testable requirement is that individual outputs make sense in the context of prior inputs and other outputs. But what determines which outputs would and would not make sense in which contexts? That is, what determines which overall patterns render their constituents intelligible under an interpretation, or which input/output constraints count as cogency conditions? I have said that in appropriate circumstances, people can "just tell"; they can come to understand insightfully.

This is not to say that insight is itself some impenetrable mystery, which we are forever barred from explaining. But once we appreciate that it is a genuine problem we can ask whether an IPS explanation could account for it. Now, we can understand how an IPS comes up with the reasonable outputs that it does, because we know how it works; in particular, we know that it works through a rationale for each output, and we know that it makes sense to say this of it because each of its interacting component IBBS consistently accords with certain cogency conditions. If we did not have that kind of story to tell, then we would have no IPS explanation of the overall IBB's abilities.

So if an IPS explanation is to account for an object's having insight, then there must be a rationale for the insightful outputs. More specifically, if the insight is that certain new constraints constitute a kind of cogency, then there must be a rationale, according to the kind of cogency that the object and its components already exhibit, for why the new conditions count as cogency conditions. It seems to me that there could be such a rationale only if the new conditions were equivalent to, or a special case of, the established ones. For example, there could be no rationale according to chess-player cogency conditions for why adding-machine outputs make sense, or vice versa. If this is right, then an IPS with general insight into what makes sense would itself have to operate according to some cogency conditions that are ultimately general (so that the others which it recognizes could be given rationales as special cases).

There are two reasons to doubt that human insight can be explained that way. First, there is a sense in which it would preclude any radically new ways of understanding things; all new developments would have to be specializations of the antecedent general conditions. But I think the invention, say, of derivational-nomological explanation (around the time of Galileo) did constitute a *radical* advance in *ways* of understanding, in just the sense that the cogency of the new accounts could not be defended with a rationale which was cogent by prior standards. Medieval Aristotelians had explained (and understood) the motions of various kinds of bodies in terms of their efforts to get where they belonged, and their thwarting of each other's efforts. Galileo, Kepler, Newton, et al, didn't simply add to or modify those views. They invented a totally new way of talking about what happens, and a new way of rendering it intelligible; mathematical relationships and operations defined on universal measurable magnitudes became the illuminating considerations, rather than the goals and strivings of earth, air, fire, and water. I don't think a medieval IPS could have come to understand the new theory unless it had had it latently "built-in" all along. The same would be true of every IPS child who comes eventually to understand science, the arts, politics, and so on.

The second doubt has to do with this latent building-in—essentially, the ultimate general cogency conditions. We really have no reason to believe that there is any final characterization of what it is to make sense, except that it would facilitate a tidy account of intelligence. Barrels of philosophical ink have been spilt in the search for it, but so far without success. People who regularly make convergent decisions about the reasonableness of theories and interpretations don't explicitly work through rationales for their judgments. So we're back to postulating some mysterious and magnificent unconscious IPS. But once we admit that the phenomenon of insight is simply mysterious and unexplainable at present, then all we have to go on are the prima facie indications that IPS explanation is inadequate to the task.

It seems to me, however, that there is yet a deeper side to this: understanding pertains not primarily to symbols or rules for manipulating them, but to the world and living in it. Linguistic articulation can be a vehicle for such understanding; and perhaps articulateness is prerequisite to any elaborate understanding. But cases where facility with the symbols is plausibly sufficient—like well-defined games, mathematics, and AI "micro-worlds"—are very peculiar, and (I think) parasitic. Paradigms of understanding are rather our everyday insights into friends and loved ones, our sensitive appreciation of stories and dramas, our intelligent handling of paraphernalia and institutions. It is far from clear that these are governed by fully explicable rules at all. Our talk of them is sensible because we know what we are talking about, and not just because the talk itself exhibits some formal regularities (though that too is doubtless essential).

When the rationalists took cognition as the essence of being human (*res cogitans*), they meant especially theoretical cognition, as in mathematics and mathematical physics. The understanding manifested in arts and crafts was not, in their view, a different phenomenon, but just imperfect theory, sullied by obscurity and confusion. Cognitivism is heir to this tradition: to be intelligent is to be able to manipulate (according to rational rules) "clear and distinct" quasilinguistic representations—only now they're sullied by omissions, probabilities, and heuristics. Deported from the immortal soul, however, they forfeit their original epistemic anchorage in the honesty of God and the natural light of reason. So, bereft of credentials from above, the distinction of certain procedures as "reasonable" floats adrift, unless it can otherwise be explained. Evolution comes vaguely to mind, but much more needs to be said. My own hunch is that the intelligibility of rational "theorizing" is a derivative special case of an antecedent, atheoretical, intelligent practice—a prior "grasp" of how to get along in a multifarious existence. If articulate theory is one developed derivative, there can be others: the appreciation of fine art, a subtle sense of personality, the "mastery of metaphor" (Aristotle), even creativity and wisdom. We will understand understanding when we understand its many forms, primordial and refined. In the economy of understanding, words are merely money.

In this section I have raised three issues which it seems to me cognitivists must face, and which it is not yet clear they can handle. It is of course possible that successful treatments will eventually be found. On the other hand, if the approach is doomed to failure, I suspect that these are tips of some of the icebergs on which it will founder.

8 The state of the art

Needless to say, the eventual fate of cognitive psychology will be settled empirically—not by armchair philosophizing. But the way in which experimental results bear on scientific theories, let alone whole approaches to the form that such theories take, is seldom straightforward. In this concluding section, I will venture a few general points about cognitivism and its relation to empirical observations.

It is illustrative to begin with cognitive simulation, a sub-discipline where cognitive psychology overlaps with artificial intelligence. A generation ago, the prospect of building intelligent computers inspired a lot of enthusiasm and brilliant work; but everyone must agree that results to date fall well short of early expectations. General problem solving programs have long since hit a plateau. Mechanical language translation has proven so elusive and frustrating that even military funding has dwindled. Advances in pattern recognition are painfully small, and mainly confined to contrived special "universes". Even game playing, a relative bright spot, is a disappointment against once confident hopes and predictions. About the only thing which exceeds original forecasts is the amount of computing power which has become available—and yet it isn't enough. Does all this constitute an empirical refutation of the possibility of artificial intelligence? Not at all.

Perhaps the lesson is just that the problem was initially underestimated; soberer judges are now gratified by smaller steps in a longer trek, and disillusioned pessimists may still be exposed as carpenters who blamed their tools. On the other hand, if there were indeed something fundamentally misguided about the whole project, then recurrent bottlenecks and modest sparse successes are just what you would expect. The empirical record is simply ambiguous, and the real problem is to wrest from it whatever morals it does hold, as clearly and as helpfully as possible.

Cognitive simulation is not merely an incidental offshoot of cognitive psychology. It is a powerful and important research tool, because it provides a new and unprecedented empirical testing ground. Any IPS, or at least any one which is reducible to some level or dimension on which component input/output functions are expressible mathematically, can in principle be simulated on a computer. That means that simulations can function as concrete checks on whether particular proposed IPSS in fact have the abilities that they are supposed to explain. This is valuable when the proposed explanations are so complex that it is otherwise practically impossible to determine whether the things would actually work as claimed. In effect, the computer makes it feasible for cognitivist theories to be more intricate and complicated than their predecessors could be in the past, and still remain under detailed empirical control.

By the same token, however, computer simulation serves as the front line where fundamental difficulties not resolvable by further complication would first show themselves. This is not to say that psychological experiments, and programmatic theories formulated with their guidance, are beside the point; quite the contrary, they form an essential high-level ingredient in the whole endeavor. But if one were genuinely to entertain the hypothesis that cognitivism is misconceived, then the stumbling blocks empirically discovered by cognitive simulationists would be the first place to look for clues as to what went wrong. How else than by struggling to build chess players could we have found out so definitively that the skill of deciding which moves to consider is not a simple matter of a few readily ascertained heuristics? What laboratory experiment could have shown more clearly than the mechanical translation effort that the hardest thing to account for in linguistic performance is understanding what the discourse is all about?

If cognitivism proves to be the wrong approach after all (that's still a big 'if', of course), then the genius who makes the next basic breakthrough in psychology will probably take his or her cue from difficulties like these. Empirical indications of what cannot be done often pave the way for major scientific progress—think of efforts to weigh phlogiston, to build a perpetual motion machine, or to measure the speed of the Earth through the luminiferous aether.

A sense of history can give us perspective in another way. Until the rise of cognitivism, behaviorism reigned almost unchallenged in American psychology departments. It could boast established experimental methods, mountains of well-confirmed and universally accepted results, specialty journals carrying detailed technical reports, and a coherent "philosophy" within which it all fit together and seemed inevitably right. In short, it had all the institutional earmarks of an advanced and thriving science. In retrospect, however, behaviorism seems to have made little positive contribution to our understanding of the human psyche, and to be hopelessly inadequate to the task.

Kuhn's notion of a scientific paradigm (1962/70) can be extended in a way that sheds light on a situation like this. A *paradigm* is a major scientific triumph, so impressive in breaking new ground, and yet so pregnant with unfulfilled possibilities, that a technical research tradition coalesces around it as a model. Thus the achievements of Thorndike and Pavlov inspired a vigorous and sophisticated investigation of the conditioning of birds, dogs, and rats—and also of people, to the extent that they are similar. But most of the interesting and important aspects of intelligent behavior, exhibited especially by humans, turn out to involve processes qualitatively different from those discovered by Thorndike, Pavlov, and their followers. So when behaviorism was taken as an approach to psychology in general, its paradigm became a kind of impostor; experiments, concepts, and methods which were genuinely illuminating in a limited domain posed as the model for illumination in a quite different domain, where they had virtually no demonstrated credentials, and really didn't belong.

Cognitivism is a natural development from behaviorism. It retains the same commitment to publicly observable and verifiable data, the same rejection of posits and postulates that cannot be treated experimentally, and the same ideal of psychology as a natural science. Its advantage is having shown, via the systematicity and intentional interpretation "cornerstones", how to make good empirical sense of meaningful or rational internal processes—which gives it a much richer and more powerful explanatory framework. And not surprisingly, it has now acquired the institutional earmarks of an advanced and thriving science. But cognitive psychology too can be accused of having an impostor paradigm. The concrete achievements which inspire the notion of IPS explanation, and prove it to have application in the real world, come originally and almost entirely from the fields of computer science and automatic data processing. The few cases in which people explicitly and deliberately work through a rationale do suggest an analogy; but so did cases in which people responded to conditioning.

Like their predecessors, cognitivists have made undeniably important and lasting discoveries. But also as before, these discoveries are conspicuously narrow, even small, compared to the depth and scope of psychology's pretheoretic purview. The brilliance of what has been done can blind us to the darkness that surrounds it, and it is worth recalling how many shadows cognitivism has not (yet) illuminated. How is it, for example, that we recognize familiar faces, let alone the lives reflected in them, or the greatness of Rembrandt's portrayals. How do we understand conversational English, let alone metaphors, jokes, Aristotle, or Albee? What is common sense, let alone creativity, wit, or good taste? What happens when we fall asleep, let alone fall under a spell, fall apart, or fall in love? What are personality and character, let alone identity crises, schizophrenia, the experience of enlightenment, or moral integrity? We turn to psychology if we think these questions have scientific answers; and if we shouldn't, why shouldn't we? Cognitivists are as vague and impressionistic on such issues as psychological theorists have always been. Of course, they too can buy time with the old refrain: "be patient, we're only just beginning (though so-and-so's preliminary results are already encouraging)". Promissory notes are legitimate currency in vigorous sciences, but too much deficit spending only fuels inflation.

The human spirit is its own greatest mystery. Perhaps the idea of an information processing system is at last the key to unlocking it; or perhaps the programmable computer is as shallow an analogy as the trainable pigeon—the conditional branch as psychologically sterile as the conditioned reflex. There is no way to tell yet, but we should be as ready to follow up on partial failures as we are on partial successes. The clues could be anywhere.

NOTES:

1 For instance, Cummins 1975; Putnam 1973; Dennett 1971/78; Simon 1969/81; and Fodor 1965

2 For instance, Davidson 1970/80, 1973/84; and Harman 1973; and compare Sellars 1954/63; Dennett 1971/78; and McCarthy 1979.

3 Compare Goodman 1968, chapter 4; Quine 1960, section 18.

4 Compare "structured description", Pylyshyn 1978.

5 For instance, Wilson 1959; Quine 1960, chapter 2; Lewis 1974/83; Grandy 1973; and Davidson 1973/84.

6 Compare McCarthy 1979 on thermostats.

7 For readers familiar with the work of Quine, I would like to clear up what I think is a common misunderstanding. Quine is a behaviorist of sorts, and he sometimes seems to defend that on the basis of his doctrine of the indeterminacy of translation (Quine 1960, chapter 2). Thus, it's natural to suppose that cognitivism is as opposed to the latter doctrine as it is to behaviorism. It isn't. In the terminology of this paper, Quine's claim is the following. For any IBB, there are many different intentional interpretations of the same input/output typologies, which are all equally "good" by any empirical tests; that is, they are all such that the outputs consistently make reasonable sense in context. Hence, one's "translation" of the inputs and outputs is empirically indeterminate, as least among these options. Now, it might seem that if the IBB were an IPS, and if one knew what it was "thinking" (its internal cognitive processes), then one could determine what its outputs *really* meant, and thereby undercut the indeterminacy. But if Quine is right in his original claim (and I take no stand on that), then it applies to the interpretations of the component IBBS as well. Thus the indeterminacy, rather than being undercut, is just carried inward; in Quine's terms, all the translations are "relative to a translation manual". That would no more rule out cognitivism than it would linguistics.

8 Strictly, the required relation between the two sets of constraints is weaker than isomorphism. It suffices if every input/output pattern which would satisfy the explained constraints on the

lower dimension would also satisfy the cogency conditions on the interpretation being reduced (the constraints on the upper dimension). This amounts to saying that the instantiation can explain more than the IBB ability in question—for example, not only how it manages to play chess, but also why it always neglects certain options.

9 For introductions to holograms and some of their interesting properties, see Leith and Upatnieks 1965; Herriott 1968; Gabor 1969; Firth 1972; and Cathey 1974. For further speculations about their capabilities, see van Heerden 1968; Pribram 1971, 1974; Pribram et al 1974; and Pollen and Taylor 1974. For hypothetical models of holograms realized in neurons, see Kabrisky 1966; Baron 1970; and Cavanagh 1972. For evidence that some neurons may actually behave in the required ways, see Campbell 1974; and Pollen and Taylor 1974; and compare Erickson 1974.

10 For some proposals of ips-based pattern recognizers, see Minsky and Papert 1972; and Waltz 1972.

11 See Yevick 1975, however, for a mathematician's tentative proposal of a holographically based logic.

12 De Groot 1965; Hearst 1967; Frey and Adesman 1976.

13 See Sellars 1956/63 for a discussion of this distinction in the context of a different issue.

14 Shoemaker 1975 and Block and Fodor 1972; but see also Dennett 1978a/78.

15 See, for instance, Shepard and Metzler 1971; Pylyshyn 1973, 1978; Paivio 1975; Kosslyn and Pomerantz 1977; Dennett 1978b/78.

16 See Winograd 1972, for example; and compare Greeno 1977.

CHAPTER TWO

Understanding Natural Language

The trouble with artificial intelligence is that computers don't give a damn. Or so I will argue by considering the special case of understanding natural language. Linguistic facility is an appropriate trial for AI because input and output can be handled conveniently with a teletype, because understanding a text requires understanding its topic (which is unrestricted), and because there is the following test for success: does the text enable the candidate to answer those questions it would enable competenthuman users of the language to answer? The thesis will not be that (human-like) intelligence cannot be achieved artificially, but that there are identifiable conditions on achieving it. This point is as much about language and understanding as about artificial intelligence. I will express it by distinguishing four *different* phenomena that may be called *holism*; that is, four ways in which brief segments of text cannot be understood in isolation or on a one-by-one basis.

1 HOLISM OF INTENTIONAL INTERPRETATION

Consider how one might *empirically* defend the claim that a given (strange) object plays chess. Clearly, it is neither necessary nor sufficient that the object use any familiar chess notation (or pieces); for it might play brilliant chess in some alien notation, or it might produce chess salad in what appeared to be standard notation. Rather, what the defense must do is, roughly:

1 give systematic criteria for (physically identifying the object's inputs and outputs;

2 provide a systematic way of interpreting them as various moves (such as a manual for translating them into standard notation); and then

3 let some skeptics play chess with it.

The third condition bears all the empirical weight, for satisfying it amounts to public *observation* that the object really does play chess. More specifically, the skeptics see that, as interpreted, it makes a sensible (legal and plausible) move in each position it faces. And eventually, induction convinces them that it would do so in any position. Notice that, de facto, the object is also being construed as "remembering" (or "knowing") the current position, "trying" to make good moves, "realizing" that rooks outrank pawns, and even "wanting" to win. All these interpretations and construals constitute collectively an *intentional interpretation*.

Intentional interpretation is essentially holistic. It is supported empirically only by observing that its object makes generally "sensible" outputs, given the circumstances. But the relevant circumstances are fixed by the object's prior inputs and other outputs, *as interpreted*. Thus, each observation distributes its support over a whole range of specific interpretations, no one of which is supported apart from the others. For example, a chess move is legal and plausible only relative to the board position, which is itself just the result of the previous moves. So one output can be construed sensibly as a certain queen move, only if that other was a certain knight move, still another a certain bishop move, and so on.[1]

This is the *holism of intentional interpretation*; and it is all too familiar to philosophers. Intentional interpretation is tantamount to Quine's radical translation—including, as Davidson emphasizes, the attribution of beliefs and desires. The condition that outputs be sensible (in the light of prior inputs and other outputs) is just whatever the ill-named principle of charity is supposed to capture. I have reviewed it here only to distinguish it from what follows.

2 Common-sense holism

Years ago, Yehoshua Bar-Hillel pointed out that disambiguating "The box was in the pen" requires common-sense knowledge about boxes and pens. He had in mind knowledge of typical sizes, which would ordinarily decide between the alternatives 'playpen' and 'fountain pen'.[2] In a similar vein, it takes common sense to determine the antecedent of the pronoun in: "I left my raincoat in the bathtub, because it was still wet." More subtly, common sense informs our appreciation of the final verb of: "Though his blouse draped stylishly, the toreador's pants seemed painted on."

Straightforward questioning immediately exposes any misunderstanding. Was the bathtub wet? Was there paint on his pants? And the issue isn't just academic; a system designed to translate natural languages must be able to answer such questions. For instance, the correct and incorrect readings of our three examples have different translations into either French or German—so the system has to choose. What's so daunting about this, from the designer's point of view, is that one never knows which little fact is going to be relevant next—which common-sense tidbit will make the next disambiguation obvious. In effect, the *whole* of common sense is potentially relevant at any point. This feature of natural-language understanding I call *common-sense holism*; its scope and importance was first fully demonstrated in artificial intelligence work.

The difference between common-sense holism and the holism of intentional interpretation is easily obscured by vague formulas like: the meaning of an utterance is determinate only relative to *all* of the utterer's beliefs, desires, and speech dispositions. This covers both holisms, but only at the price of covering up a crucial distinction. The holism of intentional interpretation is *prior* holism, in the sense that it's already accommodated *before* the interpretation of ongoing discourse. An interpreter *first* finds an over-all scheme that works, and *then* can interpret each new utterance separately as it comes. For example, once a holistic chess-player interpretation has been worked out, its holism can be ignored—moves can perfectly well be translated one by one.[3] By contrast, common-sense holism is *real-time* holism— it is freshly relevant to each new sentence, and it can never be ignored. Even if a perfect dictionary and grammar were available, sentences like our three examples would still have to be disambiguated in real time, by some appeal to common sense.

The point can be put another way. Prior holism is compatible with the formalist ideal of semantic atomism: the meaning of a sentence is determined by the meanings of its meaningful components, plus their mode of composition. This ideal is (nearly) achieved by chess notations, formal logics, and most programming languages; but it is only grossly approximated by English—assuming that meaning is what one grasps in understanding a sentence, and that words and idioms are the meaningful components.[4] Real-time holism is precisely *in*compatible with semantic atomism: understanding a sentence requires *more* that a grammar and a dictionary—namely, common sense.[5]

The nature of common-sense holism is brought into sharper relief by current efforts to deal with it—those in artificial intelligence being the most concentrated and sophisticated. The hard problem, it turns out, is not simply the enormous volume of common knowledge, but rather storing it so that it can be efficiently accessed and used. Obviously, it is quite impractical to check every available fact for possible relevance, every time some question comes up. So the task is to design a system that will quickly home in on genuinely relevant considerations, while ignoring nearly everything else. This is the "memory-organization" or "knowledge-representation" problem; what makes it hard is the quixotic way that odd little facts turn up as germane.

Most contemporary systems employ some variant of the following idea: facts pertaining to the same subject are stored together ("linked") in structured clusters, which are themselves linked in larger structures, according as their subjects are related.[6]

We can think of these clusters as concepts, so long as we remember that they are much more elaborate and rich than traditional definitions—even contextual definitions. For example, the concept of 'monkey' would include not only that they are primates of a certain sort, but also a lot of incidental information like where they come from, what they eat, how organ grinders use them, and what the big one at the zoo throws at spectators. It's more like an encyclopedia than a dictionary entry.

Three points will clarify how this is supposed to work. First, much of the specification of each concept lies in its explicit links or cross references to other concepts, in an over-all conceptual superstructure. For instance, part of the monkey concept would be an "is-a" link to the primate concept, which has in turn an is-a link to the mammal concept, and so on. So, the monkey, rat, and cow concepts can effectively share generic information about mammals. Second, entries in a concept can have modalities, like 'necessarily', 'typically', 'occasionally', or even 'only when ...'. The "typically" mode is particularly useful, because it supplies many common-sense assumptions or "default assignments". For example, if monkeys typically like bananas, the system can "assume" that any given monkey will like bananas (pending information to the contrary). Third, concepts often have open spaces or "slots" waiting (or demanding) to be filled up in stipulated ways. Thus, the concept of eating would have spaces for the eater and the eaten, it being stipulated that the eater be animate, and the eaten (typically) be food.

A system based on such concepts copes with common-sense holism as follows. First, a dictionary routine calls the various concepts associated with the words in a given sentence, subject to constraints provided by a syntactical analyzer. Hence, only the information coded in (or closely linked to) these concepts is actually accessed—passing over the presumably irrelevant bulk. The the system applies this information to any ambiguities by looking for a combination of concepts (from the supplied pool) which fit each other's open spaces in all the stipulated ways. So, for Bar-Hillel's example, the system might call four concepts: one each for 'box' and 'is in', and two for 'pen'. The "is-in" concept would have two spaces, with the stipulation that what fills the first be smaller than what fills the second. Alerted by this requirement, the system promptly checks the "typical-size" information under the other concepts, and correctly eliminates 'fountain pen'. An essentially similar procedure will disambiguate the pronouns in sentences like: "The monkeys ate the bananas because they were hungry" or "... because they were ripe". (Wilks 1974, 19)

The other two examples, however, are tougher. Both raincoats and bathtubs typically get wet, so *that* won't decide which was wet when I left my coat in the tub. People opt for the coat, because being wet is an understandable (if eccentric) reason for leaving a coat in a tub, whereas the tub's being wet would be no (sane) reason to leave a coat in it. But where is *this* information to be coded? It hardly seems that concepts for 'raincoat', 'bathtub', or 'is wet', no matter how encyclopedic, would indicate when it's sensible to put a raincoat in a bathtub. This suggests that common sense can be organized only partially according to subject matter. Much of what we recognize as making sense is not about some topic for which we have a word or idiom, but rather about some (possibly unique) circumstance or episode, which a longer fragment leads us to visualize. Introspectively, it seems that we imagine ourselves into the case, and then decide from within it what's plausible. Of course, *how* this is done is just the problem.

The ambiguity of 'painted-on pants' is both similar and different. Again, we imagine the sort of attire being described; but the correct reading is obviously a metaphor—namely, for 'skin tight', which is both coordinated and appropriately contrasted with the stylishly draped blouse. Most approaches to metaphor, however, assume that metaphorical readings aren't attempted unless there is something anomalous about the literal reading (as in "He is the cream on my peaches", or "… faster than greased lightning"). But, in this case, there is nothing anomalous about pants with paint on them—they would even clash with 'stylish', explaining the conjunction 'Though …'. On that reading, however, the sentence would be silly, whereas the metaphor is so apt that most people don't even notice the alternative.

These examples are meant only to illustrate the subtlety of common sense. They show that no obvious or crude representation will capture it, and suggest that a sophisticated, cross-referenced encyclopedia may not suffice either. On the other hand, they don't reveal much about what's left out, nor (by the same token) whether that will be programmable when we know what it is. The real nature of common sense is still a wide-open question.

3 SITUATION HOLISM

Correct understanding of a sentence depends not only on general common sense, but also on understanding the specific situation(s) to which it pertains. I don't have in mind the familiar point about descriptions and indexicals, that only the "context" determines *which* table is "the table" or "this table", and so on. Much more interesting is the situation-dependence of examples like Bar-Hillel's. Dreyfus (1972/ 92) points out that

> in spite of our *general* knowledge about the relative sizes of pens and boxes, we might interpret "The box is in the pen", when whispered in a James Bond movie, as meaning just the opposite of what it means at home or on the farm.   (216)

This is not just a problem about exotic contexts, where normal expectations might fail; both of the following are normal.

> When Daddy came home, the boys stopped their cowboy game. They put away their guns and ran out back to the car.

> When the police drove up, the boys called off their robbery attempt. They put away their guns and ran out back to the car.

The second sentence is not exactly ambiguous, but it means different things in the two situations. For instance, did the boys put their guns "away" in a toy chest or in their pockets? (It makes a difference in German: *einräumen* versus *einstecken*.) Could 'ran' be paraphrased by 'fled'?

So far, the role of "situation sense" seems comparable to that of common sense, though more local and specific. A fundamental difference appears, however, as soon as the stories get interesting enough to involve an interplay of several situations. A middle-eastern folk tale gives a brief example.

> One evening, the Khoja looked down into a well, and was startled to find the moon shining up at him. It won't help anyone down there, he thought, and quickly he fetched a hook on a rope. But when he threw it in, the hook snagged on a hidden rock. The Khoja pulled and pulled and pulled. Then suddenly it broke loose, and he went right on his back with a thump. From where he lay, however, he could see the moon, finally back in the sky where it belonged—and he was proud of the good job he had done.

The heart of this story is a trade-off between two situations: the real one and the one in the Khoja's imagination. The narrative jumps back and forth between them; and it is up to the reader to keep them straight, and also to keep track of their interaction and development.

In the first sentence, for example, the embedded clauses "the Khoja found the moon" and "it shined up at him", are clearly about the epistemic situation, despite their grammar. One must understand this at the outset, to appreciate the Khoja's progressive misperceptions, and thus his eventual pride. A trickier shift occurs in the clause "It won't help anyone down there ...", which must mean "*while* it's down there" (not "anyone *who is* down there"). In other words, it's an implicit hypothetical which refers us to yet another situation: a counterfactual one in which people are left in darkness while the moon is still in the well. This too is essential to understanding the pride.[7]

The important point is how little of this is explicit in the text. The clauses as written exhibit what can be called "situational ambiguity". It's as if the implied situations functioned as modalizers or implicit propositional operators for the expressed clauses. (The point is not to propose a logic, let alone a model theory, but only to suggest what might be a helpful analogy.) Thus the clause "the Khoja found the moon" would have not only the modality "the Khoja thought that ..." but also the modality "while looking into the well ...". The latter is a crucial qualification, for it (along with common sense) is what forces the former.

Given this way of putting it, two things stand out. First, rather than a fixed, lexically specified set of possible modalities, there are indefinitely many of them, more or less like sentences (or indeed, whole passages). Second, many of these have to be supplied (or inferred) by the reader—often, as in the last example, on the basis of others already supplied. That is, to understand the text, the reader must provide for each clause a number of these generalized or "situational" modalities, and must do so largely on the basis of some over-all situational or modal coherence. This demand for over-all coherence—that all the various "situations" (with respect to which clauses are understood) should fit together in an intelligible way—is what I call *situation holism*. It is a general feature of natural-language text, and coping with it is a prerequisite to reading.

Situation holism is especially characteristic of longer texts. We had a brief sample in our folk tale; but it really comes into its own in the forms of dialectic, characterization, and plot. Mystery novels, for example, are built around the challenge of situation holism when pivotal cues are deliberately scattered and ambiguous. Translators (who read the book first, naturally) must be very sensitive to such matters—to use 'ran' or 'flew' instead of 'fled', for instance—on pain of spoiling the suspense. But only the over-all plot determines just which words need to be handled carefully, not to mention how to handle them. Engrossed readers, in the meantime, are alert to the same issues in a complementary way. This is situation holism full-fledged.[8]

4 DIGRESSION: HERMENEUTICS

Hermeneutics, in the classical (nineteenth-century) sense, is the "science" of textual interpretation—that is, exegesis. It is often described as holistic, on something like the following grounds: the meanings of particular passages, doctrines, and specialized ("technical") terms, are only apparent in the context of the whole; yet the whole (treatise, life's work, or genre) is composed entirely of particular passages, containing the various doctrines and special terms. So the interpreter must work back and forth among part, subpart, and whole, bootstrapping each insight on one level into new insights on the others, until a satisfactory over-all understanding is achieved.

Hermeneutics is like intentional interpretation, insofar as the point is to translate baffling expressions into others more familiar or more intelligible. And the constraint on adequacy is again that the text, as construed, make a maximum of sense. But in exegesis, sensibleness is not so easy to determine as it is, say, in translating chess notations. For each sentence will have various presuppositions or facts taken for granted, and will make sense only in the light of these. Part of the interpreter's task, in determining what the text means, is to ferret such assumptions out and make them explicit. So hermeneutic interpretation must deal explicitly with common-sense holism (though it may be "common" only to the initiated few). But the paramount concern in formal exegesis is exposing the overall structure and purport of the original. A construal cannot stand unless it renders sensible the progression and development of arguments, examples, incidents, and the like. But this is just situation holism, made more articulate. Thus, I don't think the holism of classical hermeneutics is different from the three kinds so far discussed, but is instead a sophisticated combination of them all.[9]

5 EXISTENTIAL HOLISM

In the section on intentional interpretation, we noticed how naturally we construe chess-playing computers as "trying" to make good moves, and "wanting" to win. At the same time, however, I think we *also* all feel that the machines don't "really care" whether they win, or how they play—that somehow the game doesn't "matter" to them at all. What's behind these conflicting intuitions? It may seem at first that what machines lack is a *reason* to win: some larger goal that winning would subserve. But this only puts off the problem; for we then ask whether they "really care" about the larger goal. And until this question is answered, nothing has been—just as we now don't suppose pawns matter to computers, even though they subserve the larger goal of winning.

Apparently something else must be involved to make the whole hierarchy of goals worth while—something that itself doesn't need a reason, but, so to speak, "matters for its own sake". We get a hint of what this might be, by asking why chess games matter to people (when they do). There are many variations, of course, but here are some typical reasons:

1. public recognition and esteem, which generates and supports self-esteem (compare the loser's embarrassment or loss of face);

2. pride and self-respect at some difficult achievement—like finally earning a master rating (compare the loser's frustration and self-disappointment); or

3. proving one's prowess or (as it were) "masculinity" (compare the loser's self-doubt and fear of inadequacy).

What these have in common is that the player's self-image or sense of identity is at stake. This concern with "who one is" is at least one issue that plausibly matters for its own sake. Machines (at present) lack any personality and, hence, any possibility of personal involvement; so (on these grounds) nothing can really matter to them.[10]

The point is more consequential for language understanding than for formal activities like chess playing, which are largely separable from the rest of life. A friend of mine tells a story about the time she kept a white rat as a pet. It was usually tame enough to follow at her heels around campus; but one day, frightened by a dog, it ran so far up her pantleg that any movement might have crushed it. So, very sheepishly, she let down her jeans, gently liberated her quivering rodent, and won a round of applause from delighted passersby. Now, many people find this anecdote amusing, and the relevant question is: Why? Much of it, surely, is that we identify with the young heroine and share in her embarrassment—being relieved, at the same time, that it didn't happen to us.

Embarrassment, however, (and relief) can be experienced only by a being that has some sense of itself—a sense that is important to it and can be awkwardly compromised on occasion. Hence, only such a being could, as we do, find this story amusing. It might be argued, however, that "emotional" reactions, like embarrassment and bemusement, should be sharply distinguished from purely "cognitive" understanding. Nobody, after all, expects a mechanical chess player to *enjoy* the game or to be thrilled by it. But that distinction cannot be maintained for users of natural language. Translators, for instance, must choose words carefully to retain the character of an amusing original. To take just one example from the preceding story, German has several "equivalents" for 'sheepish', with connotations, respectively, of being simple, stupid, or bashful. Only by appreciating the embarrassing nature of the incident, could a translator make the right choice.

A different perspective is illustrated by the time Ralph asked his new friend, Lucifer: "Why, when you're so brilliant, beautiful, and everything, did you ever get kicked out of heaven?" Rather than answer right away, Lucifer suggested a little game: "I'll sit up here on this rock," he said, "and you just carry on with all that wonderful praise you were giving me." Well, Ralph went along for a while; but as the hours passed, it began to get tiresome. So finally he said: "Look, why don't we just add a little variety to this game, say, by taking turns?" "Ahh ...," sighed Lucifer, "that's all I said, that's *all* I said."[11]

Here, even more than Ralph's embarrassment, we enjoy the adroit way that Lucifer turns the crime of the ages into a little *faux pas*, blown out of proportion by God's infinite vanity. But why is *that* funny? Part of it has to be that we all know what guilt and shame are like, and how we try to escape them with impossible rationalizations—this being a grand case on both counts. It's not the *psychology* of guilt that we know, but the tension of actually *facing* it and (sometimes) trying not to face it. And actually *feeling* guilty is certainly not just a cognitive state, like believing one did wrong, and disapproving; nor is it that, with some unpleasant sensation added on. It is at least to sense oneself as diminished by one's act—to be reduced in worth or exposed as less worthy than had seemed.

Crime and Punishment, too, is "about" guilt, but it isn't especially funny. The novel is powerful and didactic: the reader's experience of guilt is not simply drawn upon, but engaged and challenged. We enter into Raskolnikov's (and Dostoyevsky's) struggle with the very natures of guilt, personal responsibility, and freedom—and in so doing, we grow as persons. This response, too, is a kind of understanding, and asking questions is a fairly effective test for it. Moreover, at least some of those questions will have to be answered in the course of producing an adequate translation.

One final example will demonstrate the range of the phenomenon I'm pointing at, and also illustrate a different way in which the reader's personal involvement can be essential. It is a fable of Aesop's.

One day, a farmer's son accidentally stepped on a snake, and was fatally bitten. Enraged, the father chased the snake with an axe, and managed to cut off its tail; and thereupon, the snake nearly ruined the farm by biting all the animals. Well, the farmer thought it over, and finally took the snake some sweetmeats, saying: "I can understand your anger, and surely you can understand mine. But now that we are even, let's forgive, forget, and be friends again." "No, no," said the snake, "take away your gifts. You can *never* forget your dead son, nor I my missing tail."

Obviously, this story has a "moral", which a reader must "get" in order to understand it.

The problem is not simply to make the moral explicit, for then it would be more direct and effective to substitute a non-allegorical paraphrase.

A child is like a part of oneself, such as a limb. The similarities include:

   i) losing one is very bad;

  ii) if you lose one, you can never get it back;

 iii) they have no adequate substitutes; and thus

 iv) they are literally priceless.

Therefore, to regard trading losses of them as a "fair exchange", or "getting even", is to be a fool.

But this is just a list of platitudes. It's not that it misrepresents the moral, but that it lacks it altogether—it is utterly flat and lifeless. By comparison, Aesop's version "lives", because we as readers identify with the farmer. Hence, we too are brought up short by the serpent's rebuke; and that makes us look at ourselves.

The terrifying thing about losing, say, one's legs is not the event itself, or the pain, but rather the thought of *being* a legless cripple for all the rest of one's life. It's the same with losing a son, right? *Wrong!* Many a parent indeed would joyously give both legs to have back a little girl or boy who is gone. Children can well mean more to who one is and the meaning of one's life than even one's own limbs. So who are *you*, and what is *your* life? The folly—what the fable is really "about"—is not knowing.[12]

A single act cannot be embarrassing, shameful, irresponsible, or foolish in isolation, but only as an event in the biography of a whole, historical, individual—a person whose personality it reflects and whose self-understanding it threatens. Only a being that cares about who it is, as some sort of enduring whole, *can* care about guilt or folly, self-respect or achievement, life or death. And only such a being can read. This holism, now not even apparently in the text, but manifestly in the reader, I call (with due trepidation) *existential holism*. It is essential, I submit, to understanding the meaning of any text that (in a familiar sense) *has* any meaning. If situation holism is the foundation of plot, existential holism is the foundation of literature.

In the context of artificial intelligence, however, there remains an important question as to whether this sets the standard too high—whether it falls into what Papert somewhere calls "the human/superhuman fallacy", or Dennett "the Einstein-Shakespeare gambit". Wouldn't it be impressive enough, the reasoning goes, if a machine could understand everyday English, even if it couldn't appreciate literature? *Sure*, it would be impressive. But beyond that there are three replies. First, if we could articulate some ceiling of "ordinariness" beyond which machines can't pass, or can't pass unless they meet some further special condition, that would be scientifically interesting and important. Second, billions of people can read—really read—and for most of the others it's presumably a socio-historical tragedy that they can't. Existential holism is not a condition just on creative genius. Finally, and *most important*, there is no reason whatsoever to believe there is a difference in kind between understanding everyday discourse and appreciating literature. Apart from a few highly restricted domains, like playing chess, analyzing mass spectra, or making airline reservations, the most ordinary conversations are fraught with life and all its meanings.

6 CONCLUSION

Considering the progress and prospects of artificial intelligence can be a peculiarly concrete and powerful way of thinking about our own spiritual nature. As such, it is a comrade of the philosophy of mind (some authors see AI as allied to epistemology, which strikes me as perverse). Here, we have distinguished four phenomena, each with a claim to the title 'holism'—not to trade on or enhance any mystery in the term, but rather, I would hope, the opposite. The aim has not been to show that artificial intelligence is impossible (though it *is*, you know) but to clarify some of what its achievement would involve, in the specific area of natural language understanding. This area is not so limited as it seems, since—as each of the four holisms testifies—

understanding a text involves understanding what the text is "about".
The holisms, as presented, increase in difficulty relative to current AI
techniques; and my own inclination (it's hardly more than that) is to
regard the last, existential holism, as the most fundamental of the
four. Hence my opening remark: the trouble with artificial intelligence
is that computers don't give a damn.

NOTES:

1 A different argument for a similar conclusion depends on assuming that the inputs and outputs are semantically compound.
   Then, since each compound will in general share components
   with many others, their respective interpretations (in terms of
   their compositions) will be interdependent. Thus the (semantic)
   role of 'P' in 'P–K4' must be systematically related to its role in
   'P–R3', and so on. The argument in the text, however, is more
   fundamental. There are fewer than two thousand possible chess
   moves. (Gardner 1979, 25–26, gives the figure 1840; but he neglects castling and pawn promotion.) These could be represented
   unambiguously by arbitrary numerals, or even simple symbols;
   yet interpreting an object using such a system would still be holistic, for the earlier reasons.

2 Bar-Hillel 1964, 158–159 (quoted in Dreyfus 1972/92, 215).

3 Cryptography is comparable: code cracking is holistic, but once it
   succeeds, deciphering goes along on a message-by-message basis.

4 Hilary Putnam, 1975, argues that there is more to meaning than
   what competent speakers understand; but his point is orthogonal
   to mine.

5 It is difficult to say what significance this has (if any) for formal
   semantics. The most common tactic is to relegate matters of real-
   time holism to "pragmatics", and apply the semantic theory itself
   only to idealized "deep structures" (in which ambiguities of sense,
   pronoun binding, case, mood, scope, and the like. are not allowed—thus saving atomism ... perhaps). A protective quaran-
   tine for semantics may or may not work out, but earlier
   experience with syntax hardly bodes well.

6 See, for example, Minsky 1974; Wilks 1974; Schank and Abelson 1975; and Bobrow and Winograd 1977.

7 There are also a number of "background counterfactuals" involved in understanding what happens. Thus, a reader should be able to say what would have happened if the hook hadn't caught on the rock, or if it hadn't broken loose. Anyone who couldn't answer, wouldn't really "have" it.

8 In AI, work on this problem has only just begun. See, for instance, Rumelhart 1975; Wilensky 1978; and de Beaugrande and Colby 1979; compare also Lewis 1979/83.

9 It can be argued (though not here) that genuine radical translation is less like the interpretation of a chess player than like a hermeneutic investigation of a whole culture—including (so far as possible) an "interpretation" of its practices, institutions, and artifacts. For a good account of what hermeneutics has become in the twentieth century (very roughly, it adds my fourth holism), see Taylor 1971.

10 There are many problems in this vicinity. For instance, people (but not machines) play chess for *fun*; and, within limits, winning is more fun. It's very hard, however, to say what fun is, or get any grip on what it would be for a machine actually to *have* fun. One might try to connect it with the foregoing, and say (in a tired European tone of voice) that fun is merely a temporary diversion from the oppressive burden of self-understanding. But that isn't very persuasive.

11 This is a (no doubt garbled) version of a story I heard years ago, attributed to the movie *Bedazzled*.

12 Rumelhart (1975) analyzes a different version of this story in terms of an interesting "story grammar", loosely analogous to sentential grammar. Significantly, however, he addresses only the continuity of the story and never touches on its moral or meaning.

CHAPTER THREE

Hume on Personal Identity

In memory of H. Paul Grice

In the appendix to his *Treatise of Human Nature*, Hume admits that

> upon a more strict review of the section concerning *personal identity*, I find myself involved in such a labyrinth, that, I must confess, I neither know how to correct my former opinions, nor how to render them consistent. (1739/1888, 633)

Commentators, however, have found it less than obvious what the labyrinth or inconsistency is. I shall offer what I think is a new interpretation, and attempt to show how the problem is genuinely rooted in Hume's overall philosophical enterprise.

The original account of personal identity (251–263), with which Hume was later dissatisfied, pertains both to our idea of the self, and to the self in fact; and it has a negative and a positive aspect in each case. Negatively, we have no real idea of an identical and simple self (because "there is no impression constant and invariable" 251); and positively: "The identity which we ascribe to the mind of man, is only a fictitious one, and of like kind with that which we ascribe to vegetables and animal bodies". (259) Thus, negatively, there *is* no real or substantial self, but, positively, only a "bundle or collection of different perceptions".

According to Hume's doctrine of fictitious identity, whenever the transitions among the ideas of several distinct objects are so smooth and easy as to be barely perceptible—that is, when they "feel" (almost) the same as no transition at all—then the mind confounds a survey of those distinct objects with a survey of *one* object continuing the same. This happens when the objects in question are strongly interrelated by resemblance, contiguity, and/or causation—which he calls "the uniting principles of the ideal world" whose "very essence ... consists in their producing an easy transition of ideas". (260) For example, what we regard as a single enduring cabbage is really a collection of distinct parts and stages; but they are so interrelated in the above three ways that we don't notice the transitions in thinking of them, and hence don't notice their distinctness.

This is a mistake, he says, but it is not due to mere inadvertence or inattention. Rather, the similarity (resemblance) in feeling between considering a strictly identical object and considering a suitably related succession generates a positive propensity (which can itself be felt) to make the confusion.[1] Hence, simply pointing it out and exposing it will not make it go away. Instead, the propensity will most likely be appeased by an *invention* of some permanent "substance" or some mysterious "real connection" among the distinct parts—thereby enshrining the mistake in a *fiction*. But even if we avoid that, we still feel the propensity, and so are never really rid of the issue.

A parallel account is supposed to work for *personal* identity, except that contiguity is not an important factor. The various perceptions which we suppose constitute one mind are in fact quite distinct; but we invent an enduring "self" to appease our propensity to confuse a survey of them with a survey of one object. A survey of one person's perceptions "feels like" a survey of a single thing because those perceptions are so thoroughly interrelated by resemblance and causation. For instance, impressions both cause and resemble ideas and memories; and all the other operations of the mind (habits, associations, propensities, feignings) are at least causal.

Already there is an apparent difficulty.[2] If the self is itself just an invention, then what is it that does the inventing? It seems that Hume's active causal story requires at least a non-fictional agent. But that misconstrues the basic nature of the account. Hume is not trying to give any ultimate explanation of *why* things are the way they are (that's what he eschews), but only to describe them in a coherent and illuminating way.

> To explain the ultimate causes of our mental actions is impossible. 'Tis sufficient, if we can give any satisfactory account of them from experience and analogy.   (22)

Presumably, the model for this program was Newton's physics, which illuminatingly described dynamic phenomena, while conspicuously *not* explaining *why*, say, $F = ma$ or masses mutually attract.

Hume, likewise, need not "frame hypotheses"—which is what positing an agent would amount to. A pure description of causal processes (without "occult powers") is just as coherent for the mental realm as for the natural. To say that the mind has a propensity to produce a certain idea in certain circumstances, is only to say that in those circumstances that idea reliably appears in the mental bundle. Such a regularity is quite observable, and can be described causally like any other. The word 'mind' no more has to name a presupposed agent here than does the word 'gravity' in Newton's theory; and it is perfectly consistent to say that when we do take it as naming an agent (that is, a substantial self), then we are only generating a fiction.[3]

This interpretation also dispels another criticism: that Hume gave an incorrect analysis of the concept of identity.[4] It is beside the point to object that 'identical' doesn't "really mean" either 'invariable and uninterrupted' or 'ideally related succession'—just as it would have been inappropriate to complain that 'fall down' doesn't really mean 'accelerate under the force of Earth's gravitation'. Conceptual analysis is not the issue; adequately characterizing what actually happens is.

> Our chief business, then, must be to prove [that is, to show],
> that all objects, to which we ascribe identity, without observing
> their invariableness and uninterruptedness, are such as consist
> of a succession of related objects.   (255)

Commentaries on Hume's own account of his problem are more helpful, but still not satisfactory. According to Kemp Smith, it is "reflecting on the train of past perceptions" which Hume can neither explain nor do without. (1941, 557) Reflection is indeed essential, for it is only in the course of considering (other) perceptions that thought could easily and smoothly transit among ideas of them. And Hume will have trouble accounting for this, if only because his treatment of the "of-ness" (intentionality) of perceptions is impoverished in general. The most he can say is that perceptions are caused by and resemble what they are perceptions of. But then an idea of an impression of an apple would stand in essentially the same relation to that impression as would an idea (which sprang from it) of the apple itself. Hume, of course, rejects any "philosopher's distinction" between objects and perceptions, and takes the hard line that "we never can conceive anything but perceptions".[5] But that's just the problem: if *all* thought is of perceptions, then how is reflective thought different from any other thought? The distinction has collapsed.

On the other hand, this does not seem to be the problem that motivated the appendix. In the first place, it's not clear why collapsing all thought into reflection would cause any particular trouble for the account of personal identity; and second, although Hume could easily have articulated the above question, he in fact never even hints at it.

MacNabb suggests that the difficulty is not reflective thought in general, but specifically thought which reflects on itself.

> If the self is only a relational unity of perceptions, ... that inner awareness of our own being, of which Berkeley speaks, remains unaccounted for; ... [W]hat is it for a perception to be aware of itself as a member of that relational unity of perceptions we call a mind?   (1952/66, 151–152)

The point is, how could any perception P count as awareness of *my* self, as opposed to mere awareness of some self or other, unless that bundle of perceptions which P is "of" includes P itself?

Though it's probably true that Hume could not account for this (is P to be caused by and/or resemble itself?), it again seems to expose only the lack of an adequate theory of intentionality. The only part of MacNabb's point that pertains directly to personal identity is the need for *self*-referential perception—a bugaboo that is peculiar to the twentieth century (and even we don't rule it out altogether). Moreover, not only does Hume not mention any "inner awareness of our own being" in the appendix, but he is in fact explicitly content to find personal identity in reflection on *past* perceptions. (635)

To judge from the text, what Hume himself despairs of explaining is the "principle of connexion" which "unites" our perceptions, or "binds them together" into selves. This becomes an issue because of the argument that each perception is a distinct existence, neither depending on nor having any real connections with anything else. Perceptions satisfy, for what it's worth, the classical definition of a substance: something that can exist entirely by itself. (233) In particular, they don't have to be in anyone's mind.

> Now as every perception is distinguishable from another, and may be considered as separately existent; it evidently follows

that there is no absurdity in separating any particular perception from the mind; that is, in breaking off all its relations with that connected mass of perceptions, which constitute a thinking being.   (207)

There are, it turns out, a few "experiments" which convince us that perceptions don't *happen* to exist apart from minds (210–11)—but the suggestion is not absurd.

So there are all these conceivably free-floating perceptions in the world, and the problem is to say what connects them into the bundles that constitute various selves. Or rather, it is to say what makes us *attribute* to certain groups of them the connectedness or unity of single selves—for there are no real connections, and the self is just a fiction. But that is precisely what the original account, based on resemblance, causation, and the resulting easy transitions, was addressed to. The question is: what went wrong?

Notice first that resemblance alone is neither necessary nor sufficient for allocating two perceptions to the same bundle. Napoleon's ideas of water and Waterloo probably weren't much alike, and we needn't imagine any graduated series of resembling intermediaries between them. Conversely, two people viewing the same apple from the same angle might have very similar perceptions. So causal relations are in each case at least necessary.[6]

That would be neither a difficult nor an implausible outcome, were it not for Hume's distinctive treatment of causality. He holds that the mind never perceives any real connection between cause and effect, and hence has no real idea of such a connection. Rather, impressions of the two are so constantly conjoined that the mind forms the habit of thinking of one when it thinks of the other, and of believing in one (an enlivened idea) when it has an impression of the other. Moreover, our (mistaken) idea of the necessity in causality derives not from any sense impression, but instead from an impression of reflection: namely, a feeling of the aforesaid habit or determination of the mind.

Right away, such an account makes one suspicious, since it seems to be explaining the phenomenon of causality in general in terms of certain special cases (determinations of the mind are causal). Moreover, it seems to explain the phenomenon by, in effect, explaining it *away*. But if mental causation is the foundation of the account, must not *it* at least be real? Again, the answer is that Hume's intent is not ultimate explanation, but only illuminating general description.

The uniting principle among our internal perceptions is as unintelligible as that among external objects, and is not known to us any other way than by experience [, which] ... never gives us any insight into the internal structure or operating principle of objects, but only accustoms the mind to pass from one to another.   (169)

In other words, he accords his own scientific ("mechanical") theory of the operation of the mind the same character and status he accords to ordinary scientific (mechanical) theories of physical objects. Those theories are fundamentally causal, and Hume has no cavil about that; why shouldn't his own theory be causal too? To be consistent, he need only allow that his own attributions of causal connection (including those connections which he says lead to the attribution of causal connection in general) come about in the same manner as any other causal attributions. That is, just as the attribution of physical causes manifests a certain observable, describable, regular pattern (among perceptions), so the attribution of mental causes manifests the same pattern. In the latter case, the pattern among perceptions is, so to speak, "second order", but it is formally the same (equally observable) pattern, nonetheless. As to *why* these second-order patterns exist, that's just as inexplicable as why the first-order ones do—why masses gravitate, for instance. They do; and that's all an empirical scientist can say.

In the appendix, however, Hume complains that he cannot render his principles consistent after all; and, in particular, he cannot account for those which "unite our successive perceptions in our thought or consciousness". (636) The problem, I shall argue, is not that the account of causation (including mental causation) is by itself incoherent or circular, but rather that it is incompatible with the account of personal identity in terms of (mental causation). In a nutshell, the question of personal identity is how we can allocate all the conceivably free-floating perceptions into various personal bundles, given that the prerequisite pattern of constant conjunctions constitutive of mental causation presupposes a *prior* bundling.

Consider the (temporally ordered) set of all the perceptions there ever were, and think back to the time when billiards was first invented. That was the time when impressions of billiard ball impacts and rebounds first entered the overall set of perceptions; and such impressions have been constantly conjoined ever since. Soon thereafter, *ideas* of impacts, *in the mind of Smith*, became constantly (habitually) conjoined with ideas of rebounds, *also in the mind of Smith*. That is, the causal mechanisms of Smith's imagination have started working in the way Hume describes. This has not yet happened, however, in the mind of Jones, who is stupid, let alone Robinson, who had to leave after the first collision. In other words, in the unallocated, overall set of everyone's perceptions, there *simply is no* constant conjunction of impact *ideas* with rebound *ideas*—Jones's slowness and Robinson's inexperience interject counter-instances which destroy the pattern (and other neophytes do the same, throughout history).

Suppose the (serially ordered) letter tokens in a text were "distinct existences", having no "real connection" to each other, or to anything else; still, it seems, they would "hang together" as a single novel, because they exhibit a coherent overall pattern—legibility, say. Now imagine "shuffling" the tokens from all the novels there ever were, preserving the serial ordering for each, but randomly interspersing its tokens among all the others. What results is not a more complicated or higher-order pattern, but illegible chaos—alphabet salad. Therefore commercial printers don't intersperse texts, but rely on a form of spatial contiguity to indicate which tokens belong together in the same book.[7] Hume, however, denies that contiguity is a factor in assorting perceptions (260), and wants the coherent patterns (mental causation) to do the whole job. Unfortunately, there *are* no coherent patterns unless the perceptions are *already* sorted—all he has is perception salad.

This construal of Hume's problem suggests several replies. First, if it's a matter of theoretical circularity—he can't account for personal identity until he's accounted for mental causation, and vice versa—then why not do both at once, fitting the data "holistically"? Thus, a given assortment into bundles, and a given discovery of constant conjunctions within them, would mutually support each other, and the theory as a whole. But this is fundamentally wrong: the set of all perceptions is not, for Hume, a data-set to which he (or some homuncular observer) is trying to accommodate a theory. Rather, he is proposing a kind of quasi-mechanical model for what this set is like, and how it grows. The trouble is: one part of the model (the negative account of personal identity) denies the set a feature (it isn't *really* bound or apportioned into bundles at all) which another part of the model (the account of mental causation) requires (at least the *patterns* must be real). This, in turn, undermines the positive account of our *idea* of personal identity—which requires mental causation (both in constituting the ersatz unity of the mind, and in generating the fictional idea). The model fails because it is internally incoherent, not because some "data" don't support it.

Stroud suggests that Hume can escape the dilemma "by appealing to the undeniable fact" that perceptions *just do* come in separate bundles: "the only 'data' available to a person for the formation of his ideas and beliefs are his own perceptions".[8] (1977, 136) This is enough to get the rest of Hume's account off the ground. The trouble, Stroud concludes, is rather "that it leaves completely unintelligible and mysterious the fact that those 'data' are as they are". Hume cannot explain "[w]hat accounts for the fact that one cannot survey in the same way *all* the perceptions that there are". (138)

But a mystery never fazed Hume; he thought all science ultimately rested on inexplicable basic facts. So there must, at least, be more to it than that. I think it is that Hume's account not only doesn't explain personal bundling, but that, when pushed to the limit, it doesn't even allow for it. And that doesn't just leave the model without a foundation, but brings it crashing down on itself. If Hume could have said that individual selves were "real", then he could have maintained that all causation, including mental causation, and specifically the generation of our ideas of causation and identity, amounted to no more than an (unexplained) pattern in each person's perceptions. Or, if he could have said that perceptions were "really connected", then he could have maintained that the self is no more than a connected bundle of such perceptions (with certain patterns in it) and proceeded as before.

> Did our perceptions either inhere in something simple and individual, or did the mind perceive some real connexion among them, there would be no difficulty in the case.   (636)

But the doctrine that perceptions are distinct existences precludes either move.

> If perceptions are distinct existences, they form a whole only by being connected together. But no connections among distinct existences are ever discoverable by human understanding. (635)

Thus, there is no principle of sorting perceptions into personal bundles; and without such sorting, the observable patterns, on which everything is supposed to rest, simply do not exist.

Holding both that perceptions are distinct existences, and that real connections among them are never discoverable, renders the account of personal identity, and with it Hume's entire empiricist "science of man", incoherent. This is what I take him to have meant when he summed up:

> In short there are two principles, which I cannot render consistent; nor is it in my power to renounce either of them, viz. *that all our perceptions are distinct existences*, and *that the mind never perceives any real connexion among distinct existences*. (636)

NOTES:

1 There is some question of what Hume takes the survey of a strictly identical object to be (or feel like), since he doesn't allow that there are any—at least not any that endure. Perhaps a continuing reflective survey of a single (fleeting) perception provides the necessary point of comparison.

2 See, for instance, Price 1940/65. In my 1977 manuscript, I also cite Strawson in this connection; but I am now (1997) unable to recover the reference.

3 Husserl is said to have regarded Hume as the first descriptive phenomenologist; perhaps this is what he had in mind.

4 See, for instance, Price 1940/65 and Penelhum 1955/65.

5 At least he does in the section: "Of scepticism with regard to the senses"—see especially pages 215–218.

6 Conceivably, all perceptions could come with little "signatures" on them, which were the same for two perceptions just in case those perceptions belonged to the same person. In that case, resemblance (in respect of signature) would be both necessary and sufficient for allocation to the same bundle. But Hume makes no such suggestion; and we can well imagine his empiricist ridicule of the idea, had someone else ventured it.

7 In principle, the tokens could be interspersed, so long as each book had its own distinctive typeface (see preceding footnote).

8 Stroud cites an earlier version of the present paper in setting up his point.

Matter

CHAPTER FOUR

Analog and Analog

When I began this paper (years ago) my concern was with the grand-sounding claim that any analog computer can be digitally simulated to any desired degree of precision. Along the way, however, I found the definitions of 'digital' and 'analog' to be tricky and interesting in their own right, and they now comprise the bulk of the paper. But the original issue returns at the end, and its resolution involves distinguishing stricter and broader senses of 'analog'—hence my curious title.

1 DIGITAL

Definitions of terms like 'analog' and 'digital' are guided first by paradigm cases, and intuitions about what these cases have in common. In the final analysis, however, a definition should be more than merely adequate to the intuitive data. It should show that the cases cited are instances of a theoretically interesting general kind, and it should emphasize the fundamental basis of that theoretical interest. An ideal definition makes manifest why the term in question is worth defining. This ideal is easier to approach for 'digital' than for 'analog'.

Standard examples of digital devices include Arabic numerals, abacuses, alphabets, electrical switches, musical notation, poker chips, and (digital) computers.[1] What is important and distinctive about these cases? Several common features stand out.

> 1 Flawless copying (and preservation) are quite feasible. For instance, no copy of a Rembrandt painting is aesthetically equal to the original, and the paintings themselves are slowly deteriorating. By contrast, there are millions of *perfect* copies

of (most of) Shakespeare's sonnets, and the sonnets themselves are not deteriorating. The difference is that a sonnet is
determined by a sequence of letters, and letters are easy to
reproduce—because modest smudges and squiggles don't
matter. The same goes for musical scores, stacks of poker
chips, and so on.

2 Interesting cases tend to be complex—that is, composites
formed in standard ways from a kit of standard components,
like molecules from atoms. Complexity can also be diachronic, in which case the standard components are actually standard steps or "moves" constituting a sequential pattern. For
example, digits of only ten standard kinds suffice, with a sign
and decimal point, for writing any Arabic numeral; moreover,
a sequence of steps of a few standard sorts will suffice for any
multiplication in this notation. Likewise, the most elaborate
switching networks can be built with the simplest relays; and
all classical symphonies are scored with the same handful of
basic symbols.

3 There can be exactly equivalent structures in different media.
Thus, the sonnets could be printed in italics, chiseled in
stone, stamped in Braille, or transmitted in Morse code—and
nothing would be lost. The same computer program can run
on vacuum-tube or solid-state hardware; poker chips can be
plastic disks, dried beans, or matchsticks.

I call these features *copyability*, *complexity*, and *medium independence*,
respectively. The question is: What do they all presuppose? Out of
what deep root do they all grow?

All digital devices involve some form of *writing* and then *reading*
various *tokens* of various *types*. That is, there are procedures for producing tokens, given the types that they are supposed to be, and
procedures for telling or determining the types of given tokens. For
example, penciling on white paper a particular inscription of the letter
'A' is a way of writing a token of that alphabetic type, which can then
be read by eye. But also, rotating a switch to a specified click-stop is a
way of "writing" a token of that setting (type); and that token can then
be "read" by determining which of the connected circuits will now

conduct electricity. These examples emphasize that the tokens don't have to be symbols (that is, represent or mean anything), and that writing and reading are here generalized to cover whatever it takes to produce and reidentify the relevant tokens.

But what makes the device digital is something more specific about the write and read procedures: they must be "positive" and "reliable". A *positive procedure* is one which can succeed absolutely and without qualification—that is, not merely to a high degree, with astonishing precision, or almost entirely, but *perfectly*, one hundred percent! Clearly, whether something is a positive procedure depends on what counts as success. Parking the car in the garage (in the normal manner) is a positive procedure, if getting it all the way in is all it takes to succeed; but if complete success requires getting it exactly centered between the walls, then no parking procedure will be positive. There is no positive procedure for cutting a six-foot board, but there are plenty for cutting boards six feet, plus or minus an inch. The 'can succeed' means feasibly, and that will depend on the technology and resources available. But we needn't worry about the limits of feasibility, because we care only about procedures that are also *reliable*—ones which, under suitable conditions, can be counted on to succeed virtually every time. With the available technology and resources, reliable procedures are in a sense "easy", or at least established and routine.

What counts as success for write and read procedures? Evidently that the write procedure actually produce a token of the type required, and that the read procedure correctly identify the type of the token supplied. But these are not independent, since usually the procedures themselves jointly function as a working definition of the types—what counts as an inscription of the letter 'A' is determined by what writers produce as one and readers recognize as one. The important constraint is that these be the same, or rather that whatever the writers produce be correctly recognized by the readers, and nothing else be recognized by the readers at all. In other words, the requirement really applies to the composite procedures for the write-read "round-trip", plus a specification of suitable environmental conditions; and there is a kind of trade-off in how stringent the various parts need to be. Thus if the write procedures are very precise, and the suitable conditions provide a very clean, noise-free environment, then the read procedures can get away with being fairly lax; and so on.

So we can define a *digital device* as:

1 a set of types,

2 a set of feasible procedures for writing and reading tokens of those types, and

3 a specification of suitable operating conditions, such that

4 under those conditions, the procedures for the write-read cycle are positive and reliable.

Note that the success condition, that written tokens be correctly read as written (and nothing else be read), indirectly requires that no token in fact be a token of more than one type. That is, the types are disjoint, and hence the relation 'are-of-the-same-type' is an equivalence relation.

Now that the definition has been given, I want to make five follow-up points, which should explain it a little further and reveal more of the motivations behind it. First, the copyability feature of digital devices is easily accounted for; indeed, the definition itself is not far from being a fuller statement of what that feature is. The original can be read positively and reliably; and these readings (type identifications) can simply function directly as the specifications to the write procedures for a new round of tokens. The new tokens can also be read positively and reliably, and hence they are exactly the same as (type identical to) the originals—that is, a *perfect* copy.

Second, (non-degenerate) digitalness is not ubiquitous. One often hears that a system is digital only relative to a description; and too often it is inferred that any object can be construed as any digital system, relative to *some* outlandish (but true) description. Being digital, however, is no more "relative" than being a fugue or an amplifier. True, the types and procedures (like the musical theme, or the input and output ports) must be specified before the definition applies; but whether there is such a specification according to which the definition is in fact satisfied is not at all relative or trivial or automatic.

Third, my definition differs from Nelson Goodman's (by which it was largely inspired) in two significant ways. He says, in effect, that a disjoint set of types is digital just in case

for any candidate token, and for *at least one of* any pair of types (in the set), it is theoretically possible to determine that the candidate is *not* a token of that type.[2]

In other words, for any candidate token, all but at most one of the types can be positively ruled out (by some theoretically possible method)—no token is ever equivocal between two distinct types.

This is most easily explained with examples. Suppose that tokens are penciled line-segments less than a foot long; let Lx be the length of segment x (in inches), and let n be an integer. Then we can specify four different systems in terms of the following four conditions on two line segments being tokens of the same type:

1 $Lx = Ly$ (any difference in length is a difference in type);

2 $n < Lx, Ly < n+1$ (segments are of the same type if their lengths fall between the same consecutive inch-marks);

3 $n + \frac{1}{2} < Lx, Ly < n+1$ (as above, except that segments between any inch-mark and the next higher half-inch-mark are ill-formed—that is, not tokens of any type); and

4 $Lx = Ly = n$ (any difference in length is a difference in type, except that only segments of exactly integral lengths are acceptable—all others are ill-formed).

The first system is not digital because, no matter what (theoretically possible) method of measurement you used, there would be indefinitely many types to which any given token might belong, for all you could tell. Similarly for the second, except that the problem cases are only the segments very close to integral length, and there are only two types you can't rule out. The third system is a paradigm case of a digital device (assuming you can measure to within a quarter inch).

The last case is the troublemaker; it is digital by Goodman's criterion, but it doesn't have the copyability feature—and that for two reasons. First, even if there were any tokens, they couldn't be recognized as such, as opposed to ill-formed scribbles (noise); and second, duplicate tokens could never be produced at all (except by miraculous accident). Both defects are remedied by requiring that the write-read cycle be positive (and reliable).

The second difference between my definition and Goodman's was hinted at in the remark about a stringency trade-off. It is common digital electronics practice to build pulse detectors that flip "high" on signals over about two and a half volts, flopping "low" on smaller signals. Since this is a sharp threshold, and not even very consistent from unit to unit or moment to moment, these detectors cannot define a digital token-scheme, by Goodman's lights. What saves the day for engineers is that pulse *generators* produce only signals very close to zero and five volts respectively, and the whole apparatus can be well shielded against static, so the detectors never actually get confused. Again focusing on the write-read cycle in the ambient conditions is the definitional remedy. But I think a broader point can be made. In making his determinations "theoretically possible", without mentioning the determination procedures, let alone the production procedures or the working conditions, Goodman betrays a mathematician's distaste for the nitty-gritty of *practical* devices. But *digital*, like *accurate*, *economical*, or *heavy-duty*, is a mundane engineering notion, root and branch. It only makes sense as a practical means to cope with the vagaries and vicissitudes, the noise and drift, of earthly existence. The definition should reflect this character.

My fourth follow-up is a reply to David Lewis, and some comments on complexity. Lewis offers a counterexample to Goodman, which, if it worked at all, would work against my definition as well.[3] Imagine representing numerical values with a variable resistance—a setting of 137 ohms represents 137, and so on. And suppose the variable resistor is constructed with a rotary switch and a lot of discrete one-ohm resistors, such that the 137th switch position connects 137 resistors in series, for a 137-ohm total. This, says Lewis, is analog representation (hence, not digital), just as if the variable resistor were a sliding contact moving smoothly along a wire with uniform resistance per unit length. But, since the switch has click-stops, he claims it would be (mis-)classified as digital by Goodman.

I think the case is underdescribed. Assuming the representations are to be read with an ohmmeter, then we need to know how accurate the meter is, how precise and stable the one-ohm resistors are, and the total number of switch positions. If there are a thousand positions, and the meter and resistors are good only to one percent, then (whether it's analog or not) the device surely isn't digital; but it satisfies neither Goodman's conditions nor mine. On the other hand, if there are only two hundred positions, and the meter and resistors are good to one part in a thousand, then it satisfies both Goodman's conditions and mine. But I think it's clearly digital—just as digital as a stack of silver dollars, even when the croupier "counts" them by height.

Lewis, however, has another point in mind. He notes (326) "the many combinations of values" that are possible when several variables are used together. For instance, a bank of six switches, each with only ten positions, could represent any integer up to a million, even with crude equipment. This is a special case of the complexity feature; Lewis calls it 'multidigitality', and proposes it as an additional condition on digital representation. To evaluate this proposal, we should see how the multidigitality (complexity) condition relates to the other conditions, whether Goodman's or mine.

Consider two similar systems for representing wagers in a poker game. Each uses different colored tokens for different denominations, red and blue being worth ten and a hundred times more than white, respectively. But in one system the tokens are standard colored disks ("chips"), while in the other they are measured volumes of colored sand—one tablespoonful corresponding to one chip, say. Though both systems are multidigital in Lewis's sense, the complexity is silly and useless in the sand case. For suppose players can measure volumes to within two percent, and imagine trying to bet 325 units. It's crazy! The expected error on the blue sand (the grains that stick to the spoon) is more valuable than the entire five spoonsful of white sand. A stack of three blue chips, on the other hand, can be counted positively and reliably (no residual error at all); so the white chips are not overwhelmed, and remain perfectly significant.

Lewis, of course, would not deem poker sand digital, any more than I would; his multidigitality is a *further* condition, not an alternative. What the example shows is rather that multidigitality only pays off in systems that are already digital in my sense—the sense in which poker chips would still be digital even if they were all one color. I take the lesson to be that my definition has already captured the basic phenomenon, and that complex systems are just an important special case, which the underlying digitalness makes feasible. I see the complexity feature not as essential to being digital, but (if anything) vice versa.

In considering complex types, it is essential that not only their constituent atomic types be digital, but also their modes of combination. For instance, the power of Arabic numerals depends not only on the reliable positive procedures for (writing and reading) individual digit tokens, but just as much on the reliable positive procedures for concatenating them left to right, and so on. In effect, syntactical structures must themselves be digital types. And this point applies equally to diachronic complexity: each individual step (transformation, move) must be a token of a type in a set whose members' tokens can be produced and recognized reliably and positively. The types in this set might be identified with executable instructions, as in computer languages, or with permissive rules, as in logical deductions or formal games like chess and checkers. It should be clear that complexity in digital devices goes far beyond arithmetic (or poker chip) multidigitality, and that the crucial dependence on reliable positive procedures rises dramatically with intricacy and elaborateness.

My fifth follow-up point is really just a footnote to the preceding. In digital devices, the main thing is eliminating confusion over the type of any token; and a primary motivation (payoff) for this is the ability to keep great complexity manageable and reliable. In such cases it is generally the complexity itself—that is, the structure, form or pattern of the complex tokens and processes—which really matters; the digital atomic tokens are merely means to this larger end. Hence any digital atomic tokens which will admit of a corresponding variety of digital combinations and transformations would do as well. Since all the relevant structure is digital, the substitute will be not just similar in form but exactly isomorphic. (The sonnets can be spelled perfectly in Morse code, and so on.) The very features which make reproduction reliable and positive also make formal transubstantiation reliable and positive. Digital devices are precisely those in which complex form is reliably and positively abstractable from matter— hence the medium-independence feature.

2 ANALOG

'Analog' can be understood in broader and narrower senses; but even in the latter, analog devices comprise a motley crew. I am not at all confident that a satisfactory general definition is possible—which amounts, I suppose, to doubting whether they are a well-defined natural kind. Standard examples of analog devices include slide rules, scale models, rheostats, photographs, linear amplifiers, string models of railroad networks, loudspeakers, and electronic analog computers. As before, we can try to extract some salient common features from these varied cases; three stand out.

> 1 Variations are smooth or continuous, without "gaps". There are no click-stops, or forbidden intermediate positions on a slide rule or a rheostat; photographs have (in principle) a continuous gray-scale, varying with two continuous position

dimensions. This is everybody's aboriginal intuitive idea of analog systems; unlike switches, abacuses, or alphabetic inscriptions, every setting or shape (within the relevant range) is allowed—nothing is ill-formed.

2 Within the relevant range, every difference makes a difference. The smallest rotation of a rheostat counts as changing the setting (a little); slight bending alters loudspeaker output; a photographic copy isn't perfect if it's slightly fuzzier, slightly darker, or slightly more contrasty. This is the complement of the previous feature: not only are all variations allowed, but they all matter (again unlike switches, abacuses, and letters). In general, however, the smaller the difference, the less it matters.

3 Nevertheless, only certain "dimensions" of variation are relevant. Slide rules can be made indifferently of metal or bamboo, and their color and weight don't (strictly) matter. The thickness of the paper and even the chemistry of the emulsion are irrelevant to a photograph as such—assuming they don't affect the distribution of gray levels.

I call these the *smoothness*, *sensitivity*, and *dimensionality* features, respectively.

Though it need not (for any theoretical reason) be the best approach, we can pattern the definition of 'analog' after that of 'digital'. That is, we start with a set of types, and consider the procedures for producing and reidentifying tokens of those types. For analog devices, the procedures for the write-read cycle are *approximation procedures*—that is, ones which can "come close" to perfect success. More specifically, there is some notion of margin of error (degree of deviation from perfect success) such that:

1 the smaller this margin is set, the harder it is to stay within it;

2 available procedures can (reliably) stay within a pretty small margin;

3 there is no limit to how small a margin better (future, more expensive) procedures may be able to stay within;[4] but

4 the margin can never be zero—perfect procedures are impossible.

So all ordinary (and extraordinary) procedures for parking the car right in the center of the garage, cutting six-foot boards, measuring out three tablespoons of blue sand, and copying photographs, are approximation procedures. But there are no approximation procedures for raising the dead, writing poetry, winning at roulette, or counting small piles of poker chips. Approximation procedures are, in a clear sense, the antithesis of positive procedures; the two are exclusive, but of course not exhaustive. There is no need to write out the definition of *analog device*—it is the same as for digital, except with 'approximation' substituted for 'positive' (and a margin of error included in the specified conditions).

The follow-up points again tell the story. First, Goodman says a scheme is analog if dense—that is, if between any two types there is a third. (See pages 160 and 136.) The main difficulty is that 'between' is not well-defined for all cases that seem clearly analog. What, for instance, is "between" a photograph of Roosevelt and one of Churchill? Yet it is easy to set resolution and linearity limits such that copying photographs is an approximation procedure. Similar observations apply to scale models.

Second, Lewis suggests that analog representation is representation in terms of magnitudes that are primitive or almost primitive in some good reconstruction of the language of physics. (324–25) He mentions only representations of numbers, and it isn't clear how he would generalize his criterion to non-numerical representations (to portraits, for instance), or to non-representational analog devices. But more to the point, I see no reason why we could not have analog representation of numbers by, say, hue (as in multiple pH paper or various flame-tests) or even by bacterial growth rate (say, in a model of a resource-limited chain reaction); yet surely neither of these is "almost primitive" (whatever exactly that means).[5]

Third, it seems to me that there is an important digital-like character to all the standard analog devices—specifically in the dimensionality feature. Speaking freely for a moment, the essential point about (atomic) digital types is that there tend to be relatively few of them, and they are all clearly distinct and separated. Though the types of analog schemes are themselves not like this (they "blend smoothly" into one another), the *dimensions* along which they vary *are* relatively few and clearly distinct. Thus for photographs there are exactly three orthogonal dimensions: horizontal, vertical, and gray scale. A string model of a rail network has exactly one string piece for each rail link and exactly one knot for each junction (none of which blend together). But the best example is a regular analog computer with its electronic adders, integrators, multipliers, inverters, and the like, each as discrete and determinate in type as any mathematical symbol, and their circuit connections as well-defined as the formation of any equation. Indeed, though the state and adjustment types of an analog computer are analog, the *set-up* types are perfectly digital—the component identifications and interconnections are positive and reliable.

This "second-order" digitalness of analog devices is important in two ways. First, it is, at least roughly, a necessary condition for the write and read procedures to be approximation procedures in complex systems. In one-dimensional devices, like rheostats and slide rules, it suffices to say that between any distinct types there lies a third. But in multidimensional cases, where betweenness is not in general well defined, it is crucial to have the determinate set of independent dimensions such that a copy which is close on each dimension is ipso facto close overall—hence the intelligible importance of resolution in photocopying, of precision components in analog computers, and so on. This is what gives *approximation* its sense.

It is also what gives digital simulation its grip, and for essentially the same reason. Everybody knows that photographs can be "digitized" by dividing the area into equally spaced dots, and the gray scale into equally spaced shades; the fineness of the spacings determines the quality of the digitizing, just as the smallness of the error margins determines the closeness of the approximation. Likewise when a digital computer program simulates an analog computer, the values of all the fixed components and the initial values of all the variables are stored in specified registers, and then successive variable values are computed incrementally, using interaction equations determined by the circuit structure. And the accuracy of the simulation is controlled (primarily) by the number of bits in all those registers, and the fineness of the time increment. If the system were not second-order digital, such simulation could not get off the ground: there would be no particular set of variables and parameters to digitize in specified registers (let alone equations for computing their interactions).

My fourth follow-up point, then, is the original sixty-four-dollar question. Is *every* analog device second-order digital? Or, is it really true that any analog device can in principle be digitally simulated to any desired degree of precision? To the extent that the suggestions in the previous three paragraphs hold up, the answers would appear to be 'yes'. Being second-order digital is equally the general condition for the possibility of write-read approximation procedures and of digital simulation techniques; and approximation procedures for the write-read cycle are criterial for analog devices.

They are criterial, that is, for analog devices in the *narrow* sense—that's all we've discussed so far. But the universal digital simulability claim is often made in a more sweeping tone, as if it applied to *every-thing*. Are there systems, perhaps "analog" in some broader sense, which are not second-order digital, and not necessarily digitally simulable (to whatever desired precision, and so on)? There are, of course, all manner of mongrel devices, analog in some respects or parts, digital in others; but these present no greater obstacle to simulation than purebred devices. If we think of digital devices as clean and resilient, and analog ones as messy and touchy (with the mongrels in between?), then the question becomes: Can there be systems even messier and touchier than pure analog—second-order messy, as it were?

I don't see why not. Consider the metabolic system of the rat, tokens of which are often used as "analogs" of our own metabolism, to predict the effects of fancy drugs, and the like. Now, some general metabolic relationships are known, and quite a few more specific local mechanisms are understood. But these by no means provide a complete description, in terms of which responses to strange chemicals can confidently be predicted. The millions of delicate hormonal balances, catalytic reactions, surface effects, and immunological responses, all interdependent in a biochemical frenzy of staggering proportions, can be catastrophically disrupted by the most peculiar of "side-effects". A minute occurrence on one side of a tiny membrane can have vastly different consequences from the same occurrence on the other side—and every rat contains billions of membranes.

There is essentially no way to gain detailed, quantitative control over such a mess—no hope of delineating a set of "state-variables" which fully characterize it at a time. Risky as long-term predictions are, I think it safe to announce that there will *never* be a digital simulation of human physiology reliable enough to supplant (or even challenge) biological and clinical testing of new drugs. And the reason, basically, is that metabolic systems are not second-order digital. Accordingly, there is also no specifying the "grain" or "resolution" of an approximation procedure for biochemical duplication of, say, healthy rats; there are no relevant dimensions along which such specifications could make sense.

Fifth and final follow-up point: "But isn't physics second-order digital? What about digital simulation at the level of atoms and molecules (quarks and leptons, ... whatever)?" I have two different replies to this question. In the first place, the idea is absolutely preposterous. Remember how impressed you were when you first heard that a computer with the capacity of the human brain would be the size of Texas and twenty stories high?[6] Well, the fastest and largest state-of-the-art computers today can be overwhelmed by the problem of digitally simulating a single large organic molecule (atom for atom); and there are more molecules in a human body than there would be pocket calculators, if the entire Earth were packed solid with them.[7] But simulating the molecules individually wouldn't scratch the surface: when their interactions are included, the required computations go up combinatorially!

But second, and more to the point, switching to the atomic level changes the subject. When the claim is made that photographs, linear amplifiers, and analog computers can be digitally simulated to any desired precision, that has nothing to do with fundamental physics; it would not matter if physicists had found swirling vortices in the plenum, or infinitely many infinitesimal monads. The digital simulability of analog devices is a claim about *macroscopic* phenomena. The range and variety of circumstances in which it holds is truly astonishing and important (the scientific revolution depended on it); but it is also important that such simulability (that is, second-order digitalness) is *not* universal. This second important fact is completely missed and covered up by the careless shift in topic to micro-physics.

3 CONCLUSION

'Digital' and 'analog' (in the narrow or strict sense) are both best understood in terms of the kind of practical procedures employed for the writing and reading of tokens of allowed types—these being positive and approximation procedures, respectively. And, sticking to the narrow sense, it is plausibly the case that any analog device can (in principle) be digitally simulated to any desired precision. But there are other cases which, though they do not fit this strict mold, still seem to be "analog" in some broader sense; and for at least some of these, the digital simulability claim is wildly implausible.

NOTES:

1 I resort to the noncommittal "devices" because anything more specific seems wrong; thus (as the above list shows) not everything digital is a representation, a process, a computer, a machine, or what have you. Indeed, even the implication of plan or contrivance in 'device' should be ignored, for some biological systems might be digital.

2 Goodman 1968, 136–37 and 161. This is a paraphrase into my terminology of his definition of "syntactic finite differentiation", which is his essential condition for being a digital *scheme*, which has similar conditions imposed on its semantics (152 and 161). I ignore the latter because in my view digital devices are not necessarily representational or symbolic.

3 Lewis 1971, 322. He actually offers two counterexamples, but they are based on the same idea; so I consider only the simpler one.

4 Quantum-mechanical limits are almost always distracting and boring; so let's ignore them.

5 Ned Block and Jerry Fodor make essentially this point in an old (*circa* 1971) manuscript which, so far as I know, has never been published.

6 I've forgotten where I heard this, or how long ago; and Lord knows how the calculation was made. But I've never forgotten the image.

7 180 lb $= 5 \times 10^{28}$ hydrogen masses; the volume of the Earth is 7×10^{25} cubic inches.

CHAPTER FIVE

Weak Supervenience

I shall argue against token identity theory, not by defending either dualism or type identity theory, but rather by promoting a variety of physicalist monism—"weak supervenience" I call it—which is so weak that it entails no kind of identity theory, and yet preserves a suitable "primacy" for the physical. The argument proceeds in three broad stages. The first (sections 1 and 2) is a rebuttal of Davidson's influential argument in favor of token identities of mental and physical events. The second stage (sections 3 and 4) is a demonstration that physicalism without identity theory is a coherent position. And the third (sections 5 and 6) is a series of examples, designed to show how implausible token identity theory is, once one appreciates what it claims *vis-à-vis* the alternative.

1 THE ARGUMENT FOR ANOMALOUS MONISM

I begin with Davidson's (1970/80) argument not merely because of its wide influence, but (mainly) because the points to be raised will be important in the remainder of the paper, and are also of some interest in themselves. Davidson considers only events, and his aim is to show that every mental event is also a physical event. He relies on an intuitive test for whether an event is mental or physical: mental events are just those which are describable in mental terminology, and physical events are those describable in physical terminology. This test is only intuitive, both because the respective kinds of terminology are not precisely defined, and because the conditions on *describability in a* given terminology are not fully specified. The latter is more serious than it seems, because all the conditions that first come to mind turn out to be way too inclusive, which could trivialize the result (for instance, if *all* events counted as physical, by definition). Still, the test is reasonable on an intuitive level, and it suffices for present purposes.

The fact that the test is description-relative, however, is important to the argument; for subsumption under scientific laws is also description-relative, and everything turns on that connection. A law (whatever else it is) is a statement, in the terminology of the relevant science, to the effect that all events (say) of such and such a sort are thus and so. But an event will be of the specified sort just in case it satisfies the *description* in the expression of the law. So, if it could be shown that all events in a certain class must be subsumption instances of the laws of physics, and hence must have descriptions in the terminology of physics, then it would have been shown that all those events are physical events—by the given intuitive test. This essentially is Davidson's strategy.

There is one more preliminary: the distinction between "strict laws" and mere "practical lore". A *strict* law is a member of a closed, comprehensive system of laws, each of which is perfectly precise, explicit, and exception-free. In other words, there is nothing hedged, or approximate, or incomplete about systems of strict laws—they say everything there is to say about their domain, and they say it exactly. Practical lore, by contrast, is little more than a compendium of rules of thumb—rough generalizations which are only loosely related to one another, are by no means comprehensive, and are always padded with escape clauses like "more or less", "by and large", or "other things being equal". There are, of course, intermediate gradations, including most of science; and it may well be that *nothing* we now know how to say is a genuine strict law. Davidson holds, however, that mathematical physics provides the paradigm of what strict laws should look like; and it is, moreover, our *only* viable candidate for being on the track of some. That is, we have reason to believe that the laws of "ultimate" physics will be strict laws, and no reason to believe that there will be any other strict laws.

With this groundwork laid, Davidson can state three plausible premises from which his conclusion seems to follow directly.

1 (At least many) mental events are causally related to other events.

2 Any two events related as cause and effect must be subsumable under a strict law—that is, they must have descriptions under which they instantiate such a law.

3 Strict laws can be framed only in the terminology of (ultimate) physics—which, in particular, will not include any
"mental" terms.

The argument is this: from 1 and 2, (at least many) mental events
must have descriptions under which they instantiate strict laws; and
from 3, these descriptions will have to be in the terms of ultimate
physics. Thus, by the original observation that physical events are just
those describable in physical terms, (at least many) mental events are
also physical events. Though he declines to argue for it, Davidson in
fact admits to the view that *all* mental events enter into causal relations, and hence are all physical. Since it will simplify exposition, and
make no other difference to what follows, we will henceforth stick to
this stronger, unqualified view.

Davidson calls his position *anomalous monism*—"monism" because
it entails that every event is a physical event (though some may be
mental events as well); but "anomalous" because it entails—in premise
3—that no strict laws can be framed in mental terminology (mental
events, *described as such* are "lawless"). The idea is that, although mental event predicates and physical event predicates range over the same
domain of events, the (actual and possible) extensions of the former
are so gerrymandered with respect to those of the latter, that no *strict*
generalizations can be expressed in terms of them. Essentially the
same view is also often called *token identity* theory, in contrast to the
older *type identity* theory. (See, for instance, Fodor 1974/81.) The claim
is that each separate, particular mental event ("token") that actually
occurs is numerically identical to some particular physical event
(token); but the "kinds" or "types" intended by mental event predicates are not nomologically or necessarily equivalent to any kinds or
types intended by physical event predicates (no matter how complex).

2 ROBUST VERSUS MATHEMATICAL EVENTS

One might, of course, dispute any of Davidson's premises; the third is
particularly controversial. I want to focus, instead, however, on the
use of the term 'event', which is, I believe, equivocal between the first
two premises.

In ordinary usage, an event is an occurrence or happening which is
somehow noteworthy, important, or conspicuous. Thus we speak of
"current events", the "main event" of the evening, an "eventful day",

and so on. This isn't terribly precise; and besides, what counts as "noteworthy" is very much a function of the situation and interests at hand—the slightest twitch could be a crucial turning point, in the right circumstances. Clearly, no airtight set of necessary and sufficient conditions is forthcoming for this notion; but the following should do for our purposes.

> An *event* is a relatively abrupt change in the state or course of things, which therefore stands out against a local background of things proceeding smoothly, or without interruption.

So, in this sense, the switch tripping and the light coming on are both events, as are decisions and sudden realizations, battles and billiard ball collisions. But the Mississippi River continuing to flow quietly as usual (past Memphis at noon) is not an event; nor is it an event that the moon stays in orbit at midnight, or that the light stays off at some moment when no one touches the switch. So long as nothing "happens" to a billiard ball, it remains "uneventfully" on course.

Most of physics has *nothing* to say about events in this ordinary sense. To be sure, one can use, say, classical mechanics to predict the occurrence of an eclipse, or the results of a billiard ball collision. But such events are *not* the subject matter of the theory; none of the variables in any of Newton's laws ever takes an eclipse or a collision as its value. Rather, the values of these variables are always the magnitudes of the various relevant quantitative physical variables and parameters (forces, masses, distances, and so on); and the laws simply state that certain mathematical relationships *invariably* obtain among these magnitudes—no matter what (if anything) "happens". Events like eclipses and collisions can be predicted on this basis, even though the laws say nothing about them, just because their occurrences happen to be perspicuously correlated with certain conjunctions of the quantitative values.

Nevertheless, the traditional view in philosophy has always been that science is concerned with the causal relations among events; and so, to accommodate that view, another sense of "event" has been extorted from English.

> An *event* is an instantaneous valuation of the applicable physical variables at a point (or, perhaps, in a region).

So in this sense, the velocity of the Mississippi at Memphis at noon (that is, the velocity's being such and such) *is* an event; likewise, the mass, momentum, and average temperature of the moon at midnight are events, and its traversing a kilometer in a second is an infinite set of such events—or, alternatively, a single complex event. By definition, these are the "events" which are related by the laws of physics; but, on the face of it, they bear little resemblance to what are called 'events' in the more ordinary usage described above. To avoid confusion, I will call events in the ordinary sense (where something "happens") *robust* events, in contrast to the sense just described, which I call *mathematical* events. The laws of physics relate mathematical events, but they do not apply (at least not directly) to robust events.[1]

Likewise, we may distinguish a special usage of "cause" to go with strict laws and mathematical events; instead of the robust "instigator" or "bringer about" (the explosion caused the shock wave which caused the avalanche), we have the "cause" as the mathematically sufficient condition, given the laws (the state of a closed system at t *causes* its state at $t+\Delta t$). Finally, the term 'physical' itself plays a double role. It can be used strictly for that pertaining to the theoretical *science* of physics—in which case, physical events are mathematical events characterized in the same terms that appear in the laws of mathematical physics. But at least as often, 'physical' is used as a sort of catch-all term for everything contingent and "substantive" which isn't expressly set aside in some special category like the mental, the functional, the ethical, or what have you; here we find also the "merely" physical, or that pertaining to "mere things". Though explosions and avalanches (and mouth movements and arms going up) may not be the stuff of mathematical physics, they are surely *physical* events in this larger and more amorphous sense, which is also widely used in philosophy. The point is that the terms 'event', 'cause', and even 'physical' must be handled just as carefully as the term 'law' in arguments about physics and physicalism.

With this in mind, consider what 'event' means in Davidson's argument. To support his first premise, that mental events are causally related to other events, he gives a common sense example:

> [I]f someone sank the *Bismarck*, then various mental events such as perceivings, notings, calculations, judgements, decisions, intentional actions, and changes of belief played a causal role in the sinking of the *Bismarck*. (208)

These, obviously, are events (and causal roles) in the robust, rather than the mathematical sense. But the second premise states that events related as cause and effect must be subsumable under a strict law, and strict laws apply only to mathematical events (and causation). Thus, it seems that 'event' is used in two different ways in the two premises; and, if so, the argument equivocates, and is invalid.

It might be replied that "really" *all* events are mathematical events—robust events are just very complex mathematical events—so there is no equivocation. To assume at the outset that mental events are mathematical events, however, is tantamount to assuming the conclusion; for mathematical events were essentially invented to be whatever events mathematical physics talks about. A safer reply (because it will always work against any charge of equivocation) is to say that the term 'event' is used *generically*—it denotes on each occasion everything which is an event in either sense. This strategy builds the implicit assumption of univocality into the premises. For Davidson's argument, the second premise would end up shouldering the entire burden; for it would then say, in effect, that robust events are mathematical events. Though this would remove any question of a *logical* flaw, it would raise questions about the exposition. Davidson gives no indication that he means 'event' in this curious generic way, nor that he means the second premise to conflate the specific senses; and he offers not a word of support for the second premise—suggesting that he does not regard it as the crucial move.*

3 SUPERVENIENCE WITHOUT TOKEN IDENTITY

Problems with the argument notwithstanding, Davidson's *conclusion* remains attractive; for it seems a last safe haven for physicalism, given the sorry fate of various definitional and nomological reductions. Even if there is no systematic way to line up mental *predicates* (kinds, types) with physical counterparts, still each mental *individual* (token) has got to be identical with some physical individual—on a one-by-one basis. The situation is reassuringly asymmetrical, since though every mental individual is physical, not every physical individual is mental. And it preserves our inchoate but compelling sense that the universe is basically physical—if you took away all the atoms, nothing would be left behind. The question is: Can this intuition of "the primacy of the physical" be preserved with any position *weaker* than

---

* Regarding the argument in this section, see the appendix (added in 1997).

the token-identity thesis? I will try to show, in this section and the next, that such a position can be defined and that it is logically tenable (coherent).

The initial clue comes from a passage of Davidson's.

> Although the position I describe denies there are psycho-physical laws, it is consistent with the view that mental characteristics are in some sense dependent, or supervenient, on physical characteristics. Such supervenience might be taken to mean that there cannot be two events alike in all physical respects but differing in some mental respect, or that an object cannot alter in some mental respect without altering in some physical respect. (214)

The problem with this passage as it stands is that, in characterizing supervenience, it takes the token-identity thesis for granted. Thus it says, if two events are alike physically, then *they* (the *very same* two events) cannot differ mentally; again, it is one and the same object that cannot alter mentally without altering physically.

Kim (1978, 1979) gives an explicit definition of 'supervenience' (with Davidson's remarks clearly in mind), but he makes the same assumption.[2]

> A family of properties M is *supervenient upon* a family of properties N with respect to a domain D *just in case*, for any two objects in the domain D, if they diverge in the family M then necessarily they diverge in the family N; that is to say, for any x and y in D if x and y are indiscernible with respect to the properties in the family N, then necessarily x and y are indiscernible with respect to the properties in M. (1979, 41)

The properties in M and N are understood to be properties of the *same individuals*, from the same domain D—which is all the token-identity thesis requires.

Supervenience, however, can (and thus should) be defined without building in token identities. The central intuition is that "fixing" the physical fixes everything, or that nothing could have been otherwise without something physical having been otherwise. There is no reason whatsoever to tie this intuition down to any particular domain of individuals; that is, expressing the intuition need not at all be confined to the form: "For each individual, *it* could not ..." The idea that fixing the physical fixes everything need not be broken down on an individual-by-individual basis—it can be, so to speak, "world-wide". Just as objectors to so-called type-identity theories urge that physics need not capture how the mental is "carved up" into kinds, I urge that it need not capture how the mental is "carved up" into individuals. The essential constraint is on sets of *truths*, without regard to how (or even whether) those truths are decomposed into properties of individuals.

So removing the offending references to individuals (other than the whole world), Davidson can be paraphrased roughly as follows.

> It could not have been the case that the world was just as it is in all physical respects, but different in some mental respect; or, the world cannot alter in some mental respect without altering in some physical respect.

To formulate an analogous paraphrase of Kim, we consider languages whose sentences are evaluated at possible worlds in set W, and define discernibility this way.

> Two worlds in W are *discernible with* language L just in case there is a sentence of L which is true at one, and not true at the other.

Then *weak* supervenience—that is, supervenience that does not (explicitly) entail the token-identity thesis—can be defined as a relation between two languages (relative to a set of possible worlds).

> K *weakly supervenes on* L (relative to W) just in case any two worlds in W discernible with K are discernible with L.

There is no mention here of the individuals (if any) in the domains of K and L. (Notice also that the modality in Kim's definition has been absorbed into the quantification over possible worlds.)

It remains to be shown that weak supervenience does not entail the token-identity thesis *implicitly*; that is, that it is consistent to affirm the one while denying the other.

4 WEAK SUPERVENIENCE AND TOKEN IDENTITY

To show that weak supervenience is compatible with the denial of the token-identity thesis, it suffices to produce one consistent model in which the former holds and the latter is false. For this purpose, let the *possible worlds* in W be infinite white sheets of paper, each with a finite number of non-intersecting "loops" inscribed on it in black—where a *loop* is a simple closed curve (figure) with a finite perimeter. For simplicity, we suppose that polar coordinates are defined for each world; that is, the *center*, the *unit of radius*, and the directions *north* and *positive rotation* are determined. Relative to these worlds, we consider two languages, each a first-order theory with identity.

The *arrow language* has in its domain (that is, the objects it is intended to talk about) the real numbers and the "arrows". An *arrow* is a ray, starting from the center of the world, and extending in a straight line without limit. There are three primitive predicates in the arrow language.

$Sxyz \ =_{df} \ x$ is the sum of y and z.

$Pxyz \ =_{df} \ x$ is the product of y and z.

$Barv \ =_{df} \ a$ is an arrow v revolutions from north and black at radius r.

With these resources, various functions and relations (including numerical inequalities) can be defined; and the existence of certain figures (for instance, circles concentric with the universe) can be asserted indirectly. However, infinite expressions (such as infinite sums) are not allowed; so trigonometric functions, in particular, cannot be defined.

The *loop language* has in its domain only the loops. It has any number of primitive predicates, of which the following five are to be taken as typical.

$Cx \ =_{df} \ x$ is circular.

$Qx \ =_{df} \ x$ is square.

$Exy \ =_{df} \ x$ encloses y.

$Lxy \ =_{df} \ x$ is larger (in area) than y.

$Mxy \ =_{df} \ x$ and y are geometrically similar (in shape).

In case there is doubt about which other predicates are relevantly "like" these, then restrict the language to these only.

The loop language supervenes on the arrow language. If there is so much as one point which is black in one world, and white in another, then those two worlds are discriminable with the arrow language; but any two worlds discriminable with the loop language would have to differ at least that much. However, the token-identity thesis is false relative to these two languages; for the sets of objects describable in them (their respective sets of "tokens") are completely disjoint. Hence, supervenience does not entail token identities.

The foregoing counterexample depends on the token-domains which were stipulated when the arrow and loop languages were defined; and it might be thought that those stipulations were artificially narrow. Perhaps, for purposes of token-identity theory, the domain of a language should be closed under compounding—that is, it should contain all compounds or complexes of its members. Such enrichment would make no difference to the present case, however; for whatever a "compound" is, it must *at least* be the (mereological) sum of its components, and no loop is the sum of any set of arrows and/or numbers. A different suggestion is that the domain contain every individual whose existence could be "required" by a sentence of the language. Thus, though there is no way to *say explicitly* in the arrow language that there is a circle of radius *r* concentric with the world, this can be "said implicitly" with the following sentence.

$$(\exists r)(\forall v)(\exists a) \; Barv.$$

But this strategy will not work in general. For instance, it takes trigonometric functions to describe a square in polar coordinates, and these functions are unavailable within the resources of the arrow language; hence no sentence of the arrow language can require the existence of any square—not to mention irregular loops shaped, say, like amoebas.

Does this merely show that the arrow language is too impoverished? If the full resources of classical mathematics were added, then, of course, it would be possible not only to assert the existence of squares (and many other figures) but also to describe them in glorious detail, and prove all kinds of theorems about them. But that is beside the point in the present context. We are concerned with what *supervenience* entails, and the arrow language is *already* rich enough for the loop language to be supervenient on it. The whole aim of the exercise is to show what a *weak* constraint (weak) supervenience is; and, toward that end, we want to impoverish the "subvenient" language as much as we can get away with. Of course, this particular example only works because we know that arrows and loops are both identical to (sums of) sets of points—that is, to the individuals in the domain of some "point language", on which the loop and arrow languages both supervene. But there is no reason to suppose that there must always be such a third language, whenever one language supervenes on another. We have only chosen such a case here, because it makes the *proof* that supervenience does not entail token-identities so straightforward.

A much more important question is whether this weak constraint is strong enough to capture our intuitions, ill-formed and elusive though they be, about the "primacy of the physical". One significant factor which has not been addressed is the special "comprehensiveness" of physical *laws*. So far, weak supervenience requires that the terminology in which these laws are expressed be *descriptively* sufficient to "fix" the world *at a time* (in the sense that the world could not have been different without there having been a difference describable in these terms). But the laws themselves are comprehensive in a further sense: roughly, they are sufficient to "fix" the progressive alteration or development of the world *through time*—at least insofar as it is fixed at all (that is, not random). If we believed in strict determinism, we would say:

> The history of the world could not have been different (physically) at one moment, unless it had been different (physically) at each moment.

The apparent failure of physical determinism, however, makes the relevant special authority of the physical more difficult to express. The basic idea seems to be that all the alternatives that are left fundamentally undetermined by physics (such as quantum indeterminacies) are *genuinely* undetermined—that is, nothing else determines them in lieu of physical factors.

We attempt to capture this idea with a notion of "nomological" supervenience. Let W be the set of *instantaneous* possible worlds (possible world "slices"), and H be the set of *possible histories*, each of which is a function from the real numbers of some finite interval into W. Intuitively, a possible history is the world developing over a finite time period from a certain starting condition; and the point is that only some possible histories will be "allowed" by any set of laws which govern how the world changes. Consider two languages, each associated with a set of such laws (expressed in the terms of that language); then:

> K is *nomologically supervenient* on L (relative to H) just in case every member of H disallowed by the laws of K is also disallowed by the laws of L.

That is, no alternative possible histories allowed by physics are ruled out by any other laws. Note that nomological supervenience does not entail weak supervenience, because there might be two members of *W* which were descriptively discriminable with *K* and not with *L*, but which were, so to speak, equivalent with regard to all the *laws* of *K*— that is, for any history where one is allowed, there is an exactly similar history in which the other is allowed.

The punch line is that even the conjunction of weak and nomological supervenience is insufficient to entail the token-identity thesis— as a simple modification of our earlier example will show. Add a time parameter to each of the nonarithmetic predicates in the loop and arrow languages, and promulgate the following *law* in the arrow language:

$$(\exists\omega)(\forall a,r,v,v',t,t')\{(Barvt \ \& \ v'-v = \omega(t'-t)) \supset (\exists a')Ba'rv't'\}$$

In effect, this says that the whole world rotates with constant angular velocity, ω. There might be any number of laws expressed in the loop language, of which the following is typical:

$$(\forall x,y)\{(\exists t)Exyt \supset (\forall t)Exyt\}$$

(That is, if *x* ever encloses *y*, then it always does.) The new loop language is nomologically supervenient on the new arrow language— indeed, the latter is strictly deterministic—and yet the token identity thesis fails, just as before.

Quite a different philosophical question remains about relying on the notion of supervenience to characterize the special status of the physical. What is the sense of "possible" in which the worlds in *W* are *possible* worlds? If it meant just *logical* possibility, then we would know at the outset that the mental is *not* supervenient on the physical; for example, it would not be *contradictory* to hold that there are some nonphysical angels whose attitudes are discriminable in mental terms. On the other hand, we must be careful not to equate possibility with *physical* possibility in too restrictive a sense, on pain of trivializing the thesis. The answer is not to look for some "neutral but natural" sense of "possibility" with the aid of which supervenience can be defined, but rather to turn it around and regard the thesis of supervenience as a contribution to our understanding of *genuine* possibility. Thus, we let the possible worlds in *W* be all those which are physically possible, in the weakest sense—no physical laws are violated, but there might be all manner of nonphysical angels, and so on, about which these laws say nothing. Then, the thesis that the mental supervenes on the physical amounts to a further culling of this set; it says that some of these worlds are not really possible after all, because they still do not bear a close enough relation to the physical. Supervenience provides a way of tightening the grip that the physical has on the possible, without having to say that only propositions expressible in the language of physics can be true, or that only individuals in the domain of physics can exist.

5 WAVE HITS: A SIMPLE EXAMPLE

So far, I have argued two points: (i) that Davidson is unconvincing in his "proof" that every mental event (token) is also a physical event (token); and (ii) that it is coherent to deny the token-identity thesis, while still maintaining the supervenience of the mental on the physical. These are flank attacks on the token-identity thesis, meant to sap its defenders of their will to resist. I have yet to confront the thesis directly, and give positive reasons to believe that it is, in fact, false. The strategy in this final phase is to examine a selection of cases in a way which, I hope, exhibits the gross implausibility of token identity theory—now that we have seen that supervenience can be maintained independently. Let's begin with a case that has nothing to do with the mental.

Suppose that you and I each make a crisp, single-crested wave, starting from opposite ends of a swimming pool. These radiate outward from us, progressively bobbing tiny corks which are strewn across the surface of the water. Each "wave-hit" on a cork—or to be more precise, each passage of a wave crest under the center of gravity of a cork—is an uncomplicated robust event. The basic question is: With *which* mathematical event could such a robust wave-hit be identical? The serious difficulty of this question, however, is most conspicuous in a slightly trickier variation. Whenever your wave and mine hit the same cork at the same time, then there are *two* quite distinct (though spatio-temporally coincident) robust events. At the level of description of wave-hits, there is yours and there is mine, and (at that level of description) these are not the same. Hence, if each is identical to a mathematical event, then these must be *distinct* mathematical events (since identity is transitive).

What's the most likely candidate for a mathematical event—an event describable in the language of ultimate physics—which is identical to one of our wave-hits? Presumably, it's some complex of enormously many (perhaps infinitely many) instantaneous positions and velocities of water molecules, at the relevant place and time. (We needn't worry about the fuzziness of the vicinity, since there are harder problems.) *Which* instantaneous positions and velocities are to be included in this complex? If only one robust wave-hit were involved, we might be tempted to duck the nitty-gritty details, and grandly include *all* the molecular events in the relevant vicinity. But such cavalier indiscriminateness is manifestly impossible when there are two coincident events which must be kept distinct. Of course, distinct complexes can have constituents in common; but it would be a clear cheat to make much of that in the present case. Your wave-hit, and mine are not mostly the same event, differing only on some peripheral technicality. At the level of description of waves hitting corks, these are quite distinct events, with entirely different causal histories, and correspondingly different counterfactual properties. So, though they might have some common micro-physical components, they had better be largely disjoint.

When we turn up our microscope, however, and *look* at the positions and velocities of the water molecules, there isn't a trace of either wave-hit to be found anywhere. The individual molecules are racing around in all directions, crashing into and careening past one another at speeds far greater than that of any water flow or wave propagation. When the water moves macroscopically, there is just a slight statistical imbalance in the frenetic turmoil at the molecular level. Crudely, we might picture such an imbalance as 1001 molecules going up (at a certain moment) for every 999 going down. Put this way, it is painfully obvious that you can't ask *which* of those 1001 rising molecules is "the unbalanced one". Or (what comes to the same thing) if the ratio is 1002 to 998 when two waves coincide, there is no allocating one particular molecule to each wave (and 1998 others to the normal thermal chaos. *None* of the particular positions or velocities at the molecular level is determinately a constituent of one wave-hit (or the other, or neither)—though each makes a tiny contribution to the overall effect.

In other words, *there is no* "complex" of such microscopic mathematical events which is literally *identical* to any robust wave-hit. Wave-hits simply don't "hang together" as determinate individuals (no matter how "complex") at the level of particle physics.[3] My conclusion, then, is that the individuals or tokens of which our sentences are true are just as "relative" to the level of description as are the kinds or types into which those sentences sort them. The world does not come metaphysically individuated, any more than it comes metaphysically categorized, prior to and independent of any specific descriptive resources—which is not to say that these individuals (and categories) aren't perfectly genuine and objective, once the language is specified; nor is it to say that the languages themselves are in any sense arbitrary. It is only to say that the individuals we can discuss in one way of talking need not be identified with the individuals we can discuss in another way of talking, even if the latter way of talking is somehow "basic and comprehensive". That is, we need another way of accounting for the basicness and comprehensiveness of physics than the identity theory.

6 THE MENTAL AS SUPERVENIENT

The relations between robust water-wave phenomena and the phenomena of ultimate physics are about as uncluttered and well-understood as relations to ultimate physics are likely to get. This is in stark contrast to the case with mental phenomena. There are three reasons for beginning with the simpler case. First, it makes it obvious that objecting to the identity theory—even token identity theory—does not require any peculiar or controversial metaphysical categories; there is nothing scientifically intractable, let alone metaphysically spooky, about water waves. In other words, the problem lies with expressing the primacy of the physical in terms of *identities*, and not with the (various) extraordinary properties of the mental. Second, it would be bizarre to maintain that, although identity theory fails for ordinary undulatory phenomena, it nevertheless holds for the mental. Typically, in fact, mental phenomena are cast as the last holdouts against a clean sweep for physicalism—making their capitulation seem both more important and more inevitable. The wave example and the definition of weak supervenience combine to remove that pressure. Third, the very simplicity of the example makes it easy to see how it works. It turns on the interplay of two factors: (i) the "swamping" of macro-individuals by all the irrelevant micro-turmoil; and (ii) the "coincidence" of all the candidate constituents of distinct macro-individuals. We can now be on the lookout for a comparable interplay in more difficult cases.

Thus, if the physiological is an intervening level between the mental and the (strictly) physical, then there might well be such an argument against mental/physiological event identities. Given the passing of the neat wet-flip-flops view of brain functioning, there is less reason to suppose that the metabolic constituents of mental events can be identified in the midst of all the irrelevant physiological housekeeping; and there is more reason to suppose that distinct mental events will each "supervene on" (the activity in) extended brain regions, which may largely, or even entirely coincide. I will not pursue this point, however.

Rather, I will adapt an example of Dennett's (1977/78, 107) to make an even stronger point. In the spirit of Lettvin's remark, that the information processing model in psychology is "the only straw floating", assume that the mind can be understood as roughly analogous to a computer chess-player; and consider such a chess-player which works on the following general principles.

1 It has a number of heuristics for evaluating any given chess position as it stands (that is, without look-ahead).

2 It can construct a tree of possible future positions from any given position, using the heuristics to prune unpromising branches.

3 It can choose a "best" move in any position, by evaluating the ultimate positions in the (pruned) tree, and then mini-maxing back to the current options.

Such a machine will not only play chess, but play with a recognizable style, which might naturally be described in intentional terms.

1 It "thinks" it should get its queen out early.

2 It "prefers" a free-swinging, wide open game.

3 It tends to "choose" an aggressive posture over a defensive one.

Dennett's point is that intentional descriptions, such as these, are based on the machine's overall behavior, and need carry no specific implications at all about the content of any internal representational structures.

That is, though there are data structures in the machine interpretable as expressing various facts and goals about the game—say, that bishops are three times as valuable as pawns, or that mobility and center control are about equally important—there are no data structures even remotely interpretable as: "It's good to get the queen out early," or "The best defense is a good offense." Instead, the characteristics noted in 1 to 3 "emerge" as "net" attitudes from the collective action of all the different detailed heuristics, without themselves being expressed internally at all.

Suppose now that three coefficients in the machine's evaluation heuristics are adjusted slightly (either by us or by its own "learning" routines).

1 Knights are boosted in value relative to bishops.

2 Pawn coordination gets more weight *vis-à-vis* piece mobility.

3 The value of linking rooks is reduced a little.

It is entirely possible that these three adjustments together (but no two of them without the third) would result in the reversal of each of the preceding emergent attitudes. That is, after the adjustments, the machine thinks its queen should be held back, prefers a tight, close game, and tends to emphasize defense over offense. It seems to me that each reversal of attitude is plausibly regarded as a distinct event at the intentional attribution level of description; but at the level of internal information processing, there is no distinguishing *which* "micro-events" (coefficient adjustments) are constituents of which attitude changes. In other words, intentional level events attributable on the basis of external behavior need not be *identical* with information processing events (no matter how complex)—even if they supervene on them. Needless to say, relations between the mental and any "information processing level" in people are likely to be rather messier than this (assuming a level like the latter can be discriminated at all—compare Dreyfus 1979, chapter 4). And, of course, computational or information processing models are widely regarded as the last best hope for any clean, general science of psychology. The only point here, however, is that even if psychology were in that good a shape, it would be no salvation for the identity theory.

I have argued that Davidson has failed to demonstrate the token identity thesis (because he equivocates on the term 'event'); that the primacy of the physical can be captured by the notion of *weak supervenience*, which does not entail the token identity thesis; and that several examples render the token identity thesis very implausible in fact. I do not claim that these examples (the wave-hits, and the chess-player attitudes) confute the token identity thesis by themselves, because there is too much room for philosophical maneuvering by desperate defenders. The earlier sections are meant to show that desperate defense is not worth the effort, since physicalism doesn't hang on it; and in that context, the examples may be persuasive. The overall point is not that there is anything special about the mental, which exempts it from the comprehensive claims of the physical, but rather that these claims can be expressed without recourse to the notion of identity, and that there are reasons to prefer doing so.

APPENDIX (ADDED 1997)

The charge in section 2 that Davidson equivocates on the word 'event' is unjust. For he certainly could, and surely did, mean to use it in what I go on to call a "generic" sense. My observation that this effectively puts the entire burden of the argument on the principle of causality (his premise 2) remains correct. But Davidson is forthright in saying that he is simply going to rely on this principle without defending it; so his argument as it stands is unexceptionable.

I still believe that the distinction between mathematical and robust events is important and to the point in bringing out the strength and implausibility of that premise; but a revised version of this paper would need to argue against the causal principle more directly. (The examples in sections 5 and 6 can be seen as illustrations of what's wrong with it.)

NOTES:

1 I admit to some uncertainty about particle physics. Disintegrations, annihilations, and quantum jumps are perfectly robust events, despite their tiny scale, and they seem more central to quantum mechanics than eclipses, collisions, and so on, do to classical mechanics. Still, such events are at most a part of the subject matter even of micro-physics; wave equations and the like relate only mathematical events, and, of course, most of the motions and interactions of these particles are described by more or less classical equations of motion and electrodynamics.

2 Kim takes his definition to be a development of Hare's (1952) usage; but Hare points out (in conversation) that it is not. His concern was that an evaluative judgment, such as deeming something "good", involves an element of personal commendation or commitment, which is over and above describing the object's actual properties. There is never an inconsistency or contradiction, he says, in conceding an object's factual characteristics, while declining to commend it. There would be, however, another kind of "inconsistency" in commending one object and refusing to commend another, while agreeing that the two objects are just alike descriptively. This is the sense in which, for Hare, evaluative judgments *supervene* on descriptive judgments. Nevertheless, despite Hare's prior claim on this term, I will follow in general the usage of Davidson and Kim.

3 It might be supposed that the language or level of description with which we refer to robust wave-hits is not itself sufficiently well-defined or scientifically respectable for the token identity theorist to have to worry about it. But the only consistent way to maintain this line is to be an "eliminative materialist" about wave-hits (that is, there "really" aren't any such events), which is just the sort of desperation maneuver that I hope to show unnecessary.

CHAPTER SIX

Ontological Supervenience

I BACKGROUND

A couple of years ago I wrote and published a paper entitled "Weak Supervenience" (1982). Unbeknownst to me, several of the important theses in that paper had been clearly stated some years earlier in a pair of joint articles by Geoffrey Hellman and Frank Thompson (1975 and 1977). Better late than never, I would now like to acknowledge their priority, and apologize for not having done so sooner. Further, now that I am apprised of their pioneering work, I would like to take up explicitly certain additional issues that they raise.

Hellman and Thompson (and I) seek to articulate the basic intuition of physicalist materialism in a way that does not imply too much; in particular, we all want to avoid any formulation that entails traditional reductionism. They propose a conjunction of two distinct theses, which they call the principles of *physical determination*, and *physical exhaustion*, respectively. Physical determination is quite similar to what I (later) called "weak supervenience"; and despite various differences, I am (not surprisingly) largely sympathetic.[1] The principle of physical exhaustion, on the other hand, has no analog in my paper; and, moreover, I am not very sympathetic. So that's what I want to discuss.

A little history first. Many recent authors have rejected so-called "type-type" identity theory (and the closely related reductionism), on the dual grounds that it is implausibly strong, and that it is not necessary for materialism. All that's needed, they say, is a weaker "token-token" identity theory. The idea is this: even if psychological (or whatever) *types* (kinds, properties) cannot be identified (or nomologically correlated) with physical types, still individual psychological *tokens* (particular events, states, and so on), might be identifiable with individual physical tokens, on a one-by-one basis; and that would suffice for a materialist metaphysics.

The question now is whether even token identity theory might be too strong, and unnecessary for materialism. I think it is, and that the determination/supervenience principle is sufficient by itself. That principle may be roughly paraphrased as follows:

> The world could not have been different in any respect, without having been different in some strictly physical respect—that is, in some respect describable in a canonical language of physics.

The thing to notice is that this makes no mention of any particular individuals (other than the whole universe); hence, unlike earlier definitions,[2] it doesn't *explicitly* presuppose token identities. The main thrust of my paper was to argue that supervenience and identity theory are in fact independent, and that the latter is probably false. Hellman and Thompson agree about the independence,[3] and they are also dissatisfied with common versions of the identity thesis. But, rather than reject identities, they propose a new and significantly more sophisticated theory.

2 HELLMAN AND THOMPSON'S PHYSICALISM

Many philosophers, myself included, had been content to regard as physical any entity of which some "suitable" physical predicate is true—leaving it for another day to say just which predicates those are. Hellman and Thompson have a similar intuition, but a much better strategy. They begin only with "basic" physical predicates—like: 'x is a neutrino', 'x is an electromagnetic field', 'x is gravitationally attracting y', and so on. They assume that positive instances of basic predicates are uncontroversially physical, and that collectively these constitute the whole physical universe. We are still not told just which predicates are "basic"; but they are clearly less problematic than "suitable" predicates in general. In fact, as near as I understand it, the single predicate, 'x has non-zero mass-energy', would suffice, according to contemporary physics.

In any case, the essential innovation lies in what comes next: using the calculus of individuals (that is, of parts and wholes) to *construct* all physical entities out of positive instances of basic predicates. First, the physical universe is defined as the fusion (that is, the sum or spatio-temporal agglomeration) of all those instances; then all and only physical entities are parts (spatio-temporal portions) of that universe. The point of fusing and then repartitioning the universe is that there are no constraints on the "boundaries" of the new parts. They may be arbitrarily (perhaps infinitely) complex and bizarre; and they need not be definable, implicitly or explicitly, in any particular language.

Those arbitrary parts of the physical universe are the physical "tokens" for Hellman and Thompson's identity theory. Since there are almost certainly more such tokens than there are predicates in any (finitistic) language, they provide not only a better specified physical basis than before, but also a larger one. The principle of physical exhaustion, however, is not quite the same as the token-identity thesis, for it also delimits abstract entities—namely, to what I will call "physically based" sets. These are just the sets appearing in a set-theoretic hierarchy, all of whose ur-elements (ultimate individuals) are physical tokens.[4] Thus, all that really exist, according to Hellman and Thompson, are physical tokens and physically based sets.

This is manifestly a superior formulation of the identity thesis, both sharper and weaker than its antecedents; and it makes a tidy companion for the determination/supervenience principle. The question remains: does that principle *want* a companion? That is, in our effort to articulate our somewhat inchoate sense of materialism, is there reason to augment physical determination with physical exhaustion? I don't think so—though, I confess, it's not altogether clear to me how best to argue the point.

3 REASONS TO BE MATERIALISTS

A plausible beginning is to ask why we want to be materialists in the first place. Then we could consider which (if either) candidate principle satisfies those original motivations. The common rationales for materialism, it turns out, are a surprisingly mixed bag; and that fact alone may make a modest catalog of them worthwhile. I have distinguished six loose categories, which I will list, and then briefly comment on.

1 THE CALL OF THE ONE. Some folks take seriously a so-called "unity of science". Now, if this unity is supposed to be an established fact that needs explanation, then I simply don't see it. If, on the other hand, it's proposed as a desideratum or goal, then we can wish its

seekers all luck and happiness; but their fondest hopes are hardly a *reason* for adopting materialism. In fact, I think, only people who are materialists already are inclined to hope for a "unification" of science; and all they really mean by it is that their materialism would be vindicated.[5]

A different unity issue, however, is more interesting. Without lingering over details, we may roughly categorize entities three ways: (i) those which (almost) everyone agrees are physical; (ii) those which are disputed; and (iii) those which (almost) everyone agrees are not physical. The third category includes numbers, sets, Platonic forms, and the like—that is, *eternal* or even *necessary* entities, in the sense that means not subject to generation, variation, or decay. By contrast, the first two categories comprise the *temporal* or *contingent*—that is, entities that we might generically call "occurrences" subject to generation, variation, and decay. Now this temporal/atemporal contrast is quite significant, metaphysically; and it puts all the disputed cases on the same side as the clearly material. To take a pertinent example, beliefs and feelings are like mountains and molecules (and unlike numbers and sets) in being temporal, contingent occurrences. The same could be said of institutions, moral actions, and what have you.

Now this, plausibly, *is* a fact to be explained; and materialism might be brought forward as the explanation. What is the principle of unity of the temporal/contingent? Matter! Cutely: if we ask, with Kant, why time is the form of *both* inner and outer sense, we can answer, contra Descartes (not to mention Kant), that time (not space) is the essence of matter—and everything (sensible) is material.

2 SEDUCTIVE ANALOGY. A novel, or even a drawing, can be filled with courage, conflict, pathos; it can break new artistic ground, while excitement and beauty leap from every page. Yet, in some sense, each copy is "nothing but" ink and paper; vaporize that paper, and you have eliminated that copy—snuffed it right out of being. Eliminate all the copies, and (in one way or another) you eliminate the work. Now, aren't people (and cultures and whatever else) just like that—vaporize their material embodiment and you snuff them out entirely? Sounds right to me.

3 THE WAY THE WIND BLOWS ("PROGRESS"). Negatively: many opponents of materialism seem like die-hard stragglers, clinging desperately to some old system that's hit the metaphysical skids. More positively: science marches on. First they decided the stars are just

(ordinary) matter; then came the synthesis of urea, the theory of evolution, the double helix, ... and now the *avant garde* want to talk to their computers. Again and again, it looks as if matter in motion wins out—with nothing else needed. And, naturally, we'd all rather be winners than die-hard stragglers.

4 FEAR OF DARKNESS. Denizens of the mental, some say, are unclear, shadowy, elusive, and generally spooky—*hence* ontologically suspect. Not quibbling over the premise, we may inquire about the inference: *why* can't dark, slippery things be real? Well, it is a venerable (if peculiar and not always acknowledged) principle of metaphysics that: *To be is to be intelligible.*[6] It's hard to know what to make of that. It seems presumptuous on the face of it (in the absence of intelligent creation); but I'll still bet its root runs under a lot of philosophical dirt.

Be that as it may, the argument from mere spooklessness to materialism can go several ways. One line has it that understanding is the product of explanation, and that the only really clear explanations we have are in the physical sciences. So, unless the other sciences start shaping up, their domains had better identify with the physical, on pain of gloomy non-being. A different tack maintains that intelligibility presupposes cognitive meaningfulness, which in turn always rests on objective observation. Then, supposing that only material objects (states, events, and so on) can be observed objectively, only they can be intelligible, hence real.

5 THE SCROOGE INSTINCT. How many's the poor son gone to debt and ruin for frittering his metaphysical accounts? In principle, of course, Ockham's famous razor, "Don't multiply entities beyond necessity", gets its edge from Beetle Bailey's more incisive "Don't do *anything* beyond necessity". But in practical New England, the moral is keenly economical: "In all commitments, be as frugal as possible— nay, even parsimonious. Buy a basic physics if you must, but avoid every frilly extravagance. And never, *never* squander your precious fluids in profligate hypostasis!"

I have occasionally wondered what makes ontology so expensive, or what limits our budget, or, indeed, what exactly we are spending. Having dwelt more summers in the southwest than the northeast, I feel no great longing for desert landscapes; and frankly, Ockham's razor cuts little ice out there anyway. Perhaps, however, I can abide a prudent California compromise: We shall assume no entity before its time.

6 Law and order. Physics strives (and promises) to be *strict*; that is, to provide a closed, comprehensive system of exception-free laws.[7] In other words, setting aside any implications about other domains, physics takes care of its own very nicely, thank you. At the appropriate level of description, physical phenomena can be *fully* explained *physically*. This promise, in turn, fuels a standard criticism of interactionism: if physical phenomena are already fully explicable in their own terms, then how can anything non-physical (anything mental, for example) make any difference to them? Only, it seems, by breaking the laws of physics. Moreover, the mental had better be able to affect the physical (for instance, in deliberate action), or it won't be much use. Unfortunately, therefore, the price tag on having mental entities be both non-physical and effective appears to be the internal strictness of physics itself. That'll never sell in Boston.

4 Why these aren't reasons for identity theory

That completes my little catalog of rationales for materialism; needless to say, some considerations impress me more than others. Now we can return to the problem of formulation. In particular, do these motivations support the identity theory, in addition to the principle of physical determination? It's easiest just to go through the list again in order.

1 Call of the one. Explaining the unity of the temporal/contingent is a tantalizing metaphysical prize, and a big plus for materialism. But what exactly in materialism promises us this prize? It seems to me that the principle of physical determination says it explicitly. For that principle addresses precisely whatever *could have been different*: in other words, essentially the temporal/contingent. And it is all and only this category that the principle ties down to the physical—thereby explicating the unity of the category, via the common supervenience on matter (as described in canonical physics).

I don't see that physical exhaustion would add anything to the foregoing; but it might offer an alternative account. For it entails that every entity is either a physical token or a set, and that division could plausibly be aligned with the temporal/atemporal distinction. Saying that temporal occurrences are all and only physical tokens would explain both the unity of the category, and also its connection with time (since physical tokens are spatio-temporal fragments of the universe). It's less obvious, however, how well this strategy accommodates temporal events, processes, and states. They would have to be identified with physical tokens (not sets), on pain of undermining the point; and that seems likely to cause problems.

In passing, I should warn against an attractive simplification. It's tempting to reformulate supervenience in terms of possible *changes*:

> The world could not change (become different) in any respect without changing in some (canonically describable) physical respect.[8]

Unfortunately, there are clear counterexamples. Thus, a person can change from married to single, or an item can change from your property to mine, at the stroke of midnight, when some prior legal decree takes effect—there being no physical change *at that time*, save, so to speak, the ticking of the clock. Of course, what the materialist wants to insist upon is physical changes back when the decree was promulgated (as well as many others during the evolution of matrimonial, proprietary institutions, and so on). Consequently, the general statement of supervenience must be made "world-wide" through time as well as at each instant; hence, the looser formulation in terms of how the world (*in toto*) could have been different.

2 SEDUCTIVE ANALOGY. As everyone knows, the painting/story analogy is vulnerable to a dismissive ploy: there's no real pathos in the story—the story is just pathetic. By the same token, there are no real stories, but only story-like inscriptions; and, according to some philosopher-like organisms, "real" mental entities can likewise be eliminated. I, however, find that all arch and boring.

So, suppose we take the analogy at face value: what does it really suggest? Well, basically, if you disintegrate enough material structures, you can wipe out lots of other entities as well. But *which* entities are liable to such extinction? Not, presumably, numbers, sets, and Platonic forms; in fact, potential victims seem limited exactly to the temporal/contingent—that is, to the very entities that supervenience binds to the physical. Indeed, the impossibility of any temporal realm at all without a physical realm is just a coarser way of expressing the intuition behind the principle of physical determination.

3 HOW THE WIND BLOWS. Marching with the winds of science won't help here until we have an independent argument about what scientific successes entail. Achievements like synthetic urea and statistical

thermodynamics are awkwardly strong, if taken as a basis for induction—for they are *reductions*, and we've given up trying to generalize that. On the other hand, instances like the theory of evolution and functional psychology (if that counts as a success) are metaphysically ambiguous. At most they show that it's only "because" matter got arranged as it did, that there exist life forms, minds, and so on. In other words, if certain material structures vanished or fell apart, various lives and thoughts would go with them. But that doesn't imply that each particular mental (or biological) occurrence is identical with some particular material structure. Instead, the conclusion is simply that disintegrating enough material structures will wipe out lots of other entities—which is what we just discussed.

4 FEAR OF DARKNESS. Consider denizen of darkness, D, seeking materialist sanctuary from crusading scotophobes. Now, classical type-reduction of D-kind would indeed flood them all with the prophylactic light of physics. But materialists no longer offer reduction *carte blanche*; some petitioners must settle for less. Is there safety in physical determination? Well, it forces D to hew the physical line rather closely; for D could not have been different, without the physical world having been different as well—and, this goes, of course, for each possible difference in D. That suffices, I think, to rule out demons, ghosts, disembodied spirits, magical auras, and miscellaneous other sleazy shades—without necessarily eliminating thoughts, feelings, customs, institutions, and the like. On the other hand, it must be confessed that determination throws no particular *light* on the entities it spares; supervenience may thin the ranks of the immaterial, but it doesn't illuminate the remainder.

What about physical exhaustion? Being identical to some arbitrary fragment of the physical universe won't render D, *qua* D, a whit more intelligible either. And, remember, the exhaustion principle does not imply that D has any other identifying description than *qua* D; in particular, even if D is exhausted by the physical, it need not be describable in the language of physics. In other words, *neither* materialist clause (short of reductionism) guarantees the physical *intelligibility* of all that is. And, in that case, identity theory fills no gap left open by supervenience.

5 SCROOGE. Beetle Bailey's razor cuts both ways. To be sure, one corollary is: "Don't multiply entities beyond necessity." But another, just as sound and important reads: "Don't multiply *principles* beyond

necessity." The difficulty with each lies in deciding what's "beyond necessity". A spendthrift's need is a skinflint's poison. I have been urging that identity theory is not necessary for an intuitively satisfying materialism. And one of my claims is that mere parsimony in the entity account is, by itself, no reason at all to impose shotgun unions with the physical.

6 LAW AND ORDER. This argument must be handled carefully. To say that the motion of a certain molecule is "fully" explicable physically is to say that all the *physical* forces on it determine its motion completely: no other forces are needed or allowed. But that doesn't rule out other *explanations*. The very same molecule might be lodged in my thumbnail, and might therefore rise three feet *because* I decide to raise my hand. The strictness of physics does not forbid such explanations; it only forbids that any decision contribute an additional *force* on any molecule. In other words, the psychological explanation is not allowed to interfere with or modify the physical one—but only to supplement it, by providing another point of view.

Consider, in a similar spirit, the punctuation mark printed at the end of this very sentence token. It's a little blob of ink; and the forces exerted on it by nearby paper fibers fully explain its present spatial location (in some reference frame). But one can also explain why that period is where it is by citing its terminal juxtaposition to a declarative inscription (which reflects my reasons for putting it there). Both of these explanations are perfectly correct; they are nowhere near equivalent; and they are *not competitors*. Strict completeness means only that physics brooks no intrusions on its own turf; it does not mean that physics is the only explanatory game in town (or the only good one, or the only one we really need).

What does this tell us about the mental? If physics is complete in its own terms, then there could have been no difference in the mental (that made any difference to the physical), without there being concomitant differences in the physical itself (that sufficed to explain everything, at the level of particles, fields, forces, and whatnot). But this is just a special case of the principle of physical determination (by strict physics); physical exhaustion is beside the point.

One might, however press a stronger interpretation. It's not just that there must be some "concomitant" physical difference or other; but rather, there must be some physical difference that makes the *same* difference—causes the same effects. Then add some hocus pocus about causal roles being nature's ownmost principle of individuation, and token identities spill right out. But hold fire.

For *each* physical effect (each molecular motion, for instance), precisely described in the language of physics, there must be a strict physical account, expressed in that same language. But a decision to act (say, to raise my hand) "involves" untold numbers of molecular motions in and around my body. The strictness of physics in no way requires that these can be *sorted* into:

1 the effective cause, as an integral unit (a complex physical token, identical to my decision);

2 the relevant effect, as an integral unit (a complex physical token, identical to my act); and

3 the innocent bystanders (such as my blood circulation, the thermal vibrations in my thumbnail, protein synthesis in my cortex, and so on).

Yet, each of these distinctions is necessary to the token identity thesis: they are practically a statement of it, for the case at hand.

The point is not that the "boundaries" of decisions and actions are micro-physically fuzzy, indescribable, or even negotiable. Rather, there are no such boundaries at all: decisions are not distinguishable (even in principle) as separate individuals *at the level of micro-physics.* Or, at any rate, the strictness of physics does not entail that they are. So, again I conclude that a familiar rationale for materialism supports the determination/supervenience principle, but not identity theory or physical exhaustion.

5 OTHER EXPLANATORY WILLS-O'-THE-WISP

There can, of course, be independent arguments for holding the identity thesis (over and above supervenience), even apart from the general reasons for materialism. I will consider two. First, one might suppose that the principle of physical exhaustion is needed to *explain why* the mental (and whatever else) is determined by the physical. But no such explanation is forthcoming: the two principles are, as Hellman and Thompson point out, quite independent. Supervenience is a relation between bodies of truths or facts; and, as such, it makes a strong claim on the expressive power of the "subvening" language—theoretical physics, presumably. Physical exhaustion, on the other hand, makes only a minimal claim on physics: a handful of "basic" predicates are required, but beyond that, the relevant theory could be very weak and inexpressive.

In the meantime, it would be peculiar to ring in a whole new principle merely to explain an already established one. In other words, if there are *further* grounds for identity theory, well and good (let them justify it). But, if not, then supervenience is evidently all the materialist metaphysics we need. It can perfectly well be a "principle" all by itself: exhaustion is no more fundamental that it is, and would add no useful support.

The second argument is trickier. Physical determination (even conjoined with strict physics) seems quite compatible with parallelism, epiphenomenalism, and similar ghosts of philosophy past. Doesn't it take identity theory to stuff these back into their graves? Naturally, I doubt it. Let's consider a couple of other hypotheses at the same time:

1 Once every few millennia, the universe pauses—stops stock still—for about ten minutes, and then resumes its motion exactly as it had been going; this last occurred just before William of Ockham was born.

2 Each sub-atomic particle actually has its own rich and unique personality, which it expresses in deep, fervent conversations with its neighbors. Unfortunately, radical translation is of no avail, because the particles' quantum-mechanical behavior is never affected—except in statistical indeterminacies.

These hypotheses have much in common with parallelism and epiphenomenalism; in particular, they are scientifically unmotivated, magically undetectable, and thoroughly bizarre. In my estimate, that is enough to damn them already. But, we can make a gesture of principled generalization, by articulating a *new corollary* (hitherto unnoticed, I think) to Bailey's razor: "Don't get weird beyond necessity." Needless to mention, this corollary (like Ockham's before it) is essentially a dialectical foil, useful mainly for transferring burdens of proof to other people.

Identity theory looks, at first, like a happier, more positive answer. With it, parallelism and epiphenomenalism come out not merely peculiar and unproven: instead, they are contrary to the principle of physical exhaustion—a genuine no-no. Appearances, however, can be deceiving. For, suppose we change the example to a (roughly) Spinozistic monism.

> There is really only one substance, God, but He has infinitely
> many attributes, each of which is complete and infinite, and
> corresponds perfectly with each of the others; two of God's
> attributes are mind and matter.

Thus, when we speak of physical tokens, we are speaking of God—specifically of His modes under the attribute matter. Likewise, when we speak of anything else, we are also speaking of God—the *very same* God. In other words, no matter what we talk about, it is *ontologically* the same thing as (identical to) what we talk about when we talk about physical tokens. Of course, unlike Hellman and Thompson's, Spinoza's system is symmetrical: it entails mental exhaustion as well.

The point is that brilliantly kooky metaphysics knows no bounds. (If the seventeenth century doesn't persuade you, try the nineteenth.) I don't think any definitive principle will ever suffice to rule out all and only those systems that are currently embarrassing. In other words, I expect that we will need our new corollary to handle arbitrarily many peculiar schemes that are compatible with supervenience, physical exhaustion, or what have you. And, if that's the case, then dismissing an odd fraction of them seems tenuous grounds for identity theory after all.

6 PHYSICAL EXHAUSTION AS HYLOMORPHISM

At this juncture, I would like to switch gears, and discuss the principle of physical exhaustion more directly. It rests fundamentally on two "modes of composition": spatio-temporal fusion and set abstraction. These are both ways of getting new entities out of whatever ones you already have; thus, for many collections of things, you can form their sum, and/or the set containing them as members. Moreover, according to Hellman and Thompson, these are the *only* modes of composition that have *ontological* import. Any other purported "compound" either doesn't really exist, or is equivalent to one of these (that is, a physical token or a set).

One is entitled to wonder how fusion and set abstraction got such exclusive rights. I suspect it goes back to the Greek preference for permanence, and the resulting approach to the problem of change. Forms (or essences) are top dog: eternal, hence incorruptible. Manifestly, however, ordinary things decay; so they can't be pure form. The solution is to introduce another factor, matter, that fleshes out forms to constitute temporal entities. Matter as such is also permanent, in that it is conserved; but it has no intelligible features either to keep or lose. Rather, all change is localized in the way form and matter go together—which matter has which form is a function of time.

The philosopher's weakness is to generalize. We know that, in addition to ordinary things, there can be unmaterialized forms (hipp-pogriffs, for instance); but, there is no uninformed matter. So … *everything* is either a pure form, or some hunk of informed matter. Hellman and Thompson's principle of physical exhaustion is, I think, just this generalized hylomorphism in modern (mathematical) garb. Sets are the (more comprehensive and precise) replacement for time-less forms; and arbitrary portions of physically occupied space-time are the (more comprehensive and precise) replacement for hunks of informed matter. (Mass-energy may even do for "raw" matter.)

The fatal flaw in hylomorphism is that it leaves too little room for distinctions: being concrete, individual, temporal (contingent), and material are all lumped together. That is, all and only material entities are particular, temporal concreta—everything else is an abstract, eter-nal kind. Moreover, there is only one possible relation between the two sides: inhesion (instantiation, set membership). And, finally, the modes of composition are asymmetrical: you can go horizontally or up, but not down. That is, you can take an arbitrary bunch of material individuals and fuse them into a new one; or, you can abstract away from—rise above—all their materiality, to get a pure form (set); and, with modern apparatus, you can abstract a still "higher" set from an arbitrary bunch of sets. What you can't do is go the other way, and make matter out of forms—once eternal, always eternal. The result is a rigid hierarchy, with all temporal individuals exactly on a par at the bottom.

Consider a story and its various "tokens". Written tokens are par-ticular inscriptions—temporal individuals, plausibly identifiable with hunks of ink. (I will ignore oral tokens, recitations; they only make the case harder.) But what about the story itself, of which these are tokens? If we call it a "type", we still have to explain what that means. In *some* sense, a story-type is composed or "made up" of its tokens: it has its being in and through them—without them it wouldn't exist at all. Is it made up, however, by either fusion or set abstraction? Not that I can see.

Try fusion. The story itself is just a larger and more scattered fraction of the physical universe—a bigger hunk of ink. It follows, presumably, that story types have mass and volume, which is startling, but perhaps not insufferable. More serious is collapsing the token/type relation into the part/whole relation: tokens (for instance, copies) of a story become, precisely, portions of it. That makes them comparable to, say, chapters, which (on this view) are also spatiotemporal portions of the whole. But, on the face of it, the chapter/story relation is completely different from the copy/story relation; they're not even similar. As if that weren't enough: in case there were only one copy of a story extant, the type and its token would be identical—which is surely unacceptable.

So, try set abstraction. That makes story-types like timeless kinds, which sounds congenial at first. But, on reflection, it seems to me incontestable that stories are *temporal, contingent individuals*. In the first place, they come into existence at some time, they evolve, they migrate, and sometimes they die out (possibly leaving progeny): this is not the habit of timeless kinds.

Second, stories are related as individuals, not as subvarieties, to the obvious species and genera of literature. Thus, in the sequence "Fido, spaniel, dog, mammal, …" we recognize the first step as different from the others. Fido is not a narrower classification than spaniels, but an item classified. Likewise, in the sequence "'The Sour Grapes', fable, allegory, fiction, …", "The Sour Grapes" is not a narrower classification than the others, but an item classified—that is, an individual. Hence, there seems as little hope for collapsing token/type into instance/kind or member/set as into part/whole. That's why I say there's too little room for distinctions.

Consider another homespun example. Take any dozen people from anywhere in history. There is a unique physical entity that is their fusion (or the fusion of their bodies, anyway); and there is a unique timeless entity that is the set containing exactly them. But suppose that a certain twelve people are friends with a common hobby, and they decide to form a club. Again, in *some* sense, a club is composed or "made up" of its members. But I take it as obvious, without further argument, that a club is identical neither to the set of its members, nor to the fusion of their bodies. Evidently, we need some other way(s) of composing new entities than the two allowed by the principle of physical exhaustion.

"Evidently", I hedge, because, as is well known, set theory is a boundless playground for those willing to invent astonishing interpretations for otherwise ordinary terms; indeed, the integers are a boundless playground for the truly open minded. Who knows what gawdawful set (or number) is *identical* (by somebody's lights) with "The Sour Grapes" or the Pittsburgh Quilters' Triangle? Who knows how predicates like 'is a temporal individual' might be construed so as to apply to them? And who cares? If preserving the principle of physical exhaustion is the primary motivation for such gymnastics, then I just don't feel the urge. Indeed, in such cases, I am sorely tempted to quote again our new corollary to Bailey: "Don't get weird beyond necessity!"

NOTES:

1 Hellman and Thompson actually distinguish three variants of the determination principle; weak supervenience is similar to the one they call "determination of truth". That's the only version I will be concerned with here, and also, apparently, the one of which they are most confident.

2 For instance, Davidson 1970/80, and Kim 1978 and 1979.

3 See their remark about parallelism (1975, 561).

4 This includes "pure" set theory (hence classical mathematics, as reconstructed therein), since the null set is a subset of the set of physical tokens.

5 See, for instance, the last sentence of their 1975.

6 Not usually a biconditional—but maybe sometimes (Meinong?).

7 These phrases are taken from Davidson 1970/80.

8 See my initial paraphrase of Davidson (in my 1982, page 97 = page 96 in this volume); and compare Quine on "difference *in the world*" and change (1978, 162). I am indebted to Joe Camp for a conversation during the course of which the point of this paragraph emerged.

Meaning

CHAPTER SEVEN

The Intentionality
All-Stars

All-star conundrum: How do you handle a hot Pirate with three balls on him? Metaphysical answer: You walk him intentionally, and pitch to the Padre.[1] The philosophical credentials of this strategy are impeccable; for, even though Hobbes was prepared to argue "I walk, therefore I am", Descartes held out for the more explicit "I walk *intentionally*, ..."[2] His point, of course, was that, unlike mere corporeal walking, intending is a kind of cognition—it has, in his terms, not only formal but also *objective* reality. And this ostensibly distinctive character of cognitions has remained a topic of investigation ever since—though now under the title *intentionality*.[3] Remarkably, however, neither Hobbes nor Descartes nor, indeed, any of their successors has ever noticed the significance of baseball for the alternatives and their explication. I shall attempt to remedy this startling omission.

1 Warm up

Intentionality is hard to get a glove on. It is often glossed as that character of some things (items, events, states, ...) that they are "of", are "about", or "represent" others. Thus, my belief that Babe Ruth built Yankee Stadium is about Babe Ruth and Yankee Stadium, or (better) it represents the one's having built the other. Much the same can be said for hopes and fears, wonderings and intendings, even perceptions and actions. My wanting to get some popcorn, my intending to get some popcorn, and my going to get some popcorn are all "about" my getting some popcorn. In a different terminology, to have intentionality is to have (semantic) *content*: the content of my belief is *that* Ruth built the stadium, the content of my intention (or action) is *to* get some popcorn. Note that something's content is not the same as what it is about or represents, but rather determines what it is about or represents; thus, if two things have the same content, then what they are about or represent is the same, but not vice versa.[4]

On the face of it, intentionality is (sometimes) a *relation* between whatever has the intentionality (for instance, a belief) and whatever it represents or is about (for instance, some state of affairs). But as a relation, it has the serious peculiarity that its second relatum need not exist. For instance, my belief that Babe Ruth built Yankee Stadium could be just as intentional (with the very same content), even if Ruth had never lived or hadn't built a stadium; similarly, I might go to get some popcorn, yet not get any. But how can a "relation" not be *to* anything? This peculiarity betrays another: if it's not the case that Ruth built the stadium, or I get the popcorn, then something's *faulty*—in that beliefs are not "supposed to" be false, or actions failures. In other words, the fallibility of intentionality reveals that it is not merely a factual, but also a *normative* relation.

At least as important, entities having intentionality are (sometimes) thereby related to one another. I might believe that Ruth built the stadium *because* I believe that the greatest Yankee built it, and that Ruth was the greatest Yankee; I go to get the popcorn *because* I want to, and see nothing to stop me. Yet the force of this "because" is also peculiar, in that it purports simultaneously to explain and to justify. The double purport is reflected in the double sense in the *"reason"* one does something. On the one hand, it must be *normative*, since my reasons for coming to believe or act, can always be criticized according to how good or valid they are. On the other hand, it must be *causal*, since I can have a reason to believe or do something, and do so, yet not for that reason—it's not the having of *that* reason that leads to my belief or action.[5] The difference between such a case and the usual one must be the absence of a causal relation. But how can a relation be both causal and normative?

Evidently, the most sporting question about intentionality is not "What is its definition?" but rather "How can there be any?" More specifically, given the *vapid materialism* now generally conceded (roughly: without any matter, there wouldn't be anything else contingent either), how can it be that any part or feature of the universe represents or is a reason for another? How can there be norms among the atoms in the void? How, in short, is intentionality compatible with materialism? This question is posed not as a dilemma, but as a challenge. We shall assume both that materialism is compatible with everything there is, and that there is intentionality; the aim is not to doubt or debunk, but to understand.

Cognitions, perceptions, and actions are not the only phenomena that exhibit intentionality. A line in a song, or on a plaque, can say that Babe Ruth built Yankee Stadium; and, if so, it has essentially the same content as my belief. Clearly, sentences, formulae, and public symbols of all sorts can have intentional contents, including a great deal of overlap with the possible contents of thoughts. Intentionality, however, is not all created equal. At least some outward symbols (for instance, a secret signal that you and I explicitly agree on) have their intentionality only *derivatively*—that is, by inheriting it from something else that has that same content already (such as the stipulation in our agreement). And, indeed, the latter might also have its content only derivatively, from something else again; but, obviously, that can't go on forever.

Derivative intentionality, like an image in a photocopy, must derive eventually from something that is not similarly derivative; that is, at least some intentionality must be *original* (nonderivative). And clearly then, this original intentionality is the primary metaphysical problem; for the possibility of delegating content, once there is some to delegate, is surely less puzzling than how there can be any in the first place. Now, it is sometimes maintained that all and only *mental* intentionality is original—hence, that all public symbols have their contents only derivatively. But this further claim is controversial and calls for a separate argument; it does not follow directly from the uncontroversial thesis that at least some intentionality must be original.[6]

In the good old days, a philosopher might hold that mental entities are somehow ontologically distinctive (modes of a special substance, say), and then maintain that an essential part of that distinction lies in their having original intentionality as an intrinsic property. Thus, just as material entities have mass and extension intrinsically, so mental entities have content—that's simply the way God made them (end of discussion). In the present context, this is like trying to score a run without rounding the bases; and the effect of vapid materialism is to throw it out at first. But throwing it out does raise a problem.

Whether or not "original intentionality", "intrinsic property", and "matter" ever hang separately, it is at least clear that they don't hang together: no single patch of matter can, purely in virtue of its own physical structure, and regardless of the rest of the universe, mean exactly one thing. For instance, if some cyanide molecules in the Crab

Nebula should happen to trace out the shape of the letters 'Hank Aaron', they would not name the homer Hammer (or even be the letters 'Hank Aaron'). Hence, vapid materialism seems to imply that the intentionality of any individual state or occurrence always depends on some larger pattern into which it fits—which is, of course, the principle of *vapid holism*. And, so long as the formulation of this principle remains carefully evasive, most contemporary philosophers would accept it.

The Crab Nebula example harbors a further lesson; for there might well occur, somewhere in the vast reaches of galactic dust, an arbitrarily large and enduring pattern of apparently sensible "text" or "behavior". Still, if that pattern comes about entirely by *accident*, a mere cosmic coincidence, then no part of it can have any more content than an isolated flash of 'Hank Aaron'. So vapid holism must require not merely that some "larger pattern" occur, but also that it not be just an accident. But whether something is accidental or not is relative to a level of description, and the possibility of some kind of account.[7] Thus, in terms of physics and a prior configuration, the positions of the dust particles might not be accidental at all; yet it could still be a complete coincidence if those positions happened to yield some *higher-level* pattern. Vapid holism requires that the larger pattern itself not be an accident—that is, at the very level at which it is describable as that pattern.

If vapid holism is to be the key to intentionality, the nonaccidental "larger pattern" must be specified more fully; and this fuller specification, moreover, should account for the peculiarity of intentionality as a relation, for its normative force, and for what differentiates original intentionality from derivative. Even with all these stipulations, however, there remain a number of distinct candidates—alternative specifications of the relevant "whole". And differences among them, it seems to me, are characteristic of differing basic approaches to intentionality.[8] I propose, therefore, to outline and compare several of the main positions, and to name some of their foremost defenders—to choose, in effect, an *All-Star Team* for the intentionality league. Needless to warn, the brief sketches I will offer verge on caricatures, in comparison with the positions actually held by the named players; but that is the price of mapping a real field.

To begin with the obvious: I'm pitching, and you're catching. That is, we and our teammates are the fielding team; and, though our positions are all different, we are alike in collectively facing a line-up of truly phenomenal (not merely sensational) all-star batters—which implies (though the fact is seldom noticed) that our common game plan is *phenomenology*. Actually, since time is limited, we shall discuss mainly the infield; but the rest of the team deserves a quick survey, both for completeness and for perspective. Roughly, the difference between infielders and outfielders is that infielders have (various) spelled-out proposals about *how* holism renders intentionality compatible with vapid materialism; that is, they offer positive accounts of whatever "larger pattern" makes original intentionality possible. Outfielders, on the other hand, try (in various ways) to dismiss the issue—generally by blaming Descartes for philosophy's misplaced presumptions, and remanding any remainder to biology.

So, on the intentionality team, Richard Rorty and Jacques Derrida are out in left field. They both play pretty deep, Derrida perhaps closer to the foul line. The position in a nutshell: talk about mentality and intentionality is just that: *talk*. "Intentional idioms" may, as a way of talking, sometimes be useful or entertaining; but that gives them no more claim on our allegiance than talk of sakes or goblins. What's worse, they're out of date: now that the intellectual high culture is over its infatuation with transcendence and the a priori, intentionality can slip quietly into the social-history curriculum, alongside transubstantiation, noumenal selves, and the divine right of kings.

Next, in maximum possible contrast to Rorty and Derrida, we find John Searle covering right field, maintaining that there really are *mental* brain-states, and that intentionality is what distinguishes them. When pressed for details about what this (material) intentionality consists in, however, he doesn't get far beyond calling it an occult power hitter—some mysterious causal property which biochemists are going to have to unravel (much as they did photosynthesis).[9]

Finally, way out on the warning track in center field, B.F. Skinner is up against the wall defending the view that science can explain behavior without reference to intentionality, and that therefore there is no reason to posit intentional states or entities. Hence, their status is like that of the crystal spheres or the luminiferous aether: unnecessary inventions of a naive and false scientific theory.

So much for the outfield.

2 FIRST BASE

Naturally, everyone is dying to ask: Who's on first? Well, think of it as the position just infield from Searle's. We would expect to hear, then, that original intentionality is the province exclusively of contentful internal (mental) states; but we would expect, in addition, a worked-out account of just what it is about these states that makes them contentful. Such a position can be called "neo-Cartesianism"; but its place in the all-star defense is better expressed by *right-wing phenomenology*. Stellar players at this position surely include Jerry Fodor, Hartry Field, and the philosophical foundations of cognitive science—as expounded, for instance, by Zenon Pylyshyn.[10]

Here is the basic idea: separate mental states have their contents in virtue of their systematic relations *to one another*. That is, the "larger pattern" of all vapid holism is further specified by right-wing phenomenology as a pattern of interrelations among discrete internal states. Moreover, since the intentionality of these states presupposes the pattern of relations among them, they must themselves be *tokens*, in the following strong sense: each state (and relation) has a determinate identity independent of its content—it is a concrete internal item (feature, configuration, ...) that is uniquely characterizable in nonintentional terms. Inasmuch as these tokens have contents, they are also *symbols*.

The required congruence between symbols and tokens can be spelled out more fully. Let a description or specification be *semantic* if framed in intentional terms, *formal* if framed in nonintentional terms (at some appropriate level),[11] *local* if meant to apply only to the given system, and *loose* if sensitive to context, subject to retroactive adjustment, and only approximate. Then, first, for each particular symbol there is a particular token with which it is numerically identical, and vice versa; that is, symbols and tokens are the very same entities, but identified semantically and formally, respectively. Second, there is at least a loose and local general formal specification of which entities are tokens (hence symbols). And third, at least loosely and locally, the semantics of the symbols is a systematic function of their formal character as tokens. The first clause is sometimes called "token-token identity theory". The other two are a very watered down version of "type-type identity theory".[12] Their conjunction, needless to say, is *vapid reductionism*.[13] The relation of natural dialect semantics to phonology is a familiar vapid reduction.

Because the inner states are independent tokens, specifying their symbolic contents can be regarded as *interpreting* them (in roughly the philosophical linguists' sense—that is, radical translation). Accordingly, the problem of *how* their contents depend on patterns among them can be approached in terms of constraints on viable interpretations. Speaking very broadly, an interpretation must always assign contents in such a way that the patterns turn out to be "appropriate" in the light of those contents. What does this mean?

The underlying intuition (though not the actual account) is reminiscent of the resemblance theory of pictorial representation. On that view, an individual dot can represent a certain freckle on the Queen's nose, but only in virtue of its (spatial) relations to all the other dots making up the whole picture; and these relations, moreover, must be such that all the dots together somehow visibly "resemble" Her Majesty's face. Likewise, first-base-men assign contents to individual tokens in virtue of their relations to one another in an overall pattern, which must in turn bear some relation to the world; obviously, however, these interrelations won't be merely spatial, and the relation to the world won't be pictorial resemblance.

Imagine trying to interpret some ancient inscriptions; and consider a certain hypothesis according to which they are an astronomical treatise, detailing various eclipses, equinoxes, and planetary motions, as well as theories to explain them. How do we evaluate such an hypothesis? Well, in the first place, the text (as translated) had better be internally coherent. If a passage is construed as a question and a response, then the latter should turn out, by and large, to be a plausible answer to the former; if a passage is construed as adducing considerations, then they ought, by and large, to be relevant; if a passage is construed as an argument, then the conclusion ought, by and large, to follow from the premises; and so on. Likewise, in longer segments, the discourse should develop reasonably and hang together as a consistent and sensible treatment of its topic. Such relations among interpreted tokens are broadly "rational".

Second, the claims and presuppositions of the proposed translation ought, by and large, to cohere "externally" with the world. Thus if eclipses, planetary motions, and the like, occurred just as the descriptions say they did, and as the questions and inferences presuppose, and so on, then that supports the interpretive hypothesis; but if the (alleged) discussions bear no sensible relation to actual events, then there is reason to suspect a mistranslation. Of course, the standard is not perfection: "by and large" implies only "at least in most of the most obvious cases". Thus, it would be excusable to omit an occasional eclipse, and perhaps even all eclipses visible only elsewhere on the globe; but if the interpreted text got nearly everything wrong, including the manifest and commonplace, that would undermine not so much the author's credibility as the translator's.

Apparently, then, the first-base counterpart of intrapictorial spatial relations is intrasystematic rationality, and the counterpart of resemblance is truth. Though these considerations have been only roughly indicated, they are familiar enough, and can summed up in a convenient maxim.

> PRINCIPLE OF INTERPRETATION: the tokens, as situated, should turn out, as interpreted, to make good sense, by and large.[14]

A token's "situation" is meant to include both its internal context (the other tokens) and the external circumstances of its utterance (the world). And "making good sense by and large" subsumes both internal and external coherence—that is, both by-and-large rationality and by-and-large truth.

Rationality and truth are *normative* constraints, and on two different levels. First, interpretation is supposed to construe the tokens as making sense overall; and second, the tokens themselves are supposed to make sense, as construed. In other words, not only is interpretation as such norm governed, but it also imputes these norms to what it interprets. But how can norms be *attributed*? That is, when a token fails to make sense as interpreted, how can we ever say that it is the token itself that is faulty, and not just the assignment of its content (the interpretation)? Predictably, the answer to this question invokes holism; less predictably, perhaps, it therefore *presupposes* a vapid reduction—that is, a (loosely and locally) systematic function from token types to contents.

What makes any holism nontrivial is the simultaneous imposition of two independent constraints. Thus it is easy to assign contents that make sense overall (just assign the contents of *War and Peace*, regardless of the token types); likewise, it is easy to assign contents systematically (just equate each type of token with an arbitrary English word, regardless of sense). What's hard is an assignment that's simultaneously sensible *and* systematic. Suppose, for example, that you're struggling with some alien text, and you could improve the sense by reinterpreting a few tokens. The trouble is, systematicity would then oblige you also to reinterpret other tokens of the same types; and those changes might or might not make sense, in their contexts. Of course, sometimes you can make excuses, or accommodate by making still further changes, and so on. Such juggling of readings to make maximum sense *overall* is what holism is all about; but it is nontrivial only if systematicity supplies an independent constraint. This is why holistic interpretation requires an objective pattern in the *tokens* being interpreted—thus a vapid reduction.

Whenever there are two independent constraints, they can conflict. Now, if they conflict grossly (nothing comes close to satisfying them both), then interpretation simply fails. But if you can almost satisfy both, then you get a viable interpretation with a few anomalies—a few tokens that "ought" to be different than they are. Sometimes these are just bad data, and can be discarded. But, in more interesting cases, a persistent anomalous theme will be coherently interwoven with text that is otherwise not anomalous. For instance, claims about a "thunderbolt hurler" might occur, quite rationally, in various otherwise sensible discussions of the weather, sports, crops, marriages, eclipses, and what have you. Undeniably, these symbols belong in the text and are interpreted correctly—systematicity and internal coherence both support them—yet they are faulty (false). Since the "fault" is not in the interpretation (it's as good as can be), it must lie in the very pattern being interpreted. That is, it lies in the tokens themselves—and often in quite particular ones. It's like finding a flaw in a crystal; only, since the "regularity" which the flaw violates is normative, so is the violation. This is how the norms of interpretation devolve onto the interpreted tokens.

What's more, these normative constraints on the symbols themselves illuminate the peculiar character of intentionality as a "relation". For, if I believe that Mighty Casey built Yankee Stadium, precisely what's *wrong* is that there was no Mighty Casey (hence no such state of affairs); the relata that my belief *should* have had are missing. In general, norms can apply even when they are not satisfied; and that's why symbols can have the same content even when they're faulty, and why intentionality can be "relational" even without one of its relata. Put rather crudely, the peculiarity of intentionality as a relation is a special case of the peculiarity of normative rules that they are "made to be broken".

As a neo-Cartesian account of intentional content, however, the "principle of interpretation", even understood normatively, is (so far) radically incomplete. For, in the first place, it cannot distinguish between the intentionality of text (inscriptions found in the desert) and that of real live cognitions. And second, even in the case of cognitions, the principle offers no basis for saying why, or even whether, interpretation means *exposing* (discovering) norms and contents that are already there, rather than *imposing* (stipulating) them by fiat. Both of these shortcomings point to the same omission: there is no account of the difference between original and derivative intentionality. That is to say, the holistic pattern of interrelationships among internal tokens, upon which the entire first-base position rests, has not yet been characterized in a way strong enough to support these distinctions—something more is needed.

And right-wing phenomenology is ready with an answer: the rest of the needed pattern lies in appropriate *interactions* among the interpreted tokens. That is, the relevant pattern includes not only static but also dynamic (causal) relations among the inner symbols. Of course, even ancient ink marks interact slightly (gravity, chemical diffusion, and the like), but not in any way that reflects what they mean. In a mind, on the other hand, inner symbols (thoughts) are constantly interacting in regular ways that are directly and systematically appropriate to their contents—in the course of reasoning, problem solving, decision making, and so on. In effect, the norms of internal coherence apply to the symbols not only synchronically, from one part of the text to another, but also diachronically, as the symbol structures evolve rationally through time.

To take a trivial example, if you write the premises of a syllogism on a piece of paper, nothing much happens; but if you get them into somebody's thoughts, a conclusion is likely to be drawn—not just any new notion, but (by and large) a semantically valid consequence. The only way for that conclusion to appear on a page (other than by accident) would be for someone to write it there—the tokens and paper themselves do nothing. But inside a person, the regular causal interactions among the tokens (internal "processes") systematically maintain and develop the pattern in virtue of which they can be interpreted as symbols. This causal structure is what accounts for the fact that the neo-Cartesian pattern is not an accident, and thus for the fact that rational conclusions can be generated without intervention from an outside agency. And that is precisely what inclines us to say that people understand the tokens occurring in them, whereas paper is utterly oblivious.

Call such semantically appropriate symbolic dynamism *semantic activity*, in contrast to the semantic inertness of, say, sentence inscriptions on a page. Clearly, semantic activity is a global property of "systems" of interacting tokens, together with the processes or primitive operations through which they interact. Hence, the principle of interpretation is not superceded by semantic activity, but instead enriched, in that the "contexts" of tokens now include also their temporal situations in the endless work and play of thought. Likewise, the pattern of interrelations among tokens that constitutes the essential first-base specification of vapid holism is not superceded, but simply acquires a new dimension, in patterns of interaction.

Clearly, semantic activity differentiates decisively between cognitions and mere inscriptions. It also provides a basis for saying that the intentionality of text is *imp*osed, whereas that of thought is merely *exp*osed by interpretation. For, the origin of the content assigned is plausibly identified with the source of the orderly pattern on which that assignment rests. But in the case of inert text, any interpretable (hence nonaccidental) pattern must derive from some external source—which plausibly, then, is responsible for its content. Semantically active thoughts, on the other hand, maintain their interpretable pattern all by themselves; no outside source is implicated in the pattern, hence none in the content. Thus semantic activity is also the foundation of the neo-Cartesian account of the distinction between original and derivative intentionality.

It remains to ask: How is semantic activity possible? If this cannot be answered, then there is no neo-Cartesian account of how intentionality is compatible with vapid materialism after all. Semantic activity is materially possible precisely in case rational thought processes can also be specified as formal operations—in effect, vapidly reduced. Such specification is possible in general if internal symbols and internal operations are *semantically articulated*—that is, systematically composed of atomic symbols and operations, such that the content and validity of the composites is structurally determined by that of their components. The relevant formal level, therefore, is not physical but *syntactical*, and hence also *digital*. Vapid reduction to syntactical operations and operands suffices for materialism, however, because we know independently how to reduce these to physics—or, at any rate, how to "implement" them in physical systems. An implementation of a semantically interpreted active syntactical system is, in the broadest and most proper sense, a (digital) *computer*. In other words, semantic activity is possible if thinking is an internal computational process conducted, so to speak, in a *"language of thought".*[15] This is why artificial intelligence and cognitive science belong at first base.

Our basic outline of right-wing phenomenology is now complete; but, before continuing around the infield, one further set of issues should at least be acknowledged. In specifying what is required for original intentionality, we have said nothing about minimum degrees or kinds of content or interaction; yet it seems clear that overly simple-minded systems are not "minded" at all—even if they satisfy all the above characterizations. Arguably, for instance, the symbols in most ordinary computers, including sophisticated "expert systems", are only derivatively intentional, even though they are semantically articulated and interactive, maintaining quite sensible patterns nonaccidentally. It is tempting, therefore, to introduce some further threshold in what or how the system thinks. Thus, it might be said that a system cannot have original intentionality unless it can think about itself and its own thoughts, or about the thoughts of others, or about the difference between truth and error, or about norms and values as such, or about life and death, or whatever. I shall not affirm or deny any of these, but observe only that semantic activity seems more fundamental, since: first, these special contents are all equally possible in inert text, whereas semantic activity is not; and second, special contents, unlike semantic activity, do not help explain nonaccidentalness or the difference between imposing and exposing intentionality.

3 SECOND BASE

Second-base-men, obviously, play just infield from Skinner; and *neo-behaviorist* is really a happier epithet than "mid-field phenomenologist" (though strictly either is correct). Whatever we call them, the all-star cast must include W.V.O. Quine, Daniel Dennett, and Robert Stalnaker.[16] Naturally, neo-behaviorists are suspicious of determinate (concrete) mental states; but, unlike paleo-behaviorists, they take intentional *ascription* very seriously. Characteristically, they treat an intentional system purely as a "black box"; and they specify the larger pattern of vapid holism as a pattern in the interactions between the system and its environment. These interactions, however, are not conceived merely as physical stimuli and responses, but rather as perceptions and actions—that is, intentionally.

As we have seen, when a single token is considered in isolation, there is no determining whether it is a symbol—or, if so, of what. Likewise at second base: if a single environmental interaction is considered in isolation, there is no determining whether it is a perceiving or doing—or, if so, of what. Suppose some photons land on my retina or my earlobe. Do I perceive anything? What? Suppose my body moves or changes shape. Am I doing anything? What? The holist response, of course, is to consider such interactions not in isolation, but in the context of one another, finding a pattern among a subset of them, in virtue of which these make sense as contentful.

How can such a pattern be nonaccidental? Imagine a blind chess player, exchanging moves verbally. Her environmental interactions are richly patterned in a way that makes sense of them as perceptions and actions—namely, as moves in a particular on-going chess game. For that sense not to be a mirage, however, it cannot be just a coincidence that her exchanges are so patterned. What does this presuppose? Well, she must at least "remember" the developing current position from move to move (or, conceivably, the history of prior moves); for otherwise the continued legality of her moves would be unaccountable. Similarly, the pattern may also presuppose that she forms strategic goals and plans, discerns options, foresees consequences, and makes choices in the light of them. Finally, inasmuch as she is not "hard wired" for chess, she must be understood as having come to know about the game and to want to win.

Thus, neo-behaviorists can and must ascribe content not only to overt environmental interactions, but also to relatively enduring states of the interacting agent—states which are therefore cognitive—and perhaps also to events that are changes in those states. Perceptions and actions are thus only a portion of the whole into which particular ascriptions must fit. But they are a privileged portion, in three related respects. First, the entire holistic ascription depends exclusively on the pattern exhibited in perceptions and actions; intervening cognitive states and events are themselves ascribed only on the basis of that pattern, and contribute no additional constraint. Second, it is only perceptions and actions for which, at second base, a vapid reduction must be possible; that is, only these must be identical to determinate entities that are uniquely identifiable in formal terms, in a way that systematically determines content (at least loosely and locally). Hence, third, this privileged subpattern alone must support the independent systematicity constraint that is required lest holism be trivial.

By contrast, ascribed cognitive states need not even be token-identical to states that are individually concrete and formally characterizable; it need not be possible to "individuate" them in any terms other than intentional. Beliefs and desires, hopes and fears are ascribed *en masse* to an agent as a whole, not severally to its internal parts. Accordingly, mid-field phenomenology also does not treat cognitions as semantically articulated internal symbols, and cannot understand thinking as a computational process defined over a syntactical language of thought, after the manner of classical artificial intelligence. On the other hand, however, neo-behaviorism is entirely compatible, in a way that right-wing phenomenology could never be, with parallel or neurologically inspired cognitive models based on "distributed representations".[17]

What is meant by saying that cognitions are "states of the whole"? Well, first, they are not localized—as are, for instance, (the state of having) a broken leg, a full stomach, or a tattooed shoulder. That is not to deny that cognitions might be collectively localized, say in the brain, but only to deny that they are individually and distinctly localized—as would be multiple fractures or multiple tattoos. Well, then, are cognitive states more like the being-warmed-up of an engine or the being-dehydrated of a plant? These are not localized in specific parts. But that's only because they are uniformly exhibited in and diffused throughout all the parts; cognitive states are not thus uniformly exhibited and diffused throughout a cognitive system. Perhaps, then, they are more like states of the economy. Growth, inflation, and unemployment are neither localized in individual transactions and relationships, nor evenly diffused throughout them. Still, they are basically just averages or sums of similar conditions that are localizable; a cognitive system's beliefs and desires are in no sense averages or sums of the beliefs and desires of its parts.

A more promising analogy would be the state of an engine that is running (idling), and thus ready to deliver power at the touch of a pedal, or the state of a battleship that is on "red alert", and thus ready to respond at the slightest provocation. These too are global states, but they are not simply diffused throughout or averaged over the various parts; rather, they are overall states that depend on a richly integrated system of complexly interlocking capacities and activities. Following up the analogy would suggest that, at second base, cognitive states have the metaphysical status of *dispositions*—roughly on a par, that is, with irritability, patriotism, or a natural aptitude for baseball. I believe this is fundamentally correct; but it must be dissociated immediately from all so-called "dispositional analyses". For the latter were essentially atomist and reductionist in tendency: A's believing that p was to be analyzed as A's having a complex disposition, which A could have regardless of any others, and which could be specified in principle entirely in nonintentional terms. Holist neo-behaviorism shares neither of those forlorn ideals, but only the idea that states intervening between perception and action can be understood as global states of the whole system, on the model of dispositions.

In a cognitive system, these disposition-like states must be elaborately interrelated both causally and rationally. Suppose Pete Rose wants to hit a long fly, *because* he wants to drive in runs, and believes he will drive in runs if he hits a long fly. That 'because' is both rational and causal: Rose both *should* want to hit a fly for the given reason, and actually *does*. But how is this possible, if the states are not identified with formally determinate internal tokens, and cannot even be individuated except in intentional terms? Has vapid materialism been abandoned to some peculiar intentional species of causation? I don't see why. Suppose company X out-earns company Y "because" it introduces a profitable new product, or suppose the Pirates win the World Series "because" they out-hustle the Orioles. In both cases the 'because' is causal, yet in neither case could the cause or the effect be individuated physically.[18] Perhaps in some sense the causes are specifically "economic" or "sporting"; but not in any sense that is inimical to materialism. For states of a system to be intentional, the causal relations connecting them to one another and to certain environmental interactions must account for the fact that the latter consistently make sense as contentful perceptions and actions. It is an empirical question whether unarticulated states of a material system can indeed be so causally structured (that is, whether perception and action are in fact possible without a language of thought); but, if they can, there is no conceptual barrier to ascribing them as cognitive and rational.

Ascription is like interpretation in that the overall pattern must, as construed, be somehow appropriate. But, since the primary pattern is not a corpus of syntactical tokens, but a "biography" of environmental interactions, the primary appropriateness must be different as well. Imagine a mouse circling a box of cereal, pushing on it here and there, gnawing at its edges, climbing atop it via the soup cans, and so on—until it gets in. We inevitably ascribe perceptions, actions, and even intervening states: we say the mouse is hungry, can smell the cereal, and is trying to get into the box so that it can eat. But these ascriptions are not at all like translations: intentionality is manifest in behavioral tokens not as the "reasonable sense" of a text, but as the *competence* of an agent. Hence, the primary normative standard is not truth but *success*; and the rational relations among ascribed states are not primarily logical, but *instrumental*—oriented as means and ends, not evidence and conclusions. Truth, of course, is not irrelevant, but just secondary: true beliefs are preferred in the first instance as reliable guides to action. A purely passive observer (theoretician) is unintelligible at second base.

The holistic constraints that govern ascription, holding it all together, can again be summed up in a convenient maxim—roughly analogous to the principle of interpretation.

> PRINCIPLE OF ASCRIPTION: Ascribe perceptions, actions, and intervening cognitions so as to maximize a system's overall manifest competence.

The point, in other words, is to "rationalize" the system's behavior, relative to its circumstances, by interpolating just the right mental structure to do the job—ascribing it, however, only to the system as an unanalysed black box, without any implications about what's "inside". Beliefs, considerations, subgoals, inferential steps, and the like, are not themselves systematically rooted in patterns of independently identifiable tokens, but only indirectly supported by their causal/rational role in competent environmental interaction. Thus, neo-behaviorist cognitive states are not internal in the literal neo-Cartesian sense of having determinate locations inside the system; but they might be deemed "internal" in another sense, in that they *intervene* between perception and action.

Because second base does not rely on formally determinate inner tokens, it faces a special problem: *how much* cognition should be ascribed? This will be clearer if we digress briefly to see why the same problem does not arise at first base. Given a determinate cognitive "text" to which interpretation is beholden, there is a clear basis for attributing *explicit* (or "core") beliefs, desires, and so on: the system explicitly has those cognitive states that are formally tokened in it, and no others. Then, with respect these, it is possible to attribute further cognitions that are only implicit or tacit. *Implicit* thoughts are ones that are not held explicitly, but are implied by explicit thoughts via implications that the system could follow. For instance, I may want to hit a home run, and believe that home runs embarrass pitchers, both explicitly, but without explicitly making the connection; then I want to embarrass the pitcher, but only implicitly. *Tacit* cognitions are those evinced in the cognitive behavior of the system, quite apart from whether they are held explicitly or implicitly. Thus, a system might simply be constructed so as to infer according to modus ponens, or to infer always from big bared teeth to danger; then, even though it doesn't contain any symbols that express or imply the corresponding rules, it accepts them tacitly.

Neo-behaviorists, by contrast, cannot draw these distinctions, because they do not claim that any cognitive states are ever formally tokened. At second base, all ascribed cognitions are merely "evinced" in behavior; so, in effect, they would all count as purely "tacit". Unfortunately, in the absence of any antecedent delineation of behavior and of evincing, there is no upper bound on what to ascribe. The difficulty can be more vividly presented by switching from mouse psychology to

> MOUSETRAP PSYCHOLOGY: The trap *wants* to kill mice, and it *believes* it can whenever one nibbles the bait. Further, whenever it *feels* its trigger move, it comes to believe a mouse is nibbling. It now so feels, and straightway it *acts*.

Painstaking observation reveals that the trap, as construed, has mostly true beliefs and reliable perceptions; moreover, it acts on them consistently and rationally, achieving its goals with enviable success. And, while we're at it, why not ascribe to the cheese, in virtue of its canny silence and redolence, a subtle knowledge of mouse temptations—not to mention of acoustics and chemical diffusion? Now a mid-field phenomenologist could try to maintain that such ascriptions are perfectly legitimate—though not very interesting, since mousetraps and cheese are such "simple" black boxes. But that just drops the ball. Intentionality is worth considering in the first place only because it seems so intimately involved in our own intelligence and cognition; perhaps we can share these qualities to some extent with mice, but any account that fails to rule out mousetraps and cheese *ipso facto* fails to capture whatever it is we're interested in.

There is a tension in the ascription principle itself. On the one hand, we want to ascribe as much capacity to the system as we can. For instance, if the dolphins really are scheming and communicating in sophisticated ways, we'll be missing something if we fail to figure it out. This is the point of *maximizing* the system's manifest competence.

On the other hand, the mousetrap and cheese examples suggest that we should ascribe no more capacity than we have to; if there is no countervailing minimizing constraint, ascription runs gratuitously rampant. This is the point of maximizing (only) the system's *manifest* competence. In sum, it is equally a mistake to elevate a mousetrap to the cognitive level of a mouse, or reduce a mouse to that of a trap; they are objectively different, and we require a principled way of marking that difference.

Consider *Supertrap*, an anti-rodent system with a more versatile repertoire. For instance, when a mouse is soaked with gasoline, Supertrap strikes a match; when a mouse is in a blender, Supertrap trips the switch; when a mouse is in the batter's box, Supertrap throws a bean ball; and, of course, when a mouse nibbles the bait, Supertrap snaps shut. These habits betray a common malevolent thread that is *generalizable* by (and only by) ascribing one persistent goal: dead mice. Without malice aforethought, it would be just a grisly (and incredible) coincidence that each gesture happened to be potentially lethal, not to mention exquisitely timed so as to realize that potential. How do *you* suppose Supertrap would behave if a mouse took refuge under the tires of a truck, or huddled in an empty light socket? The obvious conjectures project not from previous bodily motions, but from previous results. In other words, the projectable pattern in Supertrap's behavior can be characterized only in terms of what he is up to— what he is *doing*.

Of course, the case had better be more complicated than this. How, for instance, does Supertrap know where his little victim is hiding? Perhaps sometimes he looks it in the eye, while other times he hears a squeak or notices a careless tail. Just as diverse routes to a common result support the ascription of actions, so diverse routes from a common source support the ascription of perceptions.[19] Similarly, intervening cognitive ascriptions are better supported insofar as they figure in diverse rationalizations, combined with various others. Thus, just as murderous intent helps to explain several proclivities, in conjunction with sundry beliefs about gasoline, blenders, and the like, so also those beliefs should work together with other goals in other accounts: how Supertrap starts a bonfire or makes a milk shake, say. Still subtler combinations explain why he declines to harm cats and barn owls, even when they nibble the bait or reek of gas. Call such intricate complicity of rationalizations *semantic intrigue*; it marks the difference between merely gratuitous ascriptions and those that are genuinely required to maximize manifest competence.

Ascription, like interpretation, is a way of discerning order (non-randomness) that would otherwise go unnoticed, or be indescribable. The discovered pattern, of course, need not be perfect; but "flaws" are identifiable as such only against the backdrop of a pattern that is largely clear and reliable. (There are no flaws in chaos.) Accordingly, semantic intrigue—the interpolated pattern found in competently non-random behavior—makes possible the ascription of (scattered) *errors*. Suppose I jiggle a mousetrap's trigger with a feather, and it snaps shut. Shall we say it tried to kill "that mouse"; believed the unobvious dictum "Crush a feather, kill a mouse"; or merely took the opportunity for some target practice? None of these makes any more sense than the rest of mousetrap psychology. But if we switch to Supertrap, and if we have independent evidence that he expects some sneaky mice to don owl disguises, knows where they might get the feathers, and so on, then there could be enough intricacy to justify attributing some (particular) error. Thus, as with interpretation, the norms governing ascription devolve onto the states ascribed.

Although we have based neo-behiorist cognitive ascriptions on a system's overall pattern of environmental interactions, we have so far neglected the very special case of *linguistic* perception and action. All actions as such have content: what the agent is *doing* in behaving that way. But some actions, including especially speech acts, also have content of another sort: what the agent *means* by doing them. In his pioneering second-base account of such meaning, Grice (1957) shows how it is *derivative* from the intentionality of the agent's prior cognitive states (particularly in how the agent intends witnesses to respond). Even in the case of actions with antecedently standardized meanings (such as utterances in public languages), that meaningfulness is understood as ultimately derivative from the intentionality of agents, though in a more complex way, involving cooperation, agreement, and common expectations.

Standardly, of course, agents say only what they believe (as manifested also in their other dispositions to behave), request only what they want, promise only what they intend, and so on. These are the familiar "sincerity conditions" on illocutionary acts; and abiding by them, by and large, is a precondition on treating the behavior in question as linguistic. And there are corresponding conditions on treating responses as linguistic perceptions—as understanding what somebody says. Accordingly, from the perspective of neo-behaviorist constraints on intentional ascription, the Grice/Austin/Searle analyses of relations between cognitions and speech acts function as particularly sophisticated forms of discernible semantic intrigue.

The very fact that insincerity is possible, however, shows that linguistic and nonlinguistic dispositions are distinct and can diverge; indeed, there are many sources of discrepancy besides insincerity—such as lack of self-knowledge, psychological repression, logical or linguistic errors, unexamined slogans, and so on. Further, the language faculty itself is, of necessity, highly developed and specialized (perhaps even a separate "module" in the architecture of the mind[20]); and this raises tantalizing possibilities. There could, for instance, be cognitive states of a distinctive sort that are already formulated verbally within the linguistic faculty—*verbal* cognitions, we might call them. And dispositions specific to these states might interact among themselves in a way that is relatively divorced from the agent's other dispositions, and more narrowly "logical". Thus, we could imagine the agent engaging in private verbal ratiocination, drawing silent verbal conclusions, and so on, in an internal monologue of arbitrary complexity; and the conclusions of these deliberations would be ready for immediate linguistic expression, in a way that ordinary (that is, unformulated) cognitions are not. On the other hand, those same verbal conclusions would not affect nonlinguistic behavior, except insofar as they influence ordinary dispositions outside the language faculty—presumably through a process like that involved in understanding the speech of others.

Neo-behaviorist verbal cognitions are in some respects like neo-Cartesian explicit cognitions; in particular, they are semantically articulated and directly expressible, without additional processing. Nevertheless, the two notions are profoundly different. Explicit internal symbol manipulations at first base are the primary medium of cognition. As such, they must also be the immediate cognitive products of perceptual transduction, and the final cognitive causes of voluntary action. Moreover, they are essentially the same in linguistic and non-liguistic creatures, and essentially the same in linguistic and nonlinguistic transactions in creatures capable of both. Verbal cognitions at second base, by contrast, are fundamentally parasitic. They arise only in linguistic creatures, and only in their specialized linguistic faculty; accordingly, they are not involved in most perception, action, or cognition, but only in a peculiar special case.

Though the peculiarity of verbal cognitions raises special problems, particularly in how they are related to "ordinary" cognitions, it is also their principal theoretical attraction. Thus Dennett takes advantage of the distinction between two kinds of cognition to account for the difference between merely coming to believe or desire, and "making up one's mind"; and he suggests that the same division might form the basis of an account of self-deception and weakness of the will. Stalnaker makes a roughly similar appeal to account for the difference between the sense in which rational agents believe all tautologies, and the sense in which they do not. Finally, a second-base-man might well draw on the same distinction to differentiate between what Dreyfus calls intuitive "zeroing in" and explicit "counting out" (for instance, in the course of deciding on a chess move).[21]

4 SHORTSTOP

Wittgenstein might have been a shortstop.

5 THIRD BASE

At third base, social practices are the bottom line; so the position is most naturally called *neo-pragmatism*, though team organization again supports the clumsier "left-wing (that is, socialist) phenomenology". The all-stars include at least Martin Heidegger, Wilfrid Sellars, and Robert Brandom.[22] When these leftists flesh out the skeleton of vapid holism, the fundamental pattern becomes a culture or way of life, with all its institutions, artifacts, and mores. The idea is that contentful tokens, like ritual objects, customary performances, and tools, occupy determinate niches within the social fabric—and these niches "define" them as what they are. Only in virtue of such culturally instituted roles can tokens have contents at all.

Imagine a community of versatile and interactive creatures, not otherwise specified except that they are conformists. *Conformism* here means not just imitativeness (monkey see, monkey do), but also censoriousness—that is, a positive tendency to see that one's neighbors do likewise, and to suppress variation. This is to be thought of as a complicated second-order disposition, which the creatures have by nature ("wired in"). It presupposes innate capacities to react differentially (via sensory discrimination, say), to adapt behaviorally (that is, to learn, as in conditioning or habit formation), and to influence the adaptations of others (by setting an example, reinforcing, punishing, and such like). But conformism does not presuppose thought, reasoning, language, or any other cognitive faculty; the creatures do not in the first instance conform or censure wittingly or because they want to (except "tacitly")—they are simply built that way.

Censoriousness, despite the term, is not only negative: we adjust the behavior of children and fellows with smiles and strokes as well as frowns and blows. Censoring behavior is not in the first instance voluntary, nor is voluntary behavior particularly its object: involuntary "body language" is an effective means of shaping behavior, and is itself largely so shaped. What in general counts as censorious acceptance and rejection? Whatever community members do that promotes conformism: if they smile at conforming performances, and smiles promote repetition, if they fire electric shocks at those who err, and these shocks discourage aberration, then smiles and shocks are devices of censorship. And who are the members of this community? The members are basically whoever is brought into conformity with the rest of the group, and thereupon participates in the censoring of others.[23] Conformism—imitativeness and censoriousness together—is a causal interactive process that results in more or less permanent changes in the behavioral dispositions of its participants. Without such a process, there can be no community, no social practices, and no neo-pragmatist account of intentionality.

The net effect of conformism is a systematic peer pressure within the community, which can be conceived as a kind of mutual attraction among the behavioral dispositions of the different community members. Under its influence, these dispositions draw "closer" to each other, in the sense that they become more similar; that is, the community members tend to act alike, in like circumstances. The result is analogous to that of gregariousness in range animals: given only their tendency to aggregate, they will tend also to form and maintain distinct herds. Other factors (including chance) will determine how many herds form, of what sizes, and where; gregariousness determines only that there will be herds—distinguishable, reidentifiable clusters of animals, separated by clear gaps where there are no animals (save the odd stray).

When behavioral dispositions aggregate under the force of conformism, it isn't herds that coalesce, but *norms*. Other factors (including chance) will determine the number of norms, how narrow (strict) they are, and where they are in the "space" of feasible behavior;

conformism determines only that there will be norms—distinct, enduring clusters of dispositions in behavioral feasibility space, separated in that space by clear gaps where there are no dispositions (save the odd stray). Like herds, norms are a kind of "emergent" entity, with an identity and life of their own, over and above that of their constituents. Thus, young animals replace the old, thereby enabling a single herd to outlast many generations; likewise, though each individual's dispositions eventually pass away, they beget their successors in conformist youth, and thereby are the norms handed down to the generations.

The community-wide classes of similar dispositions that coalesce under the force of conformism can be called "norms"—and not just collections or kinds—precisely because they themselves set the standard for that very censoriousness by which they are generated and maintained. The censure attendant on deviation automatically gives these standards (the extant classes themselves) a *de facto* normative force. Out-of-step behavior is not just atypical, but abnormal and unacceptable; it is what one is "not supposed to" do, and in that sense improper. Norm-governed proprieties can be commissive or permissive, either to do something or not to do it (that is, must, may, must not, and need not). We sometimes also call norms *practices* or *customs*, depending on context. *Abiding by* a norm or custom (engaging in a practice) is behaving in the manner required by that norm, and not merely by coincidence, but as the exercise of the dispositions fostered by that norm.

Abiding by norms is not the same as following explicit rules. When a cook follows an unfamiliar recipe step by step, or a youngster builds a kit by carefully following the instructions, two things are required. First, the rule to be followed must be explicitly formulated in some code or language; and the rule follower must read the formulated rule and do what it says to do *because* that's what it says (that is, if you changed the formulation, so that the rule said to do something else, then the follower would do that instead). But conformists need not read a formulated rule (indeed, they need not be able to read at all) in order to abide reliably by elaborate norms; they simply acquire the relevant complexes of dispositions from their fellows (via imitation and positive and negative censoriousness), and then behave as they are disposed. Accordingly, as far as neo-pragmatism is concerned, formulating the norms explicitly as rules need not even be possible in principle. The distinction between norm-abiding and rule-following is important at third base, since the aim is to explain the possibility of the latter (as a special case of language use) in terms of the former.[24]

On the other hand, norm-abiding is also more than mere causal regularity. This is not to say that it is irregular or uncaused, but rather to insist that it has a significantly different status as *normal*. We can see the difference in two ways. First, when a laboratory specimen behaves in accord with some regularity, it does not do so "because of" the regularity; the regularity does not lead to or guide the behavior in any way, but merely shows up in it. By contrast, when community members behave normally, how they behave is in general directly accountable to what's normal in their community; their dispositions have been inculcated and shaped according to those norms, and their behavior continues to be monitored for compliance. Second, if a specimen deviates from some alleged regularity, then either the regularity is defective, or else it is only statistical and has exceptions; but the specimen itself is in no sense "wrong". By contrast, behavior deviating from communal norms is *wrong* in the clear and specific sense that it is subject to censure from others; abnormal behavior is not acceptable within the community.[25]

Finally, conformist norms should not be confused with conventions, in David Lewis's (1969) sense. Roughly, a *convention* is an "as-if" agreement, in which the parties have settled on a certain arranged behavior pattern, for mutual benefit. The origins of these conventional arrangements are not addressed by the account; but their persistence is explained by showing how, for each individual, it is *rational* to go along with whatever arrangements are already in place. The difference between norms and conventions lies in this explanatory appeal: conformism does not presuppose any prior beliefs or preferences on the part of individual conformists, and hence the persistence of norms cannot be explained in terms of agents' interest maximization or rational choice. Indeed, norms need not be, or even seem to be, in any way beneficial either to the individuals or to the group; the mechanism of conformism is completely blind to the character or merits of the norms engendered. This is not to deny, of course, that beneficial (or at least nonharmful) norms may be more likely to form or persist; but, if so, that will reflect the influence of additional factors—it is not built into the normalizing process itself.

Metaphysically, conformism works like the mechanism of inheritance and natural selection: it not only engenders order and structure in a domain that is otherwise comparatively amorphous, but it engenders a new *kind* of order. The order and structure in organisms and ecologies is not only greater than that in the primordial soup, but also of a fundamentally unprecedented kind—made possible by the distinctive mechanism of biological evolution. Likewise, the order and structure in cultural institutions and practices is not only vastly greater than any in genetic or adaptive ethology, but of a new and different kind—made possible by the distinctive mechanism of social conformism (and pruned, no doubt, by "cultural evolution"). In the latter case, like the former, whole new categories of phenomena emerge, including, according to left-wing phenomenology, social norms and original intentionality. To say that biological and social categories are "emergent" is not to say, of course, that they are incompatible with vapid materialism or exempt from the laws of nature. Quite the contrary: it is only because conformism is itself in some sense a "causal" process that the emergent social pattern is nonaccidental in the sense required for intentionality.

We may call the overall pattern of a community's norms and practices its common (shared, public) *way of life*. Unlike a scatter of herds, a way of life is highly integrated and structured, in that the norms which make it up are intricately interdependent. The basic reason is that, strictly speaking, what get normalized are not behaviors themselves but dispositions to behave in certain ways in certain circumstances. Thus, norms have a kind of "if-then" character, connecting sorts of circumstance to sorts of behavior. And therefore, the conforming community (in the differential responses of normal behavior and normal censorship) must effectively categorize both behaviors and behavioral circumstances into various distinct sorts. The public way of life *institutes* these connections and sorts.[26]

Imagine, for instance, that the rules of chess were not explicitly codified, but observed only as a body of conformist norms—"how one acts" when one plays chess. So, it is proper (socially acceptable) to move the king in any direction, but only one square at a time. For this to be a norm, players and teacher/censors must be able to "tell" (that is, respond differentially to) which piece is the king, what are the squares, what counts as a move, and so on; thus, the presupposed sorting of circumstances is effectively a sorting of items, features, and events within those circumstances. Meanwhile, according to other norms, the king must be protected when threatened, cannot be exposed to capture, can castle under certain conditions, and so on; and, crucially, for all of these norms, it's the *same* instituted sort ("king") that's involved. Hence, the norms themselves are interdependent via depending on the same sorting of circumstances (items, features, …). Let's call an instituted sort that is involved in many interrelated norms a *role*—the role of the king in chess, for instance. Many such roles are simultaneously instituted by the norms of chess behavior; and, in consequence, the roles too are interrelated by those norms. Obviously, in fact, all the norms and roles of chess are bound up in a complex and highly interdependent structure.[27]

Neo-pragmatists have often made these points in terms of the tools and paraphernalia of everyday life; but the upshot is the same. Hammers, nails, boards, and brackets, screwdrivers, screws, and glue are all bound up in a (large) nexus of interlocking roles, instituted by the norms of carpentry practice. And, as with a king in chess (or anywhere else[28]), what it is to be a screwdriver is essentially determined by its instituted role. What a screwdriver is *for* is turning screws. This does not mean just that it is of a suitable size and shape for turning screws, but rather that this is how it is supposed to be used. Of course, screwdrivers have ancillary roles (opening paint cans, and the like); but not everything you could do with one (even do well) would count as proper use. Stabbing laboratory mice, for instance, or carving your initials in the bleachers, would be a misuse or abuse of a screwdriver—no matter how clever or successful the endeavor. This question of propriety, I think, is what separates human use of tools from the uses animals sometimes make of handy objects. A monkey might be both clever and successful at getting some bananas with a stick, but in no sense is that what the stick is properly "for"; equivalently, a monkey could not abuse a stick, no matter what it did.[29]

In saying that tools are defined by their instituted roles, we imply that they are defined, at least in part, by their (instituted) relations to other role-defined paraphernalia; what it is to be an arrow is nonsense apart from what it is to be a bow, and vice versa. Bows *as such* are "objectively" related to arrows, via the communal norms; shooting arrows is what they're *for*. Thus, when a bow is used to shoot an arrow, the relation between them is not only factual (causal/explanatory), but also and simultaneously normative (that's how they are supposed to be used). What's more, the normative "relation" obtains even in the absence of the second relatum: my bow is still "for" shooting arrows, even when my quiver is empty. Needless to belabor, instituted relations among public paraphernalia are the third-base archetype of all intentionality. Linguistic devices are thereby included too, as a (very) special case. Dewey put the point colorfully and succinctly.

> As to be a tool ... is to have and to endow with meaning, language, being the tool of tools, is the cherishing mother of all significance. (1925/29, 154)

It remains to ask what distinguishes linguistic from other tools (that is, the specific difference of the special case), and how the intentionality of paraphernalia connects with that of cognition.

Linguistic tools—words and sentences, for instance—must be uttered to be used; in the first place and mostly, they occur only in utterances.[30] The term 'utterance' is ambiguous between the producing and the product—that is, between the uttering of the word tokens and the word tokens thus uttered. The former is a using of the linguistic tools; the latter are the tools thus used. In the case of speech (which is the more basic), this distinction can be elusive, since the tokens used are as ephemeral as the using of them; but written tokens, being more durable, are clearly distinct from the writing of them, and thereby clarify the distinction. In either case, it is these tokens produced that are the tokens of linguistic types; they are therefore also the tokens that have proper linguistic uses in relevant circumstances, hence play linguistic roles and serve as the primary bearers of semantic content.

Linguistic tools are distinctive in being essentially *double-use* tools: they have two (different but connected) uses in the uttering and in the responding thereto. It's not just that, like tandem bicycles, linguistic tools typically have two users, or that, like army pocket knives, they are multi-purpose. Rather, the basic *point* of linguistic tools is to *connect* the two uses: utterances are "meant" to be responded to, and the responses are to them as uttered. Both uses, of course, are governed by norms; and it is in the relationships between the respective proprieties of utterance and response, as situated, that the connections reside. To take the most rudimentary illustration: when the policeman directs traffic, it is proper for him to direct you on your way when and only when it is fair and safe for you to go; and it is proper for you (and, similarly, the other drivers) to go when and as he directs, and not otherwise. What's more, such proper adjustment and distribution of further proprieties is precisely what the policeman's gestures are *for*. How can this observation be generalized?

As with norm-governed behavior in general, the proper use of linguistic tools is conditioned on the circumstances: what would be proper in one situation would not in another. Obviously, for instance, the propriety of saying "Look, there's a fire engine" is closely associated with the visible presence of a fire engine. Norm-relevant circumstances, however, include more than what is presently manifest. Thus, in chess, the propriety of castling is contingent not only on the present configuration of pieces, but also on whether that king has previously moved; we can say that when the king first moves, its "status" changes: it is no longer eligible to castle. Similarly in baseball, the batter always has a status (called the "count"), reflecting how many previous pitches have been balls and strikes; and various proprieties (for various players) depend on the current count. Other pertinent statuses include place in the batting order, the number of outs so far, what inning it is, the score, and so on. Some statuses attach to individual players, others to teams or equipment, still others to the game in progress. More generally, a *status* is a propriety-determining, variable condition that is not manifest; hence, norm-relevant circumstances include not only the manifest characteristics and configurations of present items, but also their normative statuses

By leftist lights, the primary utterance use of linguistic tools is to affect the current normative circumstances, including the statuses of both utterer and audience. This is the generalization of saying they are "double-use" tools; for the use in proper response is precisely in behaving according to the new proprieties implicit in the affected statuses. Many ways in which language is used primarily to affect status and propriety are familiar and banal: promises, vows, offers, commands, requests, questions, and the like, are clearly means for altering and otherwise managing various proprieties. If I make a promise, I am committed to keeping it; and those to whom I make it are entitled to count on my keeping it. This means not merely that they may act in ways that will be proper only if I do what I promise, but that they may do so "on my account"; that is, if I fail, I am responsible not simply for breaking the promise itself, but also for the resulting improprieties of those who counted on me—they are entitled to defer that blame to me. Neo-pragmatism must offer comparable normative analyses of all other speech acts, including, in particular, factual assertion.

So: asserting that *p* is committing yourself to showing that *p*, if called upon, and entitling your hearer to pass along to you any call to show that p; that is, your hearer may act in a way that incurs a commitment to show that p, and defer that commitment to you. Thus, suppose it is proper to lock the door only if you can show that all the children are in. Then, if I say that all the children are in, you can lock the door "on my account": if someone challenges you to show that all the children are in, you can call upon me to discharge that commitment; and if I cannot (maybe one of the children got locked out), then you can defer the blame (negative censure) to me. Conspicuous among the things that the hearer can do on the asserter's account is make further assertions. Trivially, for instance, you could relay to a third party that the children are all in, deferring to me if challenged to show it. But further, if someone else has said that the adults are all in, then you could assert that everybody is in, accepting responsibility for the propriety of the inference, but deferring me and that third party for the premises.[31]

This can elaborate practically without bounds—with much conversation directly depending on and affecting only the rest of the conversation. Thus, many, perhaps most, linguistic moves are purely *intralinguistic*, in the following sense: their propriety is secured entirely by current circumstances resulting from prior linguistic utterances, and they affect exclusively circumstances determining the propriety of subsequent utterances.[32] This is why, at third base, language is so readily comparable to a game. For, the point of moves or plays in a game, like speech acts, is precisely to affect normative circumstances—that is, to make a difference to what's proper. Further, as far as the game itself is concerned, moves are always "intrasystematic" in the above sense: their propriety depends only on circumstances within the game (resulting, typically, from previous moves), and they affect only circumstances within the game (determining the propriety of subsequent moves). Crucially, however—for this is the essential difference between language and games—not all linguistic moves are intralinguistic. That is, some utterances depend directly for their propriety on nonlinguistic circumstances, and/or directly affect the propriety of nonlinguistic actions. Observation statements and promises are obvious cases in point.

At third base, as at first base, the primary bearers of content are semantically articulated symbols, occurring in appropriate dynamic patterns, and vapid-reducible to distinct and determinate formal tokens.[33] Third-base tokens, however, are external, not internal, to the systems that use them; and the holistic pattern in which they occur includes far more than just their relations to one another—indeed, it includes in principle all the interdependent relationships instituted by the way of life of which they are a part. Roughly speaking, intralinguistic proprieties involving these tokens correspond to internal coherence within a text (rationality in the broad sense), and linguistic proprieties involving extralinguistic circumstances correspond to external coherence with the world (including truth and other satisfaction conditions). Publicly instituted by all these norms are such relationships as that between (tokens of) "Babe Ruth built Yankee Stadium" and the indicated state of affairs, as well as that between 'Babe Ruth' and the man himself—relationships which, though more complicated in many respects, are metaphysically of a piece with the instituted relationship between bows and arrows, or bats and balls.

Normative statuses are by nature not manifest properties; accordingly, community members must effectively "keep track" of them, lest they be lost and cease to exist. In particular, if the point of language is to be served, interlocutors must keep track of everyone's conversational status—including especially their own. Thus, if it is to amount to anything for me to undertake, by saying that p, a commitment to show that p, then I, as well as anyone who is thereby entitled to call on me, had better keep track of that commitment; otherwise, it would be for nought. And these retained statuses are then the cornerstone for a third-base account of cognitive states—such as believing that p.[34] We cannot here pursue the development of that account, but merely mention two noteworthy consequences. First, approaching cognition from a basis in conversational status has the merit of making it unsurprising that psychological states so closely parallel possible speech acts, not only in content but also in "force"—beliefs to assertions, intentions to promises, wonderings to questions, and so on. And, second, founding cognition thus in language renders its intentionality incontestably derivative. At third base, the instituted intentionality of *public* symbols is *original intentionality*. The extant normative order in the communal pattern is *sui generis* and self-sustaining, via the mechanism of conformism; it is the fountainhead of all intentionality, public and private. Thus, insofar as this order is imposed on the behavior or states of individual community members in such a way as to confer intentionality also on them, that resulting private intentionality is *derivative*.

6 WRAP UP

Neo-Cartesians differ radically from neo-behaviorists and neo-pragmatists alike in maintaining that original intentionality is *internal*—that is, essentially a property of vapid-reducible explicit cognitions, each of which is identical to a formally determinate internal token. Hence, they naturally embrace a semantically articulated language of thought, and account for the possibility of semantic activity in terms of computational processes defined over expressions in this language. It is, of course, this character that makes right-wing phenomenology so intimately compatible with "classical" artificial intelligence and cognitive science, and so completely incompatible with the newer "distributed representation" models (with which the center and left are entirely comfortable).

Second-base-men are properly distinguished from their teammates on either side by an account of original intentionality that is basically *nonlinguistic*. Accordingly, intentional ascription is nothing like translation, the ascribed intentional states themselves are not semantically articulated, and the contents of those states need not be exactly expressible in any symbolic system. The fundamental normative considerations, therefore, are not the language-based notions of truth and logical inference, but the action-based notions of success and effective means to ends. Acting competently in the environment takes the place of saying (perhaps only in the language of thought) reasonable things about it as the basic mark of systems with intentionality.

Left-wing phenomenology is primarily distinctive in making original intentionality essentially a *social institution*—part of a way of life engendered and maintained by communal conformism. Hence, on the one hand, linguistic and other behavioral norms can be seen as fundamentally kindred, the familiar parallels between language and tools and between language and games are naturally accommodated, and the phenomenon of intentionality itself is assimilated to a broader range of instituted structures and relationships. On the other hand, however, the account is confined exclusively to social beings: the left, unlike either the center or the right, differentiates in principle between people and all other known creatures or systems—it leaves no room whatever for original intentionality in any animals, (asocial) robots, or even isolated (unsocialized) human beings.

All three positions agree that intentionality is a normative notion; but they differ subtly on the basic character of the norms. At first and second base, the relevant norms "devolve upon" intentional states along with their intentionality. Now, inasmuch as that intentionality is *original*, so also are the norms: they too are *exposed*, discovered as belonging to the systems themselves, and not merely *imposed*, tacked on at the will and convenience of the observer. Nevertheless, these norms remain "external" to the systems in another sense: they do not bring about the actual normality of the states to which they apply—the states are not as they should be *because* that's how they should be. In this regard, they are like norms of proper functioning in biological systems. Thus, the liver is supposed to secrete bile; if it doesn't, it's not just atypical but malfunctioning and defective. But livers do not secrete bile because they're supposed to; the propriety of it has no effect on the actual secretions. Likewise, the intentional norms at first and second base prescribe how the systems are supposed to be (irrationality is a defect), but have no part in actualizing what they prescribe. At third base, on the other hand, the norms as such—the extant classes of shared dispositions—causally engender and foster further normal dispositions and behavior, via the mechanism of conformism. We talk and act, work and play as we do *because* that's how it's normally done in our community. Thus, neo-pragmatist social behavior is norm-*governed* (guided and directed) in a way in which neo-Cartesian cognitions and neo-behaviorist interactions are not. To put it another way, leftist norms are, at least tacitly, understood and appreciated as norms by the creatures who abide by them.

This, moreover, is why there is nothing at third base corresponding to the principles of interpretation and ascription. At the first two bases, all that distinguishes a pattern (of token deployments or environmental interactions, respectively) as specifically intentional is that it can be "mapped onto" our own rational thought or behavior. The point is not that the intentionality of the observed system is supplied by us, or derived from our own, but rather that the only standard of what to count as intentional is comparison with ourselves. In other words, to claim that a system has intentional states is just to claim that there is such a mapping—a systematic interpretation or ascription, depending on what pattern is being mapped. But at third base, the pattern that supports intentionality is distinguished not by its likeness to anything about us, but by its distinctive ontological foundation in social conformism. The institution, via this process, of intentional relationships among sorted items is perfectly describable and intelligible quite apart from any possible or actual mapping onto our own norms and practices. Hence, no corresponding principle is required.[35]

The three positions also have interestingly different implications concerning the unity and nature of the *self*. A neo-Cartesian self, like its celebrated forebear, is essentially a thinking thing. The unity of the set of cognitions it comprises is fundamentally determined by the scope of their automatic rational interactions, or, equivalently, by the scope of the automatic cognitive processes acting over them. In effect, the self is a maximal set of cognitive states (tokens) that are directly accessible to one another in cognitive processing. Thus, we could understand two or more selves inhabiting the same "hardware" by assuming that their cognitions are suitably isolated from one another; and we could understand a single self spread over several hardware units by assuming that cognitions from all the units are mutually accessible in the course of thinking. Somewhat more complicated structures are manageable, if we imagine maximal sets of semi-autonomous "modules" that are tightly coupled within themselves and loosely coupled among themselves. But it is also easy to imagine rambling networks of interconnected structures, with various degrees of local and global coupling, and no well-defined boundaries anywhere; in such cases, the notion of an individual cognitive system—a self—loses its grip.

A neo-behaviorist self, by contrast, is essentially a rational agent; hence, its fundamental unity is that of a body of environmental interactions that can be rendered intelligible as competent by the interpolation of a coherent set of intervening cognitions. This makes it more difficult, though not impossible, to sort out multiple selves sharing hardware, or single selves in scattered hardware. Much more interesting, however, is the qualitative differentiation between two levels or kinds of mental life, within a single agent, that is made possible by the distinction between ordinary and verbal cognition. For it is tempting to suggest that the "higher" verbal level coincides, at least approximately, with that special *conscious self* that we often suppose distinguishes us from other creatures. The attraction is not merely that there are two different levels to work with, but also that certain familiar characteristics of consciousness seem to fall naturally out of the account. Thus, compared to the "unconscious processing" that must somehow be involved in ordinary skillful behavior, conscious thinking is conspicuously laborious and slow—not a lot faster than talking, in fact. What's more, it is about as difficult to entertain consciously two distinct trains of thought at the same time as it is to engage in two distinct conversations at once; consciousness is in some sense a linear or serial process, in contrast to the many simultaneous cognitions that are manifest, say, in driving a car or throwing out a base runner. Finally and notoriously, of course, conscious deliberation seems verbal to introspection—so much so that philosophers and poets have since antiquity assimilated thought to "inner dialog".[36]

A neo-pragmatist self is essentially a member of a conforming community; hence, it's unity is determined in the first place by the scope of effective imitation and censoriousness. Thus, to take a homely example, two hands belong to the same child just in case, if either is out of line, it suffices to slap either as a response; both hands are then part of a single "unit of accountability"—a single self, from the point of view of conformism. It is also this self-unit that comes to play miscellaneous social roles, and to which cognitive and other statuses attach. The mechanism of conformism, however, harbors implicitly the resources for a further understanding of selfhood. Members of the community are, of course, not only normatively censored, but also (eventually and in general) the censors; and this raises the prospect of self-censorship. Primitively, we might imagine some creature actually slapping itself after misbehaving, thereby learning from its mistake; but that would soon give way to private self-flagellation (remorse), and even anticipatory criticism, thereby forestalling misdeeds. Moreover, as the demands of diverse norms and commitments come into conflict, as inevitably some must, these too become accessible to critical scrutiny and adjudication. All of which suggests a foundation, unmatched at first or second base, for the possibility of *moral choice*, with regard not only to particular actions, but also to enduring personal roles and values. Thus, the unit of public accountability could "take over" its life, as a unit of personal responsibility and resolve—an *owned self*.[37]

Before concluding, we should pause to consider whether our three positions might be compatible. On the face or it, the answer is no. Insofar as each position puts forward a *different* fundamental pattern—among internal tokens, environmental interactions, or social institutions—as *the* pattern upon which original intentionality depends, they are not compatible at all, but mutually exclusive. There are, however, several conciliatory avenues that might mitigate or even eliminate intramural conflict. The *double-play* option, for instance, simply divides the spoils: teammates agree that there is more than one *kind* of original intentionality, each depending on its own underlying pattern. Thus, we might imagine a neo-behaviorist and a neo-pragmatist agreeing that animals and people share a certain primitive sort of intentionality (second-base pattern), and yet also that a qualitatively "higher" intentionality is possible only for conformists with a culture and language (third-base pattern). Questions could be raised, of course, about what the two sorts of intentionality had to do with one another—why, in particular, both were sorts of *intentionality*—but perhaps there would be enough similarities to justify the common term.

Other olive branches exploit the fact that, although the three positions are directly incompatible, their respective essential *patterns* are not. Hence, any player has the *fielder's choice* option of admitting the existence, and even the profound importance, of either or both of the other patterns, while still insisting that only his own favorite is the foundation of original intentionality. In other words, one pattern is accorded a necessary but subsidiary role in the implementation or genesis of another, which alone has metaphysical pride of place. For instance, a second- or third-base-man might concede that the internal first-base pattern is needed to explain how sophisticated behavioral dispositions are physically achievable—yet maintain that only the resulting interactive or social pattern can account for intentionality. It seems to me that Dennett dallies with this particular compromise, especially when he talks about "sub-personal cognitive psychology", or the brain as a "syntactic engine".[38] Finally, the most radical ecumenist is the *utility infielder*, who points out that, inasmuch as the patterns themselves are mutually consistent, any two or even all three of them could be combined into a single more encompassing pattern. The suggestion would be that none of the three "subpatterns" alone is sufficient for original intentionality, but only a larger pattern of which they are portions. Thus, someone could maintain that the neo-behaviorists' environmental interactions must be integrated with the neo-Cartesians' token interactions in order to account simultaneously for external and internal coherence. Fodor may be moving in this direction, and I suspect that Donald Davidson and David Lewis could be read similarly (Davidson, indeed, might want to combine all three patterns).

It is not my purpose here, however, to home in on the best account of intentionality, but only to sketch some contemporary positions and moves, placing them within a ballpark that shows both what they have in common and where they differ. Still, in closing, I must acknowledge one glaring omission. Counting you and me (catching and pitching), we've been through the entire defensive line-up; that is, we've considered how each position is defended vis-à-vis those phenomenal hitters at the plate. But all defensive positions are alike in confronting intentionality only from the outside—in the "third person", as it were. Some philosophers, however, have maintained that the phenomenology of original intentionality, along with consciousness and associated phenomena, is possible only from the inside—only as actually *experienced*, in the "first person". Clearly, however, the offensive side of the game requires entirely different strategies and considerations; hence, we must leave to another occasion the question made famous by Tom Nagel (1974): What is it like to be *at* bat?

NOTES:

1 For those unfortunate readers unfamiliar with American baseball, I should perhaps mention that in the annual baseball All-Star Game, star players from the Pittsburgh Pirates and the San Diego Padres play as teammates (for the National League). Generally, the opposing pitcher (from the American League) would try to avoid giving a batter a free "base on balls" (also called a "walk"); but in certain threatening situations, especially when the current batter is on a "hot streak", then that batter is "walked" intentionally.

2 This exchange between Hobbes and Descartes occurs in objection 2, from the third set of objections (written by Hobbes) to Descartes's *Meditations*, and Descartes's reply thereto (1641/1984, 122–124). I have taken certain liberties with the actual texts, in view of well-known doctrines from the *Meditations*, and purposes of my own.

3 Actually, the term 'intentional' (with more or less this sense) antedates Descartes, in scholastic metaphysics; but only much later was it reintroduced into modern philosophical vocabulary by Brentano 1874, and into the English language, by Chisholm 1957 and 1960. (The latter volume contains translations of several relevant chapter-length excerpts from Brentano.)

4 In recent years there have been numerous arguments to the effect that content (by itself) can't really determine extension after all—with attendant discussion of what to do about that. Putnam 1975 ("twin Earth") got a lot of it started; Dennett 1982/87 includes a useful survey. In my view, however, these issues won't matter in the present context; so I shan't mention them again.

5 The thesis that reasons must be understood also as causes is argued in Davidson 1963/80. Davidson considers especially reasons for action; but the point generalizes.

6 The distinction I draw between *original* and *derivative* intentionality should not be confused with a similar distinction that Searle 1980 draws between *intrinsic* and *observer-relative* intentionality. According to Searle, mental structures or states have intentionality "intrinsically", as a causal consequence of the physical/chemical properties of the brain—much as other structures or states might have wetness or the ability to photosynthesize. But this is a substantive metaphysical claim, with it is possible to disagree (see, for example, Dennett 1987a/87). According to my distinction, on the other hand, intentionality is original just in case it isn't derivative (namely, from the intentionality of something else with the same content). So, on pain of circularity or infinite regress, *some* intentionality *has to* be original—whether as intrinsic intentionality in Searle's specific sense, or in some other way. That is, it is not a substantive thesis to claim that if there is any intentionality, some of it must be original; hence, the interesting question is not whether there is any original intentionality, but how. In effect, this paper is an exploration of three *different* ways in which we might understand original intentionality (none of them the same as Searle's). (Incidentally, I know that Searle and I were discussing our respective distinctions as early as summer 1979; but I do not remember which, if either, influenced the other.) Block 1986 introduces yet another pair of terms, *autonomous* versus *inherited* meaning; however, he also seems to build into his understanding of the terminology a substantive view of how original intentionality (in my sense) is possible—namely, as conceptual roles in a language of thought. But no particular theory, Searle's or Block's or any other (my own included), is built into the original/derivative distinction.

7 For discussion of the "relativity" of accidentalness, see Dennett 1984, especially chapter 6, section 3, and the sources cited there.

8 Note in passing that the variations on holism to be discussed here are all varieties of what I called "prior holism"—in contrast to "real time holism"—in my 1979 (= chapter 2 of this volume).

9 Obviously, my swift remarks about the outfield positions are far worse as caricatures than even the oversimplified sketches I will offer for the infield; and these few wisecracks about Searle are perhaps the least just of all. They may not be entirely unfair with regard to Searle 1980; but his 1983 offers a much richer and more complicated view. In particular, his insistence in the latter that intentionality is possible only in the context of both a network of other intentional (mental) states and a background of non-intentional (but still mental) capacities and habits, strikes me as a major advance; I find it difficult, however, to reconcile this with the idea of "intrinsic" intentionality (which he retains). I am also impressed by the following passage:

> The actual performance in which the speech act is made will involve the production (or use or presentation) of some physical entity, such as noises made through the mouth or marks on paper. Beliefs, fears, hopes, and desires on the other hand are intrinsically Intentional. To characterize them as beliefs, fears, hopes, and desires is already to ascribe Intentionality to them. But speech acts have a physical level of realization, *qua* speech acts, that is not intrinsically Intentional. There is nothing intrinsically Intentional about the products of the utterance act, that is, the noises that come out of my mouth or the marks that I make on paper.
>
> (1983, 27)

This does not quite say, but certainly suggests that, according to Searle, mental states do *not* have a physical level of realization, *qua* mental states, that is not intrinsically Intentional (though he emphasizes elsewhere, for instance on page 265, that mental states *are* physically realized). I'm not entirely sure what this means (a lot turns on that "*qua*"), but it is remarkably like the *second*-base claim that it need not be possible to individuate cognitive states in any terms other than intentional. Alas, Searle does not explicitly defend either a first- or second-base (or any other) account of what it is about certain physically realized states in virtue of which they (unlike most others) can have original intentionality; and that, finally, is why he's in the outfield.

10 See, for example, Fodor 1975 and 1981, Field 1978, and Pylyshyn 1984; a number of other prominent philosophers of psychology could be counted at least as first-base sympathizers, including, I think, Ned Block, Rob Cummins, Gilbert Harman, and Bill Lycan.

11 In my 1985 I used 'formal' in a more restrictive sense than this; the present broader sense follows Fodor 1980/81 (and is, incidentally, reminiscent of Descartes's much older usage).

12 On the distinction between token-token and type-type identities, see Davidson 1970/80 and Block and Fodor 1972 (the terminology is from the latter).

13 Notice that vapid reduction is weaker than classical reduction not only in that the "bridge laws" are loose and local, but also in that there is no requirement that higher-level regularities be derivable (even loosely and locally) from lower level laws.

14 This principle of interpretation is, of course, a variation on what Quine 1960 (following Wilson) called the "principle of charity" (see Quine's sections 13 and 15). Quine used the principle as an adequacy condition on translations of alien speech; but inasmuch as interpretation is here a generalization of translation, the point transfers.

15 I do not claim to have argued that semantic activity is *only* possible if thinking is a computational process conducted in a language of thought—though that view is certainly widely held, and not implausible.

16 See, for example, Quine 1960, Dennett 1971/78 and 1981/87, and Stalnaker 1976 and 1984. Of course, there are also a number of well-known philosophers whom I suspect of second-base leanings—though, interestingly, more often from philosophy of language than philosophy of psychology; J.L. Austin, Jonathan Bennett, and Paul Grice come to mind. (I can't decide whether Gilbert Ryle plays second base way back or center field close in.)

17 For the notion of distributed representation, see Rumelhart, McClelland, *et al*, 1986.

18 Davidson 1970/80 argues that standing in causal relations *entails* token-identity with the strictly physical—at least for events. In my 1983 (= chapter 5 in this volume), I challenge that argument, and dispute its conclusion.

19 Dretske 1981 appeals to a similar notion of diverse routes from a common source in explaining his notion of "semantic content" (see chapter 6, especially the remarks on pages 187–188).

20 For an explanation of the "language module" thesis and a survey of linguistic and psychological evidence in its favor, see Fodor 1983.

21 See, for instance, Dennett 1978c, Stalnaker 1984, chapter 4, and Dreyfus 1972/92, chapter 1, part 2.

22 See, for instance, Heidegger 1927/72 (especially Division One, chapters 3–5), Sellars 1954/63 and 1969, and Brandom 1979 and 1983. As notable fellow travelers at third base, I hope to get away with tagging at least John Dewey, Hubert Dreyfus, Michael Dummett, and John McDowell. My own sympathies are also mainly here. [But see the 1997 remark added to note 37 below.]

23 In "real life", of course, it's more complicated, because we have various kinds and degrees of partial and parasitic membership. Thus young children (and certain mental incompetents) are held only to a subset of the norms, and participate in the censoring of others only in a very limited way. Also, communities are seldom sharply delineated, but overlap and merge into one another; moreover, they often comprise numerous somewhat distinguishable subcommunities with variant "normative dialects". Finally, I think we can imagine "adjunct" members who don't really participate in a community's norms—they neither censure nor are censured—but nevertheless reliably behave "normally", at least in certain respects; I have in mind, for instance, robots programmed to speak (a significant fragment of) natural English, though they can neither learn it nor teach it.

24 There is a natural extension of the notion of following an explicit rule to that of a computer following an explicit program; and it

might be held that no material system could in fact exhibit the required behavioral complexity and versatility unless it explicitly followed a complex rule (program) "internally". But this is a strong and separate claim that calls for an independent argument. The question is presumably in some sense empirical. Third base, like second base, need not be concerned with how the dispositions are "implemented"; hence, it is also entirely compatible with "distributed representation" models of how it all works.

25 The last two paragraphs are meant to summarize and show compatibility with the first seventeen paragraphs of Sellars 1954/63. He does not develop an account like mine of how norms result from conformism; but he very clearly delineates what he calls "norm conforming behavior" (also "pattern governed behavior") as distinct both from "rule obeying behavior" (what I call "explicit rule following") and from behavior that "merely conforms to rules" (what I call "regularities"). I take it as a condition of adequacy on the conformist account of norms that it support both of these distinctions.

26 As I read *Being and Time*, what Heidegger means by "the anyone" (*das Man*) is roughly equivalent to what I am here calling a *common* (public) "way of life". However, the notion of a way of life is in principle more general than this, and encompasses, when fully worked out, all of what Heidegger means by dasein. The parallel with the Wittgensteinian phrase and idea of a "form of life" hardly needs mention.

27 Note the parallels between the complexity described in this paragraph and that called "semantic intrigue" at second base.

28 The instituted structure of sorted roles and relationships extends not only to the tools and paraphernalia of a way of life, but to those who live it as well—the members of the community whose way of life it is. Thus, King of Belgium, postal clerk, committee member, and so on, can be understood as *social roles*. The parallels between equipmental and social roles—evidenced even in the common term—are obvious. Roles of both kinds are induced by conformism, and reflect proprieties regarding the behavior of, as well as behavior towards, whatever plays the roles. Nevertheless, the two kinds of role are fundamentally different, for social role players, unlike their equipment, are themselves conformists.

Community members are positively inclined to be like their peers, are subject to censure if they misbehave, and contribute to the censure of others; but tools are oblivious to how they compare with one another, are subject merely to redesign or repair if they are defective, and are never censors. Since community members are *participants* in the community, we do not say their roles determine what they are "for", nor do we speak of "using" them. More important, since the entire complexity of the way of life depends on the normalized dispositions of its participants, these participants must be considerably more versatile and flexible than ordinary equipment need be. For instance, community members can and do play many social roles at once, change their roles from time to time, and even sometimes redefine the roles they play.

29 The term 'use' here is not meant primarily in the deliberate or "on purpose" sense in which one might, for instance, use a newspaper to swat a bug, or use a cauldron as a planter. Rather, the primary sense is the way in which we "automatically" use the equipment that is most familiar to us, without paying attention or even noticing—as when a skilled driver routinely uses the pedals, or we thoughtlessly (but properly) use the knife and fork at dinner, while concentrating on the conversation.

30 Word tokens do occur (as word tokens) in, for instance, spelling bees (oral), crossword puzzles (written), and such like. I take it that these occurrences are not proper utterances, in that the words are not being used to say anything, and that they are parasitic on the use of words in proper utterances.

31 These remarks about assertion have been especially influenced by Brandom 1983.

32 In the case of speech, the normative circumstances resulting from prior utterances will be entirely in the form of current (retained) statuses—precisely because the tokens themselves do not last. Written tokens, by contrast, usually remain on the page (or chalkboard, or whatever) long enough to be part of the manifest circumstances of subsequent linguistic actions.

33 At first base, semantic articulation (in a language of thought with a digital syntax) is introduced in order to explain how semantic activity is possible; in other words, it is justified in terms of its

engineering payoff. There is an analogous payoff at third base, of course (we need only master thousands of words to master trillions of sentences, and so on); but there may be an independent account of the "articulation" as well. For the very mechanism of conformism induces a "clumping" effect in the normal sorts of behavior and circumstances it institutes. Thus, just as herds are widely scattered concentrations of animals, with at most the odd stray between them, so normalized atomic speech dispositions should naturally spread out into widely differentiated clumps in the space of makable sounds—and that's the essence of digital articulation. In fact, a neo-pragmatist might argue that this natural tendency towards articulation in social practices *explains why* sophisticated languages (which must be articulated, for the engineering reasons) emerge in all and only conformist communities.

34 Brandom, from whom I have learned much, is working out a detailed account of the *semantics* of explicit belief *attributions* (including a novel account of the *de re/de dicto* distinction) along roughly these lines.

35 It has sometimes been argued (for instance, Davidson 1974/84) that we cannot make sense of ascribing intentional states that are unintelligible to us, because (roughly) the only grounds we could have for regarding them as intentional are fundamentally indistinguishable from the grounds for understanding them in some determinate way (namely, by mapping them onto our own states). It seems to me that first base and second base are committed to this argument, but not third base. I see no reason in principle why we could not recognize a group of creatures as a conforming community, with highly developed norms and practices (including rituals, equipment, games, and even language), quite apart from whether or how far we could correlate those norms and practices with any of our own.

36 This list of considerations is adapted directly from Dennett (1984, 41), though I introduce it in a somewhat different (and much briefer) way. It must be acknowledged, of course, that an account along these lines is not restricted to neo-behaviorists alone. A "modular" language faculty, for instance, may be independently motivated, and could easily be accommodated at either first or third base; and that would generate the essential two-

tiered structure, on which the rest depends. Still, the approach is less *ad hoc* at second base, since only there is the fundamental understanding of cognition independent of anything language-like (public or private); hence, only there are ordinary cognition and talking different in kind on the face of it. Third base, however, does discriminate fundamentally between cognitive states (which are linguistic) and the many (non-cognitive) capacities and dispositions that are involved in routine skillful behavior; so the underlying third-base distinctions are in fact more like those at second base than those at first—it's just that neo-pragmatists do not deem the pre-linguistic (animal-like) states cognitive.

37 Needless to say, these last few remarks derive much more from Heidegger than from any of the other neo-pragmatists I've mentioned. My point in the paragraph, however, is that the seeds of such doctrines lie in the grounds of neo-pragmatism itself, and are not idiosyncratic to Heidegger (or "existentialism").

Remark [added 1997]: While it is surely true that what I have here called "neo-pragmatism" is not *idiosyncratic* to Heidegger, it is questionable whether it is attributable to Heidegger at all. There is a "pragmatist" strain *at most* in what he calls "The preparatory fundamental analysis of dasein" (1927/62, Division One, especially chapters III–V). Certainly the larger tendency of the work is profoundly non-pragmatist. McDowell, likewise, is not really a neo-pragmatist. (Compare chapter 13 below.)

38 For recent examples, see the entries listed under the two quoted phrases in the index of Dennett 1987. Note, by the way, that even if a neo-behaviorist were to allow internal computational tokens at the implementation level, these needn't be identical with *either* the system's "ordinary" cognitive states, intervening between perceptions and actions, *or* its "verbal cognitions" (if any) formulated explicitly in its linguistic module. The internal tokens might very well have some sort of intentionality or representational content, but it would be (on the present compromise, anyway) metaphysically derivative.

CHAPTER EIGHT

Representational Genera

A *genus* of representation is a general kind, within which there can be more specific kinds, importantly different from one another, yet generically alike. The level of generality intended can be indicated by example. Natural languages, logical calculi, and computer programming languages, as well as numerous more specialized notations, are all interestingly different species; but they are generically alike in being broadly *language-like* or *logical* in character. By contrast, pictures, though equally representational, are not linguistic at all, even in this broad sense; rather, they, along with maps, scale models, analog computers, and at least some graphs, charts, and diagrams, are species in another genus of broadly *image-like* or *iconic* representations. So the level of generality intended for representational genera is that of logical versus iconic representations, thus broadly construed.

The motive for the notion lies in the possibility of raising two kinds of question. First: on what basis are such genera gathered and distinguished? That is, what sort of likeness or disparity between two representational species determines whether they are in the same or different genera? Given an account of this basis, it should be possible to delineate the distinctive "essence" of each genus. Second: besides the two familiar genera, are there any others? In particular, is so-called *distributed* representation a separate genus, on a par with logical and iconic representation, yet as different from each as they are from one another? And, if so, what is its generic essence?

Inasmuch as distributed representations are still relatively strange and (hence?) unintuitive, the latter questions can best be approached by way of the former. Accordingly, even an investigation into the essence of distributed representation must be guided in large part by intuitions grounded in the better-known logical and iconic genera—

in effect, bootstrapping these up to a common level, which can then be extended and applied to less familiar cases. The considerations that follow are even more than usually tentative and exploratory; the results are at best preliminary and incomplete, perhaps much worse.

1 REPRESENTATION: THE "FAMILY" OF THE GENERA

An explicit account of representation as such will not be necessary; that is, we can get along without a prior definition of the "family" within which the genera are to be distinguished. A few sketchy and dogmatic remarks, however, may provide some useful orientation, as well as places to hang some terminological stipulations.

A sophisticated system (organism) designed (evolved) to maximize some end (such as survival) must in general adjust its behavior to specific features, structures, or configurations of its environment in ways that could not have been fully prearranged in its design. If the relevant features are reliably present and manifest to the system (via some signal) whenever the adjustments must be made, then they need not be represented. Thus, plants that track the sun with their leaves needn't represent it or its position, because the tracking can be guided directly by the sun itself. But if the relevant features are not always present (manifest), then they can, at least in some cases, be represented; that is, something else can stand in for them, with the power to guide behavior in their stead. That which stands in for something else in this way is a *representation*; that which it stands in for is its *content*;[1] and its standing in for that content is *representing* it.

As so far described, "standing in for" could be quite inflexible and ad hoc; for instance, triggered gastric juices might keep a primitive predator on the prowl, even when it momentarily loses a scent—thus standing in for the scent. Here, however, we will reserve the term 'representation' for those stand-ins that function in virtue of a general *representational scheme* such that: (i) a variety of possible contents can be represented by a corresponding variety of possible representations; (ii) what any given representation (item, pattern, state, event, ...) represents is determined in some consistent or systematic way by the scheme;[2] and (iii) there are proper (and improper) ways of producing, maintaining, modifying, and/or using the various representations under various environmental and other conditions. (This characterization is intended to be neutral not only among genera, but also between internal and external representations, and between natural and artificial schemes.)

Since the content of a given representation is determined by its scheme (and since the point of the facility is to be able to represent what isn't present or currently accessible), it is possible for representations to misrepresent. What this amounts to will vary with the specific scheme, and even more with its genus; but it must hark back eventually to the possibility of the system(s) using it being *misguided* in their attempted adjustments to the features of the world. But misrepresentation should not be confused with improper deployment on the part of the using system, nor bad luck in the results. These can diverge in virtue of the fundamental holism underlying what can count as a representation at all: the scheme must be such that, properly produced and used, its representations will, under normal conditions, guide the system successfully, on the whole. In case conditions are, in one way or another, not normal, however, then a representing system can misrepresent without in any way malfunctioning.

2 CANONICAL ACCOUNTS OF THE GENERA

Analyzing representation in terms of a relational structure—that which represents–representing–that which is represented—suggests looking for the distinctive essences of the genera in one or another of those elements. But they clearly do not lie in the representative tokens alone. One cannot simply say, for instance, that linguistic tokens are essentially digital, whereas images are analog, since, in the first place, speech is to some extent analog, and in the second, images are often handled digitally. More to the point, however, paradigm representations of *any* genus—logical, iconic, distributed, or whatever—can be recorded without loss[3] in strings of bits; and certainly no properties of bit strings as such can differentiate in general between the sorts of representation they record. And, on the face of it, there seems equally little hope of differentiating the genera on the basis of their represented contents. Thus, a police officer's report might well include both descriptions and photographs of one and the same crime scene; and, *prima facie*, there could be distributed representations of it as well.

Apparently, then, the essential differentia must be sought in the nature of the representing itself, the relation between representations and their contents; and, indeed, standard characterizations of all three genera take this form. I, on the contrary, however, will argue that the distinctions cannot be made out in terms of the representing relation (but are to be found in what is represented—the contents—after all). In order to appreciate what's wrong with the standard approach, we will need first to outline how it is supposed to work for each genus. These outlines can be called the *canonical accounts*, because they are what almost everybody expects almost everybody else to believe. It will not be necessary to formulate them precisely, since the underlying problem is common and structural.

Logical representations are distinctive in that they have a (generative) *compositional semantics*. This means that complete logical tokens (sentences, well-formed formulae, production rules, and so on) are complex structures, each with a recursively specifiable syntax and determinate atomic constituents, such that the semantic significance of the whole is determined by its syntax and the semantic significances of its constituents (perhaps with some situational parameters). 'Semantic significance' is here used as an umbrella term, meant to include, without being limited to, the represented contents (what the tokens represent). The respective contributions of the possible structures and constituents are fixed arbitrarily by the scheme (for instance, a language); but, given these (and any relevant parameters), the significance of the compound is not at all arbitrary.

Iconic representations are distinctive in representing their contents by virtue of being somehow *isomorphic* to them. In many familiar cases, like pictures and scale models, the isomorphism is obvious enough to strike the observer as *resemblance*. But that's not required: the isomorphisms that determine the representational contents of graphs, wiring diagrams, and analog computers are often so abstract or mathematical that we wouldn't naturally call them resemblances (though, of course, in a sense, they are). Note that there are many different kinds of isomorphism, and the ones that are relevant to any particular representation are all and only those determined by the scheme to which it belongs. Thus a picture token that happens to be entirely monochromatic may or may not represent its object as likewise monochromatic, depending on whether it belongs to a monochromatic or full-color scheme. Which isomorphisms a given scheme employs is initially arbitrary or conventional; but once they are fixed, the contents of particular tokens are not arbitrary.

Distributed representations are distinctive in that each portion of the token participates (in some broadly egalitarian way) in the representing of each portion of the represented contents. For this to make sense, there must be antecedent notions of portions, both of the tokens and of the contents; and then the idea is that the representings of the content portions are all spread out over the token portions and superimposed on one another—whence the term "distributed". What these respective portions are, and how various possible content portions can be (simultaneously) determined by various possible token portions, is, of course, settled by the particular scheme (which is arbitrary); but, given a scheme, it is not at all arbitrary what any particular token represents.[4]

Each canonical account focuses on a distinctive sort of relation between representing tokens and their represented contents— namely, a relation that is systematically determined by complex structures and a primitive vocabulary, a relation that is based on having a common abstract form, and a relation that somehow has its components all mixed up (spread out and then superimposed). There is, of course, no suggestion that these possibilities are exhaustive; it is an interesting and important question whether there are or could be other genera of representation, and if so what they are. As canonical accounts of essences, however, they should at least be mutually exclusive, so as to distinguish their respective genera. Unfortunately, they are not.

3 PROBLEMS WITH THE CANONICAL ACCOUNTS

This superficial difficulty with the canonical accounts will be exploited, via a three-stage argument, as a symptom of an underlying common failing. The first stage is a group of three counter-example sketches, designed to suggest that each account admits cases that properly belong to another genus, and hence that none of them successfully captures what is distinctive of its own genus. As with the accounts themselves, the counter-examples will be presented informally, since the point is not really to get any of them right, but rather to "see through" them, in preparation for a completely different tack. The second stage will further that cause by advancing a trio of more outlandish counter-theses, which are therefore also more transparent in their operation. In particular, it should be obvious that they all trade on failing to respect one and the same fundamental distinction. The final stage then re-examines the counter-examples from stage one in the light of this distinction, and recruits them to show that the failures at stage two lie not with the outlandish counter-theses, but with the canonical accounts themselves.

So, stage one begins with three counter-examples. Consider first a designer's floor plan, a kind of two-dimensional scale model of a room, with movable cardboard cutouts for the various furnishings, fixtures, and pathways. There are explicit rules for composing these primitives into well-formed rooms: the pieces must lie flat, they shouldn't overlap, pathways have to be connected, and the like; and, according to essentially the same rules, these room plans can then be assembled into building plans, which in turn can make up city plans, and so on (recursively), with no principled limit. For a digital variant, arbitrarily define a grid (set of axes and unit pixels) on the Cartesian plane, and assign distinct colors to a finite set of landscape features (blue to water, green to forest, and so on); then maps can be recursively defined as follows: (1) a grid with a single colored pixel is a map; and (2) a consolidation of two maps (coincident axes, no pixel conflicts, all colored pixels contiguous) is a map. In each example, the represented content of the resulting plan or map is manifestly a determinate function of its compositional structure and the significances of its primitive components—just the token/content relation that was supposed to be characteristic of logical representations. Yet floor plans and maps are paradigmatically iconic.

Consider next how abstract and general the notions of form and isomorphism are, and must be, if the canonical account of the iconic genus is to accommodate such abstract representations as graphs, analog computers, and wiring diagrams. Yet, in a sufficiently abstract sense of form, it is arguable that many other (perhaps all) tokens represent their particular contents by exhibiting the same form. Wittgenstein (1921/74), for instance, once presented a theory of meaning according to which sentences represent worldly facts by "picturing" their logical structure; and, more recently, Sellars (1963/67, 1985) has proposed an account of predication based on the idea that juxtaposition of predicate symbols is essentially a flexible way of giving different properties to terms—in a manner that "maps" the properties of the referents of those terms. Regardless of whether any such approach is viable in general, if it can be made to work for even one scheme of logical representation, then the canonical account of iconic representation fails to exclude it.

Consider finally ordinary holograms: they seem to be paradigmatic examples of the spread-out-ness and superposition that are officially characteristic of distributed representation. Thus, in the original and most familiar sort of hologram, representing a scene in 3-D, each point on the holographic plate represents (in some measure) each part of the scene and each part of the scene is represented (in some measure) by each point on the plate. Yet, in a perfectly straightforward sense, such holographic representations of scenes are patently images—just as every popular article and exhibition unabashedly calls them. What's more, as is well known, holographic techniques can also be used in error-resistant encodings of logical representations.

These counter-examples are alike in suggesting that the canonical accounts are insufficiently restrictive (each admits cases that don't belong) and hence are incapable of supporting principled distinctions among the genera. One possible philosophical response would be to try ruling out the examples by somehow sharpening the accounts; another would be to give up, and concede that the alleged genera are not, after all, essentially distinct. I am arguing instead that all three canonical accounts misfire for a single underlying reason—namely, they all mislocate the generic essences in the representing relation—and, hence, the appropriate response is neither repair nor despair but fundamental reconception.

4 The representing/recording distinction

The second stage in this argument now proceeds indirectly, through a matched set of outlandish theses whose transparently spurious justifications are designed to bring out the need for a basic distinction.

Outlandish thesis #1. It is easy to "translate" any iconic or distributed representation into an equivalent logical representation—that is, a set of sentences representing the same contents. Before considering the "argument" for this thesis, we should perhaps remind ourselves why it is outlandish. Explaining perceptual recognition—how, for instance, a system can look at a scene (or picture) and produce an articulate verbal description of what it sees—is a profound outstanding problem in psychology and artificial intelligence. It has proven exceptionally difficult, and remains substantially unsolved. Yet thesis #1 implies that it should be easy. Here's how: use a simple computer-driven scanner to divide the scene (or picture) into a large number of cells, and generate on a printer, for each cell, a sentence token of the form: "The light reflected from direction (or pixel) x, y is of intensity, hue, and saturation i, h, and s." The supposed translations of distributed representations would be equally fatuous—for instance, a list of sentences of the form: "The weight on the connection between nodes *j* and *k* is *w*."

OUTLANDISH THESIS #2. It is easy to "translate" any logical or distributed representation into a representationally equivalent image. Like perceptual recognition, this ought to be hard—harder, for instance, than the job of a police artist, for the translator would have to draw an accurate picture of the suspect, or the scene of the crime, from the description alone, without any corrective feedback from the witness. Yet thesis #2 implies it should be easy. Here's how: Obtain a clear, written copy of the relevant description, focus a camera on it, and take a picture.[5] The comparable iconic translation of a distributed representation is only marginally less contrived: choose some sensible one-to-one correlation between the connections in a given network and the cells in a graphical array, and shade or fill each cell in proportion to the weight on the corresponding connection.[6]

OUTLANDISH THESIS #3. It is easy to "translate" any logical or iconic representation into an equivalent distributed representation. To establish thesis #3, we invoke a recent invention called *Turing's piano*. This versatile instrument has arbitrarily many notes, each a pure unmodulated sine wave, ascending in a standard chromatic scale from one hertz. Remembering, then, that any text or icon can be encoded without loss in a finite string of bits, and noting that each finite string of bits corresponds to a unique chord played on Turing's piano, we conclude that any text or icon can be encoded in such a chord. The waveform produced, however, is a perfect distributed representation, according to the canonical account: each point on the waveform (instantaneous amplitude) participates in recording all of the bits, and the recording of each bit is spread over all of the waveform. Since whatever it is that is representational in the original text or icon is somehow captured in patterns of these bits, that representing too is spread out and superimposed in the waveform.

What these irritating examples have in common is most evident in the case of a photographed inscription. While the result is, in one sense, clearly an image, it is equally clearly *not* an image of whatever the inscribed text was about; rather, it is an image of the inscription itself, but in such a way that (assuming the text is still legible in the image) the ability of the original to represent whatever it represented is preserved in the image. Obviously, however, that representing remains essentially logical in character. In other words, the logical representation has in no sense been "translated" or transformed into an iconic one; instead, it has merely been "recorded" in an iconic medium. Significantly, the recording process, unlike genuine translation, would proceed just as smoothly even if the given inscription were complete gibberish. Evidently then, we must distinguish in this case between the logical *representation* and its iconic *recording*.

The scanner-generated printout of sentences describing individual pixels is basically symmetrical, but with an important added twist. In case what is scanned is an image, then that image is clearly what the sentences describe, pixel by pixel; and, as before, assuming the descriptions are fine enough, the ability of the image to represent whatever it does is preserved, but only as iconic. Thus, the image is not translated or transformed into a logical representation, but only recorded in a logical medium.[7] (And, again, the recording itself would be equally successful even if the "image" were a contentless blob.)

The new twist emerges when we consider the companion case in which what is scanned is not an image of a scene, but the scene itself. Then, it seems, we must say that the resulting sentences describe the scene, since there is no image in play for them to describe, or to record logically. Yet, they don't describe the scene in anything like the way an articulate observer would describe it; rather, the "description" is essentially the same as what the scanner would have delivered in recording a photo of the scene. Hence, even when the sentences are generated directly from the scene, what they are doing is logically recording an *image-like* representation—a *virtual image*, we could call it—from the perspective of the scanner; and it is this which the sentences describe, pixel by pixel. This characterization is already intimated, I suspect, in calling what is represented a "scene", rather than, for instance, the facts or a state of affairs.

Turing's piano, of course, can be understood in the same way. It generates distributed *recordings* of arbitrary bit strings; indeed, multiple independent strings can be simultaneously recorded in the same chord, either interspersed or concatenated. Whether, as *representations*, these recorded strings are logical, iconic, or, perhaps, even distributed, depends on something else—it is not settled by the fact that the actual waveform records the bits and the contents (if any) in a spread out and superposed manner. What else it depends on, that is, how the representational genus is determined, remains an open question.

The common moral of the examples is now clear: we must distinguish between recording and representing, and that on two levels.

Consider once more a photo of an inscription: in favorable cases, it both represents and records that text; and, meanwhile, the text itself is a (different) representation of something else. What is the difference between recording and representing, and how is it that they are so readily confused? Fundamentally, I think, recording is a *process* of a certain sort; and to be a record is to be the result of such a process. By contrast, representing is a functional *status* or *role* of a certain sort, and to be a representation is to have that status or role. These are not the same because, in general, being the result of a recording process is neither necessary nor sufficient for having a representational status or role. On the other hand, the recording process does produce an output which is a record *of* its input; and representational status does involve one entity *standing in for* another. This formal relational parallel, plus the fact that, in certain cases (such as photography), the product of the recording process can also have the status of representing the input, therefore being simultaneously a record and a representation *of* it, is the basis of the confusion.

Recording is a generalization of copying. To count as recording, a process must be reversible in the sense that there is a complimentary process—"playing it back"—which reproduces from the record a duplicate or copy of the original. Since a copy of a copy is a copy, copying is a special case of recording (in which the record and play-back processes are the same). Recording, like copying, is only partial; only certain prespecified aspects of the original are recorded. In case what is being recorded is a representation (as a representation), then the relevant aspect, what must be reproduced on play-back, is its schematic type; the criterion for successful recording of representations is preservation of type-identity.

Recording is also essentially trivial or mechanical. Describing a scene from a picture, or drawing a picture from a description, takes experience and skill, whereas the camera or scanner "merely" records the original. This notion of triviality, however, must be delineated carefully; after all, any fool can tell a story, whereas cameras and scanners require sophisticated technology. The crucial point is that recording and playing-back are completely *witless*—the processes themselves are oblivious to content (if any) and ignorant of the world. By contrast, articulate description and artistic rendition depend crucially and thoroughly on general *background familiarity* with the represented contents—that is, on worldly experience and skill. The claim, of course, is not that representations are never produced witlessly (remember photography), but only that records always are.

An apparent exception (but one that proves the rule) is a court recorder, whose task is to produce a verbatim transcript of the oral proceedings. This task is anything but witless (so far, it can't be done by machine at all, despite substantial investment). The reason is that the phonic realization of phonemic units is highly variable, and non-disjoint; that is, the same word "sounds" quite different on different occasions, to the point of overlapping with the sounds of other words. A skilled recorder, like any speaker of the language, can identify the words correctly on the basis of knowing what "makes sense" in context—the exact opposite of witlessness. But this way of putting it shows the way to the answer. A court recorder's job is actually two-fold: identifying the spoken words (non-trivial) and then recording them (trivial). The case is essentially similar to producing a typescript from someone's handwritten scrawl, or even restoring the missing characters in a spotty photocopy: identifying the words takes wits; recording them, once identified, does not.

These considerations further suggest, though by no means establish, a sufficient condition for sameness of representational genus: if the representations of one scheme can be witlessly transformed into equivalent representations from another scheme by a general procedure, then those schemes are species of the same genus.[8] Thus, Morse and ASCII coded texts are equally logical, whereas pictorial and verbal representations differ in genus. Of course, this is not a necessary condition, since distinct natural languages cannot be witlessly intertranslated, yet they are of the same genus. Even as a sufficient condition, the proposed test is so far only hypothetically acceptable, since it depends on the plausible but unsupported assumption that cross-generic "translation" always requires wits.[9] Only later will we be able to explain and support the plausibility of this assumption, and thereby defend the suggested condition.

5 The initial problems rediagnosed

The third and final stage of the argument against the canonical accounts of the generic essences returns to the counter-examples introduced at stage one. The aim is to rediagnose these examples as showing not merely that the canonical accounts are insufficiently exclusive, but more importantly (and damningly) that they themselves confuse the representing/recording distinction.

Ordinary holographic images of scenes are the easiest case. In principle, they are no different from a Turing's piano chord produced from the output of a digitizing scanner. That is, if the hologram is prepared from an ordinary image (say, a photograph), then it is a distributed recording of that image, which, qua representation of the original scene, remains iconic—even in its recorded form. If, on the other hand, the hologram is prepared directly from the scene itself (as it must be to achieve the famous 3-D effects), then, as in the earlier treatment of the scanner, it is effectively recording a "virtual image"— which is again still an iconic representation of the scene. In other words, the distributedness in the example derives from and characterizes not the genus of the representation but rather the technology with which it is recorded.

The second counter-example, the picture theory of meaning, has the same basic structure, though in a less obvious way. Suppose we have a logical scheme of representation for which some sort of picture theory provides a plausible semantics. Then a slavish parallel to the above treatment of holographic images would go like this: the representations in the specimen scheme are indeed logical, but they are recorded in an iconic form. What's more, since there have been no actual prior sentences to record iconically, we must say that the recordings are of "virtual sentences"—something like the *facts* pictured. Now, surprisingly perhaps, I think this account is basically correct. But it does call for some explanation.

Recall the strategy of the original example: first it is pointed out that isomorphism is a very general notion, and indeed must be so if the account is to capture all kinds of icons; and then it is observed that such a general notion might apply equally well to the relation between sentences and facts. But this latter is just the tip of the iceberg. Isomorphisms are everywhere: a gunslinger's notches and his trail of victims, magnetic bit patterns and character strings, cash register tapes and the day's transactions, chess transcripts and the game's moves, and so on. All of these are familiar forms of record keeping, and none of them is plausibly an image. Thus, isomorphism is a common basis for making records, and not a distinctive mark of iconic representation. (A reversible witless process is a likely candidate for a function defining an isomorphism.) Hence, a general isomorphism between the tokens of some scheme and their contents would not alone make that scheme iconic; for it might instead just be the way the contents, understood as "virtual tokens", are recorded.

But surely this is strained: we have actual logical representations (sentences) allegedly both representing and isomorphically picturing "virtual logical representations" (the "facts"); yet, the isomorphism is not supposed to have anything to do with the representing. Rather, the sentences are said also to record those same facts; and the isomorphism is supposed to be relevant only to this recording. But what then is the sense of calling the facts "virtual *logical* representations"? And what witless process could produce such a recording; indeed, isn't describing a situation a paradigm of a process that is not witless?

The appearance of paradox can be alleviated by reexamining two earlier examples. Remember first the task of the court recorder, which is far from witless as a whole, but which can be resolved into two subtasks: identifying the oral tokens, and then recording them. Once it is appreciated that only the former requires background familiarity with the contents and the world, then the recording itself can be seen as witless after all. Then return to the case of the scanner producing pixel-by-pixel descriptions, either from a photo of a scene or directly from the scene itself. It was comparison of these that suggested the notion of recording a virtual token in the first place; and, conveniently, a scanner working directly from a scene was still a thoroughly witless process. But that process too can be conceived as a composite of two others, though in this case both witless: producing a photo-like image of a scene, and recording that image pixel by pixel.

Consolidating the two examples allows us to regard describing a situation (in a language for which a picture theory is workable) as also a composite process: identifying the pictured facts, and then verbally recording them. As with the scanner, the first step yields a virtual token, but, as with the court recorder, that step is not witless—hence neither is the composite. But the second step, the recording itself, remains witless in every case. Needless to say, this story makes only as much sense as the notion of facts as virtual sentences; but that much is a burden of the picture theory already.

Finally, the example of recursively generated floor plans and maps is at least as complicated and interesting as the preceding. Note first that the generative composition is, in each case, a *process*, starting from given primitives, proceeding by formally specifiable, rule-governed steps, and yielding the representation as a product. It is precisely this process, moreover, that is cited when confronting these icons with the canonical account of logical representations. To be sure, the constructive process is not at all like that of recording a representation, whether actual or virtual; it is, however, quite like the reverse process of recovering a representation from a record of it.

To see this, consider the intermediate case of an architectural drawing created by a computer-aided design system: it is stored within the system as a set of line specifications, or, equivalently, line-drawing commands, which can be sent to a pen-plotter or display driver to execute. Now, those internal specifications are just as much a logical record of an iconic representation as are our earlier printed sentences describing individual pixels; and commanding the plotter to draw the lines is just the (witless) process of "recovering" that image. The fact that the image may never have existed in visible form before does not mean that the process of drawing it is not the inverse of recording. The commands to the plotter, however, are exactly analogous to the formal specifications of the steps by which the floor plan or map may be constructed—except that the step specifications need not actually be written down, let alone all together in advance.

That suggests the following diagnosis: recursively generated maps or floor plans are not therefore logical representations, but rather are icons witlessly recovered from (possibly "virtual") logical recordings of them. To be sure, the idea of playing back virtual recordings has a certain air of hocus pocus; but that doesn't affect the point. We want to know what it is about recursively specified maps that gives them a semblance of being logical or language-like, even though they're not; and the answer is that the recursive specification itself functions in the account just as if it were a logical recording from which the image is being restored.

Each canonical account characterizes its genus in terms of a distinctive sort of representing relation between the representations and what they represent—roughly compositional semantics, structural isomorphism, and spread-out superposition. Our diagnoses of the three counter-examples, however, have revealed these distinctive relations to be indicative more of certain recording devices or processes than of the respective representational genera. Of course, one might still undertake to revise the definitions and/or rebut the diagnoses; but the consistent pattern of results invites a more radical response— namely, to abandon the canonical accounts completely, and seek the distinctive marks of the genera elsewhere than in the representing relation. Since the argument that a bit string can be a (recorded) representation in any genus decisively rules out finding the marks in the representations themselves, I now want to explore further the prospects of finding them in what is represented—the contents of the representations.

6 SKELETAL VERSUS FLESHED-OUT CONTENT

The first question to ask is: What, strictly speaking, *are* the contents of various representations? Exactly what objects, features, or configurations in the world are represented? Often, in real-life communication, only a little need be indicated, in order to apprise the recipient of much about the world. In practice, a little representation goes a long way. But that's because the recipient is already in a position to learn much from just a little new information—perhaps by already "knowing" a lot about the current situation and/or about the world in general. How much of what derives from this "background familiarity" belongs in the represented contents as such?

In one sense, all or most of what a recipient could be expected to learn from a communicated representation could be deemed "contained" therein—that is, as part of the message. Unfortunately, such a liberal attitude is problematic in the context of qualitatively differentiating the contents characteristic of the respective genera. For, if the recipient's broader understanding is mediated by other (presumably internal[10]) representations, themselves belonging to a genus different from that of the representation being examined, then the contents broadly construed would confusedly exhibit characteristics of both genera. Since it is not possible in general to know about or control for the effects of all such mediating representations, there is no hope of finding the essences of the genera in the character of their contents, unless these contents can be delimited more narrowly.

By way of anticipation, then, let's call the strict content of a representation, that not augmented or mediated by any other, its *skeletal* or *bare-bones* content. The metaphor is intended to suggest that the full-blooded contents of everyday representations are shaped and supported by their skeletal contents, but that they are (or can be) fleshed out and enlivened through other influences. How can this distinction be made out?

Consider again the police officer's report from the scene of a crime—including both descriptions and photographs. Clearly, the room was searched; clearly, there was a violent struggle, resulting in the death of the victim; clearly, the victim was robbed; and much else besides, as anyone can tell. But, reading more closely, the descriptive report does not actually say that the room was searched; it says only that all the drawers were opened, with the clothing removed and strewn about. It says there were signs of a struggle, including spilled drinks, broken furniture, and of course, a dead body; but it nowhere characterizes that struggle as violent. Finally, though it does point out that the decedent's wallet was found on the floor, with all the cash and credit cards missing, the report omits any mention of robbery.

Of course, the officer has made numerous assumptions in describing the scattered clothing as the "removed from the drawers", in saying the cash and cards are "missing", and so on; but that's irrelevant here. What matters, in delimiting the skeletal contents of the descriptions, are rather the natural "assumptions" of the *reader*. Thus, however natural it is, perhaps even part of what the speaker intended, and prerequisite to understanding the text, for the reader to appreciate that the drawers were searched, the struggle violent, and the missing money stolen, the fact remains that none of these is strictly contained in the report itself—any more than the lurid and sensational surmises that will make of it a journalistic bonanza. The content of what is strictly said—said "in so many words"—is intuitively what we mean by *skeletal* content.

There are many difficulties with this distinction; of these, I will discuss three briefly (none adequately). First, the skeletal/fleshed-out distinction should be located relative to other and better-known distinctions, such as literal versus figurative, and explicit versus implicit. Clearly it does not coincide with the former (even adjusting for the fact that figurative excludes literal, whereas fleshed-out includes skeletal). Thus, none of the reader's natural assumptions (that the missing money was stolen, and so on) are in any sense figurative; yet they are not part of the bare-bones content. It might be, however, that (for logical representations) a figure must always be shaped and supported by a skeleton, hence that the skeletal is somehow a subset of the literal.

The explicit/implicit distinction is closer, in that (again, for logical representations) the skeletal may roughly coincide with the explicit; but whether the rest of the full-blooded content can be regarded as implicit depends on how carefully that word is used. It is not irrelevant that the connotations of 'implicit' ("folded within") run exactly counter to those of 'fleshed out': the one suggests "already there but hidden", the other "added on". More specifically, the implicit is what is implied, in the sense that it can be got or brought out by inference. But, even if this is taken broadly to include material implication (such that, from a formal point of view, common knowledge would be functioning as a suppressed premise), the merely implicit falls far short of full-blooded content. Only if "implication" is stretched to the full gamut of what can be expected from conversational skills, topical associations, critical judgements, affective responses, and so on, can it hope to encompass the sort of content routinely conveyed in the newspaper, in the board room, and over the back fence. But, quite apart from whether (as I think) that's an overstretching of the word, it remains the case that implication, like trope, is proper to logical representation, whereas the bare-bones/fleshed-out distinction is intended to apply in any genus.

Yet another potentially confusing distinction in the vicinity might be likened to that between a pig and its rider: some representations incorporate or "carry on their shoulders" others that work according to different schemes, maybe even in different genera. Here I do not have in mind cases where, within one representation, another is represented (the protesters' banners visible in the photos of the rally), or encoded (the secret formula hidden in an innocent love letter), but rather "piggyback" devices that systematically belong and contribute to the representations that carry them. Perhaps the clearest examples are the legends and descriptive tokens that often appear on maps; but the standardized symbols in medieval paintings, and the labels in political cartoons, are essentially comparable. Onomatopoeia and "graphic" textual effects (advertising copy that not only touts speed, but itself "looks" fast) are presumably analogous, in the other direction. It seems to me that the additional content in piggyback devices might in principle itself sustain a skeletal/fleshed-out distinction, and that none of it should be counted in the content (even the full-blooded content) of the underlying representation. What we have instead is a sort of hybrid, with separate but related content on two distinct levels.

Second, the idea of "fleshing out" skeletal content suggests interlocutors who, over and above grasping the content of a representation as dictated by its scheme, also bring into play general background knowledge and familiar at-home-ness in the world at large. Put this way, however, the notion seems to presuppose a scheme/background distinction, which may in turn seem tantamount to the sort of language/theory distinction that Quine warned us not to draw. But the worry is misguided. What Quine argued against is the possibility of a systematic distinction, in the grounds for what we say, between arbitrary choice or convention and empirical evidence or theory; in particular, the language in which a theory is expressed cannot be separated from that theory in such a way that some theses are defensible on linguistic grounds alone, with no admixture of theory. But that is not at all incompatible with distinguishing between what a particular thesis says "in so many words" (according to the language-cum-theory of which it is a part), and what its concrete "implications" are in the current circumstances (according to that same language-cum-theory). Still less, therefore is it incompatible with the distinction between skeletal and full-blooded content, inasmuch as the latter extends even beyond implications.

Third, and most serious: artificial intelligence research has established that natural language competence is impossible without a common-sense grasp of real-live flesh-and-blood content; that is, systems that lack such a grasp fail to understand natural discourse at all. But if language with skeletal content alone is unintelligible, then perhaps skeletal content, as a kind of abstraction from "living language", makes no sense. This argument effectively assumes, however, that each representational scheme must make sense on its own, apart from all others; but, once exposed, that assumption seems to have little ground to stand on. Why, for instance, couldn't one "living" scheme be *parasitic* on another, or two schemes be *symbiotic?* Thus, it might be granted that natural language is viable (as a means of communication, or whatever) only with its full-blooded everyday content, but this be attributed to its dependence on (or interdependence with) some other scheme of representation—presumably internal to the language users. In other words, the full content of a discourse, in terms of which it is workable at all, is simultaneously a function of two determining factors: the skeletal content of those linguistic tokens themselves, plus whatever else the relevant sensible speakers of that language can count on one another to grasp in that context. That the latter is essential in practice does not show that the former is impossible in theory, or indeed inessential.

The suggestion that language depends on inner representations has, of course, a long history. But traditionally, the idea has been that thought is the original locus of all contentfulness, and that linguistic tokens acquire contents only by having thought contents somehow conferred on them. The present notion of "symbiosis", however, is much less definite. In the first place, skeletal linguistic contentfulness need not be dependent on internal representations at all; and even fleshed-out content is dependent only in the sense that it arises in the linguistic practices of interlocutors whose usage relies also on other representations. These do not so much as imply that linguistic contents are of the same sort as those of internal representations, let alone that the former are merely conferred duplicates of the latter.

Before attempting to characterize the skeletal contents of logical representations more specifically, let's ask in a general way whether a comparable distinction can be made out for iconic representations. What, for instance, would be the bare-bones contents of the police officer's photos? On the one hand, the pictures reveal much that is omitted from the descriptions, like the shape of the bloodstain on the carpet, the color of the victim's shirt, and the cockroach in the corner. On the other hand, much that the officer explicitly said is not represented in the photographs. For example, not only do they not show the money and credit cards as stolen, they don't even show them as missing. More interestingly, the pictures don't actually represent the victim as dead, or, for that matter, as a victim—though, of course, we would be likely to appreciate these facts, if we saw the pictures.

How far does this go? The same reasoning, pressed to its limit, implies that, bare bones, the photographs don't even represent a human body lying on the floor in a pool of blood, surrounded by scattered clothing and broken furniture. These are features that an ordinary person, relying on common background familiarity with the world, could easily "tell" about the situation depicted. But, as the perceptual recognition research cited earlier has demonstrated, no system innocent of the world, lacking common sense, is capable of such telling. The ultimate conclusion would then be that all the photos "strictly" represent is certain variations of incident light with respect to direction—taking seriously, in effect, the pun in photo*graph*. Of course, the pictures surely do represent the scene of a violent robbery, just as much as the verbal reports describe one. The point is not to deny the obvious, but rather to distinguish, within the undeniable contents of everyday representations, a substructure that is skeletal—in the special sense that it does not draw upon the user's antecedent familiarity with the situation and the world, and hence cannot exhibit any admixture of characteristics from other (possibly symbiotic) representational schemes.

7 DISTINGUISHING GENERA BY CONTENTS

The motive for distinguishing skeletal from full-blooded content is to clear the way for characterizing the essences of the genera in terms of the natures of their respective contents. Fleshed-out content is not a candidate for this role, inasmuch as it may confound the traits of more than one scheme. Hence, it could at best be the general characters of the respective skeletal contents that are distinctive of the representational genera.

What is the distinctive structure of the skeletal contents of logical representations? The mainstream tradition in logic has always taken atomic sentences to be about the properties of (or relations among) things. Modern formal semantics generally remains within this tradition by explicating property instantiation in terms of set membership and/or function application, and therewith mathematically extending the approach not only to quantification and sentential composition, but also (so it is hoped) to tense, aspect, modality, adverbial modification, propositional attitude ascription, and what have you. Somewhat further afield, but still logical, are calculi of parts and wholes, systems representing condition/action pairs, notations for allocations of resources to tasks, and so on. Of course, these are not incompatible: conditions can be objects having properties, tasks can have others as parts—indeed, in its way, natural language can handle them all.

It is awfully tempting to say that these contents of atomic sentences are (possible[11]) atomic facts, somehow composed of, for instance, objects and properties; and that the contents of molecular sentences are molecular facts, composed of, or in some other way determined by, atomic facts. The difficulties in spelling out what sort of structures or features of the world such facts might be, however, are well-known and formidable. Thus, even if it is intelligible to say that a certain object's having a certain property is a structure or feature of the world, it remains unclear what kind of structure or feature it would be for an object *not* to have a property, or for it to have *either* one property *or* another, or for it to be the case that *at least one* object has some property. To be sure, each such "complex fact" is settled in any given instance by some or all of the atomic facts: since the paint is red, it isn't yellow, it's either red or green, and at least something is red. But the paint's being red isn't equivalent to any of these other facts, because any or all of them might have obtained even had the paint not been red.

Evidently, non-atomic contents cannot in general amount to particular combinations of atomic contents: since different incompatible combinations can equally well satisfy a given representation, the structure represented must be conceived more abstractly. One attractive suggestion is that the represented content is a structure or feature of the whole world that it shares with various alternative possible worlds—for instance, its belonging to a certain set of such worlds. For our purposes, however, it's irrelevant how exactly this might go; and the real lesson lies in why it's irrelevant. Insofar as *any* representation represents something about the world, and can misrepresent it, the content of that representation can be conceived in terms of a partition of possible worlds. Thus, the content of a certain map might be associated with the set of worlds of which that map is accurate. But this shows that whatever distinguishes some representations as logical gets lost if content is reduced simply to a partition of possible worlds. Or, to put it the other way around and more broadly, whatever in the content distinguishes the genera must lie in distinct general *sorts* of "possible" world. Sets of compossible atomic facts, for example, might plausibly be the worlds needed for logical content, whereas totalities of compossible shapes of terrain or compossible scenes might amount to possible "iconic worlds". But what underlies *these* differences?

The following, I believe, is the heart of the matter: the primitive elements of logical contents—whether objects and properties, components and complexes, conditions and actions, or what have you—are always identifiable separately and individually. That is, they can enter into atomic contents one by one, without depending on their concrete relations to one another, if any. It can be a fact, for instance, that the glass is broken, quite apart from whether it is larger than the cockroach, contains traces of whisky, or used to belong to the deceased. The point is not that all combinations are possible—obviously the glass can't be both broken and intact—but rather that it is not a precondition on its being broken (or representable as such) that it or its brokenness occupy any determinate position in any structured ensemble of other objects or properties; they stand in their togetherness on their own. Seen from the side of language, this self-standingness of fact elements shows up in the mutual independence of proper names and the (in this regard) namelikeness of primitive predicates. For reasons that will emerge shortly, I call these self-standing logical content elements (such as individual objects and properties) *absolute* elements.[12]

The contents of iconic representations are in general quite different. Taking a cue from graphs, and remembering the quip about photographs, iconic contents might be conceived as variations of values along certain dimensions with respect to locations in certain other dimensions. Thus, variations of temperature with respect to time, or altitude with respect to latitude and longitude, would be the contents of familiar icons. The former dimensions are called dependent, the latter independent, because, for each point in the relevant independent region, a point is determined in the dependent space, but not necessarily vice versa. The (skeletal) contents of a color photograph have two independent and three dependent dimensions; monochrome photos reduce the latter to a single dimension, and line drawings and silhouettes further restrict that dimension to two (or a few) points. Representational sculptures can be thought of as silhouettes with three independent dimensions; and scale models are much the same, but with more internal detail. Analog computers typically represent the variations of quite a few dynamic variables, all with respect to time, or time and space.

This account, however, is insufficiently specific, until the notion of dimension is further delimited. Consider, for a moment, some unstructured sequence of distinct objects as a "dimension"; and imagine a space with n such independent dimensions, and one two-valued dependent dimension. Then, for any n-adic property, a "graph" in that "space" could show exactly which n-tuples of those objects have that property. Pressing the idea to its limit: if all the primitive objects in some universe of discourse were in such a sequence, and there were as many independent dimensions as the highest "adicity" of any primitive property, plus a separate dependent dimension for each primitive property, then the entire object/property state of that universe could be represented in a single multi-dimensional silhouette. What's wrong with this "picture"? The problem lies in regarding an arbitrary sequence as a dimension.

On a genuine *dimension* (in the definition of iconic representation) the relative positions of the content elements are not at all arbitrary. Quite the contrary, those elements are always organized relative to one another in some regular structure that every representational token of the pertinent scheme essentially presupposes (and which, therefore, cannot itself be represented by any such token). For instance, both dimensions corresponding to a graph of temperature versus time are uniform measurable magnitudes that admit of simple metrics; and the very possibility of the graphing scheme depends on this. Why? Because what is graphed is the *shape* of the variation; hence, no particular temperature or instant is relevant except as placed, along their respective dimensions, relative to all the others. The point is even more conspicuous for maps and pictures: the shapes of the variations are the represented (skeletal) contents—and "shape" makes no sense except in terms of relative locations in structured spaces. With obvious and I hope illuminating contrast to the above use of 'absolute', I call the dimensionally placed elements of iconic contents *relative* elements.

The point is not that the dimensions are continuous. Thus, for a biological species that reproduces synchronously, it makes perfect sense to graph population against generation, even though both variables are discrete. The graph makes sense because generations and population sizes are themselves both intrinsically ordered. This does not mean merely that they can be assigned numbers; rather, what matters is the order in the dimensions themselves—an order that can be captured in an assignment of numbers, if desired. By contrast, a "graph" of telephone numbers versus social security numbers would be nonsense, precisely because those assignments do not reflect any underlying order. (They are, in effect, just absolute names, formed from digits instead of letters.[13]) It is also not necessary that the dimensions (or spaces), either dependent or independent, be Euclidean; they might be, for instance, curved or ramified, so long as their intrinsic structures enable relative locations and hence representable shapes.

The contents of logical representations are not, in any analogous sense, "shapes" in "conceptual space"; and the reasons show up the limitations of the spatial metaphor for factual possibilities. Only spaces in which locations are identifiable with respect to intrinsically ordered dimensions—such that relative position makes non-arbitrary sense—support a notion of *shape* at all. Objects and properties (or kinds) do not as a rule constitute such dimensions: one cannot place Mugsy "between" Toto and Lassie on the dog scale, or spaniel "above and to the left" of collie in breed space. Therefore, even if for every dog there were a breed, it would make no more sense to graph breed against dog than phone number against social security number: there's no space for such a graph to take shape in. Objects have their properties one by one, absolutely, and not as part of some shape, relatively.

Insofar, however, as contents are worldly, it may seem that logical and iconic contents can overlap or coincide. We can, for instance, say—it is a fact—that the Earth is round. Is this not the very same "structure or feature of the world" that would be represented also by a silhouette of the Earth against a bright background? I don't think so. In the first place, the sentence identifies (the fact comprises) a particular object and a specific property of that object, whereas the silhouette identifies no object or property: its skeletal content is just the overall pattern of light and dark from some perspective. But further, though the sentence is entirely compatible with the Earth being transparent or just as bright as the background, the silhouette is not; and so on.

The thesis that representational genera are distinguished according to the structure of their contents yields an unexpected dividend: it explains and therefore supports the observation made earlier that "translating" from one genus to another requires wits. If the skeletal contents of two generically different representations—say, a picture and a description of the scene of the crime—differ qualitatively, even in their basic structure, then, in particular, neither includes the other. That is, much (or all) of what the one representation represents is simply not represented at all by the other. Thus, a description of a situation does not "say" how the light values vary with angle of view, any more than a photo of those values "graphs" what objects are present with what properties. Hence, a witless conversion is not possible, simply because the content is not there to convert. On the other hand, a system with wits of its own—background familiarity with the world and the circumstances—might be able to "tell" or to "see" what that missing content would have to be, and fill it in. Often, for instance, a person, relying on knowledge and experience, could tell that a certain light pattern would normally issue only from an object with a certain property, and could thereby supply the logical content needed to "translate" an image into words.

8 CONNECTIONIST NETWORKS

Is it possible to give a comparable generic account of the contents of distributed representations? In contrast to the familiar logical and iconic genera, distributed representation is a relatively new idea, and remains largely terra incognita outside the circle of scientific specialists. So far, acknowledged examples tend to be arcane, and disputes continue as to which of their features are most significant. What's more, the distinctions between recording and representing and between skeletal and fleshed-out content, no matter how clarifying in the long run, can only add perplexity at the outset. Accordingly, it will not be possible in this case, as before, to draw out a broad characterization from a few intuitively paradigmatic examples, relying on the reader to appreciate how the generalizations work. Instead, therefore, I will attempt a concise overview of a central class of cases, and then propose a generic account that seems both parallel to and interestingly different from the logical and iconic genera considered above.

The most widely investigated examples, and those with regard to which the term *distributed representation* was first introduced, are connectionist networks. Though there are many species, the following characterization applies to a representative variety, and gives some indication of how they can differ.

A network consists of a large number of independent elementary units, each of which has a variable state, called its *activation* level.[14] Each unit also has a number of inputs and/or outputs (via connections—see below), and corresponding *transfer functions* relating these to its activation level. Often, the activation is determined as a function (possibly stochastic) of its previous value and the sum of all the inputs; and the output is a function of the current activation. Both functions tend to be simple, though they are seldom both linear. Usually, the transfer functions of all units are the same (or of just a few distinct types). More complicated arrangements, functions, and states are, of course, possible; but they have the effect of locating more of the system's "power" in the individual units, and less in the network—contrary to the spirit of connectionism.

The units of a network have a great many *connections* among them, each of which has a determinate strength, called its *weight*. As a rule, each connection connects one "source" to one "target" unit, with no two having the same source and target. In the most general such case, each pair of units is connected in each direction, and each unit is connected to itself (so the number of connections is the square of the number of units). Many networks, however, implement only a subset of these connections; and they can be classified according to which connections are included. The most significant distinction is between *cyclic* and *acyclic* nets: in the former, but not the latter, sets of connections can form closed paths (feedback loops). The general case is cyclic. By contrast, *feed-forward* networks, in which the units are effectively subdivided into two or more "layers" by implementing only connections from one layer to the next, are acyclic. (Perceptrons are two-layer acyclic nets.)

The input to a network as a whole consists of a pattern of initial activations assigned to some (perhaps all) of its units. The output consists of the final activation levels of some (perhaps the same, perhaps different) units. These final values are reached during a "run" in which the units individually adjust their activations in response to incoming values, and then broadcast outgoing values, according to the respective transfer functions. The incoming value from a connection to its target generally equals the product of that connection's weight and the value that was broadcast by its source. Thus, the output of a network is a joint function of its input and the weights on all its connections (plus, perhaps, some random factors). In the case of a feed-forward network, the input is entered on the first layer, and then each successive layer is activated, until the output appears on the last. Cyclic networks are more difficult because the feedback can generate instabilities (loops that feed on themselves chaotically); hence, they must be carefully constrained to ensure that they will settle down and yield an output.

Corresponding to this broad characterization of the networks themselves, we need a comparably broad characterization of their performance. In general, a network's inputs and outputs are both *patterns* of unit-activations: given a certain input pattern, the net will produce some associated output pattern. What makes this different in principle from a traditional look-up function (besides efficiency) is the network's fundamental tendency to group input and output patterns according to *similarities*: that is, similar inputs tend to yield similar outputs. One can get a rough grip on why this should be so from information theoretic considerations. Loosely speaking, the number of possible input and output patterns is exponential in the number of nodes, whereas the number of connections is only polynomial; so there aren't enough "bits" in the connection strengths to encode an arbitrary distinct output pattern for each possible input pattern.[15] Rather, arbitrary output patterns can be encoded for a number of relatively scattered input patterns, leaving the rest to fall where they may. Of course, the network will produce some output or other for any given input; but these associations must be more or less determined by those already encoded—specifically by "clustering" around them in some way.

Importantly, there can be multiple independent respects of similarity in play at once. Thus, a given input might be classified as belonging to (similar to) one group of possible inputs in one respect, and, at the same time, as belonging to an entirely different group in some other respect. Operationally, of course, the groupings themselves define the "respects": for two patterns to be "similar" is nothing other than for them to belong to the same cluster. The reason that the groups can be thought of as kinds (similarity groups) is that a network can "learn" them from examples, and then generalize to new cases. Depending on the training set and other details, the generalizations can be both surprising and strikingly apt. (The teachability of networks has also been important to connectionist research for a more workaday reason: trivial cases aside, there is no known practical way to determine suitable connection weights for given problem domains other than via automated training regimes.)

Different networks induce different groupings, hence different respects of similarity. How does a network induce a similarity grouping? For the simplest classifier, a domain is partitioned as follows: two inputs belong to the same group just in case they produce (exactly) the same output. But this is doubly restrictive: first, it does not allow for multiple respects; and second, it does not take account of outputs being "almost" the same—that is, similar. Both restrictions are lifted in principle by letting the outputs of one network be the inputs of one or more others. If the latter are simple classifiers, each can define an independent respect of similarity in the outputs of the first network, which can in turn induce subtler simultaneous respects of similarity in its inputs. Indeed, still another network, connected to the outputs of all the networks connected to the first, can pick up patterns in the co-occurrence of simultaneous groupings, thereby inducing still more sophisticated ("meta") groupings in the original input patterns. But all of this is just to indicate indirectly the potential power of multi-layer (or cyclic) networks.

Yet even this fails to capture the possible richness in the input/output behavior of a sophisticated network, for it ignores the potential for relevant similarity relations among the output patterns. The point is not simply that outputs can significantly cluster—though that's important—but that relative positions of output patterns within their similarity groups can systematically reflect the positions of the input patterns within their similarity groups. Thus, to take a contrived but suggestive example, imagine the input and output patterns respectively coming from and going to a ping-pong player's eyes and muscles. Major similarity clusters in the input will effectively "recognize" slams, slices, and lobs in the opponent's stroke, as well as (simultaneously) topspin, bottomspin, and lateral English, not to mention speed, direction, and the like, in the oncoming ball. Output patterns must effect major partitions among forehand, backhand, and scoop shots, and upward versus downward wrist motion, plus, of course, locating and aiming the racket. Not only must the output "choices" be coordinated in subtle ways with the input recognitions, but also—and this is the point—everything depends on finely tuned gradations within those major similarity groupings: variations and nuances in the arriving shot call for *corresponding* variations and adjustments in the return.

9 ARE THERE "DISTRIBUTED" REPRESENTATIONS?

As examples like these illustrate, connectionist networks contain two quite different candidates for status as representations. On the one hand, there are *patterns of activation* across various sets of network units—the input and output sets, obviously, but also perhaps others, such as intervening layers. So, in the ping-pong example, patterns might represent any number of concrete and abstract aspects of ball and racket motions, gathered and/or projected. On the other hand, there are *patterns of connection weight* among the units of the net. It is usually much more difficult to say what these might represent; but it is somehow they that encode the distinctive capabilities of each individual network. Thus, continuing the example, it would be the connection strengths (collectively) that "contain" the system's know-how or ability to play ping-pong. In contrast to patterns of activation, which are ephemeral (changing with the play in real time, say), connection weights tend to remain constant, or to change only slowly (with experience and practice, say).

Both sorts of pattern are commonly cited as instances of distributed representation. But in most actual research systems, input and output patterns tend to be, at best, distributed *recordings* of various determinate domain features, structures, or categories—in effect, lists or descriptions. Thus, either individual activations indicate particular features separately (not distributed at all, but "localist"), or else the representations of a number of features are spread out and superimposed on a multi-unit pattern of activation—distributed in the recording, but still, so to speak, localist in content. There is a perfectly sensible reason for this: investigators must be able to interpret inputs and outputs if they are to argue that their systems are representational at all, and to evaluate their performance. Inasmuch as descriptive (logical) representations are the most familiar, it is natural to want to interpret others as equivalent or comparable to these—especially when it is taken for granted that the generic differences lie not in the represented contents but in the representing relation. Activation patterns of hidden (non-input/output) units are often less fathomable; but even here the temptation is to look for "micro-features" or "coarse-coded" partitions.

Patterns of connection weight, on the other hand, are almost invariably quite undecipherable. These constitute not occurrent or episodic states that arise and pass away in the course of the net's operations ("thoughts"), but rather its long-term functionality or competence ("know-how")—which it is essentially impossible to express in words, except as generalities. But the fact that the best verbal characterization of a skill is an imprecise hand-wave does not mean that the skill itself lacks delicacy and detail; on the contrary, it has a "complexity" and "precision" of its own. To the extent, therefore, that connection patterns are regarded as representational at all, they are the most compelling candidates in contemporary networks for illustrating a *distinctive* representational genus—to wit, *distributed representations* (as opposed to mere distributed recordings).

Does it even make sense to regard the embodiments of a system's abilities or know-how as *representations*? Why not take them rather as just complex dispositional properties—acquired and subtle, perhaps—but, for all that, no more representational than a reflex or an allergy? Recall the characterization of representations as such adumbrated at the outset: they serve as a kind of "stand-in" for specific features or aspects of the environment to which the system must adjust its behavior, even on occasions when those features or aspects are not currently present or detectable. And consider, in those terms, a very special but important case of ability or know-how: the ability reliably to recognize the individual faces (or voices, or smells, ...) of one's regular companions. It seems to me to be unquestionably some sort of structure or feature *of the environment* that this face can look all these different ways (different angles, expressions, surroundings, and the like), another face can look all those other ways, and so on, with hardly ever any overlap. Clearly, such a "feature" could never be detected on a given occasion; yet "adjusting" to it *in absentia*, as a means to correct reidentifications, would be of great value. Accordingly, whatever incorporated the ability to recognize those faces could, by our account, be deemed a *representation* of that feature. To be sure, that initial account was formulated only casually and without argument, so nothing is proved by it; still, the consilience is not unsuggestive.

In particular, it suggests a natural generalization to other abilities and know-how. Thus, it is likewise a structure or feature *of the world*—quite determinate and intricate, albeit in some sense also highly "abstract"—that just these patterns of movement will suffice to get those ping-pong balls back over the net, a car through this traffic, or, indeed, that fresh antelope home to the cubs. Again, such structures are never presently detectable, yet adjusting to (taking account of) them in real time would be just as valuable. Surely, in fact, this separation of recognitive and performative abilities is altogether artificial: special cases aside, skillful performance is essentially adaptive to current circumstances, which is to say responsive to recognized relevant developments; and recognition in general can be nothing other than production of responses relevant to what is recognized.

Representations as such, however, must be party to a general scheme. How do patterns of connection weights, understood as representations of the subtle worldly structures accommodated by abilities and know-how, belong to a scheme? There is certainly little, if any, prospect of finding explicit interpretation or projection rules that would specify, for each "well-formed" weight pattern in some net, what all it would represent. But this is at most to acknowledge that schemes of distributed representation may not be articulately definable. It remains the case that a network, incorporated in a real-world system (an organism, for instance), and typically encoding a considerable variety of complicated responsive dispositions, *could have* encoded any of an enormous range of others, if only its connection weights had been different. Moreover, for that system, the actual weights consistently *determine* (fix) which abilities are actually encoded; whereas for a (qualitatively) different net or system, those weights might determine quite different dispositions, or none at all. Finally, there are clear possibilities of malfunction or malperformance in the reliance upon and/or management of actual weight patterns: for any of many reasons, a system can misrecognize or misbehave, even within the range of its normal abilities; and weight modifications in the light of experience (learning) can be carried out improperly, or result in degraded performance. Thus, whether an explicit "semantics" is possible or not, it does seem that weight patterns can be regarded as belonging to representational schemes.

The "elements" of the contents of distributed representations, at least as we have considered them so far, would be the various aspects or looks of recognizable individuals or kinds and the various behaviors or movements of skillful responses—that is, the elements of competent situated action. What distinguishes these essentially from the absolute and relative elements of logical and iconic contents? The answer must lie in how they belong together, in two interdependent ways. First, such elements can belong together in that they fall in the same similarity cluster—for instance, by being aspects of the same individual or executions of the same move. Second, they can belong together in that one calls for the other, or determines it as relevant or apt—for instance, when a recognized eventuality calls for a certain response. These are interdependent because: (i) it is by virtue of calling for similar responses that elements belong to the same recognition clusters, and vice versa; and (ii) it is by virtue of belonging to a certain recognition cluster that an element can call for a certain response, and vice versa. With due, and I trust understandable, trepidation about the history of the term, I call elements that belong together in this twofold interdependent way *associative* elements.

It is perhaps worth mentioning explicitly three respects in which this account of distributed representation differs essentially from classical associationism, such as Hume's. First, and most conspicuously, what are here deemed associative are elements not of representations (ideas, for instance) but of represented *contents* (structures or features of the represented world). Second, by traditional lights, the mind associates ideas because they are antecedently ("objectively") similar or otherwise related; whereas here the similarity of elements is consequent on ("induced by") a system's know-how or ability effectively casting them into the same clusters. (Note carefully: this is not incompatible with it being a structure or feature *of the environment* that such and such intricate responsive dispositions constitute competence in it, relative to given ends.) Third, and hand-in-glove with the preceding, traditional theories did not understand the different associative relations, especially resemblance and constant conjunction, as interdependent; but we have seen that clustering together and calling for a certain response make sense only in terms of one another.

10 CONCLUSIONS AND MORALS

The upshot of these considerations—tentative and exploratory, I reiterate—is, first, that representational genera are distinguished essentially by the characteristic structures of their represented contents; and, second, that the represented contents of logical, iconic, and distributed representations are structurally characterized respectively by absolute, relative and associative elements.

In conclusion it may be observed that such an account of the genera, to the extent that it is tenable, yields another unanticipated dividend: by, in effect, dividing the spoils, it may mitigate the PDP/GOFAI standoff in contemporary cognitive science. Thus, consider the following putative dilemma: either PDP networks "implement" familiar symbolic AI architectures (in which case they are *irrelevant* to cognitive theory), or else they are incapable of representing contents which we know to be cognitively representable (in which case they are *inadequate* to cognitive theory). But if it is acknowledged at the outset that logical and distributed contents differ fundamentally in kind, then proponents of network models can cheerfully embrace both horns of the alleged dilemma, without conceding any damaging consequences. For, on the one hand, people obviously speak, and can think what they can say. (And no doubt that facility is implemented in some sort of network: what else, if the brain is a "neural net"?) But that doesn't show the cognitive irrelevance of network models, unless it is further assumed that logical contents are the *only* contents important to cognition; and there's no reason to assume that. On the other hand, acknowledging the qualitative difference in kinds of content is already to acknowledge that not all contents can be contents of distributed representations. But this implies no inadequacy of network models unless it is further assumed that distributed contents are the *only* contents they can allow as important to cognition; and there is no reason to assume that. Therefore, the camps are not really at odds, unless one (or each) purports to account for everything cognitive—but there's no reason to put up with that.

Indeed, the relationship may be considerably more intimate. Logical contents require absolute elements, such as determinate, reidentifiable particulars and properties. But among the most frustrating unresolved problems of "good old fashioned" AI and philosophy of mind is how these contents are recognized in realistic situations. (Constructing explicit tests in terms of neutral sense data, for instance, has proved quite unrewarding.) *Recognition*, however, is a specialty of systems employing distributed representations—suggesting the possibility of a deep cooperation, based on an *ability* to apply names. But any partnership would be unlikely to stop there, especially insofar as language is an evolutionarily late capacity, implemented in organs originally adapted for another sort of representation. Thus, everyday speech is extraordinarily sensitive to relevance and topical surprise, yet remarkably unfazed by ambiguity, ungrammaticality, and catachresis; it is thoroughly suffused with allusion, trope, posture, and drama; it is biassed, fanciful, opportunistic, emotion charged, and generally fast and loose; and much the same could be said of thought. Yet these qualities are notoriously resistant to capture in explicit symbolic models. Perhaps, that is because they involve adjustment to contents that cannot be represented logically: sophisticated and intricate abilities that, in symbol processing terms, could only be classified as transductions or basic operations—but are hardly peripheral or primitive. Perhaps natural language is possible only as symbiotic with the distributed representations of the system it is implemented in.

Notes:

1 This use of the term 'content' is not altogether standard. Most contemporary authors (and I, in the other essays in this volume) mean by the "content" of a representation something distinct from the object it represents, and which determines that object (as sense determines referent, for instance). Here, however, I mean by 'content' that which the representation represents—the "object" itself—but *as it is represented to be* (whether it is that way or not). Thus, it is a possible object—which may in fact be actual, or similar to something actual, or neither. [Note added 1997.]

2 For instance, if (or to the extent that) particular representations are tokens of well-defined types, the scheme will determine the content of any given token as a function of its type—or, at least, these will determine how that content is determined. Thus, if any extra-schematic factors (such as situation or context) co-determine contents, then which factors these are and how they work are themselves determined by the scheme and type.

3 "Without loss" here means without loss of representational content; it goes without saying that there could be other sorts of loss, such as market value (think of a digitized Rembrandt) or convenience (a digital recording often cannot be read, heard, or viewed without special equipment).

4 The above definition is essentially that offered by Hinton, McClelland, and Rumelhart 1986, 77; and by McClelland and Rumelhart 1986, 176, but in a less binding terminology. The two-volume set—the "PDP volumes"—in which both of these essays appear has become something of a *locus classicus* for research on parallel distributed processing. The most extended and penetrating treatment I have seen of distributed representation as such is by van Gelder (1989), who argues persuasively that superposition is more fundamental than spread-out-ness. (I have retained the more usual account merely for expository convenience.) Philosophical implications of connectionism are also discussed in Horgan and Tienson 1987; Pinker and Mehler 1988; and Churchland 1989. Note, incidentally, that the notion of separate tokens for distinct contents is undermined by distributed representations, to the extent that there is just one "big" token representing many different contents at once.

5 This procedure would be anything but ridiculous if the inscription happened to be in an unknown script, such as on the wall of an ancient tomb. Because the photograph will preserve all visible features of the inscription, it will *a fortiori* preserve all representationally relevant visible features, even if no one yet knows what they are.

6 Such graphical displays of points in weight-space (sometimes called "Hinton diagrams") are common in the connectionist literature; see, for example, Hinton, McClelland, and Rumelhart 1986, 103.

7 Fourier transforms of spatial intensity functions, expressed algebraically as sufficiently long sums of terms, would be comparable logical recordings of distributed representations.

8 A general procedure here means an effective procedure that does not depend on there being an upper bound on the number of distinct representational types in either scheme. If there are such

witless transforms in both directions, the relation between the schemes may have to be even closer—perhaps as close as being "notational variants" of one another.

9 Note that witlessness is not a function of level of description. Thus, it is sometimes said that whether certain processes in the brain (or a computer) count as intelligent or sensible depends on the level at which they are described; the very same processes can be intelligent at the cognitive level, but simultaneously unintelligent and mechanical at a lower formal or physical level. Be that as it may, witlessness here means *thoroughly* witless—there is *no* level at which the process can be redescribed as other than oblivious to content and ignorant of the world

10 "Internal" here (and hereafter) means *functionally* internal, not "immanent to the sphere of consciousness", or any such epistemological/metaphysical status.

11 In general only *possible* because the sentences might be false; "actual" facts would be the contents of true sentences.

12 Two qualifications. First, to call objects and properties (or whatever) "absolute" is not to imply that they are what they are independent of the scheme in terms of which they are represented; that is, the account of logical content in not meant to bear on questions of realism. Second, the self-standingness at stake is what might be called "occasion", as opposed to "constitutive" self-standingness. Thus, it may be constitutive of the kind 'spaniel' (as identifiable in terms of some scheme) that it be a breed of 'dog' distinct from 'collie' and subsuming 'cocker'. But, on any particular occasion, whether some object is of some kind is a function just of that object and kind, and not of any determinate relationships in which either may stand (except, of course, to the extent that the kind is itself relational).

13 The point is not simply that there is no interesting correlation between phone number and social security number, as there might be no interesting correlation between blood pressure and rate of hair growth, but rather that there is nothing there to correlate. Of course, the numbers do identify particular telephones and people, respectively; but they do not locate them

along any intelligible dimensions in ways that might or might not be correlated.

14 Activations can be discrete, real, or (presumably) even complex valued, bounded or unbounded. Units can also have additional state variables, such as latency or fatigue conditions, or a kind of momentum in the activation itself.

15 The argument is "hand-wavy" in various respects, most notably in effectively assuming that the activation values and connection strengths are both only finitely precise (and to approximately the same degree).

CHAPTER NINE

Mind Embodied and Embedded

I INTIMACY

Among Descartes's most lasting and consequential achievements has been his constitution of the mental as an independent ontological domain. By taking the mind as a substance, with cognitions as its modes, he accorded them a status as self-standing and determinate on their own, without essential regard to other entities. Only with this metaphysical conception in place, could the idea of solipsism—the idea of an intact ego existing with nothing else in the universe—so much as make sense. And behind that engine have trailed the sorry boxcars of hyperbolic doubt, the mind-body problem, the problem of the external world, the problem of other minds, and so on.

Although the underlying assumptions have been under fire, off and on, at least since Hegel—including with renewed intensity in recent years—most of the challenges have been of a general sort that I will call "interrelationist". Characteristically, they accept as a premise that the mental, or at any rate the cognitive, has some essential feature, such as intentionality or normativity, and then argue that this feature is impossible except through participation in some supra-individual network of relations. For instance, accounts based on interpretation and the "principle of charity", such as those of Donald Davidson and Daniel Dennett (with roots in Quine), ascribe contentful states only as components of an overall pattern that is rational *in context*—that is, in relation to the system's situation or environment. Similarly, social practice accounts, such as those of Richard Rorty and Robert Brandom (with roots in Sellars and Wittgenstein), understand the norms that enable reasoning and content to be instituted *communally*—that is, in relation to the practices and responses of others. On neither approach is solipsism even a coherent possibility.

Interrelationist arguments are *holistic* in the specific sense that they take cognitive phenomena to be members of some class of phenomena, each of which has its relevant character only by virtue of its determinate relations to the others—that relevant character being, in effect, nothing other than its "place" in the larger pattern or whole. The obvious example is a move or play in a game: pushing around a little piece of plastic shaped like a turret could only amount to a *rook* move in an appropriate spatial and temporal context of other chess pieces and moves. To call it a rook move apart from any such context is simply nonsense. Likewise, so the reasoning goes, to regard any phenomenon as intentional or normative in isolation from the relevant whole, is also nonsense. And since, in the case of mental attributions, the relevant whole must include the individual's environment and/or community, the Cartesian independence of the mental realm is impossible.

While undeniably important and compelling, considerations like these seem to me seriously incomplete and potentially distorting. They remain theoretical or intellectual in a way that not only does not undermine but actually reinforces an aspect of the Cartesian separation that is still so pervasive as to be almost invisible. In particular, interrelationist accounts retain a principled distinction between the mental and the corporeal—a distinction that is reflected in contrasts like semantics versus syntax, the space of reasons versus the space of causes, or the intentional versus the physical vocabulary. (Notice that each of these contrasts can be heard either as higher versus lower "level" or as inner versus outer "sphere".) The contrary of *this* separation—or battery of separations—is not interrelationist holism, but something that I would like to call the *intimacy* of the mind's embodiment and embeddedness in the world. The term 'intimacy' is meant to suggest more than just necessary interrelation or interdependence but a kind of *commingling* or *integralness* of mind, body, and world—that is, to undermine their very distinctness. The challenge is as much to spell out what this could mean as to make a case for it. Indeed, no sooner does such a possibility seem intelligible at all, than ways to bring out its plausibility and significance turn up everywhere.

There is little original in what follows. The strategy will be to bring some well-known principles of systems analysis to bear on the mind-body-world "system" in a way that refocuses questions of division and unity, and then to canvass a selection of investigations and proposals—some fairly recent, others not—in the light of this new focus. The hope is that these superficially disparate ideas, none of them new, will seem to converge around the theme of intimacy in a way that illuminates and supports them all. Sorting and aligning issues in this manner has sometimes been discussed under titles like 'embedded computation' and 'situated cognition'.

2 SIMON'S ANT

The simplest introduction to the range of phenomena I want to explore is the beautiful parable with which Herbert Simon opens chapter three of *The Sciences of the Artificial*, a chapter to which he gives the subtitle "Embedding Artifice in Nature".

> We watch an ant make his [sic] laborious way across a wind- and wave-molded beach. He moves ahead, angles to the right to ease his climb up a steep dunelet, detours around a pebble, stops for a moment to exchange information with a compatriot. Thus he makes his weaving, halting way back to his home. ... Viewed as a geometric figure, the ant's path is irregular, complex, hard to describe. But its complexity is really a complexity in the surface of the beach, not a complexity in the ant.   (1969/81, 63–64)

Simon summarizes the lesson of his parable twice, word-for-word the same, except for those indicating the subject of the behavior.

> *An ant [A man] viewed as a behaving system, is quite simple. The apparent complexity of its [his] behavior over time is largely a reflection of the complexity of the environment in which it [he] finds itself [himself].*   (64–65; italics in originals.)

This lesson can be taken in two rather different ways. On the one hand, one might heave a sigh of scientific relief: understanding people as behaving systems is going to be easier than we thought, because so much of the apparent complexity in their behavior is due to factors external to them, and hence external to our problem. On the other hand, one might see the problem itself as transformed: since the relevant complexity in the observed behavior depends on so much more than the behaving system itself, the investigation cannot be restricted to that system alone, but must extend to some larger structure of which it is only a fraction.

That Simon himself took the lesson in the first way is evident from the two "hedges" that he immediately offers—both of which strike me as quite remarkable (and ultimately untenable).

> Now I should like to hedge my bets a little. Instead of trying to consider the "whole man," fully equipped with glands and viscera, I should like to limit the discussion to Homo sapiens, "thinking man." ... I should also like to hedge my bets in a second way, for a human being can store away in memory a great furniture of information that can be evoked by appropriate stimuli. Hence I would like to view this information-packed memory less as part of the organism than as part of the environment to which it adapts.
>
> (65; second hedge only in the second edition)

With these qualifications in place, Simon can safely turn his attention away not only from sand dunes and pebbles, but also from human knowledge, culture, the body, and the world, so as to concentrate on cryptarithmetic and nonsense syllables—all in support of his view that the human "information processing system" (essentially a glorified CPU) must be serial and rather simple. In effect, he wants to pare away enough of the real human being that what's left is strikingly like an ant.

The alternative reading of the parable, however, is already suggested by the history of artificial intelligence research itself. Perhaps the largest-scale trend in this history has been precisely *counter* to the suggestion of relegating knowledge ("information-packed memory") to the "environment"—that is, regarding it as external to the problem of understanding intelligence. The essential point of systems based on semantic nets, frames, internal models, prototypes, and "common sense" is that, except in very special circumstances, the intelligent performance of a system depends more directly on the *particular* interconnectedness and organization of its knowledge, than on any reasoning or processing power. Note that the issue is not the quantity of information, but its specific quality—its *concrete* structure. Everything is in the *details*—that *these* items are grouped together, that there is a cross-reference from *here* to *there*, that *this* topic appears in *that* index with *those* keys—in such a way that abstracting the form of the knowledge from its content would make no sense. In other words, according to this trend in AI, to study (or build) *intelligent* systems is, above all, to study (or build) large, concrete knowledge structures—*not* simple processors.

Until recently, however, nearly all of this research has retained the assumption that the relevant "furniture of information" is implemented as complex symbol structures that are, in many respects, just like the contents of the traditional Cartesian mind. In particular, they are internal to the individual agent, and different in kind from any physiology or hardware. The explorations that follow can be seen as trying out the second reading of Simon's parable in a more radical way. If the significant complexity of intelligent behavior depends intimately on the concrete details of the agent's embodiment and worldly situation, then perhaps intelligence as such should be understood as characteristic, in the first instance, of some more comprehensive structure than an internal, disembodied "mind", whether artificial or natural.

3 COMPONENTS, SYSTEMS, AND INTERFACES

Of course, human intelligence is embodied and embedded; nobody denies that. The question is how important this fact is to the nature of intelligence. One way to put the question is to ask whether we can in principle partition off the intellect (or mind) from the body and/or the world. "Partition off" does not this time mean isolation or removal. That is, we can grant the holist thesis that mind would be impossible in the *absence* of body and/or world, and still ask whether it can be understood as a distinct and well-defined *subsystem* within the necessary larger whole. But this requires a brief discussion of the principles for dividing systems into distinct subsystems along nonarbitrary lines.

It is a fine testimony to the depth and breadth of Simon's slender volume that, in a later chapter, entitled "The Architecture of Complexity", he addresses this very issue: On what principled basis are large systems decomposable into subsystems? And, to answer it, he invites us to

> distinguish between the interactions *among* subsystems, on the one hand, and the interactions *within* subsystems—that is, among the parts of those subsystems—on the other. The interactions at the different levels may be, and often will be, of different orders of magnitude.   (209)

What is he getting at? Consider a television set in comparison to a block of marble. The former, we are inclined to say, is highly systematic, composed of many nested interacting subsystems, whereas the latter is hardly systematic at all. Why? One suggestion might be that the TV is composed of many different kinds of material, arranged in complicated shapes and patterns, whereas the marble contains relatively few materials and is nearly (though not quite) homogeneous. This cannot be the right answer, however, because a computer microchip (an integrated circuit) is surely more systematic than a compost of rotting table scraps, even though the former contains relatively few materials and is nearly homogeneous, whereas the latter is diverse and messy.

Rather, the difference must lie in the nature of the discontinuities within the whole, and the character of the interactions across them. To see this, think of *how* the TV is organized. If we suppose that, at some level of analysis, it consists of a thousand components, then we can ask how these components are distinguished. One possible decomposition would be neatly geometrical: assuming the set is roughly cubical, divide it into ten equal slices along each axis, to yield a thousand smaller cubes, of which the entire set exactly consists. What's wrong with this "decomposition"? Well, consider one of the "component" cubes—say, one near the center. It contains half of a transistor, two thirds of a capacitor, several fragments of wire, a small triangle of glass from the picture tube, and a lot of hot air. Obviously, this is an incoherent jumble that makes no sense—even though a thousand equally crazy "pieces", put together *exactly* right, would make up a TV set. Our task is to say why.

A resistor is a quintessential electronic component. It has two wires coming out of it, and its only "job", as the name suggests, is to *resist* (to some specified degree) the flow of electricity between them. It doesn't matter how it does that job—nor, within limits, does anything else about it matter—just so long as it does that job properly and reliably, and doesn't interfere with any other components. An electronic component, like a resistor, is a relatively independent and self-contained portion of a larger electronic circuit. This means several things. In the first place, it means that the resistor does not interact with the rest of the system except through its circuit connections—namely, those two wires. That is, nothing that happens outside of it affects anything that happens inside, or vice versa, except by affecting the currents in those connections. (To be more precise, all effects other than these are negligible, either because they are so slight or because they are irrelevant.) Second, it means that the relevant interactions through those connections are themselves well-defined, reliable, and relatively simple. For instance, it's *only* a flow of electrons, not of chemicals, contagion, or contraband. Finally, it means that it is not itself a composite of components at a comparable level of independence and self-containedness: a resistor plus a capacitor do not add up to a distinct component. (However, a suitable larger arrangement of resistors, capacitors, and transistors might add up to a pre-amp—which could in turn be a component in a higher-level system.)

An electronic component's connecting wires constitute its "interface" to the rest of the system. In careful usage, the notions of component, system, and interface should all be understood together and in terms of one another. A *component* is a relatively independent and self-contained portion of a system in the sense that it relevantly interacts with other components only through interfaces between them (and contains no internal interfaces at the same level). An *interface* is a point of interactive "contact" between components such that the relevant interactions are well-defined, reliable, and relatively simple. A *system* is a relatively independent and self-contained composite of components interacting at interfaces. So the pre-amp mentioned above would be both a component and a system; such a component system is often called a *subsystem*. Though these concepts are all defined in terms of one another, they are not therefore circular or empty, because they collectively involve the further notions of relative independence, simplicity, relevance, and interaction.

An important consequence is that genuine components are in principle replaceable by functional equivalents. For instance, a resistor in an electronic circuit can be replaced by any other that has the same resistance value (and perhaps meets a few other specifications). The circuit as a whole will continue to function as before, because all that mattered about that resistor in the first place was its resistance via a simple interface—and, by stipulation, the replacement matches that. (Of course, rifles had components before Eli Whitney invented interchangeable parts. But that was basically a difference of degree—specifically, of *how* well-defined the interfaces were and *how readily* interchangeable the parts were.)

Return now to the thousand little cubes making up a TV set. Are they *components*, in the strict sense? Obviously not, because they are not even "relatively" independent and self-contained. Or, what comes to the same thing, the surfaces separating them are not proper interfaces. That is, the interactions required across those surfaces, for the set to work, are absurdly complex and irregular, with no hope of clear definition or reliable implementation. Just imagine trying to assemble a new set from a thousand such cubes taken one each from a thousand other sets! Yet a TV can easily be made out of parts taken from others, if only the divisions are made at genuine interfaces.

The point is even more vivid if we consider instead a system that moves, such as an engine or an animal: then the cubes wouldn't so much as contain the same physical hunks through time, and a consistent "interface" wouldn't even be conceivable. Yet decomposition of such systems into simpler components is perfectly standard and straightforward, if their boundaries are allowed to move with them. For instance, a connecting rod between a piston and crankshaft is relatively self-contained, and has very well-defined interfaces in its two bearing surfaces; and all that matters about them is that their axes be kept reliably parallel and a certain distance apart. Again, the component as such is delimited by its simple, reliable interfaces.

4 INCORPOREAL INTERFACES

Examples like electronic circuits, mechanisms, and even organisms can leave the impression that the boundaries of components and subsystems are set by corporeal discontinuities—virtually complete, except at the interfaces, where narrowly defined contacts are permitted. It is particularly important for our purposes to counter this impression, since the corporeal discontinuity between our bodies and the world—the very discontinuity that determines these bodies as bodies—misleadingly enhances the apparent significance of bodily surfaces as relevant interfaces for the understanding of other phenomena, such as intelligence.

That systematic interfaces need not coincide with corporeal surfaces can be shown by example. Large organizations, like governments, corporations, and universities, are almost always subdivided into various divisions, departments, and units. But the correspondence between these demarcations and corporeal boundaries is at best haphazard, and never essential. Indeed, as more and more business is conducted via worldwide communication networks, the physical locations of personnel and data become practically irrelevant. What matter instead are the access codes, permission levels, distribution lists, private addresses, priority orderings, and so on, that determine where information flows and what gets attended to. It is the structure of these, ultimately, that determines departmentalization and hierarchy.

Members of a single department or unit tend to work more closely together, sharing resources and concerns, than do members of different departments. Likewise, units of the same division interact more often and more intimately than do units of different divisions; and so on. Nothing depends, ultimately, on who is in what building, or on what continent—as Simon himself clearly appreciated.

> Most physical and biological hierarchies are described in spatial terms. We detect the organelles in a cell in the way we detect the raisins in a cake—they are "visibly" differentiated substructures localized spatially in the larger structure. On the other hand, we propose to identify social hierarchies not by observing who lives close to whom but by observing who interacts with whom. These two points of view can be reconciled by defining hierarchy in terms of intensity of interaction, but observing that in most biological and physical systems relatively intense interaction implies relative spatial propinquity. (199)

"Intensity" of interaction here means something like how "tightly" things are coupled, or even how "close-knit" they are—that is, the degree to which the behavior of each affects or constrains the other. Heard in this way, it can serve as a generic notion encompassing the mechanical integrity of a connecting rod and the electrical unity of a resistor, as well as the social or institutional cohesiveness of a group. The different parts of a connecting rod interact so intensely, for example, that they always move rigidly together; by comparison, its interactions with the piston and the crankshaft are "looser", allowing independent rotation about a common axis. Further, comparing these intensities can be the first step in accounts, respectively, of relative independence and interface simplicity; for each can be seen as a matter of less intense interaction—looser coupling—externally, as compared to internally.

5 INTELLIGIBILITY AS THE PRINCIPLE OF DECOMPOSITION

What Simon mentions only in passing, however, without the emphasis it will need for our purposes, is the *motivation* for treating systems in this way. In a brief subsection entitled "Near Decomposability and Comprehensibility", he writes:

> The fact that many complex systems have a nearly decomposable, hierarchic structure is a major facilitating factor enabling us to understand, describe, and even 'see' such systems and their parts.
>
> (218–219)

'Nearly decomposable systems' is his term for systems of relatively independent interacting components with simple interfaces between them. So the point about comprehensibility can be paraphrased as follows: *finding*, in something complicated and hard to understand, a set of simple reliable interfaces, dividing it into relatively independent components, is a way of rendering it *intelligible*.

The significance of this can be brought out by approaching it from another side. Biological and electronic systems are also in some sense physical—as, indeed, are social and (other) information systems. But in that case, more than one kind of interaction, and accordingly more than one kind of decomposition, would seem to be possible in what is somehow the same "stuff". How, then, are we to decide *which* interactions and decompositions are the important ones? Once this question is asked, however, the answer is obvious: it depends on what we're interested in—which is to say, it depends on what phenomena we are trying to understand. Thus, when we turn to the mind-body-world "system", and wonder how, perhaps, to decompose it, our considerations will perforce be relative to some prior identification of what is to be understood.

Part of the reason, for instance, that the structure of the beach is as important as the structure of the ant in Simon's parable is that the ant's actual path is determined in real time by *close interaction* between the ant and the concrete details of the beach's surface. If, by contrast, the ant were responding to an internal model or representation of the beach, instead of responding the beach itself, or if it just contained a list of steps and turns which it followed slavishly, then the importance of the beach would be reduced or eliminated. The other part of the reason, however, and in some sense the prior part, is that what we want to understand in the first place is the ant's *path*. If we were interested instead in it's respiration or its immune system, then the beach would be largely irrelevant, regardless of how tightly the ant is coupled to it when walking. In other words, *which* close interactions matter, when considering the scope and structure of systems, depends fundamentally on what we're interested in—that is, what we're trying to understand.

Here, then, is where the account of decomposition takes hold. If what we're interested in is the path, and if the ant relies mostly on its own internal structure to guide its steps, counting on the ground just for friction and support, then the ant and beach are two relatively independent components or systems, with a well-defined simple interface at the soles of its feet. If, on the other hand, there is constant close coupling between the ant and the details of the beach surface, and if this coupling is crucial in determining the actual path, then, for purposes of understanding that path, the ant and beach must be regarded more as an integrated unit than as a pair of distinct components. This is the simplest archetype of what I mean by *intimacy*.

6 Brooks's subsumption architecture

Insect examples have all the advantages and disadvantages of simple archetypes. They are, of course, wonderfully clear, as far as they go; but they don't go very far. We will try to work our way up toward more interesting cases via a series of intermediaries. Simon muses at one point (64) that if someone were to build insect-like robots, their behavior on a beach would be much like that of his ant. Little did he know that, two decades later, such a project would be in full swing in the laboratory of Rod Brooks at MIT. It is perhaps slightly ironic that part of what drives Brooks's efforts is a dissatisfaction with the symbol-manipulation approach to artificial intelligence pioneered by Simon and Allen Newell in the 1950's. As we shall see, however, this is no accident.

Brooks's best known "creature", named *Herbert* (after Simon), is a self-powered, wheeled contraption, about the size of a small trash can, with various sensors, one moveable arm on top, and surprisingly little compute power. It's lot in life is to buzz around the MIT AI Lab looking for empty soda pop cans, pick them up, and return them to a central bin. Herbert was built (around 1990) and actually worked (albeit clumsily). What makes this noteworthy, compared, say, to robots of the 1970's, is that the labs and offices in which Herbert worked were in no way specially prepared: there were no guidelines painted on the floors or walls, the typical mess and clutter of real work space were not cleaned up, people carried on with their own business as usual, and so on. So Herbert managed to negotiate a relatively inhospitable, changing environment, do its job, and stay mostly out of trouble—with roughly the proficiency of a crustacean.

What matters for us is not this modest success but the design principles on which Herbert is based. Two points deserve emphasis. First, Brooks uses what he calls the "subsumption architecture", according to which systems are decomposed not in the familiar way by local functions or faculties, but rather by global *activities* or *tasks*.

> [This] alternative decomposition makes no distinction between peripheral systems, such as vision, and central systems. Rather the fundamental slicing up of an intelligent system is in the orthogonal direction dividing it into *activity* producing subsystems. Each activity or behavior producing system individually connects sensing to action. We refer to an activity producing system as a *layer*. An activity is a pattern of interactions with the world. Another name for our activities might well be skill ...
>
> (1991, 146)

Thus, Herbert has one subsystem for detecting and avoiding obstacles in its path, another for wandering around, a third for finding distant soda cans and homing in on them, a fourth for noticing nearby soda cans and putting its hand around them, a fifth for detecting something between its fingers and closing them, and so on ... fourteen in all. What's striking is that these are all complete input/output systems, more or less independent of each other. They can't be entirely independent, of course, because, for instance, Herbert has only one set of wheels; so if two different subsystems undertake to move the robot at the same moment, one must dominate—through some interface. But the bulk of the interactions, the tightest couplings, are *within* the respective activity layers—including, as Brooks explicitly points out, *interactions with the world.*

In other words, each of the various activities of this system is like the walking of Simon's ant. Each involves constant close interaction with certain specific aspects of the environment, and can only be understood in terms thereof. So the structures of the respective aspects of the environment are at least as important as the structures of the internal portions of the corresponding layers in rendering the different activities intelligible. Herbert has fourteen relatively independent, closely knit subsystems, each encompassing *both* structures within the robot *and* structures outside of it. To put it one last way, one that foreshadows where we're going, each of Herbert's highest-level subsystems is somewhat mental, somewhat bodily, and somewhat worldly. That is, according to Simon's principles of intensity of interaction, the primary division is not into mind, body, and world, but rather into "layers" that cut across these in various ways. And, in particular, the outer surface of the robot is *not* a primary interface. (Of course, there may be further subdivisions within the respective layers, which may or may not take portions of this surface as subsidiary interfaces.)

7 PERCEIVING INSTEAD OF REPRESENTING

The second point that deserves emphasis, closely related to the first, is captured in a slogan that Brooks proposes: *The world is its own best model.* (1990, 5) This is precisely to repudiate designs like the alternatives I mentioned earlier for Simon's ant: that is, the ant should *not* contain any inner model or representation of the beach, nor an inner list of step and turn instructions. These alternatives would substitute complexity *within* the organism for intensity of interaction *between* the organism and its environment. But Brooks, as his slogan indicates, is very much against that. Why?

We can put the answer in another slogan that Brooks would probably like: *Perception is cheap, representation expensive.* Such a slogan might surprise many AI workers, who are acutely aware of how difficult pattern recognition can be. But the point is that *good enough* perception is cheaper than *good enough* representation—where that means "good enough" to avoid serious errors. The trouble with representation is that, to be good enough, it must be relatively complete and relatively up to date, both of which are costly in a dynamic environment. Perception, by contrast, can remain happily *ad hoc*, dealing with concrete questions only as they arise. To take a homely example, it would be silly, for most purposes, to try to *keep track of* what shelf everything in the refrigerator is currently on; if and when you want something, just *look*.

Why would anyone have supposed otherwise? The answer lies in two deep assumptions that have informed symbolic AI from the beginning—including the work of Newell and Simon. The first is that intelligence is best manifested in *solving problems*, especially *hard* problems. The second is that problems are best solved by a process of *reasoning*: working from a statement of the problem and such ancillary knowledge as is available to a statement of the solution. The greatest triumphs in the history of the field are its demonstrations that these ideals *can* be realized mechanically—principally via formal inference, heuristically guided search, and structured knowledge representation. But notice how they bias the orientation toward representation and away from perception. Not only must the problem and the relevant knowledge be represented, generally in some symbolic formalism, but so also all the intermediate states that are explored on the way to the solution. The generation, use, and management of all these representations then becomes the paramount concern.

Perception, under such a regime, is reduced to a peripheral channel through which the problem is initially posed, and incidental facts are supplied; it might as well be a teletype. In most of AI, in fact, the process of perception has been conceived as *transduction*: some special preprocessor takes optical or auditory input, "recognizes" it, and then produces a symbolic output for the main system—not unlike what the system could have gotten from a teletype. What's pertinent about a teletype here is that it's a narrow-bandwidth device—the very antithesis of tight coupling.

For instance, the number of "bits" of information in the input to a perceptual system is enormous compared to the number in a typical symbolic description. So a "visual transducer" that responds to a sleeping brown dog with some expression like "Lo, a sleeping brown dog" has effected a huge data reduction. And this is usually regarded as a benefit, because, without such a reduction, a *symbolic* system would be overwhelmed. But it is also a serious bottleneck in the system's ability to be in close touch with its environment. Organisms with perceptual systems not encumbered by such bottlenecks could have significant advantages in sensitivity and responsiveness. The alternative "wide bandwidth" coupling, however, is precisely what, by Simon's systems-analytic criterion, would undermine or downgrade the organism/environment boundary as an important decompositional interface—just as Brooks proposes.

Models that emphasize internal symbolic representations insinuate bottlenecks into the understanding of action, just as they do for perception, and for much the same reason. The product of a rational problem-solving process is a low-bandwidth sequence of symbol structures, which can either report the results (say, on a teletype) or send instructions to an "output transducer". But skillful or adept engagement with a situation is as likely to profit from a wide-bandwidth coupling as is responsiveness to it. (We will return to this following the next section.)

In the meantime, notice that the very distinction between perception and action is itself artificially emphasized and sharpened by the image of a central processor or mind working *between* them, receiving "input" from the one and then (later) sending "output" to the other. The primary instance is rather *interaction*, which is simultaneously perceptive and active, richly integrated in real time. Thus, what's noteworthy about our refrigerator aptitudes is not just, or even mainly, that we can visually identify what's there, but rather the fact that we can, easily and reliably, reach around the milk and over the baked beans to lift out the orange juice—without spilling any of them. This high-bandwidth hand-eye coordination—or, better, hand-eye-refrigerator coordination—is what Brooks calls an "activity" or "skill" (though much more advanced than his robots). There is little reason to believe that symbol processing has much to do with it—unless one is already committed to the view that *reasoning* must underlie *all* flexible competence.

8 AFFORDANCE AND ECOLOGICAL OPTICS

The psychologist James J. Gibson makes several related points at a level somewhat higher than insects. Early in *The Ecological Approach to Visual Perception*, he begins a section entitled "The Mutuality of Animal and Environment" by explaining that

> the words *animal* and *environment* make an inseparable pair. Each term implies the other. No animal could exist without an environment surrounding it. Equally, although not so obvious, an environment implies an animal (or at least an organism) to be surrounded. This means that the surface of the earth, millions of years before life developed on it, was not an environment, properly speaking. (1979, 8)

This is not a fussy semantic quibble, but a subtle observation about levels and units of intelligibility. We can only understand animals *as perceivers* if we consider them as inseparably related to an environment, which is itself understood in terms appropriate to that animal.

Central to Gibson's "ecological approach" is his account of *what* it is that an animal perceives and *how*. Visual perception cannot be understood, he maintains, if one starts from the perspective of *physical* optics. A system that sees—a sighted animal—is not responsive, in the first instance, to physically simple properties of light, like color and brightness, but rather to visible features of the environment that matter to it. Gibson calls such features "affordances".

> The *affordances* of the environment are what it *offers* the animal, what it *provides* or *furnishes*, for good or ill. The verb *to afford* is found in the dictionary, but the noun *affordance* is not. I have made it up. I mean by it something that refers to both the environment and the animal in a way that no existing term does. It implies the complementarity of the animal and the environment.
>   (127)

So for example, a suitably sturdy and flat surface could *afford* a place to stand or walk to an animal of a certain sort—not to a fish, of course, and what affords standing room to a sparrow might not to a cat (a matter of some importance to both). Nooks can afford shelter and seclusion, green leaves or smaller neighbors can afford lunch, larger neighbors can afford attack, and so on—all depending on who's looking and with what interests.

What's important (and controversial) here is not the idea of affordances as such, but the claim that they can be *perceived*—as opposed to inferred. "The central question for the theory of affordances is not whether they exist and are real but whether information is available in ambient light for perceiving them." (140) Intuitively, the startling thesis is this: it can be *a feature of the ambient light itself* that, for instance, something over there "looks edible" or "looks dangerous" (from here, to a creature like me). This would have to be a very complicated feature indeed, practically impossible to specify (in physical terms). Gibson calls such features "high-order invariants", and makes essentially two points about them. First:

> The trouble with the assumption that high-order optical invariants specify high-order affordances is that experimenters, accustomed to working in the laboratory with low-order stimulus variables, cannot think of a way to measure them.   (141)

In other words, if perceptual systems "pick up" high-order invariants, then the surfaces of the eyes and other sense organs cannot be interfaces—because the relevant interactions are not well-defined and relatively simple.

The second is a point that we have seen Gibson emphasize several times already, and moreover just what we would expect to follow from the lack of a well-defined interface.

> The hypothesis of information in ambient light to specify affordances is the culmination of ecological optics. The notion of invariants that are related at one extreme to the motives and needs of an observer and at the other extreme to the substances and surfaces of a world provides a new approach to psychology.
>
> (143)

This is not merely to reiterate the complementarity of the animal and its environment, but also to associate that integration with the "high-order" affordances and invariants that constitute their interaction. Specific complexity in the perceptual capacities of the organism itself is what sustains the corresponding complexity in what it perceives, via tightly coupled, high-bandwidth interaction—at the level of description appropriate to understanding perception. Thus, the culmination of ecological optics is, in our terms, the *intimacy* of perceiver and perceived.

9 TRANSDUCTION VERSUS SKILLFUL INTERACTION

So far, with the exception of the refrigerator example, all our discussions have involved relatively primitive creatures or systems. This might give the impression that intimate intermingling of mind, body, and world—in particular, lack of mental distinctness—is characteristic mainly of lower life forms, as opposed to people. Descartes, after all, held that animals have no minds at all, and are *merely* physical. The space of reasons, by contrast, is often seen as pre-eminently or even exclusively human; and it is chiefly ratiocination that seems to require input/output interfaces and transducers to enable perception and action. (Transduction, remember, is the function that Descartes assigned to the pineal gland.) So maybe the lesson is not to undermine the mind/body separation across the board, but rather to restrict it to ourselves—the *rational* animals.

On the contrary, however, I want to suggest that the human mind may be *more* intimately intermingled with its body and its world than is any other, and that this is one of its distinctive advantages. Moreover, I think that Simon's criterion of intensity of interaction, at the relevant level of intelligibility, will be just the right tool for making this visible. Let us return to the phenomenon of skillful behavior and perception, and consider its structure in more detail. In Part III of *What Computers Can't Do*, in a chapter entitled "The Role of the Body in Intelligent Behavior", Hubert L. Dreyfus writes:

> Generally, in acquiring a skill—in learning to drive, dance, or pronounce a foreign language, for example—at first we must slowly, awkwardly, and consciously follow the rules. But then there comes a moment when we finally can perform automatically. At this point we do not seem to be simply dropping these same rigid rules into unconsciousness; rather we seem to have picked up the muscular gestalt which gives our behavior a new flexibility and smoothness. The same holds for acquiring the skill of perception. (1972/79, 248–249; second edition wording)

A *"muscular* gestalt"? What have the *muscles* got to do with it? We react with questions like these, perhaps even with a trace of exasperation, because of a very seductive traditional story. When we are acting *intelligently*, our rational intellect is (consciously and/or unconsciously) taking account of various facts at its disposal, figuring out what to do, and then issuing appropriate output instructions. These instructions are converted by output transducers into physical configurations (mechanical forces, electric currents, chemical concentrations, ...) that result in the requisite bodily behavior. The transducers, therefore, function as (or define) *interfaces* between the rational and the physical. As such, they also provide a natural point of subdivision—in the sense that any alternative output subsystem that responded to the same instructions with the same behavior could be substituted without making any significant difference to the intellectual part. On that picture, then, the muscles would fall entirely on the physical side, and not be relevant to the intelligent (sub)system at all—even as "gestalts".

Well, *are there transducers* between our minds and our bodies? From a certain all-too-easy perspective, the question can seem obtuse: *of course* there are. Almost by definition, it seems, there *has to be* a conversion between the symbolic or conceptual contents of our minds and the physical processes in our bodies; and that conversion just is transduction. But Dreyfus is, in effect, denying this—not by denying that there are minds or that there are bodies, but by denying that there needs to be any interface or conversion between them.

The fateful die is already cast in the image of the intellect figuring things out and then issuing instructions. An *instruction* (according to conventional wisdom) is a syntactic expression which, by virtue of belonging to a suitably interpretable formal system, carries a certain sort of semantic content. Specifically, its content does *not* depend on how or whether it might be acted upon by any *particular* physical output system. For instance, if I decide to type the letter 'A', the content of the forthcoming instruction wouldn't depend on it being an instruction to *my* fingers, as opposed to any others, or even some robotic prosthesis. Any output system that could take that instruction and type an 'A'—and, *mutatis mutandis*, other instructions and behaviors—would do as well. The idea that there are such instructions is morally equivalent to the idea that there are transducers.

10 OUTPUT PATTERNS THAT AREN'T INSTRUCTIONS

A different—and incompatible—story might go like this. There are tens of millions (or whatever) of neural pathways leading out of my brain (or neocortex, or whatever) into various muscle fibers in my fingers, hands, wrists, arms, shoulders, and so on, and also from various tactile and proprioceptive cells back again. Each time I type a letter, a substantial fraction of these fire at various frequencies, and in various temporal relations to one another. But that some particular pulse pattern, on some occasion, should result in my typing an 'A' depends on many contingencies, over and above just which pattern of pulses it happens to be.

In the first place, it depends on the lengths of my fingers, the strengths and quicknesses of my muscles, the shapes of my joints, and the like. Of course, whatever else I might do with my hands, from typing the rest of the alphabet to tying my shoes, would likewise depend *simultaneously* on particular pulse patterns and these other concrete contingencies. But there need be no way to "factor out" the respective contributions of these different dependencies, such that contents could consistently be assigned to pulse patterns independent of which fingers they're destined for. That is to say, there need be *no* way—even in principle, and with God's own microsurgery—to reconnect my neurons to anyone else's fingers, such that I could reliably type or tie my shoes with them. It would be like trying to assemble the cubes from a thousand TV sets into a single new one. But, in that case, what any given pattern "means" depends on it being a pattern specifically for *my particular* fingers—or, to use Dreyfus's phrase, for fingers with my "muscular gestalts".

Perhaps an analogy would help—even if it's fairly far fetched. Imagine an encryption algorithm with the following three features: it uses very large encryption keys (tens of millions of bits, just for instance); cryptograms, even for quite brief messages, are comparable in size to the keys themselves; and it is tremendously redundant, in the sense that (for each key) countless distinct cryptograms would decode to the same message. Now, consider, for a given key and message, all the cryptograms that would decode to that message; and ask whether it could make any sense to speak of what *these* cryptograms have in common apart from *that particular* key. It's hard to see how it could. Yet, if individual cryptograms have any meaning at all, then these must all have the same meaning; so either cryptograms are meaningless, or they mean something only in conjunction with a *particular* key. Then the analogy works like this: each individual's *particular body*—his or her own muscular gestalts—functions like a large encryption key; and the pulse patterns coming down from the brain are the cryptograms, which are either meaningless, or they mean something only in conjunction with that particular body. Either way, they aren't instructions. This is *only* an analogy, however, because the activity of the fingers should not be regarded as "decoding neural messages", but rather as an integral part of the "processing" that the brain and other neurons also contribute to.

But even that may be overly sanguine. Whether a given *efferent* neural pattern will result in a typed 'A' depends *also* on how my fingers happen already to be deployed and moving, the angle of the keyboard, how tired I am, and so on—factors that *aren't constant*, even for the short run. On different occasions, the same pattern will give different letters, and different patterns the same letter. The reason that I can type, despite all this, is that there are comparably rich *afferent* patterns forming a kind of feedback loop that constantly "recalibrates" the system. (In terms of the above analogy, it's as if the encryption keys were not only large, but ever changing—the new ones being sent upstream all the time.) But that would mean that the "content" of any given neural output pattern would depend not only on the particular body that it's connected to, but also on the *concrete details* of its current worldly situation.

If there were simple instructions—well-defined, repeatable messages—coming down the nerves from my brain to my fingers, then that narrow-bandwidth channel could be an interface to my fingers as physical transducers. Accordingly, it would be possible to divide the system there, and substitute "equivalent" fingers, in place of mine. Such an architecture is implicitly assumed by much of philosophy and most of AI. By contrast, the alternative that I have been sketching sees these nerves as carrying high-bandwidth interactions (high-intensity, in Simon's terms), without any simple, well-defined structure. Thus, by the same criterion, we would not get two relatively independent separable components—a rational mind and a physical body, meeting at an interface—but rather a single closely-knit unity.

II SPECIFIC COMPLEXITY

Nerve fibers, of course, aren't the only high-bandwidth channel between my fingers and other parts of my body. The immune system, for instance, is extraordinarily complex and responsive. And even the circulatory transportation of metabolites and by-products carries, in the technical sense, a lot of "information". Why focus on the nerves? Once the question is asked, the answer is easy to see. When we are trying to understand intelligence—as manifested, say, in intelligent behavior—we look to the complexity that is *specific* to that behavior. The distribution of antibodies and proteins to my hands, while no doubt essential to my typing ability, doesn't differ very much depending *which* letter I type; indeed, it doesn't depend much on whether I'm typing, writing longhand, or tying bows.

But the complexity of the nervous system is task specific, and in two different ways. In the first place, at any moment, the pulse patterns needed for typing an 'A' differ from those needed for typing a 'B', not to mention from those needed for writing a 'B'. The skills in question just are the abilities to get these things done right. And getting them right—this letter as opposed to that one—depends *in specific detail* on the actual pulse patterns, in a way that it does not depend on any details of my immune defenses. Second, as I acquired these skills, various more or less permanent changes were made in my neural pathways, in implementing all the relevant habits and reflexes. (Dreyfus, remember, was discussing *learning*.) And these changes, likewise, were specific to the skills learned—in a way that, for example, increases in circulatory capacity wouldn't have been.

The point, however, is not to focus exclusively on the nervous system. Far from it. As emphasized above, actual performance depends on a number of other specific contingencies besides nerve impulses. Similarly, a range of other *specifically relevant* permanent changes are involved in the acquisition of skills. Thus, muscles of the requisite strengths, shapes, and limberness must be developed and maintained—differently for different skills. This is most conspicuous for very demanding manual abilities, like musicianship, surgery, and stage magic. Indeed, a professional violinist must acquire specific callouses, perhaps subtle grooves in the tips of her phalanges, even a certain set of the jaw.

The unity of mind and body can be promoted wholesale, perhaps, on the basis of general principles of monism or the unity of science. Such arguments are indifferent to variety and substructure within either the mental or the physical: everything is unceremoniously lumped together at one swoop. Here, by contrast, integration is offered at retail. In attempting to undermine the idea of an interface between the mind and the fingers, I am staking no claim to the liver or intestines. (Simon may be right about glands and viscera.) The idea is not to wipe out all distinctions and homogenize everything on general principles, but rather to call certain very familiar divisions into question, on the basis of considerations highly peculiar to them.

12 GETTING THE WHOLE RUG SMOOTH

If a rug doesn't fit, then flattening it out in one place will just move the hump to another. If there's no interface between the brain and the fingers, then maybe it just is (has to be?) somewhere else. One might imagine, for instance, that the efferent nerves are high bandwidth because they (along with much of the spinal cord and some of the brain) are all part of a very sophisticated physical output system—the psycho-physical interface itself being further "in". It could be that ratiocination (or representation more generally) occurs only in the cortex, or only the *neocortex*, or whatever. Then the relevant transductions would have to take place *within* the brain, between one part of it and another—not so far from the pineal gland, as luck might have it.

Now, my question is: Why would anyone ever be tempted by such a supposition? And the answer, surely, is the same *presupposition* that the mental *must be* different in kind—categorically different—from anything bodily or worldly; so, *there must be* some interface somewhere. For, without that *a priori* conviction, the obvious evidence of neuroanatomy would be decisive: the neural pathways from perception to action are high-bandwidth *all the way through*. If anything, the bandwidth increases toward the center, rather than narrowing down.

There's just no plausible constriction where well-defined instructions might be getting converted; that is, there's no place where a counterpart of the above argument against efferent transduction wouldn't apply.

Well then, might the hump slip out in the other direction, out past the fingers? It cannot be denied that the keyboard itself is a well-defined interface. No matter how complicated and various are the ways of striking the keys, the result is always limited to character codes from a set of a few hundred, in a slow, unambiguous, serial order. (It's not for nothing that a teletype was earlier our paradigm of a low-bandwidth device.) By these lights, then, the meaningful (mental) extends all the way to the fingertips—maybe a touch beyond—and *then* interfaces to the physical world. This is, to be sure, a surprising fall-back position for defenders of mental/physical transduction—certainly not Cartesian in spirit. But could it work?

The first clue that it cannot is the artificiality of the example. Typing at a keyboard, though genuinely skillful activity, is quite atypical in the digital character of its success conditions. Dreyfus speaks instead of driving, dancing, or pronouncing a foreign language. These, too, are hard to learn; but there is no simple, well-defined test for whether the learner has got it right or wrong. The point is not merely that, like cutting wood or matching colors, you can be more or less right, that errors come in degrees. Rather, for driving, dancing, and even pronunciation, there is no well-defined standard specifying the difference between correct and incorrect. This is not to deny that there *is* a difference between doing well and doing badly, or that experts can tell. Quite the contrary: the claim is that "telling the difference" is itself a skill—one that is likewise hard to learn, and for which there can be no exact specification of what is done, or how.

Even driving, dancing, and pronunciation, however, are more socially circumscribed and narrowly delimited than most of what we do. From cooking to love making, from playing with the kids to shopping in the mall, our lives are filled with activities that exhibit human learning and human intelligence, that some of us are better at than others (as the good ones can tell), but for which none of us could articulate a definitive standard. This is the character of skillful being in the world in general. The simple, interface-like definiteness of what counts as accuracy in typing or color matching is, by contrast, the special case. So the hump in the rug can't slide outward either. We have to make it *all* lie flat.

13 VICARIOUS COPING

If there is no determinate interface between the mind and the body, or between the mind and the world, does this mean that the body and the world are somehow mental, or that the mind is corporeal and mundane? Yes, in a way, both. But not in a way that washes out all distinctions, rendering the three terms synonymous, and therefore redundant. As always, it is a matter of what we are trying to understand. When we are studying anatomy and physiology, the brain is relatively separable from the rest of the organism; the organism itself is even more separable from its environment; and the mind isn't in the picture at all. When, on the other hand, our topic is intelligence, then the mind is very much to the point, and its scope and limits are part of the issue.

Intelligence abides in the *meaningful*. This is not to say that it is surrounded by or directed toward the meaningful, as if they were two separate phenomena, somehow related to one another. Rather, intelligence has its very existence in the meaningful as such—in something like the way a nation's wealth lies in its productive capacity, or a corporation's strength may consist in its market position. Of course, the meaningful, here, cannot be wholly passive and inert, but must include also activity and process. Intelligence, then, is nothing other than the overall interactive structure of meaningful behavior and objects. This is a view shared by scientists and philosophers, all the way from the most classical AI to its most radical critics—including, among others, Simon and Dreyfus. Why?

Perhaps the basic idea can be brought out this way. Intelligence is the ability to deal reliably with more than the present and the manifest. That's surely not an adequate definition of intelligence, but it does get at something essential, and, in particular, something that has to do with meaning. For instance, *representations*—especially *mental* representations—are often taken as the archetype of the meaningful, and that wherein intelligence abides. The connection is straightforward. Representations are clearly an asset in coping with the absent and covert, insofar as they themselves are present, and "stand in for" something else—something absent—which they "represent". This "standing in for" is their meaningfulness; and it is what makes intelligence possible.

How does it work? A typical sort of story goes like this. Individual representations can function as such *only* by participating, in concert with many others, in a larger and norm-governed *scheme* of representation. Then, assuming the scheme itself is in good shape, and is used correctly, a system can vicariously keep track of and explore absent and covert represented phenomena by keeping track of and exploring their present and manifest representational stand-ins. (Really, what it means for a scheme to be "in good shape" is for this coping at one remove to be generally feasible.) In effect, the structure of the extant representations, in conjunction with that of the scheme itself, "encode" something of the structure of what is represented, in such a way that the latter can be accommodated or taken account of, even when out of view.

An alternative understanding of intelligence might keep the basic framework of this account, while modifying certain specifics. Our discussion of transduction, for instance, may have cast some suspicion on the idea of mental representation, or even of mind/world separation. But it need not undermine the broader view that intelligence abides in the meaningful, or that it consists in an ability to deal with the unobvious. Could there be a way to retain these latter, but without the former? That is, could there be a way to understand the effectiveness of intelligence in terms of meaningfulness, but without representations or a separated inner realm?

14 THE WORLD ITSELF AS MEANINGFUL

Not long after the passage about skills and muscular gestalts, Dreyfus addresses exactly this question.

> When we are at home in the world, the meaningful objects embedded in their context of references among which we live are not a model of the world stored in our mind or brain: *they are the world itself.* (265–266)

There are really several (closely related) points being made in this dense and powerful sentence. First, there is, so to speak, the locus of the meaningful; second its character; and third, our situation with regard to it. The meaningful is not in our mind or brain, but is instead essentially worldly. The meaningful is not a model—that is, it's not representational—but is instead objects embedded in their context of references. And we do not store the meaningful inside of ourselves, but rather live and are at home in it. These are all summed up in the slogan that the meaningful *is the world itself.* (This may be reminiscent, anachronistically, of Brooks's later but less radical dictum that the world is its own best model.)

The first thesis, in its negative aspect, is simply a repudiation of the view, almost ubiquitous in cognitive science and traditional philosophy, that the meaningful objects amidst which intelligence abides are primarily *inner*. "Classical" cognitive scientists restrict these inner objects to *symbolic* expressions and models, whereas others are more liberal about mental images, cognitive maps, and maybe even "distributed representations". But Dreyfus wants to extend the meaningful well beyond the inner, in any traditional sense: meaningful objects are "the world itself".

It is important to guard against a possible misunderstanding. Everyone would allow that worldly objects can be meaningful in a *derivative* way, as when we assign to them meanings that we somehow already have. You and I, for instance, could agree to use a certain signal to mean, say, that the British are coming; and then it would indeed mean that—but only derivatively from our decision. (Many philosophers and scientists would hold further that this is the *only* way that external objects can come to be meaningful.) By contrast, when Dreyfus says that meaningful objects are the world itself, he means *original* meaning, not just derivative. That is, intelligence itself abides "out" in the world, not just "inside"—contra cognitive science, classical or otherwise.

The second thesis, in its negative aspect, is again a repudiation of an almost universal assumption: that the meaningful is primarily representational. As before, the target is not only the classical symbolic approach, but most of its more liberal successors. These two negative points combined constitute a rejection of what is sometimes called "the representational theory of the mind". In its positive aspect, that the meaningful is "objects embedded in their context of references", the thesis may call for some explanation. Clearly what Dreyfus has in mind are tools and other paraphernalia. What is the sense in which these are *meaningful*?

We might begin by saying, very roughly, that the meaningful in general is that which is significant in terms of something beyond itself, and subject to normative evaluation according to that significance. Then we could see representations as familiar paradigms of the meaningful in this sense. That in terms of which a representation is significant is that which it purports to represent—its object—and it is evaluated according to whether it represents that object correctly or accurately. When cognitive scientists and philosophers speak of meaningful *inner* entities, they *always* mean representations (nothing *other than* representations has ever been proposed as inner and meaningful). Descartes, in effect, *invented* the "inner realm" as a repository for cognitive representations—above all, representations of what's outside of it—and cognitive science hasn't really changed that at all.

But when Dreyfus holds that meaningful objects are the world itself, he doesn't just (or even mostly) mean representations. The world can't be representation "all the way down". But that's not to say that it can't all be meaningful, because there are more kinds of significance than representational content. A number of philosophers earlier in the twentieth century—Dewey, Heidegger, Wittgenstein, and Merleau-Ponty, to name a few of the most prominent—have made much of the significance of equipment, public places, community practices, and the like. A hammer, for instance, is significant beyond itself in terms of *what it's for*: driving nails into wood, by being wielded in a certain way, in order to build something, and so on. The nails, the wood, the project, and the carpenter him or herself, are likewise caught up in this "web of significance", in their respective ways. These are the meaningful objects that are the world itself; and none of them is a representation.

There's an obvious worry here that the whole point depends on a pun. *Of course*, hammers and the like are "significant" (and even "meaningful") in the sense that they're *important* to us, and *interdependent* with other things in their proper use. But that's not the same as meaning in the sense of bearing content or having a semantics. Certainly! That's why they're *not* representations. So it's agreed: they are meaningful in a broader sense, though not in a narrower one. The real question is: Which sense matters in the context of understanding human intelligence?

15 Knowing the Way

The third thesis is that we live in the meaningful—that is, in the world—and are at home there. Part of the point, to be sure, is that we reside in the midst of our paraphernalia, and are accustomed to it. But the more fundamental insight must connect the meaningful as such with the nature of intelligence. It is clear enough how tools can extend our capacity to cope with the present and manifest; that is more or less the definition of a tool. But how do they help us deal with the absent and covert? Or, rather: aren't those tools that do help us with the absent and covert precisely, and for that very reason, *representations?* Not at all.

Consider the ability to get to San Jose. That's a capacity to deal with something out of view—a distant city—and so just what is characteristic of intelligence. Moreover, a cognitive scientist will instinctively attribute it to some sort of representation, either an internal or external map or set of instructions, which an intelligent system either consists in or can consult and follow. But that's not the only way to achieve the effect. A quite different approach would be to keep a stable of horses, one pre-trained for each likely destination. Then all that the capable person would need to do is pick the right horse, stay on it, and get off at the end. Here we're inclined to say that it's the *horse* that knows the way, not the rider—or maybe that the full ability is really collaborative, say like Gilbert and Sullivan's. At any rate, the horse's contribution is not to be ignored.

Now let me tell you how *I* get to San Jose: I pick the right road (Interstate 880 south), stay on it, and get off at the end.[1] Can we say that the *road* knows the way to San Jose, or perhaps that the road and I *collaborate?* I don't think this is as crazy as it may first sound. The complexity of the road (its shape) is comparable to that of the task and highly specific thereto; moreover, staying on the road requires constant high-bandwidth interaction with this very complexity. In other words, the internal guidance systems and the road itself must be closely coupled, in part because much of the "information" upon which the ability depends is "encoded" *in the road.* Thus, much as an internal map or program, learned and stored in memory, would (*pace* Simon) have to be deemed *part of* an intelligent system that used it to get to San Jose, so I suggest the *road* should be considered *integral to* my ability.

Don't be distracted by the fact that the road was designed and built by intelligent engineers who, no doubt, knew the route. Even if we might want to *extend* the collaboration in this case, the engineers are not essential in the way that road itself is; for some "roads"—forest trails, for instance—need not be intelligently designed, yet the argument works the same for them. A more serious worry is how narrow the example is: intelligent navigation ought to be more flexible, allowing, say, for alternative destinations and starting points. And then it might seem that the *intelligence* lies in this adaptability—knowing how to get there from the east as well as from the north, or where to turn off to get to Palo Alto or Modesto instead—which is internal after all. But, in the first place, even that flexibility is mostly encoded in the world, in the road signs that enable one to choose and stay on the "right" road. And, in the meantime, the road itself still holds the information for getting from one junction to the next. Most important, however, is to remember the point: it's not that *all* of the structure of intelligence is "external", but only that *some* of it is, in a way that is integral to the rest.

16 ABIDING IN THE MEANINGFUL

Still, the road example is quite limited. How much of what a culture has learned about life and its environment is "encoded" in its paraphernalia and practices? Consider, for example, agriculture—without question, a basic manifestation of human intelligence, and dependant on a vast wealth of information accumulated through the centuries. Well, *where* has this information accumulated? Crucial elements of that heritage, I want to claim, are embodied in the shapes and strengths of the plow, the yoke, and the harness, as well as the practices for building and using them. The farmer's learned skills are essential too; but these are nonsense apart from the specific tools they involve, and *vice versa*. Their interaction must be high-bandwidth, in real time. Hence, they constitute an essential unity—a unity that incorporates overall a considerable expertise about the workability of the earth, the needs of young plants, water retention, weed control, root development, and so on.

The structure of an intricate and established institution can likewise be an integral contribution to an understanding of how, say, to build cars or manage a city. That the departments are related *this* way, that the facilities for *that* are over *there*, that *these* requests must be submitted to *those* offices on *such and such* forms—all of this constitutes, if not a theory, at least an essential part of the architecture of a very considerable overall competence. Such competence is as distinctively human as is any other sophisticated art or technology. Yet, not only is it not the competence of any single individual, it is also not the sum of the competencies of all the individuals—for that sum would not include the structure of established interrelationships and institutional procedures, not to mention the physical plant, which are prerequisite to the whole. The point is not merely that organizations evolve in functionally effective ways, as do insects and trees, but rather that the structure of an institution is implemented in the high-band-width intelligent interactions among individuals, as well as between individuals and their paraphernalia. Furthermore, the expertise of those individuals could not be what it is apart from their participation in that structure. Consequently, the intelligence of each is itself intelligible only in terms of their higher unity.

Even in so self-conscious a domain as a scientific laboratory, whether research or development oriented, much of the intelligent ability to investigate, distinguish, and manipulate natural phenomena is embodied in the specialized instrumentation, the manual and perceptual skills required to use and maintain it, and the general laboratory ethos of cleanliness, deliberation, and record keeping. Without these, science would be impossible; they are *integral* to it. The point is not that theory is baseless without evidence, or useless without applications. Rather, apart from its intimate involvement in highly specific complex activities in highly specific complex circumstances, there's no such thing as scientific intelligence—it doesn't make any sense. For all its explicitness and abstraction, science is as worldly as agriculture, manufacturing, and government.

I have postponed till last the most obvious externalization of human intelligence—texts, images, maps, diagrams, programs, and the like—not because I underestimate their importance, but because they are so similar to what is traditionally supposed to be in the mind. That poses two dangers. First, it distracts attention from the radicalness of the claim that intelligence abides in the meaningful *world*: not just books and records, but roads and plows, offices, laboratories, and communities. Second, it makes it too easy for a traditionalist to think: "External representations are not really integral to intelligence, but are merely devices for conveying or restoring to intelligence proper—the inner mind—contents which it might otherwise lack." By now, however, these dangers will (I hope) have abated. So it can safely be acknowledged that (to borrow Simon's phrase) the "great furniture of information" that civilization has accumulated belongs with the rest of its furniture in the abode of its understanding.

17 CONCLUSION

If we are to understand mind as the locus of intelligence, we cannot follow Descartes in regarding it as separable in principle from the body and the world. I have argued that such separability would have to coincide with narrow-bandwidth interfaces, among the interactions that are relevant to intelligence. In recent decades, a commitment to understanding intelligence as rational problem solving—sometimes assumed *a priori*—has supported the existence of these interfaces by identifying them with transducers. Broader approaches, freed of that prejudicial commitment, can look again at perception and action, at skillful involvement with public equipment and social organization, and see not principled separation but all sorts of close coupling and functional unity. As our ability to cope with the absent and covert, human intelligence abides in the meaningful—which, far from being restricted to representations, extends to the entire human world. Mind, therefore, is not incidentally but *intimately* embodied and *intimately* embedded in its world.

NOTE:

1 The "road to San Jose" example is inspired by a discussion in Batali (unpublished).

Truth

CHAPTER TEN

Objective Perception

1 PERCEIVING OBJECTS AS SUCH

I want to distinguish and characterize what I take to be a special case among broadly sensory or perceptual phenomena. Some might maintain that this case is the only genuine case of perception properly so called; but I will sidestep that largely terminological issue, and simply specify the kind of case I mean as *objective perception*—not worrying about what to call other kinds of case. It is part of my view, though not part of what I will argue for, that objective perception, in this sense, is exclusive to people. This is not to deny that, in some other or wider sense or senses, animals perceive too; nor is it to deny that people also perceive in some or all of these other senses; nor, finally, is it to deny that some other senses of perception may also be distinctive of people (such as aesthetic perception). It is only to claim that at least some human perception is "objective" in a special sense, and no animal perception is.[1] Though I will not be defending this claim, I will have it always in mind, and will occasionally take it for granted in choosing illustrations.

The qualifier 'objective' is intended to suggest perception *of objects as objects*. Thus, it is very much part of the undertaking to spell out what is meant by the *object* of a perceiving. It should be clear at the outset, therefore, that 'object' is used in a formal sense, to identify a role or position vis-à-vis (for instance) perception; in particular, it does not carry any implications about the nature of the objects perceived—such as that they be substantial, corporeal, or otherwise thing-like. Objectivity in perception is a kind of structure that involves the perceiving, that which is perceived, and the relation between them. The aim is to delineate this distinctive structure and its presuppositions.

Several familiar problem areas in the philosophy of perception will be seen to converge in this topic, among them: (i) picking out what is perceived from among the various causal antecedents of the perceiving; (ii) the normativity of objective perception (that is, the possibility of *mis*perception); (iii) the respect in which objective perception depends on an understanding of what is perceived; (iv) the relevance of language to the possibility of objective perception; and (v) the prerequisite character of the perceiving self or subject. On the other hand, a number of other important issues connected with perception will not enter directly into the present discussion, including in particular: (i) the peculiar "of-this-ness" or indexicality of perceptual content; (ii) the richness of (apparently) ineffable yet determinate detail in perceptual content; and (iii) the special connection (if any) between perception and imagery or imagination.

2 DRETSKE ON THE OBJECT PERCEIVED

It is convenient to begin with the identification of what is perceived—the "object" in a broad sense—from among the many causal antecedents of the perceiver's perceiving. We can take for granted that, at least in ordinary sensory perception, the perceived object is *one* (or some) of those antecedents. The question is: *Which* one? Or, rather, the question is: On what principled basis can we identify one among them as "the" object? For instance, if I look at and see a bicycle, part of the cause of that perceiving in me is the presence and properties of the bike—particularly those properties that determine in detail how it reflects light. But other important causal factors include the ambient light around me (as reflected in part by the bike), the source of the illumination of the bike in the first place, the source of the bike itself, the functioning of my visual system, and so on. We want to say that what I perceive, the object of my perception, is the bicycle, and none of these other factors. The question is: Why?

Dretske (1981, chapter 6, especially pages 155–168) suggests that the object of a perceptual state is whatever that state carries information about in a primary way. "Carrying information" is the operative notion. Roughly: given conditions of kind K, a's being F carries the information that b is G just in case a could not have been F in such conditions had b not been G. To put it anthropomorphically, a's being F carries the information that b is G if you can *"tell"* from a's being F (and the conditions being K) that b is G. It carries this information in a *primary* way if it does not carry it "via" any other fact, such as c's being H. Intuitively, to say that a's being F carries the information that b is G via c's being H means that it carries that information *only because* it carries the information that c is H, and c's being H carries in turn the information that b is G.[2]

Dretske illustrates the point by explaining why, when someone rings the doorbell, we hear the bell ringing but we don't hear the button being pushed. Under normal conditions, our perceptual response—what Dretske calls the "perceptual experience"—carries both the information that the button is pushed and the information that the bell is ringing. This is because we wouldn't have that experience if the button weren't pushed, nor would we have it if the bell weren't ringing. But the *only reason* we wouldn't have it if the button weren't pushed is that we wouldn't have it if the bell weren't ringing, *and* (under normal conditions) the bell wouldn't ring if the button weren't pushed. Hence, the information about the button is carried *via* the information about the bell.

To see how this works, consider the (abnormal) conditions in which the bell wires occasionally short, thereby ringing the bell without the button being pushed. Under those conditions, the same experience would still carry the information that the bell was ringing, but it would no longer carry the information that the button was pushed—precisely because the bell's ringing would itself no longer carry that information. So, even in normal conditions, when the perceptual experience does carry the information that the button is pushed, it does so only *via* the bell's ringing. Hence, the experience does not carry the information about the button in a primary, but only a secondary way. And this is why, according to Dretske, the button is not the object of the perception. Even though we can *tell* that the button is pushed, we do not *perceive* that it is (unless we happen also to be outside watching). What we *hear* is not the button but the bell.

The more interesting and difficult question is why the experience carries even the information about the *bell* in a primary way. It might be argued, for instance, that the experience also carries the information that the air or our eardrum is vibrating in a certain manner, and that, moreover, it carries the information that the bell is ringing only via this information about the air or eardrum.[3] In that case, only the latter information would be carried in a primary way; and then, by the above logic, it would have to be conceded that what we *really* hear, even under normal conditions, is the air or our eardrum, rather than the bell.

Dretske's reply to this challenge is ingenious, but ultimately, I think, unsuccessful. It has two stages. In the first stage, he points out that one thing's being the case can carry the information that another is, without carrying any information about the intervening causal processes, if (in the relevant conditions) any of several different causal processes might have occurred, and each would have had the same result. Thus, suppose that the mantle bowl only has lemon drops in it when one of the children buys some, and that the children only buy lemon drops when Grampa provides the funds. Then, if there are lemon drops in the bowl today, that fact carries the information that Grampa recently paid, but it carries no information as to *which* grandchild fetched—because they're all equally eager and able. *A fortiori*, it can't carry the former information *via* carrying the latter.

The second stage, then, is to argue that the different ways the air or eardrum might vibrate when we hear the bell ring are like the different grandchildren that might fetch the candy for Grampa. That is, the perceptual experience must have been caused by some vibration or other that could only have been caused (in the relevant conditions) by the bell ringing; but there are any number of such vibrations that would have sufficed with no difference in effect. Under those conditions, the experience would carry the information that the bell is ringing without carrying any information as to *which* of the sufficient vibrations mediated causally. Thus, the distal information (about the bell) is not carried *via* any more proximal information (about how the air or eardrum is vibrating), for the simple reason that the proximal information is not carried (by that experience) at all. And this is why it is the bell which we hear after all.

How is this argument made out? Dretske appeals to perceptual constancy effects, which, as he rightly points out, are ubiquitous. We do not perceive the table as changing shape when we walk around it, changing size when we approach, or changing color as daylight gives way to dusk and then to candles, even though the proximal stimuli— the patterns of light entering our eyes or the patterns of neuron firings in our retinas—vary dramatically. Thus, we see the table as equally square, whether our vantage is such that its retinal projection is itself square, rhomboid, or trapezoid. So, (under normal conditions) the perception carries the information that the table is square, without carrying any information as to *which* retinal projection happened, on this occasion, to mediate the perceiving causally. Accordingly, it carries the information about the table in a primary way—not via carrying information about any proximal stimulus—and hence it is the *table* which we see.

The essential difficulty here lies in the characterization of the proximal stimulus. Note that the argument depends on the claim that the *same* perceptual experience of the *same* object can be mediated by *different* stimuli; for, if only one stimulus could mediate, then the experience would carry information about it, and hence the information about the object would not be carried in a primary way. For purposes of discussion, we can accept the suggestion, based on perceptual constancy, that in some sense the experience and the object remain the same; the question concerns the sense in which the respective proximal stimuli are different. Of course, it's *qualitative* difference—difference in kind—that's at issue; and whether two instances differ in kind depends on which kinds are being considered.

Which kinds need Dretske consider? Since the argument depends on a nonexistence claim, it must, in effect, consider *all* kinds. For if there were *any* single kind of stimulus that mediated all and only the constant perceivings (same kind of perception of the same kind of object), then the perception would carry the information that the stimulus was of that kind, and hence would carry the information about the distal object only *via* the information about the stimulus. Dretske points out that there are respects in which the stimuli differ: some are rhomboid projections, some trapezoid, and so on. But that isn't enough; he must argue that there is *no* respect in which these stimuli (and only these) are all alike.

Of course, such a kind would not be as simple as the shape of an instantaneous optical projection on the retina. And Dretske even mentions (1981, 164), as plausible explanations of constancy phenomena, the existence of "'higher order' variables in the stimulus array" and "global characteristics of the entire stimulus pattern" to which our sensory systems are sensitive.[4] Unaccountably, however, he never considers the possibility that such "higher order" and more "global" stimulus *kinds* might undermine his account of why the stimulus itself is not perceived. That is, he never considers the possibility that the perceptual response carries the information that the (proximal) stimulus is of such a (higher order, global) kind, and thus carries information about the (distal) object only via that information about the stimulus.[5]

What's worse, it seems that there *must* be such kinds, if sensory perception is to be possible at all. For if one *can* reliably recognize the squareness of the table from varying perspectives, then there must be *something*—something higher order, global, relative to context, or whatever—normally common to all and only the stimuli from such objects, on pain of rendering perception magical. To be sure, perception is not 100% reliable, in part because stimuli of the relevant kinds can be produced artificially (or accidentally) even when the corresponding objects are not present. But this is no help to Dretske. Quite the contrary: it not only suggests that there *are* the stimulus kinds that his account can't allow, but also that perceptual responses track these kinds primarily, and the object kinds only *via* them.

3 THE OBJECTS OF CHESS PERCEPTION

So far, the question has been: Why, despite being *via* (proximal) stimuli, is perception *of* (distal) objects. The answer, as we have seen, cannot depend on the absence of suitable kinds for the stimuli to instantiate. Thus, presumably it must depend instead on something positive about the objects themselves, and about perceiving them. It is crucial, however, not to suppose at the outset that *objects* are an unproblematic fixed point, and the only issue is how perception gets to be *of them*. In particular, we must not tacitly presuppose that being an object is tantamount to being a temporally and spatially cohesive corporeal lump. Rather, the "objecthood" of perceptual objects and the "of-ness" of perception go hand in hand, and are intelligible only in terms of one another, something like the interdependence of target and aim, or puzzle and solution. So, the deeper question is: How and *why* is such a structure—what we might call *the structure of objectivity*—imposed on the physics and physiology of sensation?

In order to avoid the prejudicial presupposition that we know in advance what "objects" are, I shall turn temporarily to a different sort of example, one in which the temptation to equate 'object' with 'body' is perhaps less compelling. In this context, it will be possible to ask what it is about the objects that lets them be objective, without the distraction of supposed "obviousness". That is, the question can really be confronted and maybe even answered. On that basis, then, we will be able to return to the case of ordinary corporeal "things" with clearer horizons.

The special case I want to consider is chess, when the game is played in a visible medium—that is, such that one can *see* positions, threats, moves, and the like. I can, for instance, see you castling, early in the midgame; a little later, I can see your knight simultaneously threatening my queen and rook, in a so-called knight fork; and, before long, I can even see the untenability of my entire king-side defense, and conclude that I might as well resign. We should not try to imagine that these perceptual abilities are all built up out of a handful of "primitive" or "atomic" abilities, such as identifying the individual pieces and squares. I can recognize a knight fork just as "immediately" as I can recognize a knight or a square; and it may not even be possible to define 'untenable king side' in terms of pieces and locations—suggesting that they can *only* be perceived as gestalts.

What's involved in seeing these objects? An instructive first indication is the fact that dogs and cats can't see them at all. Without broaching, for the moment, the question of what exactly they *do* see, we can be quite sure that no dog or cat could see even a rook as such on the K2 square, never mind the power, daring, or foolishness of that position. And the reason is not far to find: dogs and cats don't have a clue about chess. The very possibility of such a game, and all that it entails, is utterly alien to them. We might gather, then, that some grasp or understanding of the game of chess, and maybe also of games more generally, is prerequisite to any ability to perceive the phenomena manifested in chess play. But it will be worth the trouble to proceed more slowly, and explore what such a grasp amounts to, and why it is required.

Surely no creature or system can see a given configuration as a knight fork without having some sense of what a knight fork is. To put it in a familiar but perhaps misleading terminology, nothing can *apply* a concept unless it *has* that concept.[6] Of course, having a sense (or "concept") of what something is cannot be merely an ability to detect it reliably, or discriminate it from other things; locks, for instance, reliably detect the keys that fit them, and it's not out of the question that pigeons could be trained to discriminate (for a given chess set) positions containing knight forks.

In the case of chess, however, even the discrimination problem is harder than that; for chess sets can be implemented in all sorts of styles and media, from labeled slips of paper or computer-screen icons to costumed palace servants or elaborately painted helicopters. Knight forks are equally knight forks in any of these sets; but, to see them, a perceiver would have to "abstract from" the gross and conspicuous differences of implementation, and attend only to the chess-relevant features of the configurations.

Indeed, the matter is still more complicated, because other games, quite different from chess, can be played with the board and tokens that we ordinarily call chess sets. And it could well happen that, in the course of such a game, an arrangement occurs that would be a knight fork were chess being played. But, in fact, it's nothing like a knight fork, because, in this game, the pieces move (or are used) completely differently—the token that would typically implement a knight in chess doesn't implement a knight in this domain at all. So, in order to see that a certain configuration is a knight fork, a perceiver must first be able to see, or otherwise appreciate, that it has occurred in the midst of a *chess* game.

These complementary considerations, that chess can be played in widely different media, and that widely different games can be played in the same media, together with the fact that knight forks can occur (and be perceived) in all of the former but none of the latter, show that the ability to perceive knight forks presupposes some grasp or understanding of the game of chess—at least enough to tell when it's being played, regardless of medium. The same point is even more obvious for seeing that a king-side defense is untenable; and a little reflection shows that it is equally true for seeing that some piece is a knight (a *chess* knight), or anything else that occurs only in chess games. Chess games are a kind of *pattern*, and chess phenomena can only occur within this pattern, as *subpatterns* of it. The point about different media and different games is that these subpatterns would not be what they are, and hence could not be recognized, except as subpatterns of a superordinate pattern with the specific structure of chess—not a pattern of shape or color, therefore, but a pattern at what we might call *"the chess level"*. To put it more metaphysically, the game of chess is *constitutive* for chess phenomena, and *therefore* some grasp of it is prerequisite to their perceivability as such.

The pivotal phrase, "some grasp or understanding", has so far been left dangerously vague. It is all too easy to gloss this grasp as: knowing the rules (including the starting and goal configurations) that define the game—what one might get by reading Hoyle or the instructions on the box. But there are several reasons to resist this temptation. In the first place, it's not obvious that reading (and understanding) the rules is the same as, or even sufficient for, understanding the game. Second, and more to the point, it's not obvious that *knowing* the rules is required for understanding the game, at least not if knowing is taken in a sense that implies discursive cognizance of the rules in some explicit formulation (such as one gets by reading). But third, and most important, chess is serving here just as an example; the hope, without which the example would not repay the effort, is to generalize its lessons to less specialized cases—in particular, to cases for which, though there are constitutive prerequisites, these prerequisites have never been (and perhaps cannot ever be) articulated in any "rules according to Hoyle".

4 CHESS OBJECTS WITHOUT LANGUAGE

Too often, I believe, philosophers take it on faith that what *essentially* distinguishes people is language—"essentially" in the sense that all our other interesting differentia (society, morality, objectivity, self-understanding, history, science, normativity, sense of humor, ...) flow from, or at least necessarily involve, this one. It seems to me, on the contrary, that some of these—objectivity, in particular—are fundamentally independent of language, and that we misunderstand them if we overlook this independence. Accordingly, I want now to indulge in a brief thought experiment, by imagining some creatures that are, in certain respects, intermediate between known animals and people.

These creatures—"super-monkeys", we could call them—are subhuman in that they have no linguistic facility whatever: they neither produce nor understand speech (nor any other articulate gestures or signs to the same effect). This is not to say they never cry out in pain, make warning signals, or give mating displays; but they never, for instance, tell stories, describe things, or formulate rules. On the other hand, they stand out from all other animals in that they learn and play games, including sophisticated games like chess.

Since super-monkeys are animals, and in fact a lot like us, there is no problem in ascribing to them, not only various beliefs and desires (at least in the minimal sense of Dennett's "intentional systems theory"—1981/87), but also a considerable range of affects and moods, emotions and motives. It's perfectly obvious, for instance, that they *like* strawberries (as well as the janitor who brings them), that they *enjoy* frolicking in the pool (but would sometimes rather sleep), that they get *angry* when picked on, because it *hurts*, and that's *why* they strike back. These qualities sharply differentiate super-monkeys from any current or imminent generation of "game-playing" computer.

What should we look for in super-monkeys, if we are to understand them as playing games, even though they don't talk about it? Well, of course, they must *at least* reliably go through the motions; that is, they must actually move the pieces, not merely in accord with the rules, but in a manner more or less suited to winning. And, in the spirit of the above remarks about emotions and motives, we can expect them to be pleased and self-satisfied when they do win (or gain ground), and dejected or frustrated at the opposite. This shows that, in one sense, they are not *just* going through the motions, for the outcomes evidently matter to them. But it does not yet show that the motions are specifically *chess* moves, for it has not been shown that they are made as and only as subpatterns of a superordinate pattern at the chess level. Such further specificity is not hard to add, however: we merely require that our super-monkeys also be able to play chess in various media, and other games in the same media. This is not at all a trivial or inconsequential requirement; but it does not seem to presuppose linguistic facility, so it remains within the parameters of the thought experiment.

Super-monkeys, as described so far, are clearly guided in their moves by sensory input from the chess board; and so, in at least that limited sense, they are certainly perceiving. When we ask, however, with Dretske, what the perception is *of*, the situation is more complicated. On the one hand, since the *responses* involved are not limited to (and may not even include) inner experiences, but are rather themselves also movings of the chess pieces, we have, so to speak, a new "angle" on the *objects*: they are *both* perceived *and* acted on. Of course, just as we can ask about perception, why it is of a distal rather than a proximal cause, we can ask about action why it is of a distal rather than a proximal effect—why it is an action of moving a knight, for instance, rather than of moving an arm and some fingers. But the fact that the piece on the chess board is the one place where these two causal trajectories intersect, and especially if there is continuous feedback, as in visually guided movement, strongly suggests that it is the proper object of both the perception and the action. It is this feedback linkage, I believe, that inclines us to identify, to the extent that we do, the "objects" of ordinary animal perception and action.

On the other hand, we should notice the restricted scope of this feedback argument. It applies to a chess piece only insofar as it is a sensible, manipulable token, and has nothing whatever to do with its role or character in chess. In other words, the question of whether *chess* phenomena can be the objects of perception (or action), even for super-monkeys, has not yet been touched. And, in fact, the earlier argument brought against Dretske's information-based proposal, applies here as well. For, if chess phenomena are the phenomena they are by virtue of the way they are subpatterns within a superordinate pattern at the chess level, then, *inevitably* (under normal conditions), the proximal stimulus patterns are instances of corresponding kinds, according as they are subpatterns of higher order and more global patterns in the proximal stimuli overall. These latter patterns will have to be comparable in "level" to the chess level, in that they abstract from features that are characteristic of the various different media, and depend instead on the global relationships that define chess games as chess. But there is no reason to deny the existence of such patterns, and hence of such stimulus *kinds*.

5   LETTING THE STANDARDS GOVERN

There is, however, one more requirement that super-monkeys will have to meet if they are to be recognized as genuine chess-players; and this last requirement will prove crucial also for objectivity. It can be introduced by asking what happens in the face of an *illegal* move. We have already required, of course, that, as candidate chess players at all, super-monkeys must *reliably* make legal moves; and in undertaking to play they must, in effect, be counting on this reliability in one another. This cannot mean, however, that they have to be perfect, or that they can take perfection for granted, in the sense of being unprepared to deal with illegality.[7] No system that would blithely ignore the illegality of an opponent's move could properly be deemed a chess player.

Hence, any genuine chess player—in fact, any game player—must, as such, occupy a peculiar position. A player must, on the one hand, be ever *vigilant against* illegal moves, yet, on the other hand, always *count on* consistent legality.[8] These two are more intimately related than they might seem. Let's examine them in turn.

As vigilant, a player needs two quite distinct abilities: (i) to tell in general what move is made (including any relevant context),[9] whenever a player makes a move; and (ii) to tell, for any identifiable move, whether that move would be legal.[10] These abilities together (but neither of them alone) enable players reliably to detect illegal moves—an obvious prerequisite to vigilance. The first ability, in effect, induces a field of recognizable moves (that is, identifiable phenomena that are either legal or illegal); and the second induces a partition on that field (into the legal and the illegal). Clearly, the field of identifiable moves had better include candidates on both sides of that partition, lest the vigilance be vacuous. That is: it must be possible to identify moves that would be illegal—moves, in other words, that are *ruled out* by those very rules that are constitutive for chess phenomena and their identification at all. To say that these abilities are distinct is to say that they have within them this essential possibility of *discord*.

Counting on consistent legality means more than just expecting it, but something like *insisting* on it—on pain of giving up the game. This insistence is a kind of *commitment* or *resolve* not to tolerate illegality: in case an illegal move is detected, ordinary play is breached, extraordinary measures are called for—and the game itself (that is, continued play) is at stake in the outcome. The vigilant player's insistence, therefore, is a commitment not to stand for the kind of discord (between the above two abilities), the possibility of which is prerequisite to vigilance in the first place. So the extraordinary measures, when called for, will be an attempt to eliminate this discord, by rectifying either the identification of the move or the determination of its legality. As we shall see, it is this commitment to the definitive standards constitutive for the domain as such (for instance, to the rules of chess) that transmits normative force (including the potential for correction) to the move identification ability, and hence underlies the possibility of its objectivity. Hence, the capacity for such commitment is a prerequisite character of any self or subject that is to be capable also of objective perception (or thought or action).

Suppose, for example, that Bobby Baboon is in the midst of a chess game when his "illegal-move alarm" goes off. As a genuine chess player, Bobby is antecedently disposed to take extraordinary measures in the face of such an event, and to adjust accordingly. And among those measures will be to "double check" his identification of what move was actually made. The details of this double checking are not important. But we can imagine Bobby looking over the board again, perhaps from different angles, checking for overhanging branches or bad lighting obscuring part of the board, making sure that what he took for a bishop isn't really a knight seen from the back, and so on. We can even imagine that Bobby is still getting used to an unfamiliar chess set, and sometimes has to remind himself (or be reminded) which pieces are which. (Basically similar things could be said about Bobby "double checking" or "reconsidering" his assessment that the move was illegal—perhaps he forgot about capturing *en passant*, for example.)

It is crucial that this double checking be an effort, and that "success" not be automatic. If Bobby turned up a "misperception" every time he looked for one, then the *checking* would be a sham. Rather, we must suppose that the double-checking is an extension, elaboration, or more careful mode of the primary recognition ability, together with an ability to tell whether the result is coming up different, and to adjust if so. (Still more impressive would be a capacity to diagnose what went wrong in cases where a misperception is uncovered; but I don't see that this is required.) The enabling assumption is that, almost always, this more careful mode is unnecessary, because it wouldn't make any difference. But, occasionally, it would make a difference; and, in those cases (often flagged by the alarm), the result of the more careful mode is almost always *better*.

What does "better" mean? It means: more conducive to continued chess play, in the long run. Playing a game governed by constitutive standards is a nontrivial *achievement*; dogs and ordinary monkeys, for instance, are utterly incapable of it.[11] The mark of such an achievement is not an ability to articulate those standards as explicit rules, nor is it a disposition to go through any particular motions of play. Rather, it is the ability to play in fact, while at the same time putting the game itself at stake in insisting on the standards; that is, it is the ability to *let the standards govern* the play. Thus, the aforementioned possibility of discord—a possibility which, on the one hand, is reliably avoided, but, on the other hand, is resolutely not tolerated—is fundamental. Realizing a set of dispositions that works with this structure is the achievement; and the fine tuning effected in the double checking is best to the extent that it fosters this achievement.

6 OBJECTS DETERMINE PERCEPTUAL CORRECTNESS

Notice that, almost incidentally, we have now assembled the resources needed to answer Dretske's question. What the perception is *of* is that which the constitutive standards govern: the moves, pieces, positions, and so on, in the chess game. Why? Because, when the possibility of a *mis*perception arises, what the issue turns on is telling how things stand with regard to those standards. That's what *accurate* perception is counted on to tell; it's what is checked for in the double checking; it's the way in which perceptual ability contributes to the game-playing achievement. In other words, the *norms* governing the perceptions as such, and in virtue of which they can be objective, are inseparable from the *standards* governing, and indeed constituting, the chess phenomena as such; or, to make the Kantian paraphrase even more obvious: the conditions of the *possibility of objective perception* as such are likewise the conditions of the *possibility of the objects of that perception*.[12]

To be concrete, suppose that, on a certain occasion, the actual chess position is of one kind, but (due to some quirk in the circumstances) the ambient optic array around Bobby, and hence also his perceptual response, is of the sort usually caused by chess positions of some other kind. Is his response a misperception of the chess position, or an accurate perception of the ambient array? Clearly the former—*because* what's at issue in the perceiving at all, the whole point of *looking* in the first place, is telling what the position is. And this is manifest in the fact that, if Bobby's alarm goes off and he discovers the discrepancy, he will change his response; that is, to the best of his ability, he will bring his response into line with the actual position, rather than the optic array (the entire aim and purpose of double checking). Therefore, even when there is no discrepancy, it is the position and not the array that is perceived.

This shows, I believe, that our imaginary super-monkeys are capable of objective perception—like people, and unlike any (actual) animals. The fact that these super-monkeys are completely nonlinguistic shows further that language is not prerequisite to objective perception, and hence that it is not language that fundamentally separates us from the animals with regard to the possibility of objectivity. On the other hand, the fact that putative perceptions are normatively beholden to their objects, subject to correction in light of double-checking those objects, is integral to the account. What's more, these norms are completely dependent in force and content on the constitutive standards to which the perceived objects are held, and which must therefore be counted primary. And it is, finally, the super-monkeys themselves that "hold" those objects to those standards. Such holding to standards, by simultaneously counting on it and insisting on it, is, when it succeeds, understanding. Thus, the objects of objective perception are *ipso facto* understood. *Understanding*, not language, is what separates super-monkeys (and us) from "thoughtless brutes".

7 CHESS WITHOUT LANGUAGE (REVISITED)

That there might actually be "super-monkeys" that learn and play games like chess without benefit of language is, to be sure, practically incredible. Hence, the intended point and force of the example calls for explanation. It will help first to rehearse a few notable objections. Thus, it is extremely unlikely that the cognitive and social capacities prerequisite for chess would evolve prior to and independently of those required for language. For, clearly, there is a great deal of overlap in these capacities; and they would have far more survival value if used for language than if used only for formal games. It could even be that our own ability to play chess relies essentially on species-specific "modules" that are integral to our linguistic faculty—such as our ability to parse complex structures, or to see individual tokens as tokens of digital types, or to remember a large "vocabulary" of possible constituents.

Likewise, it is almost impossible to imagine *teaching* chess, even to a creature with all the native capacities of homo sapiens, without verbal instruction and admonition. How could one hope to convey the relevant alternatives and restrictions in various situations without explicit conditionals and modal adverbs? Indeed, if genuine chess presupposes not just that the moves in fact be legal, but that the players insist on this, then they had better have a way of expressing their insistence. Expressions of insistence, moreover, cannot be the same as mere expressions of displeasure, dismay, or disapproval; for those could have any number of possible grounds, whereas insistence (as used here) can be grounded only in issues of constitutive legality. But that means that expressions of insistence must be somehow marked as such, marked as concerned with issues of legality, so as to communicate specifically that concern. And wouldn't such specifically marked, communicative expression be tantamount to language?[13]

Objections based on actual or plausible evolutionary history, however, are beside the point. Thus, it might also be that chess-like games could not have emerged until after prehensile hands; but, even if so, that wouldn't say much of interest about the games as such. The arguments that matter, therefore, are those to the effect that chess itself presupposes language, either for learning it or for playing it. But to those, I think, a simple reply is decisive. It is certainly no harder to learn and play chess than it is to learn and speak a natural language. Quite the contrary: games are clearly much less demanding than languages on all counts. In particular, languages are just as constituted by standards, hence just as dependent on speakers' *insistence*, as any game. Yet, it must be possible to learn and speak a language without benefit of (any other or prior) language, on pain of regress. So, in principle, it's possible for games as well.[14]

There remains the idea that chess itself might *be* a language. It goes without saying that languages and games are similar in many ways—to the extent that it has become a philosophical cliché to refer to languages as "games". Nevertheless, there are also many differences, including the following, which is both easy to see and crucial. Chess, like all formal games, is *self-contained* in the sense that what moves would be proper (legal) on any given occasion depends only on factors that are *internal* to the game—previous moves, the locations of other pieces, and the like. By contrast, for any genuine language, what it is proper to say on a given occasion—what is true, authorized, materially valid, and so on—depends in general on more than the specifically *linguistic* context. Therefore, no formal game is (in and of itself) a language.

Why belabor the point? I certainly do not deny that language is characteristic of people, and centrally important to what we are. But I want to resist what strikes me as an all too prevalent tendency to make of language a magic fulcrum on which every human quality turns—as if language were the whole essence of what distinguishes us from machines on the one hand, and beasts on the other. That, I believe, is a grave distortion, for many reasons, most of which go beyond the present discussion. Even in the context of a theory of perception, however, it is important not to overestimate the role of language (if only because *correct* perception is prerequisite to dialog itself).

Playing chess, like speaking, involves interacting with items and structures in ways that depend—not just causally but normatively—on their types (roles), their reidentification as individuals (histories), and their relations to other items and structures ("contexts"). The ability to engage in such interaction is at least the greater part of what is meant by a *conceptual* grasp. Granted, a person who can talk and theorize might have more and richer concepts of chess phenomena than could a nonlinguistic super-monkey. Yet the basic concept of, say, a rook is determined by its role in the game; and any creature that can play must have mastered that. Concepts are in general articulated by their relations to one another, as expressed in the detailed contingencies of acceptable practice. Often these contingencies are primarily linguistic, and, in particular, inferential. But, as the chess example shows, they need not be: proper chess play itself, without verbal accompaniment, is sufficiently structured to institute a conceptual articulation of the corresponding phenomena.

8 SCIENTIFIC COMMITMENTS AND OBJECTIVITY

It must be acknowledged that chess is not a typical example of a perceptual domain. The question therefore arises whether the account of objectivity, in terms of constitutive standards, insistence, and achievement, might be limited to games and their ilk. We ask, that is, whether the account depends essentially on any features peculiar to such domains, or whether it depends only on features characteristic of objective perception more generally. The following stand out as distinctive of chess and the like—in contrast, for instance, to scientific observation and everyday perception of sticks and stones.

1 Chess is defined by constitutive standards (rules) that are arbitrary human inventions; they do not have the character of empirical discoveries, liable to refutation. (Even so, the rules of a playable game must be consistent, complete, and followable—an achievement that is not at all automatic.)

2 When chess players insist upon legal moves, this is understood primarily in terms of rule-compliance by other players—agents who can be held to account for their behavior. (Less often an issue, though just as important, is insistence that the board and pieces function properly—by not melting, wandering around, or such like.)

3 It is almost always easy to tell what move has been made in a chess game, and whether that move is legal—because the game is digital, explicitly defined, and relatively simple. (On the other hand, further perceptual skills, such as recognizing strategic weaknesses and opportunities, are not easy and may well not be reducible to these basic discriminations.)

Science, by contrast, seems anything but arbitrary an invention: its discoveries are a paragon of the empirical and refutable. Moreover, scientists never hold observable phenomena to account for their behavior: if some observed phenomenon fails to accord with scientific expectations, it is the observation or expectations that are at fault, not the phenomenon itself. Finally, scientific investigation is difficult: it takes years of training plus painstaking effort, both to perform reliable experiments and to tell with confidence what results are acceptable.

This, however, is not to deny that the objects of scientific study are held to standards. Donald Davidson (1970/80, 211 and 219–222), for instance, more or less defines the *physical* as that which can be picked out in terms drawn exclusively from a closed, comprehensive theory with strong constitutive elements and precise, explicit, exception-free laws.[15] This is as much as to say that being subsumable under such a theory—*strict subsumability*, we might call it—is a constitutive standard for the physical: to *be* physical is to be strictly subsumable.

Speaking in a similar vein, but of the history of chemistry, Thomas Kuhn writes:

> Changes in the standards governing permissible problems, concepts, and explanations can transform a science. In the next section I shall even suggest a sense in which they transform the world.   (1962/70, 106)

And, in the next section, he continues:

> For Dalton, any reaction in which the ingredients did not enter in fixed proportion was *ipso facto* not a purely chemical process. A law that experiment could not have established before Dalton's work, became, once that work was accepted, a constitutive principle that no single set of chemical measurements could have upset. ... As a result, chemists came to live in a world where reactions behaved quite differently from the way they had before.   (133–134)

In other words, the principle of fixed proportions became a constitutive standard for what it is to *be* a chemical reaction—and thereby also for being an element or a compound. Kuhn, however, unlike Davidson, is concerned not merely with the notion of standards for *entities*, but with the implications of this view for the conduct of science.

> Finally, at a still higher level, there is another set of commitments without which no man is a scientist. The scientist must, for example, be concerned to understand the world and to extend the precision and scope with which it has been ordered. That commitment must, in turn, lead him to scrutinize, either

for himself or through colleagues, some aspect of nature in great empirical detail. And if that scrutiny displays pockets of apparent disorder, then these must challenge him to a new refinement of his observational techniques or to a further articulation of his theories.

(42)

Scientists, that is to say, are *scientists* by virtue of their *commitments*—in particular, commitments that require what we have earlier called *vigilance*. "Pockets of apparent disorder" are nothing other than apparent breaches of the relevant constitutive standards, the exact analog of apparent illegal moves; and scientists must simultaneously be on the lookout for them, and resolved not to tolerate them. Scientists *insist* that the scientifically observed world be orderly (strictly subsumable, for instance). Moreover, their alternatives in the face of an apparent breach are essentially the same as those available to a chess player: refinement of observational technique, further articulation of the theory,[16] or giving up the game (scientific breakdown and/ or revolution).

The constitutive standards for the objects of scientific research—whether local to particular disciplines, like combining in fixed proportions, or global throughout science as such, like displaying an order with precision and scope—are not arbitrary inventions. On the other hand, they are not exactly empirical discoveries either; for, as Kuhn is at pains to show, accurate observations and discoveries presuppose them, and they are not readily dislodged. They are somehow *both* empirical *and* invented—"synthetic a priori", Davidson says (1970/80, 221). Standards for the constitution of objects are worked out by fits and starts over many years, such that, in accord with them, ever more objects can be scrutinized in great empirical detail and ordered with precision and scope. "It is hard", Kuhn notes (135), "to make nature fit a paradigm"; and a fundamental component in that difficulty is coming up with paradigms that nature can be made to fit. Scientists may invent the recipe; but experiment is the proof of the pudding. Like chess—only far more so—science is an *achievement*.

It is an old problem in the philosophy of science to say just what is measured by a scientific instrument. In particular, in what sense can it be said that so-called "theoretical" entities and properties are measured, as opposed to "phenomenal" or "observational" properties or states of the instrument itself? Notice that this question has essentially the same structure as Dretske's question about how we can say that we hear the bell, and not the vibrations in the air or our eardrums. And the solution, it seems to me, is essentially the same too. What the measurement is *of* is that which the constitutive standards govern: the entities, properties, and relations in terms of which the theory is expressed. Why? Because, when the possibility of a *mis*measurement or experimental *error* arises, what the issue turns on is telling how things stand with regard to those standards. That's what *accurate* instrumentation is counted on to measure; it's what is checked for in double checking; it's the way in which experimental ability contributes to the scientific achievement. Successfully holding those entities to those standards, in the face of ever more precise and detailed experimental testing, is scientific *understanding*—understanding what the entities *are*.

Philosophers of science speak more often of explanation than of understanding, but these come to the same: to *explain* is to render intelligible—to show that and how something can be understood. Thus it is that explanations are of two sorts. An entire domain of phenomena can be constituted and explained when standards to which they can be held are grasped and successfully insisted upon. (Such a success is a *paradigm*.) And, within a domain, particular phenomena, or particular classes of phenomena, are explained by showing how they in particular can be held to the constitutive standards. In case the pertinent standards include strict subsumability, those internal explanations will be, in part, deductive nomological. In case the domain-constituting standards are otherwise—for instance: the Davidson/Dennett notion of rationality, the integrated operation of functional systems and organisms, or the historical/institutional dynamics of cultures and subcultures—then the explanations and intelligibility will be of different sorts. What they have in common is the structure of *insistence*: practitioners have the ability to recognize phenomena that are ruled out by the standards that are constitutive of that recognizability, and will refuse to accept them.

9 EVERYDAY OBJECTIVITY

Can the same account be extended also to the objectivity of everyday perception, say of sticks and stones? It would be here, presumably, if anywhere, that dogs and cats would have perceptual abilities comparable to our own. No doubt, we share with higher animals various innate "object-constancy" and "object-tracking" mechanisms that automatically "lock onto" medium sized lumps—especially ones that are moving and/or staring at us. The question is whether, for us in contrast to animals, there is any more to the objectivity of perceivable "things" than that they trigger such mechanisms—in particular, whether there are constitutive standards to which we, as perceivers, hold them.[17] It seems to me that there are, though they are somewhat vague and difficult to formulate. The essential tenet is something like: *things* are integral bearers of multiple properties. Integrity is the way the properties belong together in space and time, in (at least) two respects: cohesively and compatibly.

A thing is a cohesive spatio-temporal unit. At a time, a thing occupies—that is, its properties are instantiated at—exactly one place, a place which has a definite size and shape, and which is occupied by no other thing. Through time, the place of a thing can vary, as can the properties collected in it there. But mostly these variations can be only gradual—that is, relatively slow and continuous. For otherwise, it would cease to be well-defined which properties belong together as properties of which things; their staying identifiably together in one continuing thing is what fixes their belonging together at all.

The properties of a single thing must always be mutually compatible, and they can be interdependent; that is, some combinations of properties and/or lacks are not permissible in one thing. But no properties or lacks in distinct things are incompatible; that is, any individually possible things are compossible with any others, or none at all (Leibniz not withstanding). This is to say that things are what they are independently of one another, that their properties are intrinsic to them. Properties *as such* are "proper to" the things that have them.[18]

Can we make sense of the suggestion that human perceivers (but not animals) *hold* things to some such standard—*insist* upon it? Consider first (before turning to things) how the members of a family are perceivable (on a corporeal level): each has his or her own characteristic visual appearance, sound of voice, odor, way of moving, and so on; and, of course, their various parts stay attached in the same way. But suppose, one day, all these aspects started permuting: what looks like Sister sounds like Father, moves like Grandma, and smells like Kid Brother. Even the parts could mix up: Mother's head (but Father's hair) on Uncle's torso with Baby's limbs—or just two heads with no limbs or torso at all (sounding like a truck and smelling like a watermelon). And moments later, they switch again, with new divisions and new participants. What would you say?

Surely something like: "Egad! Am I going crazy? Am I being tricked or drugged? I can't *really* be seeing this—it's *impossible*". That is, you would *reject* what you seemed to perceive, you would not accept them as *objects*. Now suppose that, instead of you, it were the family dog who came home to this. We can't ask what it would say, because dogs can't talk; and, of course, any estimate of its reaction at all is bound to be largely conjecture and prejudice. But, by way of counterpoint to sharpen the main point, I'll express my own prejudice: I think the dog would *bark*. I expect it would be disoriented and distressed, maybe even frightened. But I can't imagine any part of a dog's reaction amounting to a rejection of the scene, a discounting of its reality, on the grounds that it's impossible. Though Fido can tell Sister from Brother, and humans from cats, I don't think he can distinguish in any sense between possible and impossible. And this, I believe, is the same as to say that he holds no objects to constitutive standards, and therefore understands nothing.

The integrity of family members—people—is certainly a different matter from that of things. Yet analogous permutations of the sensible properties of rocks and blossoms, comets and waterfalls would be equally fantastic. We might occasionally accept, even relish, such disintegrated phantasmagoria in dreams or hallucinations; but no one who understood what it meant could accept them as objective things. That is, the experiences, whatever else they might be, could not be objective perception. To perceive things as objects is to insist upon their coherent integrity—the constitutive standard for thinghood— just like insisting upon legality in chess, rationality in interpretation, and ordering with precision and scope in empirical science.

NOTES:

1   This is not intended as a conceptual or definitional point, but as a factual claim. It could turn out, I suppose, that dolphins or extraterrestrials are capable of objective perception; but (at least in the case of the former) I'm highly dubious.

2   Abbreviate "*a*'s being F carries the information that *b* is G" with "$Fa \Rightarrow Gb$". Clearly, for a fixed specification of the conditions, this relation is transitive: If $Fa \Rightarrow Hc$ and $Hc \Rightarrow Gb$ in the same conditions, then (in those conditions) $Fa \Rightarrow Gb$. More, however, is required for $Fa \Rightarrow Gb$ to be *via* Hc than that $Fa \Rightarrow Hc$ and $Hc \Rightarrow Gb$ in

the same conditions—because, intuitively, it might be that $Fa \Rightarrow Gb$ independently of Hc. Suppose, however, that there are some conditions in which $Fa \Rightarrow Hc$ but not $Hc \Rightarrow Gb$, and some in which $Hc \Rightarrow Gb$ but not $Fa \Rightarrow Hc$, but the only conditions in which $Fa \Rightarrow Gb$ are those in which both $Fa \Rightarrow Hc$ and $Hc \Rightarrow Gb$. Then, plausibly (and according to Dretske), it is only *via* Hc that $Fa \Rightarrow Gb$.

3 It would not be difficult to contrive "abnormal" conditions in which the air or eardrum were vibrated in such a manner as to cause the perceptual experience, even without the bell ringing— for example, using an audio recorder.

4 The terminology is reminiscent of Gibson, whom Dretske in fact cites, in a slightly different context, on the following page.

5 In terms of the earlier illustration, this amounts to suggesting that, although the presence of the lemon drops does not carry any information about *which* child fetched, it does carry the information that *some* child fetched (so, 'child' = the higher-order kind); and, moreover, it carries the information that Grampa paid only *via* the information that some child fetched. (Note, by the way, that 'some child' is not in general equivalent to any disjunction: 'child *a*, or child *b*, or …'.)

6 This way of putting it may be misleading because, as I will argue in sections 4 and 5, it is possible in principle for nonlinguistic creatures to play chess; the reader, therefore, should not suppose that I intend this mention of conceptual ability to entail linguistic ability. (I will suggest in section 7 that conceptual understanding is possible without language.)

7 An existence proof for illegal moves is not required: Murphy's Law is the best confirmed generalization in all of empirical metaphysics.

8 This counting-on and vigilance are to be understood as implicit in persistent behavioral dispositions, and not (at least, not necessarily) as conscious conviction, or deliberate being on the lookout for.

9 For nonlinguistic players (like our super-monkeys), *telling* what moves are made will be exhibited, in the first instance, in their

own legal move making (in the light of that move, so to speak). But it could also take the form of producing the equivalent moves (and positions) in various alternative media—in effect, "transliterating" them.

10 In chess, of course, both these abilities are already required in normal play, and are exhibited in a player's ability to make legal moves of its own. Note that these two abilities "to tell" amount to abilities to *recognize*, respectively, the subordinate and superordinate patterns mentioned in section 3.

11 If I'm wrong about ordinary monkeys (or even dogs), then so much the better for them; what's important is that there's a line to be drawn, not where.

12 "...the conditions of the *possibility of experience* in general are likewise conditions of the *possibility of the objects of experience*..." (1781/1929, A 158/B 197).

13 This paragraph is based closely on a conversation with Jim Conant.

14 It could be argued that a first language is learnable only by bootstrapping. That is, only a minimal initial "core" is learnable without benefit of language; the remainder of the language is not so learnable, because learning (and/or speaking) it relies on the core. Then, if it were further maintained that chess is essentially more difficult that this core, the argument in the text would fail. What I find highly dubious in this line of thought, however, is the suggestion that anything *essentially* less sophisticated than chess (and similar formal games) could be in any proper sense a language. Yet, without that, the challenge collapses.

15 I say "more or less" because Davidson, in fact, nowhere offers an explicit definition of the physical, nor do the various remarks on which my attribution is based quite add up to one.

16 For a scientist, of course, "further articulation" can include more than just a better ability to tell what is and isn't permissible; it can include modest modifications ("friendly amendments") to the theory itself. (There is no analog to this for chess players.)

17 By 'things' here I mean mere things, *realia*—like sticks and stones. "Things" in the sense of paraphernalia or equipment, things

constituted by their roles and appropriate uses, are also held to constitutive standards, but different ones. Accordingly, the most proper perception of them as objects, and what is insisted upon in such perception, is also different

18 A fuller discussion would: disengage locatedness at a particular place from the togetherness (collocation) of cohesion; add a requirement for concreteness (complete determinacy) to that for compatibility; connect locatedness and concreteness with actuality (as opposed to mere possibility), and therefore with each other (and with particularity); and so on. But exactly how is another question.

CHAPTER ELEVEN

Pattern and Being

Daniel Dennett's landmark "Real Patterns" (1991) is an essay in *ontology*: its topic is the being of entities. Ostensibly, it is prompted by questions about the reality of intentional states, and about the implications of Dennett's own seminal account in "Intentional Systems" (1971/78). But these are pretexts: the issue is not intentionality at all, except in passing, but rather *being*. Intentional states—beliefs, desires, and the like—frame the discussion, motivating it in the introduction, and secured by it in the conclusion. But all the main points are made in a more general way, in terms of *patterns*. Intentional states are just a special case, and there can be other special cases as well, the status of all of which we will be able to understand once we understand the ontology of patterns more generally. In the same spirit, I too will mention the intentional only incidentally, and will focus instead on the general case. (Also, I will take it for granted that the reader is familiar with Dennett's work, especially the two articles just cited.)

I PATTERNS AND THEIR ELEMENTS

From the beginning, Dennett's ontological investigation of patterns exhibits a perplexing vacillation between two levels. It can be brought to the fore with the following question: What are the *entities* the status of which is to be illuminated? Are they the patterns themselves, or are they rather the elements (components) of the patterns? This distinction should not be confused with another: namely, that between patterns considered abstractly or concretely. For instance, a melody is a pattern of notes, varying relative to one another in pitch and timing. Abstractly, the melody need be in no particular key, register, or tempo, not to mention at any date or location. But in any concrete instance (of which there can be arbitrarily many), these and all other character-istics must be determinate. The vacillation is between the pattern and its elements, the melody and the notes, not between the abstract form and its concrete instances.

On the one hand, the title "Real Patterns" suggests that it is the patterns themselves, rather than their component elements, whose ontological status ("reality") is to be explained and defended. This interpretation is reinforced by the initial example of a visible pattern of dots within a frame: the status of the dots is never questioned, but only that of the pattern of black and white stripes that they make up. Dennett says: "I take it that this pattern, which I shall dub *bar code*, is a real pattern if anything is" (31) and then asks the essential question: "what does it mean to say that a pattern in one of these frames is real, or that it is really there?" (32) Again, the invocation of mathematical randomness, or the incompressibility of a bit map (32–33), presup-poses the bits or the "data". Only the status of the pattern itself is in doubt: "A pattern exists in some data—is real—if there is a descrip-tion of the data that is more efficient than the bit map, whether or not anyone can concoct it." (34)

On the other hand, Dennett introduces his catalog of "different grades or kinds of realism" about beliefs by asking: "When are the elements of a pattern real and not merely apparent?" (30) Indeed, in assimilating the intentional stance to radical interpretation and radical translation (30 and 46), Dennett is inevitably (and willingly) commit-ted to the brand of holism that understands intentional items in terms of the ordered wholes they participate in (not any wholes they might individually comprise). That is, the intentional items, such as beliefs and desires, are not themselves the relevant patterns, but are rather the elements of the relevant patterns. Hence, to inquire after the ontological status of intentional states is to inquire after the status of pattern elements, not patterns. These are the two levels between which Dennett vacillates.

It is tempting to suppose that the opposition must somehow be false, that the ontological status of the pattern and its elements must go hand in hand—because (as one wants to say) "each is defined in terms of the other". Insofar as this is right, however, it is a posing of the problem rather than a solution. The problem is: How can such a "going hand in hand" make nontrivial (non-question-begging) sense? In resolving this problem, it should become clear for the first time what patterns have to do with *ontology*.

2 To be is not just to "count as"

It is important to avoid at the outset an attractively easy false start. What, after all, are the bits in a bit map, or the pixels in a picture? As was pointed out above, these elements are taken for granted—their "reality" is not in question—when we ask about the status of mathematical or visual patterns of them. But, of course, their status *as bits or pixels* is not at all independent of those patterns. A particular flipped flip-flop or black dot on white paper would not *count as* a bit or pixel except insofar as it is a component in some relevant mathematical or visual pattern. Likewise, nothing could *count as* this sort of mathematical or visual pattern except insofar as it is a pattern of such bits or pixels. Accordingly, it seems, the patterns and their elements are defined in terms of one another, and their respective statuses go hand in hand.

But this misses the point: the *being* of the bits or pixels is not at issue at all, but only whether the terms 'bit' or 'pixel' apply to them—that's what "counting as" a bit or pixel means. Thus, whether it's a pixel or not, the dot is still there; its status as an entity (namely, a dot) is quite independent of whether it counts as a pixel in some visual pattern. The corresponding approach to intentional states would be to say that they are (for instance) structures in the brain, identifiable neurophysiologically or syntactically, but so related to one another in an overall pattern that they also *count as* beliefs and desires. The being, the "reality", of such states would be nothing other than that of those brain structures—for they would be identical. Such an account (a version of token identity theory) would be ontologically straightforward and familiar. It might well be Fodor's view, or even Davidson's; but it surely isn't Dennett's.

It bears mentioning, therefore, that the analogy that Dennett still proposes between beliefs and centers of gravity (27–29) is completely misleading, and should be discarded. A center of gravity is nothing other than a spatial point at a time, or a point trajectory through time. Hence, its ontological status is exactly on a par with that of any other spatial point or trajectory—including the center of the smallest sphere containing all the socks Dennett has ever lost. Whether a given point or trajectory *counts as* a center of gravity, or a lost-sock center, depends on its position relative to certain masses or socks; but its *being* is spatial, and independent of what else it counts as.[1] Accordingly, the greater usefulness, in scientific calculation, of centers of gravity does not confer on them any further *ontological* status; they are no more "real" than lost-sock centers—just more worth keeping track of. This is not at all analogous to the claim about beliefs: as just noted, Dennett never suggests that beliefs are simply a subset of the set of all brain structures (or computational states, or anything else independently specifiable) which, by virtue of participating in some pattern, also *count as* intentional.

3 PATTERNS IN THE LIFE WORLD

Centers of gravity and bit patterns, however, are merely preparatory for Dennett's richest and most developed example: patterns in the Life world.[2] Although the lessons will ultimately be quite different, Life looks at first to be little more than a kinetic variant of a pattern of pixels. Thus, much as a black dot is a black dot, whether or not it counts as a pixel in some image, so also a Life cell is a Life cell, whether or not it counts as a component in a glider, eater, or other pattern in the Life plane.[3] Moreover, the same point can be made at successive higher "levels." For instance, if a Turing machine is implemented (as can be done) as a higher-order pattern of gliders, eaters, and so on, then each glider is the glider it is, whether or not it also counts as (say) a token on the tape of that Turing machine. Though its status as a tape token depends on its participating in the higher-order pattern, its own status as an *entity*—a glider, as it happens—does not.

A glider, as its name suggests, moves across the plane from moment to moment; so it cannot be identified with any fixed set of cells or cell states; but, somewhat like a trajectory, it might plausibly be identified with a temporal sequence of sets of cell states. The trouble with such an identification is that it ignores the *motivation* for picking out this particular kind of sequence. Thus, there are any number of definable sequences of sets of cell states—which, when they occur, are all equally "actual" or "real".[4] But some few of these kinds of sequence, including gliders, are very special. Roughly, they *persist* as reidentifiable nonempty configurations against an empty background.

One way to think about this special persistence is *from below*, as a consequence of the kinetic law governing cell state changes in the Life world. This law entails that if, at a given time, all the cells in the Life world are off except those that would be on for a single glider at that time, then the sequence of sets of cell states for that glider will occur in the future of that world—that is, the glider will persist. Further: the effect of the kinetic law is entirely local, which means that the glider will persist for as long as those cells sufficiently nearby are all off (what's happening far away doesn't matter at the moment). To put it another way, the law guarantees that once a glider sequence is started, and so long as it is not interfered with, it will continue. Very few of the definable sequences of sets of cell states have this feature of guaranteed persistence; hence those that do are special.[5]

A different way to think about persistence is to consider, not what makes it possible (and rare), but what makes it noteworthy or important—to ask, in effect, what's so *special* about persisting configurations. Dennett speaks of their *"salience as real things"*, and says this means that one can "proceed to predict—sketchily and riskily—the behavior of larger configurations or systems of configurations". (40) In other words, persistent patterns and structures are special because they can be relied upon as *components* of higher-order patterns or structures—such as tokens on Turing machine tapes. This is to think about the persistence, or, more broadly, the *specialness* of certain patterns *from above*, in terms of what they participate in or contribute to.

In a Life-world implementation of a Turing machine tape, the gliders are, at the same time, patterns and components of patterns. They fall, therefore, on both sides of Dennett's initial vacillation. As we shall see, it is precisely in this double or bivalent position, including "specialness from above", that patterning can have ontological import—that is, confer status as an entity. But this will require more careful attention to the notion of 'pattern'.

4 PATTERNS AND PATTERN RECOGNITION

Relatively early in his article, Dennett inserts a remarkable passage, one with little evident connection to the remainder of the text.

> ... I propose that the self-contradictory air of "indiscernible pattern" should be taken seriously. We may be able to make some extended, or metaphorical, sense of the idea of indiscernible patterns (or invisible pictures or silent symphonies), but in the root case a pattern is "by definition" a candidate for pattern *recognition.* (32)

Nowhere in the ensuing discussion, however, does he tell us anything about what pattern recognition *is*, or why it should have this definitive significance. On the contrary, no sooner has he acknowledged the implication of an "unbreakable link to observers or perspectives" than he turns instead to "discernibility-in-principle" and the mathematical definition of randomness—two ideas that seem as observer independent and nonperspectival as one could hope to find. Tracing this ambivalence will show, by steps, that Dennett understands 'pattern' in two different ways, that he needs *both* of them to make his ontological point, and that this is what "stances" are all about. But, to get there from here, we first have to ask what it means to *recognize* something.

Recognizing, as the quoted passage indicates, is *at least* discerning or discriminating. To recognize something is to respond to it in a way that distinguishes it from other things; to recognize is to tell apart. But differential response cannot be the whole story, for two deeply related reasons. First, what is recognized is always some determinate item, feature, or characteristic of the confronted situation, whereas a given response can equally well be taken as a response to any of several distinct things. Second, recognition, unlike response, is a normative notion: it is possible to *mis*recognize something, to get it *wrong*, whereas a response is just whatever response it is to whatever is there. These are related because: only insofar as something determinate is supposed to be recognized, can there be an issue of recognizing *it* rightly or wrongly; and it is only as that which determines rightness or wrongness that the object of recognition is determinate.

Thus, in order to understand recognition, as distinct from mere differential response, we must understand these interrelated phenomena of object determinacy and normativity. Consider an automatic door: it responds to an approaching pedestrian by opening, and to the pedestrian's passing through by closing again. Of course, it might respond identically to a wayward shopping cart, or a large enough piece of plaster falling from the ceiling; and we can even imagine it being triggered by the magnetic fields of a floor polisher passing near its control box, across the hall. Are such incidents *misrecognitions*? Has the door *mistaken* plaster or a floor polisher for a pedestrian, say? Obviously not, for pedestrians, plaster, and polishers are nothing to a door. Therefore, even in the usual case, we cannot say that it has recognized a pedestrian.

Should we conclude instead that it recognizes pressure on its floor pad, the current in some wire, or—in the limit—a force adequate to open it? Again, no; for if the possibility of error is systematically eliminated, then it's vacuous to speak of correctness or recognition at all. Rather, whenever the door opens, there is an extended set of relevant causal factors (some proximal, some distal) any of several of which might equally well be identified as "the" factor to which it responded—depending on what we're interested in at the time. But since the door doesn't get any of them right or wrong—it just responds as it does—none of the responses amounts to recognition. The same can be said about a trout striking at a fly (whether natural or hand-tied), and, in my view, about a hound chasing a rabbit (whether across a field or around a racetrack).

If, on the other hand, opening for anything other than a pedestrian would amount to an *error* (regardless of what pressures or currents did or didn't intervene), then, in the ordinary case, the pedestrian (and not any pressure or current) would be the *object* of the response; that is, the system would *recognize* pedestrians. (This is just what the situation would be if the "system" were a human employee.) To put it more generally, if some specific causal factor can be singled out as making the difference, from case to case, between correct response and error, then, in any given nonerroneous case, this same factor also can be singled out as *the object* recognized. And likewise vice versa: if a response has a determinate proper object—if it is a recognitive response—then, absent that object, the response is an error. In sum, recognition, object determinacy, and the possibility of mistake belong together.

Thus, to comprehend the full content of the suggestion that patterns be regarded as candidates for recognition, we will need to understand the normative standards according to which they can stand individually as criteria for *correct* recognitions.

5 RECOGNIZABILIA OR ORDERLY ARRANGEMENTS?

There are really two notions of 'pattern' at work in Dennett's article. On the one hand, there is the idea that patterns are "by definition" candidates for discernment or recognition; on the other, there is the idea that a pattern is some sort of orderly or nonrandom arrangement—the opposite of chaos. The first idea invites an operational or practical definition, via an account of recognizing and correctness; the second invites an explicit or theoretical definition, in terms of what's arranged, what arrangements are possible, and which of those arrangements are orderly. The mathematical definition, as well as all the pixel examples, are of this latter sort. The obvious question is: Why have both? In particular, why bother with the looser operational definition when the explicit theoretical definition is available?

One advantage of the "operational definition" in terms of recognition is that it does not presuppose or depend on any determination of what the pattern is a pattern *of*. The mathematical definition, by contrast, only makes sense if the "bits"—or, more generally, the possible types and relations of its elements—are specified in advance. But recognition needs no such prespecification: you just have to "know one when you see one". For instance, when I recognize the faces of my friends, or the expressions on their faces, or the genre of a book, there are no particular bits or other elements that these are patterns of. A delighted smile is not a pattern of epidermal cells, still less of pixels or light waves; if anything, it's a concurrence of cheek lift and brow movement, of lip shape and eye sparkle. But these are no more antecedently determinate than smiles themselves, perhaps less so. Smiles, as the definition suggests, are what they are because we recognize them to be, and not the other way around. Likewise, the recognizable mystery or romance in a novel is not a pattern of words, still less of letters, but of something more like characters, situations, and mood—again, because readers reliably take them so.

The recognition-based definition is liberating in a second respect as well: it is not oriented exclusively to the "internals" of the recognized pattern. Thus, when I recognize something as a reassuring or a cautionary gesture, my response is influenced not only by the specific character of the gestural motions, but also, and perhaps largely, by the circumstances in which they are made. "Context dependence" of interpretations is, of course, familiar; but it is frequently understood on a broadly inferential model:

1 Any instance of *I*, in context *C*, would be (or count as) an *R*.

2 Here is an instance of *I*; and it is in context *C*.

3 So, here is an *R*.

This presumes, however, that *C* and *I* are identifiable as such independently, and that the recognition of *R* is then just drawing a conclusion—not really a *recognition* at all. But very often, I think, context-informed phenomena (gestures are but one example) are recognized for what they are, quite apart from any *independent* recognition of the context or of anything which is "in" the context. Indeed, if there are to be any inferences, they, can just as easily go in the other direction. Joint recognizability of instance-cum-context yields a notion of pattern notably divergent from that of an orderly arrangement of parts.

In the meantime, requiring determinate prespecification of the bits or elements, as the mathematical definition does, can be a philosophical embarrassment, in more than one way. First, many relevant patterns—conspicuously including the behavioral patterns that support intentional interpretation—do not seem to be made up of well-defined bits or elements. Just which causal commerce with the environment amounts to perception and action is by no means specifiable in advance, nor can it be precisely delineated in any case. Second, the account of patterns as orderly arrangements of predetermined elements is an invitation to metaphysical reductionism: the thesis that these patterns are "nothing but" their elements as arranged. Clearly, however, (whatever else one thinks about it) this runs counter to Dennett's motivating insight that "real patterns" might be of distinctive ontological status and interest. Third, if (in spite of all the foregoing) an attempt were made to merge the two notions of pattern, such that recognizable patterns *must* at the same time be arrangements of prior elements, then, arguably, their recognizability would have to be *via* prior recognition of those elements; and that would be a version of epistemological foundationalism.

No sooner are these observations made, however, than the outline of a rapprochement becomes roughly visible. For if the independent identifiability of the elements of an orderly-arrangement pattern is problematic, and if, at the same time, the identity of a recognition pattern can be context dependent, then the one hand may wash the other. Rather than merging (so as to coincide), the two notions of pattern join forces, to mutual advantage. In this larger conception, the "elements" of an orderly arrangement need no longer be thought of as *simple* ("elementary"), like bits or pixels, or even as independently identifiable. On the contrary, they might be quite elaborate, elusive, and/or subtle—so long as some relevant creatures are (or can learn to be) able to recognize them. This recognizability, in turn, can perfectly well depend, in part, on their participation in the arrangement (= the context) of which they are the elements.

In effect, we have "patterns" at two different levels, one level for each of Dennett's two definitions—but in such a way that (artificially simplified cases aside) each requires the other. That is, both of the definitions are integral to a single unified account. What's more, this one integral account reveals how Dennett's ambivalence between the two notions of 'pattern' is deeply connected with his initial vacillation between considering patterns and considering their elements; for both involve the same distinction of "level." But we still must see how their integration enables his ontological insight.

6 THE NORMATIVITY OF RECOGNITION

Recognition, we noted, is subject to normative appraisal, and has a determinate (purported) object. These related characteristics are what distinguish it from mere differential response. But what they are and how they are possible has yet to be explained. If, however, recognizable patterns are understood as elements of orderly-arrangement patterns, then the resources may be available to supply that explanation. For the elements of an orderly arrangement are by no means arbitrary: the order itself, in conjunction with the other elements, imposes strict constraints on what any given element can be. In particular, it sharply—as a rule, uniquely—limits which among the causal antecedents of a response could possibly be such an element. This limitation, in other words, picks out a single factor in the causal background of the response as having a special status and importance, vis-à-vis the larger orderly arrangement; and then, if that single factor could be identified as its *object*, the response would amount to a recognition.

To pick out which factor, if any, would have the status of object, however, is not yet to show that any factor *does* have that status. For that, something else about the larger, two-level picture must be brought out, something in terms of which responses can be deemed right or wrong according as they track that object. Or, to put it differently, it is yet to be shown how this singled-out factor, the candidate object, can serve as a *criterion* for the *correctness* of the response.

Return to the Life world. Since a universal Turing machine can be implemented in it, so can any other computer architecture, and any program on any such computer—indeed, in many different ways. Dennett imagines a chess playing system implemented (several levels up) in a vast "galaxy" of gliders, eaters, and so on; and then imagines setting it up to play against itself. (41) The point of the exercise is that an outsider might adopt any of a variety of perspectives on this assemblage, including, at the highest level, the intentional stance.

... one can shift to an ontology of chess-board positions, possible chess moves, and the grounds for evaluating them; then, adopting the intentional stance toward the configuration, one can predict its future *as* a chess player performing intentional actions—making chess moves and trying to achieve checkmate. Once one has fixed on an interpretation scheme, permitting one to say which configurations of pixels count as which symbols ..., one can use the interpretation scheme to predict, for instance, that the next configuration to emerge from the galaxy will be such-and-such a glider stream (the symbols for 'R×Q', say). (41)

There are in fact three distinct perspectives or levels mingled in this dense passage: (i) the chess ontology (board positions, possible moves, and so on); (ii) the ontology of symbols for chess moves ('R×Q'); and (iii) the intentional ontology (actions, tryings, and the like).

Focus, for the moment, on the chess ontology: certain subpatterns in this galaxy *are* chess pieces and positions, and appropriate changes in them are chess moves. What makes them so? Clearly the basic requirement is that, understood as chess phenomena, they be found reliably to accord with the rules of chess—the pieces must be those defined for chess, they must start in the standard starting position, the moves must be legal (and not too bad), and so forth. Implicit in these are also certain "enabling" prerequisites, such as that the pieces and positions be reidentifiable, that they be changeable in the ways permitted by the rules, that they be otherwise reliably stable, and so on. Consistent with those, anything whatever can serve as a chess set—including, but by no means limited to, subpatterns in a galaxy of flashing cells in the Life plane.

Chess phenomena, constituted as they are in accord with these preconditions, are a perfect example of what was earlier described as *specialness from above*—something's being noteworthy *as a pattern* not by virtue of how it's built out of elements, but by virtue of how it participates in or contributes to something else. Hence, in our larger unified account, chess pieces, locations, and moves, would fill the bill as *recognition* patterns, functioning as elements in the orderly-arrangement pattern defined by the rules of the game.[6] The rules of chess, moreover, are paradigmatically normative.[7] Consequently, at least for domains with this particular structure, a credible source is at hand for the corresponding derivative norms of recognition. Two main things, therefore, remain to be shown. First, how this derivation works; that is, how the standards that govern chess phenomena as such induce norms for the recognition of those phenomena. And, second, how the account, introduced in terms of rule-governed games, can be seen to generalize to other domains as well.

7 CHESS PLAYERS AND THEIR COMMITMENTS

A fundamental limitation of Life-world chess is that one can at best observe it as an outsider; there is no provision for interactive input to the system, hence no way to play against it. So consider instead a more congenial system, such as a computer that accepts opponents' moves via keyboard input, and continuously displays the current position on a screen. Again, what makes these display patterns *chess* pieces is not that they look like old-fashioned chess pieces to us (indeed, they may not), but that they are positioned and moved according to the rules. Only this time we're not just observing, we're *playing*—so some of those moves are our own. What difference does that make?

If you want to play chess, you have to play by the rules, and insist that your opponent also play by the rules—you have to *commit yourself* to the game proceeding in accord with the rules. In any given instance, that means you have to be able to tell what the current position is, what move is being made (considered), and whether that move is (would be) legal in that position. And you must be resolved to resist if it isn't. In other words, in taking on a commitment to the legality of the game, you inevitably also take on a commitment to *recognize* the pieces, positions, and moves—and recognize them *correctly*—for only in that way can legality be judged and maintained. This is how the norms that govern chess phenomena as such can induce norms for the recognition of those phenomena.

More specifically, a concord of two potentially discordant factors is required. If we ask *which* recognitions are correct, and why, we might answer that those recognitions are correct that find the positions to be stable and the moves legal—because these are the conditions on there being chess phenomena to recognize at all. But this risks vacuity; for if there were no *other* constraint on correct recognition, then arbitrary patterns could be gratuitously "recognized" as the moves of any legal game you like. The first leaf falling today could be white's opening, P–K4; the second leaf could be black's reply, also P–K4; and so on, at tournament level. Obviously, what keeps recognition from being thus vacuous is its being *beholden* somehow to what is ostensibly being

recognized, yet in such a way that the criteria of correctness are induced from above.

Here lies the true import of the phrase "you know one when you
see one": recognition is essentially a *skill*. It can be easy or arduous to
acquire; but once mastered, it can be performed reliably and consistently. What's more, competent practitioners can almost always tell
when they're having difficulty; and, in such cases, they can much
improve their performance by taking extra care, making multiple attempts, asking for help, and so on. This conscientious, sometimes
painstaking, practical exercise is the concrete way in which recognition holds itself to its object. The constitutive standards for a given
domain—the rules of chess, for instance—set conditions jointly on a
range of responsive dispositions and a range of phenomena: if they are
both such that the former consistently find the latter to accord with
the standards, then the former are recognition skills and the latter are
objects in the domain. But such eventual concord is anything but
vacuous: it is rare and, in general, a considerable *achievement*.

It amounts to an achievement precisely because skillful practitioners—*observers* are a special case—can tell if it isn't working, and
sometimes rectify it. Thus, whatever form the chess pieces, positions,
and moves take, players who play with them would have to be able to
tell if pieces were disappearing, positions randomly changing, or the
moves illegal. And not only could they tell, but they wouldn't stand
for it. At first, an apparent breach would elicit a more thorough
examination, double checking, perhaps excuses or explanations—all
geared to correcting the recognitions, in case there were some mistake.
But these attempted corrections are themselves just further exercises
of the same recognitive skills constituted along with the recognizable
phenomena according to the standards for the domain. This means
that the efforts may well not succeed: it may turn out that the alleged
chess phenomena are not reliably stable or legal after all—which is to
say, they may not be chess. Thus, insistence on the constitutive standards is on pain of giving up the game. The fact that this could
happen is what makes it an achievement when it doesn't.

More generally, if a larger arrangement pattern is constitutive for
the domain of its elements, and is as such insisted upon by skillful
practitioners, it can induce the norms by which those elements can
themselves be recognition patterns. That is, the elements can be *criterial* for the correctness of their own recognition, and in that sense
objects.

8 ONTOLOGY WITHOUT EQUIVOCATION

The term 'object' brings connotations of "objectivity" and "autonomy": an object is an entity "in its own right", quite apart from us—which is *why* it can stand over against us as a criterion, hence *why* we can be wrong about it. Though Dennett does not use the word 'object' in this privileged way, he unmistakably endorses these connotations in his pervasive talk of ontology, realism, and "salience as real things". His purpose, of course, is to explicate and defend his own long-standing position on the ontological status of intentional entities, a position he now wants to call mild, intermediate, or semi realism. I am not happy with any of these expressions. I do agree with Dennett's final assessment that the view itself is clearer than the labels (51); but that, it seems to me, is not merely a credit to the view, but also a discredit to the labels.

Let us begin by considering the reality of chess pieces. The first temptation, always, is to think of chess pieces as the familiar manipulable figurines—conventionally shaped lumps of wood, plastic, or whatever—and these, of course, are paradigmatically real. Being *real*, after all, is being *thingly*, being in the manner of the *res*; and the cohesive, enduring corporeal lump is the paradigm thing. We should, however, be very hesitant to identify chess pieces with things.

Traditional metaphysics interprets the thing as substance: the individual perduring bearer of multiple variable properties.[8] The substantial thing is *independent* in a strong sense, as that which needs nothing else in order to be.[9] This gives the metaphysical meaning of 'property': that which is "proper to" or "owned by" a substance all by itself, that which a substance "has" regardless of anything else.[10] In the case of corporeal substances, their spatio-temporal continuity and integrity is the basis of their identity and individuality; and their properties include mass, shape, hardness, temperature, and the like. By contrast, market price, functional role, ecological niche, and so on, are *not* properties of things: they can never "belong to" an individual independently and all by itself.[11] The fact that this ontological understanding remains vague in important respects, and has evolved in a variety of distinct traditional directions, should not blind us to its very considerable specificity and definiteness. It is anything but tautologically empty and noncommittal.

What then about chess pieces—rooks, pawns, knights—are they substantial things? Manifestly not. A chess piece is "defined", *what it is* is determined, by how it moves around the chess board in relation to other pieces, how it threatens, protects, captures, and is captured by them. Apart from its participation in chess, a rook makes no sense, and could not be: to be a rook is to play the part of a rook in a chess game. That is why *patterns* in the Life plane or on a computer display can *be* rooks. The point is not that such patterns are "insubstantial", so at least some rooks are. Rather: *no rook is a substance.* No matter how the metaphysical notions of independence and property are worked out, they will not apply to rooks. Nothing about a rook is determinate, not even its "rookness", apart from its participation in a chess game.

It is equally important to resist the thought that rooks, in contrast to corporeal things, are "abstract". Insofar as abstraction concerns the consideration of properties apart from any particular instantiations in things, then it has nothing to do with chess pieces. But if we broaden the abstract/concrete distinction to mark the difference between general characteristics or possibilities and their determinacy in particular individuals, then rooks can be considered either way. Considered in the abstract, rooks—any rook, "the" rook, rooks as a type—always start in a corner of the board, move only along ranks and files, tend to be more valuable than knights, and so on. But at a particular point in a particular game, this particular rook is a fully concrete individual: everything that can be determinate for a rook is determinate for this one—the particular square that it's on, the particular other pieces that are threatening or blocking it, its particular history of prior moves, its particular strategic value in the current position, and whatever else.[12]

Must we not acknowledge, however, still speaking of this particular rook, that it is *identical to*—the very same entity as—this particular lump of black plastic? Further, having granted that the lump of plastic is a thing, must we not concede after all that the rook, this particular rook token, is a thing too—the very same thing? Whatever the fate of token identity theory in other domains, I believe it is demonstrably false for chess pieces. Chess imposes quite definite identity conditions on its pieces, and they simply do not coincide with those for lumps of plastic. For instance, a game begun with the plastic set in the garden, can, after lunch, be carried on with the ivory set in the library. Now, the rule for castling stipulates that one cannot castle with a rook that has previously moved, even if it has since returned to its original square. And, clearly, for one continuing game, black's queen-rook would be the *same* piece in the garden and in the library; that is, black couldn't move it in the garden, and then castle with it later in the library, claiming that it was a *different* rook. But the plastic and ivory lumps are quite distinct (all day long); hence neither can be identical with that (or any) rook.[13]

Dennett's double notion of pattern gives us also another way to see past the token identity theory. As the account has been emerging, individual chess pieces are recognition patterns serving as the elements of rule-constituted games, themselves understood as orderly arrangements. But recognition patterns need have no separate identifiability at all (as patterns *of* anything else, for example), apart from their recognizability in context. There must, of course, be ways of double-checking these recognitions, perhaps from multiple angles or by multiple observers (with insistence on the rules inducing the normative force). Even so, ultimately, it is (or can be) *just* a matter of recognition—knowing one when you see one. If, with all due care and attention, that can't be made to work, then the game breaks down, and objectivity vanishes. But until then, everything's fine. In other words, there need in principle be no determinate candidate in any *other* domain (such as corporeal substances or arrangements of pixels) for token identification.

So, are chess pieces *real?* It depends on how the term is meant. If it's used in its strict (metaphysical) sense, then, no, chess pieces are not at all real, not even a little bit. But if it's used in one of its more colloquial senses, to pick out all and only what there is—what there "really" is, as opposed to the posits of hallucinations, superstitions, and false pretenses—then, of course, there really are chess pieces, lots of them, all over the world. On neither reading, however, is the reality of chess pieces "intermediate" or "halfway": they are not *substances* at all, but they are genuine, full-fledged *entities*, one hundred percent. As far as I can see, the idea of "mild realism" depends on running together these two distinct senses of 'real'—and, consequently, is much more likely to confuse than to illuminate.[14]

9 STANCE AND BEING

It would be a misunderstanding, therefore, to take the analogy between intentional states, on the one hand, and patterns and game phenomena, on the other, as a way of mitigating or watering down the ontology of the mental—as if to say they're "no more real" than these. The distinctions among the ways of being, and, in particular, between the being of the intentional and the being of the physical, are, of course, central to the account; and it is to illuminate these that patterns and games are discussed. But the inner coherence and genius of Dennett's position lies not in the analogies among these distinctions, but the underlying unity that binds them all together, that makes them *all* distinctions among *ways of being*.

Famously, Dennett introduces and explicates intentionality in terms of what he calls "the intentional stance". A *stance*, on the face of it, is a kind of posture or attitude that somebody can take toward something, a specific way of regarding and dealing with it. That intentional systems should be defined in terms of a possible attitude toward them has misled many into thinking the point is to downgrade their status, to imply that the intentional is somehow secondary, observer relative, or artificial—in contrast, say, to the physical. But, in this respect, Dennett puts the intentional and the physical exactly on a par: each is understood in terms of a possible stance. To be sure, the physical stance is importantly different from the intentional; but it is a stance, nonetheless. And there are others: Dennett discusses also the design stance, and later considers the possibility of a moral or personal stance.[15] Presumably, he would be equally receptive to stances for evolutionary biology, cultural anthropology, macro economics, and so on.

Officially, a stance is a strategy that one might adopt in order to predict and explain the behavior of something. Which stance one adopts in a given case is, of course, constrained by which strategies can be expected to work; but it is otherwise optional—a pragmatic decision, based on interests and purposes. Thus, a person might be treated as a physical object when calculating elevator loads, as a designed system when performing surgery, as an intentional system when offering coffee, and so on. The phenomena predicted and explained from the respective stances are not the same. Purposive action, for instance, is not the same as physiological movement; and both are distinct from physical motion. Indeed, each stance has its own peculiar vocabulary, and, in general, even its own observational and explanatory methodology. So, from the design stance, one speaks of what the various structures and processes are *for*, and explains how their organized complexes *work*; and, in this context, one can say also that something is malfunctioning, the wrong size, out of kilter, or broken—terms that make no sense from either the intentional or the physical stance.

But a stance is more than just an attitude toward or a perspective on things, more even than a method and terminology for dealing with them. Adopting a stance is *taking a stand*. Why? Because it is this alone—*commitment* to constitutive standards—that allows that toward which the stand is taken to stand out as phenomena, to stand over against us as objects. Such standards determine the *being* of the objects: what it is for them to be, *and* what is possible and impossible for them. Practitioners' insistence that the objects accord with the standards presupposes an ability to tell whether they do, and a resolve not to stand for it if they don't—either by finding out what went wrong and fixing it, or (failing that) by "giving up the game". Only in the light of this commitment can it be said nonvacuously, when things go right, that *phenomena* have been discovered, that *objects* have been constituted.[16] Only against a genuine and determinate possibility of failure can there be any meaningful success.

Dennett discusses only the intentional stance in any detail. For the intentional domain, *rationality* is the constitutive standard—"rationality is the mother of intention" (1971/78, 19). Although Dennett speaks of a *presumption* of rationality, rather than a commitment to it, the force is the same.

> The presumption of rationality is so strongly entrenched in our inference habits [about people] that when our predictions prove false, we at first cast about for adjustments in the information-possession conditions (he must not have heard, he must not know English, he must not have seen *x*, been aware that *y*, etc.) or goal weightings, before questioning the rationality of the system as a whole. In extreme cases personalities may prove to be so unpredictable from the intentional stance that we abandon it ...
>
> (1971/78, 32)

In other words, for intentional attribution, we *insist upon* rationality: in confronting apparent breaches of the standard, we first attempt to rectify them (that is, to explain them away in terms sanctioned by the standard itself); and, failing that, we give it up. This, I claim—and I intend it fully in the spirit of Dennett's stances—is the essence of all science, and, indeed, of all objective knowledge.

10 OUTER AND INNER RECOGNITION

To bring out the essential shape of "Real Patterns", I have so far suppressed the noise in it. Yet noise is an integral component of Dennett's insight. Intentional systems, as he is constantly reminding us, do not have to be *perfectly* rational—just mostly (a lot better than chance). Ultimately, in fact, the notion of "perfect rationality" (or, for that matter, perfect accord with constitutive standards more generally) need not be well defined. This is one of several respects in which the "chess stance" can be misleading, if taken as more than an introductory example; for digital games are quite exceptional in the explicit precision with which their constitutive standards can be articulated, and the corresponding absoluteness of the demand for compliance. Even physics, notable as it is for ontical precision, is less well spelled out in its ontological foundations than is chess, and more tolerant of anomalies in its concrete practice.

To see the possibility of unarticulated (perhaps inarticulable) constitutive standards, we turn again to Dennett's definition of 'pattern' in terms of recognition, only this time from the inside out. What we have hitherto called "recognition patterns" are patterns that can be recognized, so to speak, from the outside, when the pattern as a whole is present. These have served, in the two-level account, as the elements of a larger "arrangement pattern", which is the global structure of the domain as prescribed by its constitutive standards. In principle, however, there need be no articulate specification of these standards: all that is really essential is an ability to tell, in any given case, whether the standards are being met. Thus, for chess, it would suffice in principle if the players could tell which moves were legal, regardless of whether they could spell out the rules that define legality—or, indeed, whether there were any such rules.

So we can distinguish two fundamentally different sorts of pattern recognition. On the one hand, there is recognizing an integral, present pattern from the outside—*outer recognition* we could call it. On the other hand, there is recognizing a global pattern from the inside, by recognizing whether what is present, the current element, fits the pattern—which would, by contrast, be *inner recognition*. The first is telling whether something (a pattern) is *there*; the second is telling whether what's there *belongs* (to a pattern). When chess players recognize pieces, positions, and moves, it is outer recognition of the constituted phenomena; when they recognize these phenomena as legal or illegal, it is inner recognition of the constitutive standards. What these have in common, as species of *recognition*, is that "you can tell by looking"—that is, in both cases, it's the exercise of a practical, learnable *skill* (not an inference or a rule-application).

What is crucial for objectivity is that the two recognitive skills be distinct. (They cannot, of course, be independent, inasmuch as what is recognized in the one way is constitutive for what is recognized in the other.) In particular, skillful practitioners must be able to find them in conflict—that is, simultaneously to outer-recognize some phenomenon as present (actual) and inner-recognize it as not allowed (impossible). For only in the face of such potential discord does it make sense to *insist* that the patterns accessible to outer recognition accord with the pattern accessible to inner recognition; and only on the strength of such insistence can the latter pattern be a *standard* according to which the former are constituted as *objects*.

The essential but perhaps elusive distinction between these two recognitive skills is reflected in the equally essential but sometimes elusive distinction between knowledge and understanding. Roughly, knowledge is outer recognition, understanding inner. That is, phenomena are *known* insofar as they are recognized as present with their respective characteristics and relations; they are *understood* insofar as they are recognized as being in accord with the standards constitutive for their domain. If understanding is lord of the domain, explanation is concierge: to *explain* a phenomenon is to "show it in", to exhibit its allowability according to the standards, to let it be. This is what lies behind Dennett's saying that a stance is a strategy for explanation. A stance, as a commitment to the relevant standards, as made concrete in the respective recognitive skills and insistence on their concord, is nothing other than a strategy for showing that the observable phenomena fit the overall constitutive pattern. The centrality of explanation in the philosophy of science has exactly the same provenance.

Herein lies also, I think, the ultimate limitation of the *intentional* stance. For, if the foregoing is correct, then neither knowledge nor understanding is possible for a system that is itself incapable of adopting a stance—that is, insisting that objects accord with constitutive standards. By this test, neither extant animals nor current computers can know or understand *anything*. This jibes with—I suspect, accounts for—widespread intuitions to the effect that "genuine" or "full-fledged" intentional states cannot properly be ascribed to animals and/or computers. They may exhibit, one wants to say, behavioral regularities that are best characterized as informed goal directedness; but they don't *understand* what they're doing at all. Dennett has hoped to demystify such notions as belief and desire by assimilating them to the posits of the intentional stance—being careful all the while to acknowledge the differences of degree between more and less sophisticated intentional systems. But "beliefs" and "desires", in the complete absence of any understanding, indeed the absence of any possibility of understanding, what they are about, could hardly be of the same order as what we ordinarily understand by these words. So the differences are not of degree; and the demystification fails.

Yet, in a larger sense, it succeeds. For the true achievement lies not in the account of the intentional stance in particular, but in the account of stances and objectivity in general. If the so-called "intentional states" ascribed in the so-called "intentional stance" are not genuinely *intentional*, that indicates no worse than a misnomer—and certainly not a misidentification or mischaracterization of an important domain of objective inquiry. But further, if intentionality proper is ever to be understood as an objective phenomenon, then it too must be constituted in accord with a standard-setting stance. Whether this stance, as itself a stance toward standard-setting as such, must be in some unique way a stance toward itself and its own finitude, can here be left open. In that direction lies the existential analytic of dasein, an undertaking which Dennett has only just begun.

NOTES:

1 This is not, of course, to pretend that spatial being is unproblematic, nor that it is unconnected with physics and/or everyday life. The point is merely that counting as a center of gravity or a lost sock center is not, on the face of it, an ontological determination.

2 Note: "the Life world" here refers to the realm of possible structures and processes in the two dimensional formal system called "The Game of Life"; it has nothing to do, not even as a pun, with Husserl's *Lebenswelt*.

3 Though Dennett makes nothing of it (nor will I), it is interestingly difficult to say just which cells (at a time) are components of a pattern such as a glider or an eater. Clearly, they must include not just the cells that are "on" there and then, but also at least

some of the adjacent "off" cells; for were those not off, it would be a different pattern. But exactly which cells need to be in which states is not always clear, and may even depend on spatial and temporal context—as when an eater is in the process of consuming something else.

4   The phrase "when they occur" is what differentiates this example from trajectories. A given trajectory through space-time may or may not be the center of gravity for some extended mass; but there's no sense in which the trajectory itself "occurs" or not, depending on this—it's just "there", as a continuous, one-dimensional manifold, either way. A sequence of sets of cell states, by contrast, actually *occurs* only if the relevant cells are in fact in the relevant states in the relevant temporal order; otherwise, it isn't "there", it isn't "realized" at all.

5   Actually, since Life is deterministic, every configuration has a guaranteed future, as long as it's not interfered with; and one might say that this total future amounts to one "pattern" which persists. But gliders and a few other patterns persist in the much stronger sense that they are periodic: that is, the *same* momentary configurations (perhaps translated) recur in the same order indefinitely.

6   Whether anyone could, in fact, recognize them as implemented in the Life plane is a separate question; but the essential point could be made as well with a less formidable implementation.

7   But see the distinction between regulations and standards in chapter 13; the former are clearly normative, the latter not. [Note added 1997.]

8   Compare this with Quine's definition: "To be is to be the value of a bound variable"—meaning that identifiable unity of which an arbitrarily complex open sentence is true.

9   In part one, paragraph 51, of his *Principles of Philosophy*, Descartes writes: "By *substance* we can understand nothing other than a thing which exists in such a way as to depend on no other thing for its existence." (1644/1985, 210)

10 Relational properties, if not rejected as incoherent, can be conceived as proper to a plurality of substances—but, again, *proper to*

them, regardless of anything else. Extrinsic properties, properties that individuals have by virtue of their relations to others, are then not, strictly speaking, *properties* at all, but rather abbreviated ways of speaking about pluralities.

11 This, no doubt, is why philosophers from time to time try to explain them away—they're not "really real".

12 In just this spirit, I believe also that Dennett should avoid speaking (as he does, for instance, on page 29) of beliefs as *abstract objects*. Beliefs, of course do not belong to the *thing* category any more than chess pieces do; but, in the broadened sense of the abstract/concrete distinction, surely beliefs can be discussed either in abstraction or in the concrete. Thus, one might (as in logic) consider beliefs only with regard to their content, "abstracting away" from the degree of conviction with which they are held, the source of the evidence on which they are based, their reception as good news or bad news, and so on. Concretion for beliefs, by contrast, is to be fully determinate in all such possible regards.

13 The rules for *en passant* and stalemate also depend on the identity of pieces from move to move. I think the same argument implies that there is no piece identity from one game to another, and hence that there are no chess pieces at all except in the midst of games—in the box, there's just plastic. This is to say, in another terminology, that the that-it-is of a chess piece (its being "in play") is just as dependent on chess as is its what-it-is (its "chess role"). Note that token identity theory for chess pieces breaks down just as thoroughly when the pieces "are" Life-plane or screen-pixel patterns as when they "are" lumps of plastic; in other words, this 'are' cannot be the 'is' of identity, but must be something else. Perhaps we should say that the pixels or plastic "serve as" or "implement" the pieces, or some such.

14 A further confusion possibly lurking in the progression from "milder than mild" to "industrial strength" realism is the suggestion that ontologies come in "degrees", arrayed along a single dimension. But I see no reason whatever to suppose that the respective ways of being ("reality") of intentional states, functional components, physical particles, chess pieces, everyday paraphernalia, works of art, institutions, people, and whatever else there is, form a one-dimensional series in any interesting sense.

15 See Dennett 1973/78, 240–243.

16 This suggestion that objectivity is contingent on a commitment
(eventually) to "give up the game", if it cannot be made to work in
practice, is similar in structure and intent to Popper's proposal of
falsifiability as the mark of the scientific; but it is, so to speak, a
level up (ontological rather than ontical). Thus, Popper addressed
his criterion to *hypotheses* (particular candidate bits of doctrine),
thereby presupposing an already constituted vocabulary for expressing the hypotheses, and an already constituted methodology
for testing them. A *stance*, by contrast, effectively *is* a vocabulary
and a methodology, coupled with a demand for what will in fact
be found—or, more to the point, what will *not* be found. Hence,
what is up for rejection in case of failure is not any particular
hypothesis but rather the entire constituted domain (at least in
the current situation).

CHAPTER TWELVE

Understanding:
Dennett and Searle

1 RECONCILIATION

I want to attempt here what may seem the impossible: to agree with *both* Dan Dennett and John Searle about the mind—or, at any rate, about *intentionality*. I don't mean agreement on every detail, of course; that would be too much to hope. Rather, the idea is to outline a view that accommodates (what seem to me) the most central and the most important of their respective insights and intuitions, at the expense of a few others. As it happens, the effort to achieve unity will entail the occasional point of disagreement with both of them, as well as the introduction of some exogenous material which I can only hope is compatible with what's already there.

We can begin with some obvious and acknowledged common ground. Dennett and Searle agree in regarding intentionality as an entirely *natural* phenomenon, and in their commitment to a *scientific* understanding of nature. Moreover, they are each materialists, at least to the extent of holding that (as a matter of fact, so far as we know) matter, suitably arranged and interacting, is necessary and sufficient for intentionality. In other words, two worlds that were materially identical would be mentally identical as well; but if you took away the matter, or sufficiently rearranged it, you would destroy all intentionality too. On the other hand, neither Dennett nor Searle is sympathetic to traditional physicalist reductionism. That is, neither holds out any prospect for strict definitions of mental or intentional concepts in physical terms.

Where they diverge, then, is in the way they characterize that "suitable arrangement and interaction" of matter, and hence in their accounts of which systems might have it, and how we can tell. The appearance of conflict, however, is artificially heightened by overemphasis on a few strategic examples—particularly computers and AI. Better, I think, to concentrate on basic principles as much as possible, with the hope that controversial cases will not simply be "decided" but illuminated. The ideal outcome would be not an adjudication but an explanation of why those cases are controversial in the first place—that is, why they pull in both ways. But, before we can make any headway with that, we will need a brief overview of the two approaches under consideration.

2 Dennett on intentionality

Dennett introduced his notion of the *intentional stance* to articulate his view that intentionality is, in a certain sense, in the eye of the beholder. The sense is this: a system has intentional states—paradigmatically, beliefs and desires—just in case its behavior exhibits a specific sort of observable pattern. (1981/87, 25–29) The intentional states aren't the same as that observable pattern, or, at least, not the observable part of it; rather, they are a kind of completion of the pattern that is more or less necessary for it to stand out clearly in the first place. So it's roughly as if you were given every other letter of a text, or a scattered fraction of an image, and you "fill in" the "missing" pieces. Without that filling in, the visible part seems irregular and disjointed; yet its structure becomes conspicuous and compelling, once the remainder is interpolated. Furthermore, in terms of the new whole, the original part can itself be redescribed (namely, in intentional terms).

It is important to understand, however, that this is not "inference to the best explanation". Dennett is *not* saying that the rest of the pattern is "really there" though, for some reason, invisible—so we must infer it from the part we can see. In particular, he's not saying that beliefs and desires are determinate brain configurations or processes, which, as it happens, we are (so far) unable to observe. Rather, intentional states and processes are, in principle, *nothing but* our projected filling in of the pattern, in such a way that it makes sense overall. This is the way in which they are "in the eye of the beholder"—or perhaps it would be better to say, in the sense of the understander. But note well: this by no means renders them fictional, gratuitous, or arbitrary. In any given case, the attribution of intentional states is strongly constrained, both by principles and by facts—

so strongly, indeed, that it is a nontrivial *achievement* to succeed at it at all. (24–25)

The essential principle of the intentional stance is a constitutive standard of *rationality*. This, in effect, defines the *kind of sense* that can be made of a behavior pattern by interpolating intentional states and processes into it, and simultaneously redescribing the behavior itself in intentional terms—for instance, as perceptions and actions. Rationality is a global property of a system's behavior *in context*, including actual truth and success. (17–21) Moreover, it must be understood as projectable (in Nelson Goodman's sense—that is, it supports counterfactuals). That is why it is a constraint on a *pattern*, and a strong enough one to support interpolation and a new descriptive vocabulary. Perception and action make sense *as such* as, and only as, rational. The intentional stance is the descriptive and projective stance adopted by someone—the "observer"—who, by counting on this pattern and using its vocabulary, *understands* the system as intentional (rational).

3 SEARLE ON INTENTIONALITY

Searle will have next to none of this. Above all, he rejects the idea that intentionality is *in any sense* in the eye of the beholder. (1992, 7 and 78) It's just as real—right there in the brain—as any other higher-order property of complex systems, such as liquidity, digestion, photosynthesis, or life itself. (14 and 28–29) The microstructure of the brain is causally responsible for its mental (and any other emergent) properties, in just the sense that the microstructure of water is causally responsible for its liquidity—though, of course, in a much more complicated way. This offers a perfectly straightforward solution to the traditional problem of mind-body interaction, while preserving certain other attractive features of that tradition. Thus, since mental states and events just are physical states and events, only described at a higher level, there is no mystery about how they can interact causally with other physical states and events. At the same time, however, these interactions are entirely contingent, and are in no way constitutive of the mental as such.

So, for instance, it would be metaphysically possible—though appalling—to have mental states and events without any actual connection to perception or behavior. By the same token, it makes perfect sense—though it strains credulity—to imagine a system that behaved exactly as if it had mental states, but in fact had none. (65–71) This is

the basis of Searle's rejection of the Turing test. It's not that he believes that AI is on the verge of producing systems that act just like
people, even though they're zombies "inside". There are plenty of
reasons to be sceptical of that. The point is rather that the Turing
test—and by implication, the intentional stance—is incompetent to
decide what, if anything, is inside. Intentionality is, in Searle's terms,
intrinsic to the systems that have it. No amount or kind of behavior is
either necessary or sufficient.

Finally, Searle emphasizes, in a way that Dennett does not (and
cannot), that intrinsic intentionality is essentially *subjective*. (93–100)
Obviously, "subjective" doesn't here mean observer-relative or in the
eye of the beholder—as when we say that aesthetic tastes are "subjective". Rather, it means that intentional states—again, paradigmatically beliefs and desires—always *belong to* somebody, a *subject* who has
them. Subjectivity, according to Searle, is entails *consciousness* in the
following way: any genuine subject, at least sometimes, has some of its
intentional states consciously (and could, in principal, have any of
them consciously). That is, no system incapable of consciousness is a
subject or has any intentional states (except derivatively).

Thus, in Searle's terminology, the difference between him and
Dennett is that he regards intentionality as intrinsic and subjective,
whereas Dennett regards it as observer-relative and objective. Subject
to some qualifications about how these terms are to be understood, I
think this characterization is fair enough; and, moreover, put this way,
I think Searle is closer to the truth. Predictably, however, the qualifications I have in mind are not altogether trivial, nor necessarily acceptable to Searle. Indeed, as my introductory remarks hinted, the net
effect will be to make Searle's position rather closer to Dennett's than
either of them might expect (or, perhaps, appreciate).

4 NORMATIVITY AND ASPECT

Everyone agrees that intentionality is somehow *normative*. For Dennett, this comes out in the appeal to rationality as the criterion for
adequate interpretation. (1981/87b, 51–54) The point, of course, is not
that the interpreter must be rational, but rather that the system being
interpreted must, as interpreted, be rational. That is, the normative
standard is imposed on the intentional system as such. Still, it's being
imposed—that is, it's observer-relative. For Searle, the normative element shows up in what he calls the *satisfaction conditions* for intentional

states; and, needless to say, he maintains that the having of satisfaction conditions is itself also intrinsic to intentional mental states. (1992, 51 and 238) But, for both authors, the mental just *is*—or, at any rate, supervenes on—the physical; and Searle has no more to say than Dennett about *how* a physical system might have *normative* properties *intrinsically*. In fact, Dennett might well claim it as an advantage of his "eye-of-the-beholder" approach that it needn't address this question (or, anyway, so it seems). Searle, on the other hand, can't get off so easily.

To say that intentional states are normative—are subject to norms—is to say that there is a way that they're *supposed to* be, which may or may not be the way they are. Moreover, it is characteristic of the specific normativity of the intentional that whether any given state is as it is "supposed to be" *depends on* some determinate condition or state of affairs outside of it—namely, its satisfaction condition (sometimes also called its "intentional object"). Finally, however, all intentional states (that we know of) are *finite*; that is to say, they do not and cannot depend on *everything* about any concrete particular, but can only depend on *specific aspects* of it. Searle calls this the *aspectual shape* of intentional states.

For example, I believe that Mugsy is a brown dog. As an intentional state, my belief is subject to norms; more specifically, as a belief, it is supposed to be *true*. Whether it is in fact true, however, depends on something outside of it—namely, Mugsy. But it does not and cannot depend on everything about Mugsy, because Mugsy has infinitely (or, at least, indefinitely) many concrete determinations, and I am incapable of beliefs with infinite determinate content. Instead, my belief depends on only two of Mugsy's determinations: her color and her biological species. That is, it depends only on whether she is brown and a dog; this is its aspectual shape. (The term 'aspectual shape' suggests a visible "look"; and Searle does associate it with "seeing as", "perspective", and "point of view". But I think the argument from finitude, which Searle does not give, is both more general and more fundamental.)

5 A SPECIAL CASE: CHESS PERCEPTION

So the question is: How can naturally evolved physical brain configurations be normative in this way *intrinsically*? This is the question that I want to sketch an answer to—an answer that superficially sides with

Searle against Dennett, but more deeply brings the two of them together. I will begin by considering a special case and a special problem concerning it—a problem which I will try to solve in the special case. Then I will suggest that the case, the problem, and the solution all generalize. The special case is visible *chess phenomena*: pieces, positions, moves, and the like. The special problem is how these phenomena can be the satisfaction conditions of perceptual states.

Why is that a problem? Well, suppose that I am looking at the current position, and I see that your knight is threatening my rook. In virtue of what is it the case that my perception is *of that*—in other words, has *those* satisfaction conditions? Science, of course, has learned a lot about vision. We know, for example, that ambient photons bounce off the surfaces of the knight and rook, enter my eyeball, and stimulate a complex pattern of pulses in my optic nerve, which ultimately causes my perceptual state. Moreover, had my bishop been where my rook is, then the photon and pulse patterns would have been different, and (most likely) I would have seen your knight as threatening my bishop instead.

So causal histories are highly relevant to what we perceive. Nevertheless, they cannot be what determine the content of our perceptual states, for two closely related reasons. In the first place, the pieces on the board are only one stage in those causal histories, and nothing in the histories themselves picks out that particular stage as more important than the others, even counterfactually. That is, the causal histories as such give no reason to say that I perceive the chess pieces, as opposed to the photons or even the pulses in my optic nerve. Second, and more to the heart of the matter, causal histories are not normative. The content of my perception, its satisfaction condition, is what is *supposed to* have caused it, regardless of what *actually* caused it. Misperceptions and illusions, after all, are caused too—just not by what they purport to be of. (Deviant causal chains complicate things even more; but they can be set aside in the present context.)

What we need, then, is an account of *why* my perception is *supposed to* have been caused by your knight threatening my rook, and why that normative condition is *intrinsic*—that is, not observer-relative. (Such an account would also explain why *that* stage in the causal history is the relevant one.) To understand the normativity of perception, we must understand what perception is, and what is required of it. This is where the artificiality of the chess example helpfully clarifies and simplifies matters. Perceiving chess phenomena is clearly an integral part of playing chess—along with making moves, weighing options, developing strategies, and so on. (Of course, one can also be a spectator at a chess match; but that capacity, surely, is parasitic on the ability to play.)

6 Constitutive commitment

Consequently, we must make a brief digression about what it is to play chess. Two points will be important for what follows. First, chess phenomena cannot be identified with any particular shapes, colors, materials, or other low-level properties; rather, they are ontologically constituted by higher-order standards that are spelled out in the rules of the game. So, on the one hand, chess pieces do not have to be the familiar wooden or plastic figurines: they can be marks on a piece of paper, costumed servants, patterns of light on a computer screen, or what have you—just so long as they are moved consistently according to the rules of chess. And, on the other hand, the pieces of an ordinary chess set could easily be used to play some quite different game—in which case they wouldn't be *chess* pieces or phenomena. Hence, whether there are chess phenomena there to be perceived at all depends on whether the standards constitutive for chess are in fact being met.

Second, the chess player/perceiver cannot be indifferent as to whether these standards are being met. If I am to see something as, say, a knight threatening a rook, I must be *committed* to it being part of a larger pattern of other things I can or could see—other pieces, moves, positions, and so on—that consistently accord with the rules. This commitment, I believe, is precisely what Dennett calls a *stance*— not an intentional stance, of course, but rather a *chess stance*. The constitutive role of the rules of the game exactly parallels the constitutive role he assigns to rationality-in-context for the intentional stance. Without adopting such a stance (that is, committing to it) it would be impossible to see anything as a chess phenomenon at all.

Commitment to constitutive standards means at least three things. First it means that if something does not seem to accord with them, then one had better double check to make sure there's no mistake. Second, if the anomaly persists, and no mistake can be found, then one must either modify the standards, or give up on them (and the corresponding perceptions) altogether. But, third, modifying or giving up on established constitutive standards is not a matter to be taken lightly. For instance, I might believe that you had made an illegal move if, say, I mistook your bishop for a pawn, or got confused about the icons on our new computer. But if something does seem illegal to me, I can't just ignore it. I need to find (and correct) my mistake (if any), because if there's no mistake—if you are in fact making (what would be) illegal chess moves—then this isn't chess. Either you're playing a different game, or none at all. Finally, however, I shouldn't give up too easily, because constituting a domain of phenomena according to standards is a nontrivial and valuable *achievement*—and, in the case of established standards, one with a history of reliability.

7 OBJECTIVITY (TRANSCENDENTAL PHILOSOPHY)

The stakes, however, are higher than just rule-governed games. The idea of constituted phenomena goes back to Kant; and the idea that there can be multiple phenomenal domains constituted according to different and perhaps contingent standards is a staple of twentieth-century philosophy—as the litany of terms like 'regional ontology', 'framework of entities', 'conceptual scheme', 'scientific paradigm', and now 'stance' should make obvious. While these are not all equivalent, what they have in common is a conviction that the *objects* of perception, thought, and action are *intelligible* as the objects they are only in terms of some prior commitment on our part to the limits of what they *can* be. And the terms provided (constituted) by that commitment are precisely the *aspects* under which those objects can be the objects of intentional states.

And that brings us back to Searle and the normativity of perception. Suppose there is something odd about the pattern of photons bouncing off your knight into my eye. For some reason, from my current angle of view, that pattern is much more like what would usually come from a bishop than what would usually come from a knight. So I have the response that I would usually have if there were a bishop there. Is that a *mistake*? The question can be put more sharply. Have I *misperceived* your knight, or have I *correctly* perceived the photons? The account of constitutive standards provides the answer. What I am committed to is playing *chess*. Chess standards constrain pieces, positions, and moves on the chessboard—*not* photons. Accordingly, the questions of misperception and correctness that can arise (and must be resolved) in the context of chess concern only those pieces, positions, and moves—*not* the photons. This is *why* my perceptions are *supposed to* be of the pieces, positions, and moves—not the photons. In other words: *objectivity* as such is constituted.

8 SUBJECTIVITY (TRANSCENDENTAL PHILOSOPHY)

But is it *intrinsic*? Yes! Commitment to standards is the very foundation and essence of intrinsic intentionality. To see this, we must examine what is meant by 'intrinsic'. Obviously, the intentionality of some particular belief or desire cannot be intrinsic to that individual state all by itself. That would be incompatible with the holism of intentionality and its essential dependence on the background—two theses which Searle (among others) has espoused for years. (1992, 175–178) Rather, the intrinsicness must pertain at once to all the intentional states of a single system; and it means that the intentionality of those states is independent of any other intentionality—that is, the intentionality of any other system. For instance, printed marks on a page, or the states of an adding machine, may have various meanings—but only because we assign those meanings to them. Their intentionality is *derivative* from ours, and in that sense *observer* (or user) *relative*. Intrinsic intentionality is not thus derivative. (78–82 and 211–212)

That, however, is merely a negative characterization: it says what intrinsic intentionality is *not*. A genuine positive characterization would have to show how intentionality that is not derivative is even possible—that is, *how it is possible* for any system to have intentional states *on its own*. (This amounts to showing how intentionality is possible at all, since derivative intentionality only makes sense if there is some nonderivative intentionality for it to be derivative from.) It's worth remarking in passing that what counts as a single "system" is so far a free parameter in the account; Searle often speaks as if the relevant systems are individual brains, but that's not built into the theory. What matters is that the unity of the system follow from the same positive account of how such a system could have intentional states on its own—that is, intrinsically.

But that's precisely what commitment to constitutive standards provides. The unity of the system is the unity of a single consistent commitment in terms of which a plurality of intentional states can be normatively beholden to their constituted satisfaction conditions. Moreover, it is the basis of the necessary *subjectivity* of intentional states. 'Subject' here cannot just mean grammatical subject: even an adding machine is the "subject" if its states in that sense. Rather, 'subject' means something like "author and owner"—someone who is responsible for the states in question, and to whom they matter. Surely that subject is none other than the one who is committed to the very standards that render these states intentionally normative in the first place. My commitment to getting my intentional states "right" is what *makes* their intentionality my *own*—that is, *intrinsic* to me.[1] In other words: *subjectivity* as such is constituted.

It might even be that commitment throws some light on the relevance of consciousness; for one of the characteristic features of consciousness is that, though it's not always reflective, it's always *potentially* reflective. The self is, so to speak, always there in the background. But commitment to constitutive standards likewise lurks always in the background. When I am playing chess, I am not constantly double-checking my perceptions to ensure their accuracy; but I am always quietly at the ready. I am always, so to speak, "on guard", so that whenever there's an anomaly, then the issue *can* come to the fore.

9 UNDERSTANDING

I have, in effect, been urging Dennett's hallmark notion of a *stance* onto Searle, as the foundation of his own account of intentionality. But I have not actually been urging Dennett's own position. For Dennett understands intentionality in terms of a particular stance—the intentional stance—adopted *toward* a system; whereas I am suggesting that we understand intentionality in terms of a stance—any stance—adopted *by* a system. Dennett himself discusses what he calls "higher-order" intentionality, which would have to involve a system adopting the intentional stance, adopting the stance that something else is adopting the intentional stance, and so on. (1983/87, 243–250) But this is not quite the same as what I'm talking about, nor does Dennett make anything like the use I'm trying to make of it.

Here is why I think adopting a stance is prerequisite to intentionality. Any number of different states and arrangements of matter can be regarded as carrying information about things other than themselves. This can be a consequence of natural causal dependencies, as when clouds inform us of imminent rain; or it can be a matter of tacit or explicit convention, as when a badge informs me that someone is a police officer. More interestingly, complex systems can be built that record, transmit, combine, and otherwise usefully manipulate such information bearing states in ways that systematically preserve their status as reliable bearers of information. For instance, an automated business accounting system can be built such that its manipulations preserve correct arithmetic relationships (according to the relevant interpretations of its states), thereby extracting many useful results. This is what we now call *computation*.

What is conspicuous about all such systems, whether automated or not, is that they themselves do not have a clue about the information that (from our point of view) they carry. Clouds do not understand anything about rain, nor do badges about police. Likewise, a computer has no understanding whatever about business, accounting, or even arithmetic. *Understanding* a domain and its entities is understanding the principles according to which that domain and those entities are constituted; and such understanding can be nothing other than a *commitment* to those principles. Intentionality presupposes a committed stance because intentionality—meaning—presupposes understanding.

Searle once said of computers, including AI—what I call good old fashioned AI, or GOFAI—systems, that they understand exactly nothing; they are not in that line of business. (1980, 288) I like the straightforwardness of this claim; and, what's more, I agree with it completely. GOFAI systems (including, of course, computer "chess-playing" systems) are utterly incapable of any sort of commitment: nothing is at stake for them. They are never in a position of having to figure what their own "mistake" could have been, on pain of having to modify the standards, or "give up the game". Therefore, they understand *nothing*.

For what it's worth, I have no reason to believe that connectionist or any other approaches to AI are any better off than GOFAI in this regard. But I make no principled claim as to whether artificial systems of any sort will ever understand. Who knows?

10 Ersatz intentionality

Nevertheless, I do not agree with Searle about computers and other systems entirely. It seems to me that he makes too few distinctions, in a way that results in some misclassifications. He describes three different ways in which we talk about intentionality: (i) *intrinsic* intentionality; (ii) *derived* intentionality; and (iii) *as-if* intentionality. The first is the real thing; it is what we and the higher (that is, conscious) animals share. The second is intentionality, but only, so to speak, delegated or borrowed from some prior intrinsic intentionality; it is what computers and public inscriptions share. For instance, a printed sign that says "No smoking" really does *mean* "No smoking", but *only because* we give it that meaning; it can mean nothing all by itself. The third category is not really intentional at all, but only a sort of metaphor, as when we say that water "seeks" its own level, or the saplings are "trying" to grow up to the sunlight.

Now I have no problem (for the moment) with the classifications of people, signs, and water. But animals and computers, it seems to me are more difficult, and might better be handled by an intermediate classification, which I propose to call "ersatz intentionality". Consider a GOFAI robot of a sort not too far from current technology. It wanders around campus avoiding obstacles, keeping track of which paths are blocked (so as to stay up to date on the quickest routes), recharging its batteries periodically, and perhaps delivering packages or recording how long each parked car has been where it is. This system not only contains a large number of representations, but it modifies them in direct response to its environment, relies on them to help it reach various goals, manipulates them internally in various combinations to "figure out" what to do and how to do it—all without human intervention.

It seems to me that the relation of this robot to its representations is importantly different from the relation that a piece of paper bears to a message written on it. There is a clear (even if limited) sense in which the robot is actually making and using those representations *as representations*—that is, as aids to dealing vicariously with other things that are not themselves present. If the representations were different, the robot would behave differently; if they were false, it would perform more poorly (or, perhaps, correct them). None of this, or anything like it, is true of the piece of paper. So it does not seem to me that the robot and the paper should be classified together. (Here I am agreeing with Dennett, while disagreeing with Searle.)

On the other hand, not only are all of the robot's resources and goals preprogrammed by its designers, but also, and more important, all of the standards for what are treated as objects, adequate representations, goals, success, and so on, are tacitly presupposed and "hardwired" in that design. The point is not that the standards are *given* to the robot; rather, the robot doesn't "have" them at all—they remain entirely external to it. So, even though it's actual intentionality is not merely delegated (like that of the words on a page), nevertheless the standards in virtue of which those states can be understood as intentional and normative are conferred from the outside. Hence, its states do not belong to it (as a subject) in the way that ours belong to us. This is why I want an intermediate classification between genuine and merely derived intentionality—namely, *ersatz* intentionality. (*Neither Dennett nor Searle acknowledges such an intermediate status.*)

11 ANIMALS

Once ersatz intentionality is distinguished and characterized, however, it becomes apparent that there are candidates for it besides GOFAI robots. In particular, I want to suggest that (as far as we know) the intentionality of animals is entirely ersatz (except for purely tropistic creatures, whose intentionality is at best "as-if"). That is, we can understand animals as having intentional states, but only relative to standards that *we* establish for them. This makes animal intentionality exactly analogous to biological teleology. We say that the "purpose" of the heart is to pump blood, that it's "supposed to" work in a certain way, that functional descriptions are "normative", and so on. This is not mere as-if teleology (mere metaphor or *façon de parler*); nor is it any delegation of our own purposes and norms—like those for tools (by many accounts). But finally, of course, the heart does not have any *purposes* in the way that a person does, nor does it accede to any *norms* on its own responsibility. Extending my new terminology, I could say that biological systems have only *ersatz* teleology and normativity.

Searle might agree with this characterization of biological teleology. (Compare pages 237–239.) Dennett will not only agree (it's the design stance, after all), but accept the proposed affinity with animal intentionality. But there the congeniality ends. For Searle maintains that animal intentionality is intrinsic, just like our own (and unlike robots), whereas Dennett wants the intentional stance to apply to us, animals, and robots all in the same way—leaving no distinction for 'ersatz' to mark. By splitting the difference between them, I abandon both.

By my lights, animal intentionality is ersatz because (or to the extent that) animals do not commit to constitutive standards, hence do not submit themselves to norms, and do not understand anything. This is not to say that they do not perceive, remember, desire, learn, strive, and so on, but only to say that it's all ersatz—just as it would be for (advanced) robots. The fact that higher animals are much more similar to us than are robots physiologically, ethologically, and even

phylogenetically, is not necessarily significant when considering intentionality. After all, animals are also very different from us in many
other ways, such as morality, tradition, art appreciation, commerce,
technology, and so on. Indeed, in a few respects, like the employment
of structured representations and certain kinds of problem solving,
machines are, on the face of it, more our kin than are monkeys.

The point is that none of these observations carries any probative
weight unless and until there is some prior account of which kinds of
considerations are relevant. And that prior account could itself only
be based in a philosophical explication of what intentionality is and
how it works. I have sketched one possible explication in terms of
commitment to constitutive standards. According to this approach,
however, all of the above comparisons are equally irrelevant. With
regard to what matters for intentionality, robots and animals are more
similar to each other than either is to us. Only people have intrinsic
intentionality.

12 CONCLUSION

I have suggested that there is more in common to Dennett and Searle
on intentionality than meets the eye—including, I think, *their* eyes.
Pivotal to the envisioned *rapprochement* is Dennett's basic notion of a
stance, but used in a way that neither he nor Searle anticipates. If a
stance is conceived as a constitutive commitment, then it can be seen
as a transcendental ground of objectivity, subjectivity, and normativity—all of which are prerequisite to intentionality. A committed
stance is the essence of *understanding*—hence (the colon in) my title.

NOTE:

1 Compare this discussion of Searle and intrinsic intentionality to
chapter 7, note 9, above. I am in effect suggesting here that the
term 'intrinsic' should be reserved for that special case of original
intentionality (in my old sense) in which the intentional system is
committed to a constituted domain—otherwise I call it 'ersatz' (see
sections 10 and 11 of the present essay). I have, however, no reason
to believe that Searle (or Dennett) would accept this suggestion.
[Note added 1997.]

CHAPTER THIRTEEN

Truth and
Rule-Following

1 EXHIBITED AND GOVERNING RULES

What we understand by 'rule' and by 'rule-following' go hand in hand. Different sorts or conceptions of rules go with different sorts or conceptions of following. I want to consider the sorts of rule and rule-following that are most fundamental to our telling what's what—telling the truth—about worldly entities (objects). As will emerge, this cannot mean simply identifying one special sort of rule-following that is more basic than any others. Rather, even the most rudimentary (perhaps prelinguistic) objective truth-telling presupposes an integrated structure of rules of several different and interdependent sorts. The aim is to begin to spell this out.

Toward that end, it is helpful first to rehearse some preliminary classifications. Perhaps the broadest distinction among rules is between those that we understand as merely *exhibited* in what happens, and those that we understand as, in some way, *governing* or *determining* what happens. For those rules that are expressed verbally (or in some similar notation), this exhibited/governing distinction corresponds roughly to that between descriptive and prescriptive rules; but there is no need to build verbal expression, or even expressibility, into the conception of rules and rule-following. Various physical patterns, rhythms, regularities, and propensities would be paradigmatic rules in the exhibited or descriptive sense, whereas social mores, official regulations, design specifications, and recipes would be paradigmatic governing rules.

The distinction can be seen as kin to one that G.E.M. Anscombe (1957, section 32) draws, and John Searle (1979) elaborates and names, between world-to-word and word-to-world "directions of fit". Exhibited rules are understood as having a *world-to-rule* direction of fit, in the sense that, if there is a discrepancy between a supposed rule and what actually happens, then that reflects only on the rule—either it isn't really a rule after all, or it must somehow be limited in accuracy, scope, or probability. Governing rules, by contrast, are understood as having a *rule-to-world* direction of fit, because discrepancies can reflect instead on the discrepant phenomena—as somehow out of order, unruly, or faulty. In other words, there is only one intelligible sort of nonfollowing for an exhibited rule: the rule itself is limited or inapplicable. But there are two intelligible sorts of nonfollowing for a governing rule: besides limitation or inapplicability of the rule,[1] there can also be failure or breach in the phenomena—that is, a default rather than an exception.

This suggests a third way to frame the basic distinction. Exhibited rules are understood as *factual*: they are just how things turn out or are likely to be. Governing rules, on the other hand, are understood as *normative*: they are how things ought to be, in some relevant sense of 'ought'. Putting the point in this third way makes it easy to ask two related questions about governing rules. First, where does the "normative force" of governing rules come from? What is their "authority" or their claim on compliance? And second, how does it come about that the phenomena do in fact accord with governing rules (to the extent that they do)? How is the "force" brought to bear or made effective? Differing answers to these questions yield different understandings of what it is to follow various governing rules, hence also a basis for sorting the rules themselves further into species and subspecies.

For instance, official regulations carry legal or institutional authority, enforced, perhaps, by sanctions. The authority of a recipe, on the other hand, is grounded in its author's experience and expertise, enforced, presumably, by threat of failure. This difference marks regulations and recipes out as quite different sorts of governing rule. They are importantly alike, however, in another respect: namely, in the manner in which compliance comes about. This similarity has two related components. First, regulations and recipes govern the behavior of determinate agents: reidentifiable rule-followers to which or to whom the phenomena governed somehow belong (as "their" activities or actions). Second, they are explicit rules: they are expressed in some general scheme or notation—such as natural-language sentences— and the rule-follower complies with them by complying with tokens of these expressions.[2] Following rules by following explicit expressions of them raises a familiar explanatory issue.

2 Expressions and basic governing rules

Let's first acknowledge a distinction between those explicit rules that are *just* expressed and those that are *articulated*. A rule is articulated, in this sense, if it is one whose expression specifies multiple steps that are to be carried out in some orderly way. Thus, articulated rules (recipes are a prime example) are not only explicit but explicitly complex. To follow such a rule, a rule-follower must both perform the right steps and perform them in the right order. By contrast, the instruction "Pencils down!" (given at the conclusion of an exam) is not explicitly complex. Examinees do not comply by performing several steps in an order specified by the rule; they simply put their pencils down. One might say that the instruction tells them what to do, but not how to do it.[3]

Now, complying with a rule by way of responding to an expression of it (whether articulated or not) is itself a matter of following rules—rules that are in general distinct from the one expressed. They are the rules that determine the scheme or notation in which that expression is couched. These rules are also governing rules. That is, they are normative in at least the sense that they concern what is supposed to happen in response to a token of an expression, rather than what is likely to happen. If there is a discrepancy between the rule and what actually happens, that reflects not on the rule but on what happens, the rule-following—and hence (in these cases) on the rule-follower.

The idea of complying with a rule by complying with an expression of it—following a rule by following other rules—raises an obvious question: How is the latter compliance to be understood? On pain of vicious regress, compliance with an expression of a rule cannot itself always require yet further expressions to be complied with. More generally, for each sort of governing rule, it cannot be the case that, in order to comply with any rule of that sort, it is always necessary first to comply with some other rule of that sort. Hence, for each sort of governing rule, at least some rule compliance must be intelligible as *basic*, in the sense that the rule is not complied with by (that is, by means of) complying with some other rule(s) of that sort.[4] This regress in itself will not be of particular concern here. Rather, what is important is to discover and show which sorts of *basic* governing rule (or basic compliance with governing rules) ground the possibility of truth-telling.

There is no intrinsic difficulty with the notion of basic governing rules as such. Indeed, there is more than one kind of basic governing rule, and at least several of these are fairly well understood. The question is rather whether those basic governing rules that are essential to truth-telling can be understood in any of these familiar ways. In order to suggest a negative answer to this question, I want to summarize two different accounts of basic governing rules, each of which is plausibly adequate in its proper domain, and either of which might seem initially promising as a route to understanding the foundations of truth-telling. Showing how they nevertheless fall short can then be a guide to what is required instead.

3 BIOLOGICALLY EVOLVED NORMATIVITY

Consider first the normal operations of functional structures and organs in natural organisms. We understand these operations as following or according with governing rules. The very fact that they are called *normal* operations, in a sense that clearly contrasts with potential *ab*normalities, is a signal that they are understood in normative terms. Thus, it is not merely an exhibited regularity or propensity that hearts pump blood. Rather, they're supposed to pump blood; and when they don't, there's something wrong with them (or with something else that they depend on).

When we understand the rules of biological functioning as normative, where do we understand their normative force as coming from, and how do we understand that force as taking effect? Roughly, our understanding of the normative force is part of and integral to a larger account of how individual organisms of that kind work as a whole on the whole; that is, we understand it as deriving from the systematic contribution made by that proper functioning to that overall working in general. In other words, the understanding is holistic and statistical: the norms governing the component functions are intelligible together in terms of their interdependent roles in enabling the whole system to succeed—that system-level success being understood in turn in reproductive or evolutionary terms.[5] Thus, the mechanism of natural selection is how, in the fullness of time, the normative force is effectively brought to bear. Of course, natural selection does not operate on individuals, or in a single generation. But, retrospectively, we understand it as the mechanism by which proper functioning has been rendered typical in the current population.

I do not know how common it is in biological systems for an organ or subsystem to follow a rule by complying with an expression, or even an articulation, of that rule. I suppose that protein synthesis under the direction of genetic codes is a plausible candidate; control of growth, metabolism, and behavior by hormones and other messenger chemicals may be another; and response to signals in a nervous system is yet a third. There may even be structures within biological systems that are initially plastic, and come, in some rule-governed way, to express or articulate further rules in response to specific contingencies in the organism's life experience. This could be a kind of learning or behavioral "programming" that enhances fitness by fine-tuning each individual to its concrete circumstances.

Note merely that, in each of these cases, and in any others like them, the *basic* rule-following—the (equally normative) rule-following that is complying with the expressions as such—is itself also perfectly intelligible in biological terms. There is nothing problematic about it. Whether that basic rule-following is reductively explainable, or even just redescribable, in other (nonbiological) terms is not at issue here. Either way, its normative character, which derives from its functional role in the (not atypical) organic whole, makes sense biologically.

Not only can biological systems or states carry instructions (express rules) that other systems are supposed to follow; they can also carry *information*, about the state of something else, for the benefit of other systems (or the organism as a whole); and it can be their proper function to do so. To say that it is the *function* of a system to carry information about something allows an important distinction to be drawn. In the so-called information-theoretic sense, a signal either carries information about something or it doesn't; there's no such thing as misinformation. But if it is the function of a certain signal to carry certain information, then, if it *mal*functions, or if something else goes wrong, it can *mis*inform. In other words, biological functional *norms* make misinformation intelligible.

But there is another important distinction that biological norms do not enable. That is the distinction between functioning properly (under the proper conditions) as an information carrier and getting things right (objective correctness or truth), or, equivalently, between malfunctioning and getting things wrong (mistaking them). Since there is no *other* determinant or constraint on the information carried than whatever properly functioning carriers carry, when there is no malfunction, it's as "right" as it can be. In other words, there can be no biological basis for understanding a system as functioning properly, but nevertheless misinforming—functionally right but factually wrong, so to speak.

Imagine an insectivorous species of bird that evolved in an environment where most of the yellow butterflies are poisonous, and most others not; and suppose it has developed a mechanism for detecting and avoiding yellow butterflies. Then the point can be put this way: if a bird in good working order (with plenty of light, and so on) detects and rejects a (rare) nonpoisonous yellow butterfly, there can be no grounds for suggesting that it *mistook* that butterfly for a poisonous one; and similarly, if it detects and accepts a (rare) poisonous orange butterfly. Suppose further that (due to the way it is implemented) this "yellow-detecting" mechanism, even when working properly, happens also to give positive responses to a certain unusual pattern of red and green stripes, and indeed does not respond to yellow when it has a certain unusual mottling. Then, in such cases, we could not say that the birds mistook the stripes for yellow, or the mottled yellow for another color. For there is nothing that the response can "mean" other than whatever *actually* elicits it in normal birds in normal conditions.

Here is another way see the same point. Natural selection and the evolution of species can give sense to a kind of norm for individuals: a given specimen, or its particular circumstances, can be abnormal or out of order if it is contrary to what is normal for the relevant species. But no comparable sense extends to any idea of the species itself or the whole habitat (generation after generation) being out of order or "wrong". Thus, we cannot say of the above bird *species* that it is biologically abnormal in that its members cannot discriminate certain stripe patterns from yellow. The most we could ever do would be to suggest that its discrimination capabilities reflect a general design limitation (or compromise).

4 SOCIALLY INSTITUTED NORMATIVITY

Consider, now, a second example: social norms or mores, understood as instilled in succeeding generations through a process of training by their predecessors. This training and the response to it, the "learning", both follow rules, possibly of various sorts, even including social norms. But an analog of the foregoing regress argument shows that the learning itself cannot *all* be governed by social norms (unless children are born socialized, which would undermine the point of the account). Likewise, the learning cannot all be understood as following explicit rules (unless children are born able to use a language or similar notation).[6] So, at least some of the learning rules must be nonsocial, and at least some not explicit. An obvious candidate, since they are known to be operative in animals and humans anyway, are the rules of conditioning, habit formation, and the like—presumably themselves understood as biologically normative (functional).[7]

In my preferred variation on this theme, the emergence and maintenance of basic social norms is to be understood in terms of a package of (in the first place, biological) dispositions—or, rather, meta-dispositions—that I call *conformism*. The central idea is that community members effectively promote similarities in how they and their fellows are disposed to behave relative to circumstances. This presupposes that they can tell who behaved how in what circumstances, and how that compares with what others would have done; it also presupposes that they can modify their own and each other's dispositions in the direction of conformity. (Conditioning enters as a plausible component in the latter ability.) Assuming the dynamic parameters are compatible with stability, this *institutes* a community with a common set of social customs and mores.

We understand these customs as governing rules, as normative mores, because of the manner in which they are instituted and sustained. When an individual is deemed out of step, other community members intervene so as to restore compliance (in a way that, by assumption, is likely to be effective). Thus, in very concrete terms, there is a rule-to-world direction of fit: the discrepancy reflects on the individual, not the rule. The "normative force" of these mores is essentially majority rule: deviant behavior is what one is not supposed to do (abnormal, out of bounds) in the specific sense that it's what the community members on the whole will not allow. It is brought to bear—made effective—via peer pressure actuating the mechanisms of behavior modification (conditioning or whatever).

It isn't only the norms as such that are socially instituted, but also the respective behaviors and circumstances that those norms "connect". Thus, what it is to greet someone, and what it is to be a circumstance in which a greeting is appropriate, are nothing other than what the community members accept and deem as such—which is to say, they are themselves instituted along with the normative practices in which they occur, and by the same socializing process. This allows for considerable intricacy and interdependence—especially if community members can keep track of particulars and what has happened to them. For such tracking makes it possible for current behavior and circumstances to incorporate not just "manifest" recognizabilia, but instituted statuses and roles, accrued over time. Social rank and office can be instituted in this way, as well as finer-grained actions, rights, and responsibilities, such as those contingent on whose turn it is, who owns what, which water is holy, or how the teams stand in the league.[8]

Presumably, social customs and mores are in some sense grounded in biological functions such as sensory discrimination and behavioral conditioning. But they differ essentially from biological norms in the mechanism by which compliance is brought about, and therefore in the character of that to which they apply. One way or another, compliance with social norms is induced in individual community members via the monitoring and interference of others—at the outset, elders. And what the others (elders) press for is primarily a function of how they themselves were socialized.[9] In other words, each individual starts out as largely plastic, except for its susceptibility to socialization, and some tendency to pass it on. Therefore, whatever determinate institutional structure results is not constrained in detail by any biological raw materials, but rather emerges historically, in the form of a tradition.[10] (The passing on of customs to succeeding generations amounts to a new mechanism of reproduction, hence a possible new medium of selective evolution, analogous to but fundamentally distinct from that of genetic transmission.)

This same difference in mechanism is also the basis of a further and more striking difference in structure. Since the foundation of socialization is community members taking an interest in each others' behavior, including keeping it in line, it is of the essence that particular behaviors be assigned to particular perpetrators—namely, those very perpetrators who will have to be induced to change their ways, in case the behavior is inappropriate. In other words, socialized community members (unlike biological organs) must be understood as *agents*, to whom their behavior *belongs*, in the sense that they are accountable and can be taken to task for it.

As with some biological norms, it can be that some conformist social norms are followed by complying with expressions or articulations of them. Further, the prerequisite basic norms governing the scheme(s) of expression can themselves also perfectly well be social. (As before, it is not at issue here, and beside the point, whether the following of social norms is explainable, or even redescribable, in any other terms.) Finally, and again analogous to their biological counterparts, social norms can institute behaviors the proper social role of which is to carry information; and this underlying social normativity can likewise fund a distinction between information and misinformation. A light that is green when it *should be* red does not merely fail to carry information; it *misinforms*.

Here, then, is the pivotal question: can *social* norms as such—whether understood in conformist terms or in some others—enable, *unlike* biological norms, a distinction between proper performance and getting things right? I will argue that they cannot, as a last prelude to an exploration of what is required instead.

5 TELLING YELLOW

'To tell' can mean many things: to convey information, to instruct, to recount, to reveal. I want to pick up on (what I take to be) the core senses around identifying and discriminating: telling what (who, when, where, whether, ...) something is, telling things apart, telling the differences between them, and so on. Telling in these senses can often be expressed or reported in words, but is not in itself essentially verbal. People can tell things, and act accordingly, without ever verbalizing them; this, indeed, is the bulk of cases. People can tell things for which they have no words, including things that are hard to tell, things that are culturally determined, things the telling of which takes years to master.

More specifically: telling is a *responsive* rule-following (perhaps called for in the course of following some other governing rule) in which the propriety of the response (or what is done in following the other rule) depends on something external to the performance itself.[11] The telling is the responding to that something in the required way. Thus, telling is itself a following of a governing rule, and, as such, has a rule-to-world direction of fit, in the sense that performances can be faulty—performed improperly. But insofar as there is also a kind of propriety or correctness of a telling that is a function of that worldly something to which it is supposed to respond, there would seem, in addition, to be a world-to-*telling* direction of fit: in case of a discrepancy, it is the telling that is at fault, not whatever it is supposed to respond to. The essential question is whether—or rather how—these two governing norms, proper performance and getting things right, with their respective directions of fit, can ever be genuinely distinct. Can it ever be—and, if so, how—that a telling is performed properly (in proper conditions) and yet its response is wrong *about the world?*

Let's put words to what we want, and then see what we can get. The trouble with the insectivorous birds is that there is no definition of that to which they are *supposed to* respond except as that to which they *do* respond when everything is functionally in order. There is really only one type of norm at work, the biological norms governing that responsive function. The colors of the butterflies have no normative status at all apart from their involvement in that normal functioning. What *objectivity* demands, by contrast, is that the "objects" of objective tellings should have a determinacy and normative standing *independent* of the performance norms for those tellings, such that the tellings could be performed properly, and still get their objects wrong. In other words, there must be two distinct types of norm for objective tellings: *propriety* of the performances as such, and *correctness* of the results vis-à-vis their objects. And the objects themselves must stand as *independent criteria* for that correctness.

As noted in the previous section, social conformism institutes not only performance norms, but also the performances themselves and the conditions in which they would and would not be proper. Thus, hand in hand with a greeting norm, go not only the normal behaviors that amount to greetings, but also the normal conditions that call for them. And learning to greet properly involves learning to tell when these conditions obtain. But, as with the yellow butterflies for the birds, the normative status of those conditions is nothing other than their involvement in the social norm for proper greeting. So there is no room for a greeting—including telling when the appropriate conditions obtain—to have been performed correctly, according to the instituted norms for greetings, and yet to have got those conditions wrong. There is really only one type of norm at work: the instituted conditions themselves have no *independent* criterial status at all.

Here's another way to look at it. While instituted conditions are indeed independent of any individual's tellings, and even, on isolated occasions, of everyone's tellings, they are not, and cannot be, independent of the "general telling" of the community at large. Thus, there are two relevant generalities: the usual responses of any given individual, and the common responses of most individuals. It can happen that isolated individuals are consistently out of step with their peers; and it can also happen that, on isolated occasions, all or most members of the community (by an amazing coincidence) happen to misperform in the same way at the same time. What *cannot* happen is that all or most of the community members systematically respond wrongly to a certain class of instituted conditions—for their common systematic responses define the very conditions in question. Thus, the "independence" of instituted conditions can extend no farther than usual consensus. Since this consensus is nothing other than what determines propriety of performance, there is no room for *distinct* norms of propriety and correctness. Accordingly, there is a fatal flaw in any proposed account of objectivity that cannot give sense to the possibility of *everyone* being consistently wrong about something.[12]

A pair of contrasting examples will illustrate this point and bring out its urgency. They have the following common outline. In a certain community, everyone learns to *grock*[13] when it is proper—that is, in grock-worthy circumstances—and not otherwise. In so learning, they learn how to tell which circumstances are grock-worthy, how to tell when someone is grocking, and how to grock by themselves. And through the mechanisms of conformist normalizing, or something like them, they all acquire the normal dispositions of proper grocking. In this way, grocking, grock-worthiness, and the norms connecting them are all socially instituted together. In terms of these institutions, we can understand what it would be for a member of this community to tell grock-worthy circumstances *wrongly* (or even for everyone to be wrong once in a while).

But could they ever *all* be wrong in some systematic way? Or, more poignantly, could they all be wrong but one? Until a few weeks ago, say, everyone concurred in telling grock-worthy circumstances. But then poor Pat began to diverge: sometimes everyone grocked but Pat; sometimes Pat grocked and no one else did. Pat protested and persevered against the tide for a while; but, conformism being what it is, everyone agreed again soon enough. Now, is there any chance that, during the disturbance, Pat was right and the others wrong? Would it so much as make sense to imagine that initially they had it right, but then, somehow, Pat led them all astray? Or, could it be that, initially, everyone had it wrong, until Pat finally got it right, and then brought the others around? On what basis could these alternatives even be differentiated, let alone be decided among? It depends.

Suppose, for the first case, that grocking is a special maneuver that is called for, according to the villagers, in a certain circumstance that occasionally arises in a rather free-form folk dance. Outsiders have a hard time telling when these circumstances arise, not to mention whether the relevant dancer grocks; and the villagers are not very good at explaining either one. But—until the incident with Pat, anyway—they never had any trouble telling what was going on, and agreeing among themselves. In this case, it seems to me that mere conformist norms are the only norms intelligibly in play. If all the other villagers consistently disagree with Pat, then they are right and Pat is wrong, in the only sense of right and wrong that I can understand as pertinent. This remains so regardless of whether there is any independent way for *us* to determine which dancing is the "same" as which, or who changed when. That is, it doesn't matter whether Pat changed, the (other) villagers changed, neither, or both, or even whether this makes sense to ask; at all events, the villagers are authoritative about their dance.

Suppose, for the second case, that grocking is pronouncing the word 'yellow', and that grock-worthy circumstances are those which, in the face of something yellow, call for a color-identifying response. If there is anything to objective truth-telling, a case like this had better be different from the folk dance. On the one hand, of course, which sign is to be used for yellow—'jaune', 'gelb', a certain handwave—is entirely a matter of public consensus, just like the dance step. There is no way everyone could be wrong about that, or Pat right and everyone else wrong. On the other hand, however, that some particular object *is in fact* yellow is not a matter of consensus: it's an objective state of affairs, quite apart from any and every response to it. Accordingly, once the customs have established that 'yellow' (or whatever) is the proper way to identify the color of yellow things, Pat's systematic responses to that object could perfectly well be right, and everyone else's wrong; or they could all be wrong.

The trouble is, instituted norms alone cannot sustain this distinction. If what it is to be yellow were itself instituted along with the norm for responding properly to it, then the consensus could no more be wrong about what is yellow than about the proper (customary) response thereto. Imagine a charismatic florist who, without affecting any other color responses, convinced everyone that a certain jonquil is sacred, and that the proper color response to it is not 'yellow' but 'scarlet'. In thus determining the general disposition, the charismatic florist would *ipso facto* just (further) determine what it is to *be* "yellow" (and "scarlet"), for purposes of proper color response in this community—and, if the norms are merely instituted, what other purposes could be relevant? By the same token, however, such responses would not be *objective* color reports (that is, not really *color* reports at all).

Approaches to normativity that take its bases to lie in social institution may be termed *pragmatist*. My aim here is not so much to argue the inadequacy of pragmatism as to sketch an alternative. But the motivation for this aim might be illuminated by what I take to be an historical parallel with *psychologism*.

All sides agree that thought processes are not and cannot be random or gratuitous. Impressed by the achievements of natural science (and abjuring divine guidance), naturalistic psychologists (such as Hume and Mill) argue that the necessary order could only be a matter of natural law, on a par with physical regularity. Impressed more by the possibility of doing science than its results, antipsychologists (such as Kant and Frege) retort that there must be two fundamentally distinct sorts of necessary order: the laws of nature and the laws or norms of reason. To collapse the rational normative into the natural nomological is to obliterate the essential character of thought.

Sensitive to both of these pulls, contemporary pragmatists (such as Rorty and Brandom) agree that thought is essentially norm-governed, but hold that normativity too can be understood in a way that is not incompatible with an appropriate naturalism—namely, in terms of socially instituted proprieties.[14] Likewise sensitive to both pulls, but convinced that genuine science is more than a social institution, antipragmatists (such as Heidegger and I) retort that there must be two fundamentally distinct sorts of normative constraint: social propriety and objective correctness (truth). To collapse correctness into propriety is to obliterate the essential character of thought. Indeed, the two retorts are equivalent if one supposes—as I do, and as I believe Kant and Frege did—that the norms of reason and of objective truth are ultimately the same.

How, then, can norms of objective correctness be understood (in a spirit of naturalism, appropriately construed[15])?

6 Constitutive rules and regulations

Some years ago, John Rawls and John Searle each introduced a distinction between two senses of 'rule' (and hence also of 'following'). Although the purposes and specifics are different, both distinctions are drawn within the general class of governing rules, and they more or less coincide on one side. Broadly speaking, the distinction in each case is between, on the one hand, rules that govern phenomena that already make sense as what they are, independently of those rules, and, on the other hand, rules that define or constitute the phenomena that they govern—phenomena which, therefore, could not make sense independently of those rules. It is these latter, *constitutive* rules, that Rawls and Searle concur on, and that matter here. Though is no part of what they intended, it will be my purpose to show that constitution can be essentially more than mere institution.

Rawls (1955, section 3) distinguishes rules in the sense of 'maxims' or 'rules of thumb' from what he calls 'the practice conception of rules'. *Maxims* are guides to action that summarize the results of earlier analyses and/or the wisdom of experience. Their point is efficiency and convenience, particularly in situations where it isn't feasible (or worth the trouble) to figure out exactly what is optimal; hence, they carry the force of advice or prudence. So, for instance, "Have a physical exam annually" and "Don't take candy from strangers" are maxims. Notice that the phenomena of having exams, taking candy, and so on, are perfectly intelligible apart from these and other such rules.

By contrast, rules in the *practice sense* are definitive or constitutive of the very phenomena that they govern. Rawls invokes games, especially baseball, to illustrate the difference. Here's an example: in American baseball, there's a rule according to which, when a batter gets three strikes, he or she is out. This rule is not a guideline based on previous analysis or experience, and it is in no sense advice. Rather, this rule, along with others, defines the very notions of batter, strike, out, and so on. It's not just the words or concepts that are "defined", but the phenomena themselves: they only *make sense* as *being what they are* in terms of their according with these rules. This is what is meant by saying that the rules are *constitutive*. Apart from these rules that constitute the game of baseball, there could be no such thing as a batter, a strike, or an out.

Of course, there could be—indeed, are—games more or less similar to American baseball ("hardball"), with roles and phenomena analogous to these, and even called by the same names. But nothing important hinges on when or how we decide whether to construe such phenomena as the same or different. Is a "strike" in Finnish baseball, or sandlot softball *the same thing as* a strike in American hardball? Well, roughly, but not exactly, depending on the aim of the question. To say that games are constituted by rules, and that these rules therefore define the phenomena of the game, is not to be committed to any tendentious sort of essentialism. Strikes in all of the above forms are constituted phenomena, whether precisely or loosely defined, whether deemed the same or different.

Searle (1969, section 2.5) distinguishes between what he calls "regulative" and "constitutive" rules. *Regulative* rules are regulations: they stipulate how, in relevant circumstances, some agent or agents may or must act. Unlike maxims, regulative rules are genuine imperatives and permissives: they carry the force of some antecedently legitimate authority. So "You must be in bed by 10 o'clock" and "Thou shalt not bear false witness" are regulative rules. But again, the phenomena of being in bed and bearing false witness, like those of having an exam and taking candy, are perfectly intelligible apart from such rules.

Like Rawls, Searle uses games—especially chess and football—to illustrate the notion of constitutive rule. And he makes many of the same points, including that constitutive rules define and make possible the very phenomena that they govern. But there is one important difference in Searle's account that is a symptom, I think, of an underlying problem in both. According to Searle, constitutive rules are a special case of regulative rules: every constitutive rule is also regulative (but not vice versa). For instance, the rules of chess or football stipulate how the game is to be played: they specify what the players *qua* players are required and/or permitted to do.

Rawls could not (and does not) make a parallel claim, because constitutive rules are obviously not maxims. (There are, to be sure, plenty of prudential maxims in constituted games—when to bunt, or when to develop one's queen, say—but these are not the rules constitutive of the game.) This difference between Rawls and Searle, however, reflects only the fact that maxims are not regulative; it does not show that rules in Rawls's practice sense are not a special sort of regulation. Indeed, reliance on game examples tends to focus attention on the rules governing the *players*, and hence positively invites the subsumption of constitutive rules under regulations—as much for Rawls as for Searle.

This is but one instance of how the use of games as examples is fraught with philosophical peril. In order, therefore, that the advantages of such examples—especially their structure and (relative) transparency—not be distorted or destroyed, it will be necessary to spell out several distinctions and qualifications.

7 CONSTITUTIVE STANDARDS

There are, I believe, at least four distinct sorts of rule and rule-following telescoped into what Rawls and Searle, relying on game examples, have called "constitutive" rules. First, of course, there are the "rules of the game", which regulate the actions of the players within the game, stipulating what they may or may not, must or must not do. These are the rules that one has in view when one thinks of "playing by the rules"; and they are clearly what is foremost in the minds of Rawls and Searle. To avoid confusion, I will call constitutive rules in this sense *constitutive regulations*—just as Searle's terminology suggests. The normative authority of such regulations derives from an (often tacit) agreement or convention (mutual deontic commitment) among the players, and is enforced by threat of ejection from the game.

Constitutive regulations, however, governing only the actions of the players, are not the same as what I will call *constitutive standards*, which govern *all* the phenomena that occur within the game, and determine what they are. This distinction can be hard to see. For instance, a baseball player can become a base-runner by first being a batter and then hitting a pitch into fair territory, being hit by a pitch, or receiving a base on balls (a walk). A base-runner (who has not been tagged, forced, or caught out, and whose side has not been retired) may advance from base to base, but only in order, and only when the ball is in play or the pitcher has begun to pitch. These rules, *qua* regulations, govern the actions of the players. But, at the same time, *qua* specifications of what can and cannot happen in the game, they effectively determine what it is to be a base-runner. It is only in this latter capacity that I call them constitutive *standards*. The reason that the same rules—or, at any rate, what seem like the same rules—can wear both hats (thereby making the hats hard to distinguish) is that the players' actions are among the phenomena that can occur within the game.

But not all the phenomena that can or must occur within a game, and are constituted as such, are actions of the players. For instance, a baseball game needs bases and a ball. The bases must lie on the ground (in a diamond, 90 feet apart), remain visible, and not move. The ball, when pitched, must sail through the air toward the strike zone, deviating at most slightly from a ballistic trajectory; when hit by the bat, it must rebound (not stick to the bat or explode) and sail off in another direction; and so on. These requirements are not regulations governing the actions of any players; yet they are constitutive of what it is to be bases and balls, hence, indirectly, also of other baseball phenomena. Similarly, chess pieces must be amenable to the players' moves, and must remain where and what they are when not being moved. Here we have constitutive standards that are clearly not constitutive regulations.

It is easy to underestimate constitutive standards. In games like chess and baseball, all the "action" is initiated and largely controlled by the players; the constituted paraphernalia, by contrast, are required merely to remain suitably at their disposal—a kind of compliance and inertness clause. Thus, the standards governing how rooks may move, thereby constituting what it is to be a rook, are (apart from that inertness clause) little more than an isomorph of the regulations governing how players may move their rooks. And since, if there were no players playing by the rules, there would surely be no games, moves, or pieces at all, it looks as if the regulations are primary, the standards being just a shadow they cast in a certain analytic light.

As a step toward working free of this impression, consider *semiautomatic* chess, which is just like chess except that random legal moves are automatically inserted between the moves made by the players (a random white move before white plays, and a random black move before black plays). In effect, half of the moves are made by the pieces themselves. Given the needed equipment, this is a perfectly playable game, maybe even interesting. But precisely because automatic pieces must sometimes move themselves—and then only legally—much more is required of them than mere compliance and inertness. Thus, the constitutive standards defining them are far from mere shadows of regulations governing what the players may do.

The point can be made all the more vivid by imagining more elaborate variations—call them *automatic* chess—such as games in which the moves that the pieces can make on their own are qualitatively different from those that the players may make with them, or games in which many or even most of the pieces move exclusively by themselves, only a few being movable by the players. There need not even be a requirement of taking turns; and some or all of the players may be cooperating instead of competing. But none of these variations would undermine the idea that what the pieces are is *constituted* by the standards governing how they can move in the game. The difference is that those standards are so conspicuously distinct from, and potentially more important than, the regulations governing how the players may play, that the tables are perhaps turned. So far from the standards being mere shadows of the regulations, it may rather be that the regulations themselves are constitutive only because they enjoin the players to move the pieces in accord with the pertinent extant standards—which would be to say, they are simply constitutive of the players as players.

8 CONSTITUTIVE AND MUNDANE SKILLS

By *know-how* or *skill* I mean a reliable, resilient ability to abide by a governing rule correctly and reliably. *Resilience*, as here intended, is related to reliability, but is not the same, and maybe a little harder to explain. It's a kind of perseverance born simultaneously of adaptability and self-assurance. I have in mind, as a paradigm of resilience, an expert who "knows full well" that he or she can do something—and *so* is not turned aside or discouraged at the first, or even the second, sign of recalcitrance. Adjust a bit here, try that a little longer, don't fall for every semblance of trouble: these are the stuff of resilience as we admire it in physicians and mechanics, scientists and school teachers. But everyone is a skillful expert at lots of things. Nearly all of us can tie our shoes in the cold, describe one friend to another, tell whether the roast is done—and because we know we can, we stick to it in the face of initial difficulty.

Needless to say, people have skills of many different sorts. I want to distinguish two general sorts of skill—*constitutive* and *mundane*—that are (as I shall argue) quite different from one another, and yet essentially interdependent. The classification is meant to be exclusive; but it is far from exhaustive. I will introduce them first in connection with understanding games; indeed, the whole point of talking about games has been to set up an account of this distinction and the relational structure that supports it. But the eventual goal is to reinforce and elaborate that structure, while leaving games behind.

Constitutive *skills* are the third of the four sorts of rule and rule-following that (along with constitutive regulations and constitutive standards) Rawls and Searle had telescoped together in their accounts of constitutive rules. A *constitutive* skill is a resilient ability to tell whether the phenomena governed by some constitutive standard are, in fact, in accord with that standard. So, for chess, the constitutive skills are those skills that each player has, and must have, to tell whether any specified move is or would be legal. Clearly, no one who lacked these skills could play chess: to be a chess player, one must be able to tell not only whether the candidate moves that one is considering would be legal, but also whether the moves that one's opponent actually makes (or attempts) are in fact legal.

To exercise a constitutive skill is itself to follow a rule—indeed, a governing rule. But the rules that are being followed in exercising these skills are not at all the same as the rules—namely, the constitutive standards—compliance with which is being monitored in those exercises. Telling whether a chess move is legal is quite different even from making a legal move, never mind being one. Accordingly, the normative authority of these rules, and the way it is brought to bear, must also be distinct from the standards. (We will return to this topic in section 16.)

Note that a player need have no further knowledge of the constitutive standards beyond this ability to tell whether they are being followed in practice. A chess-player need not be able to recite the rules of chess, to assent when somebody else recites them, to refer or defer to somebody who can recite them, or anything else apart from being able to apply them in practice, in exercises of constitutive skills. On the other hand, ability to recite the rules in their fullest precision and glory would be for nought in actual play without the ability to apply them. This suggests that, with regard to the standard-governedness of constituted phenomena, constitutive skills have a kind of practical priority over any articulate expression, or even expressibility, of the standards.

Mundane skills, by contrast, are the resilient abilities to recognize, manipulate, and otherwise cope with phenomena within the game, including other players, as required and permitted by the rules—in effect, the ability to engage in play. Thus, in order to play chess at all, a player must be able to tell, for each piece, what kind of piece it is, what square it occupies, what squares it threatens, and so on, as well as to move and capture pieces on the board, keep track of whose move it is, and a few other things. (A better player needs to be able to tell and do much more than that.) The mundane skills required for baseball are rather more challenging: not only to run, hit, throw, and catch, but also to tell whether a pitch will be (or was) a strike, whether a base-runner will (or did) beat a throw, whether a fielder will (or did) make a catch, and so on. Baseball also requires the ability to keep track of several on-going statuses that are not present and manifest, such as the batting order, the score, the inning, the number of outs, and the count on the current batter.

Constitutive skills depend in an obvious way on mundane skills: in order to tell whether constituted phenomena are in accord with the constitutive standards, it is necessary to be able to tell what those phenomena are. A chess player could hardly tell whether a given move is legal without telling which piece is moving and how, not to mention what other pieces are where on the board. The three-strikes-and-you're-out rule could hardly be applied if no one could tell a strike from a ball, or keep track of the count.

Mundane skills depend, in a different but equally obvious way, on constitutive skills. There could be no telling which pieces are where on the board if there were no such things as chess pieces—which is to say, if there were no constitutive standards applicable in practice via constitutive skills. To put it another way, if nobody could tell a legal from an illegal chess move, then nobody could tell a chess rook from a chess knight, because there would be no chess games, hence no such pieces. Likewise, there would be no baseball strikes and outs to tell if nobody could tell what is and isn't required and allowed in baseball.

There is another aspect of the relation between mundane and con-stitutive skills, implicit in the foregoing, but important enough to spell out. Mundane skills are, in an oblique or extended sense, game phenomena themselves. The sense is this: they are what they are only in connection with the game and with its phenomena in the strict sense. The abilities to recognize or move a rook, to call or throw a strike, make no more sense apart from chess or baseball than do rooks or strikes themselves. The reason the sense is oblique or extended is that the skills as such are not governed by the constitutive standards (at least not directly); so they are not constituted in the same sense as the phenomena in the strict sense are. We might instead think of mundane skills as "co-constituted" along with the phenomena that their exercises respond to, manipulate, and cope with.[16]

The strategy from now on will be to show how some mundane skills, understood in this sense as interdependent with constitutive skills, can therefore also be understood as *objective*—that is, as having independent objects that are criterial for their correct exercise. By 'object' I mean in general that which occupies a certain position *vis-à-vis* such skills, and not any specific character. Thus, objects need not be corporeal, substantial, or particularly thing-like. Rather, they are "objective phenomena" in the following three-fold sense: (i) mundane skills are responsive to and/or can affect them (they are *accessible*); (ii) they have normative status as criterial for the correct exercise of objective skills (they are *authoritative*); and (iii) they are independent not only of particular exercises but also of any mere consensus (they are *autonomous*[17]). The idea then is: *constituted* phenomena, and *only* constituted phenomena, can thus stand as accessible independent criteria, hence *be objects*—and therefore also that this is what we ordinarily and scientifically understand by 'object'.

What, then, is constitution?

9 LETTING BE

To constitute is to bring into being. This formulation, while strictly defensible, is deliberately provocative. For it seems to force a choice between two hopeless ways of understanding the idea that ordinary objective phenomena are constituted, one incredible, the other self-defeating. That provocation sets a stage on which the merits of a more careful formulation—constituting is *letting be*—can come into view.

According to the incredible reading, bringing into being means creating—that is, causing to be. Causal creation might be *ex nihilo*: "And God said, 'Let there be light'; and there was light." Or it might be fashioning or generating out of some available materials, by giving them some different or additional form. A poet creates a poem by arranging extant words in a new order; a builder makes a house out of provided lumber by cutting and reassembling. Likewise, it might be suggested, ordinary phenomena (objects of experience, for instance) are constituted by us as follows: we have or are given some raw materials (raw sensory data, perhaps), and we *make* objects out of them by imposing on them some suitable objective form.[18]

Constitutive standards, on this approach, would amount to success conditions. In the most straightforward case, they would just be the imposed forms construed as antecedent specifications on the objects to be created. And those objects would be nothing other than the given materials, as shaped or formed by us—hence literally our creations. Never mind whether or how creation could account for the objectivity of objects—that is, for their standing as accessible autonomous authorities. For, to take the suggestion seriously at all would be to maintain that constituted objects simply do not exist until the moment of their constitution. While such a consequence might be plausible for *some* constituted objects (chess pieces, for instance), it would be utterly incredible in any account of the constitution of many ordinary things (not to mention the objects investigated by most sciences).

The apparent alternative is to suppose that the objects as such are already there, and that constitution just means taking them to be— "counting them as"—something *else*, over and above what they already were. Thus, they aren't brought into being altogether, but only *as* what they newly become. Unlike creation out of available materials, bringing into being by counting-as doesn't rearrange or give new form to what's already there, but only accords it some new status, qualification, or role. So constitutive standards would be, in effect, the definitions of these new statuses, construed as preconditions on counting as having them. For instance, letting little figurines figure as pieces in a chess game doesn't form them in any way or rearrange what they're made of, but rather—so it is tempting to say—simply allows them to fill specified roles for the duration of a game. (Both Rawls and Searle explicitly connect constitution with counting-as.)

This second alternative, however, is philosophically self-defeating. Never mind how it could account for the constitution of sticks and stones, protons and quasars. (What already accessible entities could be "counted as" such things?) The approach is broken-backed for a more basic reason. The project is to understand the objecthood of objects—their standing as criteria for objective skills—in terms of their constitutedness. But counting-as *presupposes* the objecthood of the objects that are counted as something else, and merely adds onto those objects some new relative features (relative to whatever they are counted as). On this line, for example, a rook would just *be* a certain figurine (or whatever) for as long as the latter is so counted—with all its chess features relative to that counting. But it would really be the figurine itself that stood as the independent criterion for the players' perceptions or actions: they would have to locate and identify the figurine correctly, in order to tell where the rook is, or to move it. In other words, if all constitution were mere counting-as, it would always presuppose, hence could never contribute to, an account of objectivity—which would forfeit the point.

Letting there be light, or *letting* figurines be pieces, are at best special cases of the constitution of objects as objects. How can we understand constitution—letting be—more generally, such that it is neither incredible nor self-defeating as the basis of an account of objectivity as such?

10 Esoteric chess

The temptation to understand constitution as creating or counting-as (making or taking) is another of the perils of starting with games. As before, the first step on the road to recovery is to tinker with the examples in such a way as to make unnoticed but important characteristics conspicuous. Consider, for this purpose, *esoteric* chess, which differs from ordinary chess only in the "medium" in which it is played. Like all chess players, players of esoteric chess must learn to recognize and move the pieces, in the course of playing the game; only, for them, it's much harder than for ordinary chess players. It is this peculiar difficulty that makes the game esoteric.

The relevant point can be brought out through a pair of complementary analogies. On the one hand, there are the "chicken-sexers" of epistemological lore: semi-skilled laborers who, through long training, can learn to tell the sex of a newly hatched chick. But they don't know *how* they can tell; it's as if they acquire a new perceptual primitive. On the other hand, there are various "hidden picture" puzzles and novelties: arrangements of line and color that seem, at first, to be mere random jumbles or scatters, but in which, though diligence and practice, one can come to be able to see, often with startling clarity, an image that was previously quite imperceptible. In both cases, the resulting ability is a resilient and reliable responsive skill.

The analogies are alike in that the ability to perceive something comes only slowly and with difficulty, but then becomes easy. They differ in what makes them compelling. The chicken-sexers have no idea why some chicks strike them as male and others female; but there is an independent and conclusive test for whether they're getting it right: letting the chicks grow up. By contrast, when one "gets" a hidden image, there is no doubt about why one takes it to be an image: it looks remarkably like other images with which one is already familiar. But there is no comparable independent test for getting it right—just the concurrence of other viewers (and perhaps the puzzle's designer).

Esoteric chess players, after enough training, can also "just tell" the positions, moves, and pieces when they *see* them—even though untrained eyes can't discern anything (a cloud, a jumble, a mass of digits, ...). The ability to *make* moves calls, of course, for comparable training—the uninitiated can't get the hang of it at all for a while, but once mastered it's practically effortless.[19] What would make these abilities similarly compelling? Unlike chicks, esoteric pieces never "grow up". Nor can it be that, once seen, they look remarkably like chess pieces; for there's nothing that chess pieces as such look like. What makes chess pieces the chess pieces they are is not how they'll grow up, nor what they look like, but rather how they can move in a chess game—that is, the constitutive standards by which they abide, and in terms of which they are thus intelligible.

Therefore, esoteric chess skills will be "compelling" just in case, via them, the players can and do actually play chess with one another. If the players can play chess, then not only must they be able to tell and make moves, but also the pieces themselves must be abiding by the standards. The players will be playing via their esoteric skills—that is, using the esoteric pieces—if they are relying on them to produce and keep track of the positions (instead of, for instance, playing by memory, as in blindfold chess). Some regime like the following might help to show that they are really doing that: player-one makes a move in the absence of player-two, and then exits; player-two enters and does the same; and so on. Under these conditions, a legal game could ensue only if each player could actually make moves (changes in the position) that the other could then perceive. And even outsiders could confirm that the game was legal if the players were also discreetly recording or confiding their moves as they made them.

In an earlier example, we saw that communal agreement is necessary and sufficient for determining proper dance performances and recognitions. Esoteric chess is similar in that the moves are what the initiates make and accept from one another as such. But, unlike grock'n roll, esoteric chess depends also on the behavior of the pieces themselves. If the pieces were not in fact movable by the players, and if they did not in fact sit still and stay the same between moves, the game could not be played. Hence, consensus regarding the identity of moves and pieces also *depends on* this behavior, and cannot be sufficient to establish it or make it the case. *Because* the constitutive standards for the game are more than mere shadows of regulations governing what the players do, correctness regarding game phenomena is more than mere consensus. In effect, the compliance and inertness clause is the "empirical content" of esoteric (and ordinary) chess.

Letting esoteric chess pieces be is neither creating them nor counting other items (already objectively intelligible) as them. In particular, esoteric chess players do not first see jumbles or masses of digits (as others might) and then "count them as" chess pieces, any more than you or I first see sense data or colored surfaces and then "count them as" a tomato. They don't see jumbles or digits at all (and, indeed, they may never have), but only chess pieces. Letting esoteric chess pieces be is *finding* them—learning to find them—by finding that chess can be played with them. In playing chess with them, one finds (and shows) that they are intelligible and usable chess pieces, in accord with the constitutive standards of chess. Constituting objects is letting them be by finding and showing that they make sense in some determinate way, and can consistently be told and otherwise coped with as such.

This is just as true for ordinary as for esoteric chess pieces. Letting them be the objects that they are, namely chess pieces, is nothing other than making sense of them as chess pieces by playing chess with them. The fact that they coincide for a while with—are "implemented in" or "carried by"—plastic figurines (or whatever) is a practical convenience and an ontological distraction. Chess pieces are no more figurines than words are sounds, or thoughts are brain states. Esoteric chess makes vivid, what can remain concealed in ordinary chess, that what chess players perceive and move, the *objects* that stand as criteria for the correct exercise of their mundane skills, are chess pieces, not figurines.

II EMPIRICAL CHESS

To pick out and specify the objects of chess skills is not yet to explain *how* they can stand as such objects. In other words, the philosophical work of understanding objectivity has not been accomplished but only, so to speak, located. Perhaps the most stubborn obstacle standing in the way of games as a model for objectivity is the fact that they are made up—they are our own inventions, tailored to our own tastes and purposes. Surely this is, on the face of it, the antithesis of genuine independence and objectivity. What's worse, constitutedness itself seems deeply connected with this very made-up-ness that jeopardizes independence (autonomy). How, then, can constitution, as extracted from and explicated via game examples, form the basis of an account of objectivity?

This final challenge will be met with the ultimate tinkered example. *Empirical* chess is esoteric *and* automatic chess, only more so. Automatic chess, remember, is a game (or class of games) in which most of the moves are made by the pieces themselves, and most or all of the rules—that is, standards—according to which their moves are legal differ from those according to which the pieces moved by the players may move. (Also, there need be no turn-taking, and the players may be cooperating instead of competing.) What has so far been left unspecified, however, is where the rules come from, and why the pieces abide by them.

Approaching the example as a *game* encourages one to suppose that the rules are stipulated, or at least understood, in advance, and that the pieces abide by those rules because they have been constructed, or at least selected, in advance to behave that way. But these suppositions are not necessary. Imagine that the interesting challenge is not so much winning the game as figuring out what it is—that is, how to play it. Or—more to the point—it can be part of the challenge to ascertain whether there's a game at all or not, and, if so, what belongs to it and what doesn't. Such an exploratory pursuit would be, I think, *empirical* in a full and proper sense; this is what I mean by "empirical chess". (By the same token, of course, it is "chess", or even a game, in at best a stretched or metaphorical sense.)

The conspicuous "self-action" exhibited by automatic chess pieces is an extrapolation of the inconspicuous compliance and inertness that is prerequisite in ordinary game paraphernalia—thus, of what was earlier called the "empirical content" of such games. Empirical chess is an extrapolation of another easily overlooked feature of ordinary games as well: some imaginable games are (would be) playable, and some not. For instance, there could not be a variant of baseball in which the pitcher is required to make the ball "hang" for a second or two in front of the batter, before hurtling on to the catcher. The problem is not in getting the pitcher to comply, but in getting the *ball* to comply. A game with such a rule could not in fact be played. What that shows is that the rules of even so "made up" a game as baseball are not entirely up to us—far from it, in fact.

Finding that a game is playable—or, better, finding a game that is playable—is therefore a kind of *achievement*, one that includes an element of "discovery" about the world. This element of discovery is quite different, of course, from the sort of discovery that is possible *within* a game: that one's rook is indefensible, or that the batter is trying to bunt, for instance. Rather, it's something like a prior or "meta" discovery to the effect that indefensible rooks or attempted bunts are intelligibly possible at all, and how they are possible. If we call such "meta discovery" *disclosure*, we can reserve the word 'discovery' for ordinary or mundane findings within the game.[20] What is disclosed, then, is the playable game as such, including the intelligible domain within which its phenomena make the sense they make.

Manifestly, finding a version of empirical chess that is playable would be much more of an achievement, much *harder*, than finding that ordinary (or even esoteric) chess is playable. Accordingly, the element of disclosure would be larger, more impressive—it would seem much more like *finding* something. Yet empirical "chess" remains a constituted domain that can only be entered into by those who have mastered unobvious ("esoteric") mundane skills—skills the proper exercise of which can only be gauged by others who are already initiated. Except, unlike the original esoteric chess example, now even the rules and standards are problematic and at stake. So *how*, exactly, can this alleged "achievement" *be hard*? What keeps anybody honest?

12 THE EXCLUDED ZONE

Return, for a moment, to ordinary (or merely esoteric) chess. Rooks are pieces that move in a certain way, in the context of a game; bishops, knights, and so on, are pieces that move in their respective different ways. Just such pieces are what the players must, with their mundane skills, be able to recognize as rooks, bishops, knights, and the rest. Further, of course, the players must be able to recognize various positions and moves on the board—not to mention, to "make" some of them.

Now, recognizing that something is a rook cannot amount simply to recognizing that it is presently moving along a rank or file. For one thing, other pieces sometimes move along ranks or files; and, for another, rooks need to be recognizable even when they're not moving. Likewise, and for similar reasons, recognizing that a piece is presently moving along a rank or file cannot amount simply to recognizing that it is a rook. In other words, the skills for recognizing pieces and moves must be separate and exercisable independently of one another. So, to recognize a piece of a certain type moving in a certain way requires (at least) three recognitive abilities: for the type of piece, for the way it is moving, and for, so to speak, their combination (in the *same* piece).[21]

Not all recognizable combinations of recognizable pieces and moves would be legal; in fact, most wouldn't. For instance, were a rook to move along a diagonal, or a bishop to move otherwise than along a diagonal, the players would be able to recognize as much, even though either would be completely illegal (that is, contrary to the constitutive standards). Indeed, the recognizability in principle of illegal moves (or purported moves) is prerequisite to constitutive standards and legality as such. For if, in principle, nothing recognizable could ever be illegal, then the "standards" would impose no difference, and legality itself would be without content.

Yet the very idea of an illegal move flirts with paradox. That there should be chess phenomena at all *presupposes* that they accord with the rules (standards) that constitute chess as such. Nothing is so much as intelligible, let alone recognizable, as a chess phenomenon outside of the domain constituted according to those standards. In a perfectly straightforward sense, the rules delimit everything that is intelligibly *possible* in a chess game; anything not within those limits is precisely *ruled out*. Hence, strictly speaking, illegal moves are impossible. Yet they must be recognizable—and hence (in at least that sense) something that conceivably *"could"* occur—if the ruling-out is to be nonvacuous. That's the paradox.

Evidently, there must be two distinct senses of 'can' or 'possible' associated with any constituted domain—one wider and one narrower. The wider sense, which we might call the *conceivable*, comprises everything that the players, *qua* players, would have the resources to recognize or otherwise cope with, were it to occur. It is, in effect, the scope or compass of all the mundane skills needed for and thus belonging to the domain.[22] The narrower or stricter sense, for which we can now reserve the term *possible*, includes only that which would accord with the constitutive standards, were it to occur. Thus, in this sharpened usage, illegal moves are conceivable but not possible. On the other hand, whatever is possible in a domain is conceivable in it. (Note that the conceivable, as here defined, is always tied to the skills belonging to—co-constituted with—a particular domain; it does not mean the conceivable, let alone the imaginable, "at large".)

Yet there remains a peculiarity, even after the distinction. For consider that zone of the conceivable that lies "out of bounds" for some domain—that which, though conceivable, is impossible in the strict sense. Let's call it the *excluded zone*. As we have noted, the extent of this zone cannot be zero; on the contrary, the conceivable must extend well beyond the possible, lest the constitutive standards be vacuous, and the domain itself devoid of form. At the same time, however, anything that is conceivable in a domain at all is so only in relation to the mundane objective skills that belong to that domain. And these skills, in turn, along with the constituted phenomena that are supposed to stand as criteria for their correct or successful exercise, only make sense insofar as those phenomena *in fact* abide by the constitutive standards. In other words, the very intelligibility of the excluded zone depends on its being *actually empty* (or virtually so).[23]

Every constituted domain requires an excluded zone—a non-zero extension of the conceivable beyond the possible—that is *in fact* empty. It is excluded in the sense that "phenomena" in it are not possible; they are ruled out by the constitutive standards. But such phenomena are nevertheless conceivable (hence, the extent of the zone is non-zero) in that, were they to occur, they could be recognized by exercises of the mundane skills that belong to the domain. *Therefore*, the crucial requirement that they don't in fact occur is subject to empirical test. The availability of such tests is what lets disclosure be *hard*—lets it be an *achievement*—because it is vulnerable, liable to fail.

So far, however, this notion of empirical testability is very general. In order to elaborate it into an account of objective correctness (truth), at least three issues remain to be addressed: (i) how, given that general liability to failure, individual skills and results can be tested; (ii) how such testability can vest normative authority in the objects (objective phenomena) themselves—let them be criteria; and (iii) how that objective authority (force) is in fact brought to bear and made effective.

13 PRECARIOUS EQUILIBRIUM

Prima facie, a test is a confrontation between exercises of two (or more) mundane skills; a failure is an incompatibility between the findings (or other results) of those exercises. Incompatibilities are excluded combinations—a rook moving along a diagonal, for instance—where excluded means ruled out by the constitutive standards. But constitutive standards are brought to bear in practice via exercises of constitutive skills. It is by exercise of constitutive skills that players can tell when something has gone wrong. So, more deeply, a test is a confrontation among exercises of two or more mundane skills *and* at least one constitutive skill.

In the face of a challenge, either a particular exercise of a skill, or that skill itself, can come into question; that is, it could be either that the performance was somehow erroneous (in a sense that is so far neutral between impropriety of performance and incorrectness of result), and should be revised (rectified), or else that the skill itself is somehow defective or inadequate, and should be repaired (modified and improved). Accordingly, there are four basic responses to a failure: mundane or constitutive revision or repair. As a matter of principle, none of these can be taken lightly. If performances or skills are "revised" or "repaired" casually, at the first sign of trouble, then nothing is seriously excluded, and all "testing" is a farce. This is *why* the skills must be *resilient*: they must be able to stand up to one another, and hold their ground, lest any contentions among them be hollow and inconsequential.

On the other hand, resilience cannot mean complete obstinacy or rigidity; for that too is incompatible with meaningful testing. Suppose, for instance, that two observations or measurements are found (by exercise of some constitutive skill) to be incompatible. Other things equal, neither should yield to the other right away; they should both be resilient. But suppose further that a third mundane result turns out to be compatible with the second, but not the first; and then a fourth is compatible with both the second and third, but still not the first; and so on. It does not matter in principle whether these findings are made all by one investigator, or by several. Before long, that first result begins to look pretty lonely, and as if *it* must have been a/the error. (This example illustrates another important point as well: test failures had better be relatively isolated; and that is *why*—and also *what it means* that—objective skills have to be *reliable*.[24])

The role of the constitutive skill(s) is distinctive and fundamental. The account of errors depends essentially on incompatibilities among mundane findings. But in and of themselves, no two (or more) actual findings are incompatible. There is, for instance, no immediate incompatibility between recognizing a rook and seeing it to move along a diagonal. Only given the standards of chess, which rule out such moves, is there any incompatibility in that. Indeed, only given the standards of chess, is there any incompatibility in recognizing a rook and then seeing *it* to be *not* a rook—for, in some games (and, for pawns, even in chess) pieces can sometimes legally change their types.

Therefore, constitutive skills are not, and cannot be, just further mundane skills. They must be "meta" or "monitoring" skills vis-à-vis the results of mundane performances; for their essential exercise is to watch out for incompatibilities among those results—an exercise of *vigilance*. So, though there can be a "confrontation" among several mundane findings and a constitutive finding, there can be no incompatibility between the former and the latter. Rather, it is at most the mundane results that are mutually incompatible, and the constitutive finding "confronts" them by, so to speak, accusing them of that.

To point out that constitutive skills are essentially different from mundane skills is not at all to suggest that their exercises are immune to revision, or that they themselves are immune to repair. Players can certainly misunderstand or inadvertently misapply constitutive standards; a chess player might forget, for instance, about capturing *en passant*, or overlook that a castling rook is threatened. As with mundane errors, constitutive errors are likely only to be noticed in the face of something supposedly impossible; and the resolution, after further testing and rechecking, is again accession to the preponderant.

In contrast to rectifying particular performances, repairing and improving the skills themselves is a matter of changing how they are performed in general, altering the relevant abilities and dispositions. As resilient, objective skills must be resistant to repair, just as they are to revision, and for the same reason. Repairs, unlike revisions, are prompted not by isolated discrepancies, surrounded by results that agree, but rather by persistent and recalcitrant patterns of discrepancy. If things keep going wrong, maybe the problem is not individual errors in performance, but deficiencies in the skills themselves. (If you keep seeing rooks moving along diagonals, and bishops along ranks and files, maybe the problem is that you can't tell a rook from a bishop, or have them mixed up; or maybe they aren't rooks and bishops at all.)

A repair makes a difference to which performances were and will be proper or correct. That's the point, after all: to root out a persistent pattern of problems, past and prospective. But repairs also carry, therefore, a distinctive risk and burden. In changing a skill itself, *all* its performances are potentially affected, including those that were not previously problematic. But it's of little use to eradicate one pattern of difficulty at the expense of introducing another, as bad or worse. What's more, it can easily happen that the best (or only workable) option is to modify several skills at once, so that what would have led to additional problems in any one of them alone is offset by the others, and problems are reduced overall. In effect, skill repair is just the sort of multi-factor trading off or equilibrating that is familiar from holist epistemology.

Constitutive skills are subject to repair too, and are, in their own way, part of the same balancing act. Modifying constitutive skills and modifying constitutive standards are not fundamentally separable: ultimately and concretely, the standards just *are* what the players recognize in exercises of the skills. To modify or repair the constitutive skills is to change the game itself—slightly or radically, as the case may be. Such an option may not loom large for routine recreational games; but it can become central when, as in empirical chess, the primary challenge is to figure out whether there's a "game" (intelligible domain) at all, and, if so, what it is, what belongs to it, and how to play it. If, in order to maintain or regain equilibrium, a number of constitutive and/or mundane skills must be modified together, the effect is apt to seem "revolutionary".

In sum, then: against the background of an established and stable equilibrium, individual mundane performances can be tested through comparison with others, according to constraints set by constitutive standards (as imposed by exercises of constitutive skills). This yields a clear, new sense for the idea of isolated mundane errors (and, at a higher level, of isolated constitutive errors), a sense that transcends merely instituted consensus. What has not yet been shown, however, is how mundane error in this new sense can be understood more specifically as objective incorrectness.

As has often been noted in related contexts, individual errors are intelligible as such only given a lack of error—or, as we should rather say, a lack of incompatibility—on the whole. That such by-and-large agreements, as here understood, are not *merely* coherent and consensual is already anticipated in the fact that the background skillful equilibrium upon which they all depend is itself vulnerable in the face of patterns of errors—in the fact that any achieved equilibrium is always empirically *precarious.*

14 POWER TO THE PHENOMENA

The excluded zone is what makes the difference between constitution and institution. Constitutive standards and the zone they exclude give sense to a distinctive sort of potential incompatibility among particular mundane exercises. Constituted objective phenomena are the loci of these potential incompatibilities. Such loci are what constitution *lets* phenomena *be*—namely, as we shall see, empirical *objects*.

Here's why. These same incompatibilities—excluded conceivable combinations—also ground an equally distinctive sort of error. Mundane exercises are, of course, skillful performances; and, as such, they can be done properly or improperly. If, for instance, the skills are handed down in a tradition, or disseminated within some community by deliberate training, then the collective judgement of the relevant experts (communal elders, perhaps) is authoritative about performance propriety—essentially the structure of institution. But, as we just saw, mundane performances in a constituted domain can also be found erroneous in another and quite different way. If all but one in a group of related mundane results turn out to be compatible with one another, but incompatible with that one, then the outlier stands to be rejected as erroneous. That such a result is an error is not simply a matter of a consensus of experts; indeed, they might all agree that each performance was properly executed. Rather, the error is a matter of a structure of relations among a number of actual mundane findings—actual responses to the constituted phenomena. In other words, the phenomena themselves might confound the experts (or everybody).

What is authoritative for this new sort of error is not any consensus or collective judgement but rather the locus of incompatibility among those related exercises—which is to say, the constituted object. It is that locus, that point of intersection, at which the many results concur, and the one stands apart. But the kind of potential error for which the object itself is authoritative—normatively criterial—is nothing other than *objective incorrectness*. Therefore, the excluded zone enables a normative distinction between objective correctness and incorrectness that is quite different from that between propriety and impropriety of performance.

To be sure, it is to be hoped and expected that most objective mistakes will be traceable to failings in the skillful performances that produced them. (If not, then perhaps some skills are in need of repair;

indeed, the whole point of improving observation and measurement techniques is to bring performance propriety into line with objective correctness of results.) But what is important first is not that the two kinds of error will tend to occur in tandem, but rather that there really are *two* kinds, and either *can* occur without the other. In other words, for mundane exercises in a constituted domain, there are *two* types of norm in play, not just one.

The point can be seen also from the side of the phenomena. Merely instituted phenomena, such as dance steps, greetings, and the appropriate occasions for them, are what they are only in relation to consensual proprieties of performance. Thus, it can never be the case that everyone is systematically wrong about them, takes them to be other than they are; for, if everyone systematically took them some other way, then that's what they would be. Such phenomena have, therefore, no independent normative standing over against the general skills and customs for producing, recognizing and interacting with them. And, consequently, they can never "resist" or "stand up to" those skills—they can never show proper performances to be in error, or the skills themselves to be in need of repair.

Constituted phenomena, by contrast, *can* stand up to mundane skills. By virtue of the constitutive standards imposing constraints on *combinations* of results, individual loci of incompatibility can resist and refute particular proper (or improper) performances—show their results to be incorrect. In effect, the standards, by ruling out the bulk of conceivable combinations, bind the totality of actual results within the narrow bounds of possibility. And this binding together allows them, so to speak, to "gang up on" isolated performances whose results are incompatible with—impossible in the light of—the overwhelming majority. Figuratively, we can think of the phenomena as gaining the power to resist by "locking arms" against the skills, with the constitutive standards providing their grip or their ability to lock together. Thus, in another image, an excluded zone is how a complex practice can stick its neck out empirically, by giving constituted phenomena this power to resist or refute it.

Objective correctness is a normative rule governing the results of mundane skillful exercises, distinct from the norm of proper performance. The constituted objects themselves are authoritative in regard to—that is, they stand as normative criteria for—objective correctness.[25] But where does this authority, the normative force of the rule, come from? And, how is it brought to bear? How does it take effect?

15 First-person involvement

To understand the normative authority of objects, its source and its effectiveness, is to understand objectivity. In order to pursue this understanding, however, it will be necessary to make an apparent, and perhaps surprising, digression into *subjectivity*.

Much of twentieth-century philosophy has been driven by a rejection of any special standing or epistemic authority for subjects or other "insiders"—favoring instead evidence that is publicly available from a third-person perspective. Accordingly, there is a tendency, almost a professional reflex, to consider a question about, for instance, the objectivity of esoteric or empirical chess exclusively as *outsiders*—to ask, that is, how "we" (noninitiates, detached spectators, scientists, ...) could reliably tell whether "they" (initiates, involved participants, natives, ...) are really perceiving objects, or are merely being agreeable and consistent. But such "radical" post-empiricism runs together two quite different issues about subjectivity, and thereby distorts both.

The move to the third person in epistemology and the philosophy of mind is methodological, motivated by concerns about the character of *evidence*—to avoid such shopworn "myths" as unmistakable data, privileged access, the transparency of meaning, and so on. The trouble is that the spectators' and participants' perspectives differ in other ways than what is (allegedly) evident from them; and the distortions lie in obscuring these other differences. Thus, to return attention to the first-person position need not be, and is not here, an attempt to rehabilitate any supposed epistemic security or privilege. It is rather to recover something *else* that gets lost when one restricts consideration to what is outwardly observable—namely, the participants' own *involvement* in what is going on.

First-person involvement, I shall argue, is a crucial element in the structure of objectivity. Therefore, objectivity must be considered in its relation to subjectivity. This doesn't mean reliance on introspection or autobiography. It means rather that the *topic* is first-person involvement, as opposed to observable behavior, or what can be pieced together therefrom by radical interpretation. Note in this connection that the first person doesn't mean particularly the first-person *singular*. The return in our considerations from the third to the first person is not a return from publicness to privacy, any more than from what is overt to what is covert, but rather a return from detachment to personal involvement, from the position of the spectator to that of the participant(s).

Thus, reverting to game examples for a moment, the way to consider esoteric chess is not to imagine that we are anthropologists observing esoteric chess players engaged in a game, and then ask what we could learn philosophically. Rather, we should imagine that we are ourselves esoteric chess players engaged in a game, and then ask what we can learn philosophically. From this latter perspective, unlike the former, our (imagined) involvement in the game can come into view as something that might be relevant.

Obviously, for instance, there is more to playing chess than just moving ostensible pieces in accord with the rules (even if that accord is counterfactually projectable). For one thing, the players should be trying to win. Now I make no claim as to whether or how the presence and significance of such a feature in some activity could be established by radical interpretation. I claim rather that it is beside the point. The aim is not to certify that anyone is playing a game, or even to see how such certification is possible, but instead to understand what game-playing—and eventually science—amounts to, in its essential aspects. Trying to win is one way that players are essentially involved, in the first person, in (some) games; but it is not the only way, or even the most fundamental.

Any player of chess, esoteric or otherwise, has an investment in the legality of all the moves in the game, regardless of whose moves they are. If the "moves" made by your opponent, for example, are not all (or virtually all) legal chess moves, then you cannot understand the pieces being moved, or, by extension, *any* of the pieces, as *chess* pieces. The very existence and continuation of the game depends on the legality of the moves. In other words, if you are to keep playing—you who are *involved* in this game as a player—then you must *insist* that both your own and your opponent's moves be legal. This insistence on legality is a kind of first-person involvement that is even more fundamental to game playing than istrying to win.

16 EXISTENTIAL COMMITMENT

To undertake a game in earnest, to engage seriously in play, is to make a *commitment* to the rules that define or constitute that game. Now commitment can be understood in a deontic sense and in what, for want of a better word, I shall call an "existential" sense. Both are relevant in the case of games, but they are different, and the difference matters.

A *deontic* commitment is a socially grounded obligation or duty: something that is incumbent on one, a way one is supposed to behave, in virtue of one's relations to others. Making a commitment to the rules of a game means, in this sense, undertaking an obligation to play by the rules—say, by entering into (or implying) an agreement. Someone who fails to abide by such a commitment is corrected, or, if incorrigible, rejected as a player. (To engage in a folk dance is to undertake a comparable, if less articulated, commitment—likewise on pain of rejection.)

Existential commitment, by contrast, is no sort of obligation but something more like a dedicated or even a devoted way of living: a determination to maintain and carry on. It is not a communal status at all but a resilient and resolute first-personal *stance*. (Marriage and monastic vows may be deontic commitments; love and faith are existential.) Such commitment is not "to" other players or people, or even to oneself, but rather to an ongoing, concrete game, project, or life. Thus, it is no more a psychological or an intentional state than it is a communal status; rather it is a *way*, a *style*, a *mode* of playing, working, or living—a way that relies and is prepared to insist on that which is constitutive of its own possibility, the conditions of its intelligibility.

Insofar as existential commitment includes insistence on the standards constitutive of some domain, it can as well be called *constitutive* commitment. This (at long last) is the fourth of the four sorts of rule and rule-following that, along with constitutive regulations, constitutive standards, and constitutive skills, was telescoped into the original idea of constitutive rule. Constitutive regulations, so prominent at the outset, have, by now, rather receded as a derivative and special case. Existential constitutive commitment, on the other hand, will come to the fore as fundamental. What kind of "rule-following" is this?

Clearly, existential commitment is a governing, and not just an exhibited rule; for an individual can fall away from or fail to live up to it. Equally clearly, however, its "governance" is peculiar and in a class by itself—*sui generis*. The governing or normative "authority" of an existential commitment comes from nowhere other than itself, and it is brought to bear in no way other than by its own exercise—that is, by self-discipline and resolute persistence. A committed individual holds him or herself to the commitment by living in a resilient, determined way. Thus, its authority is sui generis in a stronger sense than just "of its own genus": it is of its own genesis, self-generated. (Another word for 'sui generis' in this stronger sense is *authentic*.)

Corresponding to the distinction between deontic and existential commitment, we can draw another between deontic and existential *responsibility*. Every commitment entails responsibilities. A promise to look after a child, for instance, entails accepting responsibility for the child's whereabouts, safety, entertainment, and such like. *Existential* responsibility, on the other hand, is responsibility for the conditions on which the sustainability of the commitment itself depends. It entails, therefore, insofar as that commitment is also constitutive, responsiveness to the constituted phenomena, in particular with regard to their compliance with the standards in accord with which they are constituted. It is the responsibility, in other words, to take seriously—that means, neither to ignore nor easily to acquiesce in—apparent breaches of those standards.

Only in this existential-constitutive sense (as opposed to the deontic sense) can the character and behavior of objective phenomena belong to the "content" of anyone's commitment—what he or she is responsible for. One can be deontically responsible only for the character and consequences of one's *own* behavior (and omissions). By contrast, a chess player as such is committed not only to following the rules of the game, but also to seeing that the rooks and bishops themselves abide by the constitutive standards—for otherwise the game cannot go on. ('Seeing that' is here neutral between 'finding that' and 'seeing to it that'.) Constitutive commitment to chess is not an agreement to play by the rules, on pain of being rejected, but rather an involved insistent *way* of responding and playing, so of finding things and dealing with them, on pain of "giving up the game".

More precisely and more generally, the content of—the issue for—any existential constitutive commitment is maintenance of the relevant precarious equilibrium. It is this commitment that stands behind the *unacceptability* of incompatible mundane results, as determined by exercises of constitutive skills. (For instance, commitment to a chess game is what stands behind the unacceptability of illegal moves.) Accordingly, it also stands behind the ability of objects to *resist* mundane findings, to show them up as incorrect. And therefore, finally, it is the driving force behind all efforts to resolve apparent incompatibilities, whether by exposing them as merely apparent (revising incorrect results), or by repairing the system so as to avoid such results in general (changing the mundane or constitutive skills themselves).

Here the artificiality and ultimate inadequacy of chess and all game analogies come most blatantly into the open. Playing legal chess is not hard; nor is giving up on a game likely to be costly. Still less—and this is the important point—is the playability of the game as such ever in question. It's *just* a game. *Empirical science* (for which empirical chess has been my rhetorical stalking horse) is another matter entirely. Unlike playing a game, even to carry out a research program *properly* and to obtain *correct* results (never mind to succeed impressively or find anything interesting) is a difficult endeavor, not to be taken for granted either before or after the fact. And giving up on a science can cost a career, perhaps many.

Yet what is most important, the *essential* difference between science and games, is that the enterprise itself is always in question. In science, unlike in any game, the repair and improvement not only of mundane but also of constitutive skills is always potentially (and often in fact) an issue. The responsibilities entailed by an empirical constitutive commitment thus necessarily extend to the very skills and concepts that are the form and substance of the domain itself. It is this empirical responsibility for the terms in which the enterprise can so much as be conducted, grounded in an existential constitutive commitment, that most deeply distinguishes genuine empirical research from all other human endeavors.[26]

The questions left at the end of section 14 are now easily answered. The normative authority of objects, by virtue of which they can stand as criteria for the correctness of mundane results—and thus as binding on judgements and assertions—devolves upon them from the commitment to the standards in accord with which they are constituted. Note that this is not to suggest that the authority of objects is somehow "delegated" or "ceded" to them by those committed to the standards. That would be to suppose that the latter already had the relevant authority and could then give it away, neither of which makes clear sense. Rather it is to say that, in committing to a constituted domain, and thereby finding objects, those who are thus committed necessarily also *find* the objects as *authoritative*, and acknowledge them as such. The authority is implicit in the structure of the finding. That normative authority of the discovered objects, derived from but not at all the same as the sui generis normative authority of the constitutive commitment, then takes its effect via the responsible responsiveness of the mundane skills.

This completes the basic account of objectivity and truth.

17 MERE COHERENCE

It remains to show that this account of truth is not a coherence theory in disguise. Initially, one might suppose that all incompatibility must reduce to contradiction, and hence that all insistence on constitutive standards reduces to insistence on logical consistency or coherence among explicit propositions. For instance, the incompatibility between being a rook and moving along a diagonal might seem to reduce to the contradiction between "Rooks never move along diagonals" and "There's a rook moving along a diagonal."

There are two things wrong with this idea. First, it gratuitously presupposes, what is surely tendentious, that all the relevant skills (or findings) can be expressed adequately in sentences. But second, and more fundamental, if the thesis is understood as an account of how incompatibilities can be recognized at all (rather than just a claim about how they might be described by an articulate observer), then it founders on a regress not unlike those mentioned in section 2 above. For, if a contradiction is itself to be recognized, the respective propositional expressions and also their contradictoriness must be recognized. But abilities to recognize those conditions amount to mundane and constitutive skills for the domain in which assertions are possible. Thus, recognizing a contradiction is a special case of recognizing an excluded incompatibility in a constituted domain. If those recognitions in turn require propositional expression and recognized contradiction, then the regress starts. But, if they don't, then why suppose that all other recognitions of incompatibility require expression and recognized contradiction?

Still, it might seem that 'precarious equilibrium' is just another name for coherence in a deeper sense. Here's a way to bring the worry into focus. If objects are supposed to stand as criteria for correctly telling what they are, then they had better be independent of those tellings (and related skills). Now, all chess phenomena—and, in this, they are surely representative of constituted phenomena in general—are constituted in terms of how they relate to one another, as required and allowed by the constitutive standards. So any given chess object, a certain rook for instance, is what it is in terms of how it fits into a legal chess game: how it relates to the board, the other pieces, and so on. But these relationships and other pieces are themselves accessible only via further exercises of the same body of mundane skills in terms of which the rook itself is recognizable. Therefore, it seems, the identity of the given rook is not independent of mundane skillful exercises after all, even when the role of the standards is taken into account; the dependence is just shared with that of other pieces, and spread out over a lot of skills.

Spread-out dependence, however, is not independence. If that were all precarious equilibrium could offer, it would indeed reduce to the sort of holism that is merely internal coherence—not so much an account of objectivity as a quitting of the field. To be sure, there is no way to check a skillful exercise except by other skillful exercises. This is the truth behind Donald Davidson's remark that "nothing can count as a reason for holding a belief except another belief".[27] And he expressly intends this thesis to characterize the sort of coherence theory that he endorses. But endorsing coherence as the *only* mark of correctness is the problem, not the solution. For, in that case, independent objects and objectivity would simply drop out. What we want is a way to acknowledge that all objective checking (testing, validation, confirmation, and so on) is "internal" to its domain—at least in the sense of not being alien to it—while maintaining that objective correctness is importantly independent of the practices constituting that domain.

The spectre raised by "mere" coherence is that, in a constituted domain, all the mundane skillful exercises are *internal* to one and the same well-oiled story—hence that all the passed "tests" are as mutually confirming as the synchronized alibis of a gang of thieves. To put it another way, if those skills themselves are subject to "revision and improvement" in the course of maintaining the equilibrium, what's to keep them from becoming mere "yea-sayers" to whatever it is that the standards demand, the despot's trusted scouts who have been selected over the years never to bring unwelcome news? Honest objectivity, by contrast, would seem to require some *external* constraint, tying correctness to something other than coherent in-house self-congratulation.

As Wilfrid Sellars (1956/63) showed, it is not sufficient to understand such constraint in terms of bare—that is, nonnormative—causal responsiveness to things. For the issue is not how our responses can be responses, but how, as responses, they can be right or wrong about what they are responding to. It is *correctness*, not responsiveness, that coherence seems to promise too cheaply. All the same, causality is not simply to be set aside. Skills, including recognition as a responsive skill, are essentially *causal too.* (Even inference is ineliminably causal:

unless a conclusion is accepted *because* the premises are, it isn't inferred from them.) *Correct* responses are still and necessarily *responses*.

All is therefore lost if, from the outset, object and response are understood in terms of fundamentally disjoint conceptual frameworks—the causal/law-governed and the normative/rational, say. For then the relation between them could not intelligibly be *either* causal *or* normative; whereas any external constraint that is to transcend mere coherence must be *both*. (It is no solution to propose causal/normative "dual citizenship" for object and response; for then, barring reduction, it is at best a coincidence if what is caused is what is right. I say *at best* a coincidence, since, at worst, such duality—"token identity"—makes no sense at all.)

In a constituted domain, however, skills and objects are *made for each other*: the objective skills are *co-constituted* along with the objective phenomena, and the latter are precisely what the former respond to (and otherwise deal with). At the same time, as we saw in section 14, those same objects stand as normative criteria for the objective correctness of the results of exercising those skills. Therefore, the spectre of mere coherence will be exorcized if and only if it can be shown that those objects, hence the constraints that they afford on correctness, are *external* in the appropriate way.

18 TRUTH AS BEHOLDENNESS

Since the phenomena by which the performances are constrained are themselves *constituted*, hence are, in at least that sense, *internal* to the domain, it hardly seems that any constraint they might afford could be appropriately *external*. In other words, that same character of these phenomena—their constitutedness—that makes it intelligible how (co-constituted) responses can be related to them both causally and normatively, threatens also to drag them back within the orbit of the very coherence that those relations were intended to transcend. Indeed, one might suppose that, whatever the details, such a collapse is inevitable. For either the desired constraint is *really* external or it isn't. If it is, then its putative role as a normative criterion is unintelligible; if not, then everything relevant is internal, and mere coherence reigns again unchecked.

But this, as we are now in a position to see, is a false predicament. It trades on an equivocation in the word 'external'. On the one hand, an external constraint might be one that is *alien*—"utterly" or "conceptually" alien—to a domain. For instance, a gravitational influence would be altogether alien to a chess position, or a political influence on the composition of the asteroids. A purely *physical* causal impact on rational norm-governed phenomena would be alien in this sense also. To whatever extent such influences can occur at all, it is only as surd intrusions; in particular, they are not intelligible as the objective constraints that check coherence.

On the other hand, however, an external constraint might be one that is *independent*, in the sense that the limits or demands it imposes are not under the control of, or already prearranged by, that which is supposedly constrained. An independent constraint precludes complacency and fiat: it will catch slips and failings, and might well impose unwelcome or even disruptive changes. An external financial audit, for example, is not one conducted in the alien terms of, say, physics or chess, but rather one that cannot be controlled or manipulated by the organization being audited—in other words, one with the independent capacity and authority to expose error, incompetence, or rampant corruption. A genuine independent constraint is one that could, in the end, bring the system down.

The false predicament, then, is the supposition that, even though an alien intervention is unintelligible as a normative check, only such an intervention could serve as an external constraint on coherence. The resolution is to notice that a genuine external check need not be alien at all, but instead *independent*, and that an independent normative check is perfectly intelligible. For precisely what the excluded zone and constitutive commitment confer upon mundane tests is the capacity and authority to expose failings, all the way from routine mistakes up to and including systematic incompatibilities that undermine the whole. And that just *is* independence in the required sense: the witness has not been bought off, the jury can indeed convict. To put it another way, objective phenomena are both accessible as normative criteria and literally *out of control*. The constitution of the domain determines what it comes to for them to be or to behave in this way or that; but whether they then *do* or not is "up to them"—and skillful practitioners can *tell*.

Ordinary or "mere" coherence, taken as a characteristic of a set of propositional attitudes and/or speech acts, whether individual or communal, lacks this element of independent constraint. It leaves no intelligible space for the objects that the propositions are supposedly about to *resist* those propositions, to show them up as *false*. If constituted domains are regarded as a variant sort of coherent set, with constituted phenomena and skillful responses in place of or added to propositional contents, and constitutive exclusion replacing or augmenting noncontradiction, then it is crucial to see this difference: constituted objects themselves, unlike any beliefs or statements allegedly about them, can "talk back". Since constituted criterial objects can be independent in this way, skillful mundane performances can be normatively *beholden* to them for the correctness of their results. We might call this a *beholdenness theory of truth*.

19 OBJECTIVE THINGS

The bare notion of an *object*—a locus of potential incompatibility in a constituted domain—is scrupulously formal, in the sense that it lacks any specific or determinate content. That is because there are and can be no antecedent restrictions on the character of constituted domains, apart from those essential to the structure of constitution as such. (There is, of course, much more to that structure than has been indicated here.) Thus, whether the relevant loci have the ontological character of ordinary things, or some other and quite different character, is a function of the domain in question. I believe, for instance, that the main lesson of Daniel Dennett's (1991) "mild realism" about beliefs and desires is that (according to his account of their constitution in the intentional stance) they are simultaneously quite objective and not at all thing-like. Nevertheless, things are an exemplary case.

The paradigm *thing* is an integral individual bearer of multiple variable properties.

Integrity in a thing means that it "hangs together" in a determinate and regular (nonarbitrary) way. It has two basic components. First, a thing is spatio-temporally *cohesive*, occupying a well-defined, connected trajectory, no part of which overlaps that of any other thing. Thus, at each moment during which it exists, it has a definite size, shape, and location; and any variations in these are continuous and regular (or nearly so) throughout its existence.

The second component of a thing's integrity is full and regular *coherence* among its properties. Each property of a thing must be compatible with each other property that it has, and with the absence of each possible property that it lacks, at each moment of and throughout its existence. Of course, some combinations of properties and/or lacks that would be ruled out at the same time may be allowed at distinct times, and vice versa. To say that the coherence among the properties of a thing is full is to say that the presence or absence of each possible property is determinate at each moment of its existence; in other words, integral things are always *concrete*. The regularity of cohesion and coherence shows up in practice as predictability.

To say that a thing is an *individual* is to say that, as long as it exists, it is (in principle) identifiable at any moment as *one* thing—"this" thing—in distinction from any other, and reidentifiable as the same (numerically identical) thing at any other moment. The regularities constitutive of a thing's integrity—cohesiveness and coherence at and across times—are the basis for its identifiability and reidentifiability.

The essential notion of a *property* combines at least three elements. First and foremost, properties are *proper to* their bearers. (Particular pluralities of things can jointly bear relational properties, such as similarity, relative location, or interaction.) This means that whether a thing (or plurality of things) has some property or not is a function only of it (or them), and not of anything else. Properties are, in this sense, "atomistic" or "intrinsic". Thus, the mass of a thing, unlike its weight, is proper to it—for the mass depends on the thing alone, and on nothing else.[28] The gravitational attraction between two things depends only on them, and so is proper to the pair (that is, a relational property). Shape, chemical composition, temperature, color, hardness, and so on, are other typical properties.[29] By contrast, being hidden, unusual, dangerous, defective, notorious, or expensive are not properties of things, strictly speaking, because they depend on factors, needs, or circumstances other than the thing in question.

Second, the properties of things are *determinations of how they interact* with anything else—including, in particular, with observers. Properties are therefore *accessible*; the properties of a thing are what can be told about it, either directly or via their effects on other things. It is primarily as having its various properties that a thing can be known. Though there may be practical impediments, and perhaps occasional exceptions, it is essential that, as a rule, properties can be told in more than one way, and that multiple properties can be told together (that is, as coinstantiated in one and the same thing). Perceptible properties can be told without (much) instrumentation or inference (though perhaps only by trained observers); imperceptible or theoretical properties can be told only in less direct ways.

Third, properties are *general*. Generality can be characterized in two ways. The usual way is to say that a general property can be had (borne, instantiated) separately by any number of distinct things (including, perhaps, none). Thus, being the highest mountain on Earth, Edmund Hillary's greatest triumph, or Mount Everest, cannot be properties strictly so called, because at most one thing can be such. The other way to characterize the generality of properties is to say that whether a thing has a property never depends on *which* thing it is—that is, on its identity as one particular individual, rather than another.

The second characterization of generality is less restrictive, but maybe more basic, than the first. It precludes being Mount Everest as a property; but it does not preclude being the Earth's highest mountain or Hillary's greatest triumph. The latter two, on the other hand, but not the former, *are* precluded as properties by the requirement that properties be proper to their bearers: being the highest mountain and Hillary's greatest triumph are not proper to Everest, but being Mount Everest (presumably) is. That a property must be such that any number of distinct things can instantiate it follows from the stipulations that properties are proper to their bearers, and never depend for their instantiation on which particular individuals those bearers are.

These last few paragraphs amount to a rough and ready sketch of the constitutive standards for the domain of ordinary objective things and properties. It seems to me that something like these standards is built into (modern western) common sense—which is not to say that ordinary people could articulate them, or would assent to them if articulated. It is only to say that, to a first approximation, they are applied—that is, insisted upon—in everyday practice. So, for example, "things" that seemed to pop into and out of existence, to change their properties radically and capriciously, to differ in character depending on who looked at them or how, or to be accessible only to specific individuals or under peculiar circumstances—such "things" would be, ceteris paribus, repudiated as *unreal*. This is exactly the basis for the common-sense denial of reality to hallucinations, dreams, delusions, occult phenomena, and the miracles of charlatans.

It does not affect this point that you can fool some of the people all of the time, or even all of the people some of the time. What matters is that the standards are in place—that is, that they are imposed in practice mostly, and that mostly they work. In some sense, there needn't have been a world in which phenomena abide by the standards of enduring things and their variable properties; no logic or metaphysics can prove its necessity. But, given that we have indeed disclosed such a world, by successfully (if tacitly) insisting upon its standards in how we live, then there are indeed things with objectively accessible properties.

A charismatic florist, therefore, *cannot* make a yellow jonquil scarlet by convincing everyone to call it that. For there are established *standards* governing the colors of things: colors don't depend on what anybody says (and especially not on cajoling); the color of something doesn't depend on which individual thing it is; there are multiple ways to determine colors; there are known relations between color and light frequencies, chemical composition, and visibility under various conditions; colors seldom change unprompted, especially without passing through intermediate hues; and so on. Thus, the color of the sacred jonquil could be told by a colorimeter, by examining it under various lamps, by comparing its composition and microstructure with those of other jonquils, or by showing it to people who don't realize which jonquil it is. If these or similar tests are performed by those who call it scarlet, incompatibilities will soon appear, and constitutive commitment will insist on a resolution. Or, if no such tests are performed, then what would have happened would have happened; and so much the worse for the fools.

20 PLAYING CHESS WITH NATURE

Scientific standards may have their roots in the ontology of things; but they tend to be more specific, more explicit, and, above all, stricter (more exclusive). In *The Logic of Scientific Discovery* (1935/59), Karl Popper proposed to demarcate science from other cognitive endeavors by a criterion of falsifiability. A theory is *falsifiable* to the extent that it rules out (by being logically incompatible with) basic or test statements. Thus, falsifiability comes in degrees; and a theory is more objective, says more about the world, the stricter or more falsifiable it is—that is, the more it rules out. Theoretical science aims at obtaining theories that, on the one hand, are highly falsifiable, in the sense that they rule out almost all logically possible basic statements (that is, they permit only a narrow range of possibilities), but, on the other hand, have not in fact been falsified, despite assiduous efforts to refute them with various tests.[30] (See sections 6–8, 31, and 82.)

Basic statements, on this view, are singular positive existentials (to the effect that an event of a certain type occurred at a certain place and time) that trained observers are motivated to accept by experience. Popper is quite clear that basic statements are never *justified* by experience; rather, their acceptance is (logically) a matter of free decision— decisions which, however, may be (psychologically) well-adapted reactions to events or experiences.[31] This does not mean that basic statements cannot be challenged or justified at all, but only that, when they are justified, it is by appeal to other statements, basic and theoretical. Such justification has no natural end; rather it is carried on to, and only to, the point at which the relevant investigators agree. (See sections 27–30.)

Obviously, the excludedness of what I have called "the excluded zone" is a descendant of Popperian falsification. Insistent vigilance corresponds roughly to the requisite effort to refute; and the constitutive/mundane divide among skills is clearly analogous to that between theoretical and basic among statements. But the two positions are not the same. Details aside, the principal difference lies in the notion of constitution: Popper has no counterpart to the idea that the *objects* of science are themselves *constituted normative constraints*, and therefore also no counterpart to my account of objectivity and truth.

In differing from Popper in this way, I am expanding instead on a difficult and controversial theme in Thomas Kuhn's *The Structure of Scientific Revolutions* (1962/70). In a passage typical of several he writes:

> In a sense that I am unable to explicate further, the proponents
> of competing paradigms practice their trades in different worlds.
>   (150; compare 111, 121, and 129)

The "worlds" are different because the constituted objects are different; that is, they belong to different domains. It seems to me that the notion of distinct constituted domains encompasses everything that was ever properly meant by distinct conceptual schemes and incommensurability. Contra Davidson (1974/84), it does not presuppose anything like what he calls a "dualism of scheme and content".

Constituting is neither creating nor counting as, but rather letting be. Disclosure of a domain is allowing a range of phenomena to make sense—or, perhaps better, allowing the sense that the phenomena can make—such that they can be noticed, recognized, or discovered as what they are. Thus, it is *finding* them in their (perhaps newfound) intelligibility. What does it mean for phenomena to "make sense"? It means that they are accessible not just in their actuality but in their *possibility*. For the possible, as a (severe) restriction of the actual, can account for the fact that—show *why*—within the conceivable, the actual has the determinate character it has, rather than various others (namely, others that are conceivable but ruled out as impossible).

When actual phenomena are recognized as what they are, by the correct exercise of mundane skills, they are *known*. When phenomena are recognized as possible, by the correct exercise of constitutive skills, they are *understood*.[32] Such exercises, hence such intelligibility, can be either with or without regard to a concrete situation. If some actual phenomenon is recognized as "concretely" possible—that is, as possible given the details of its actual situation—then its *actuality* is (to that extent) understood. If, on the other hand, some conceivable kind of phenomenon is recognized as possible (either in general or with regard to a kind of possible situation), then that *kind* of phenomenon is understood. This is what it means for phenomena to make sense.

To say that the excluded zone is empty is precisely to say that actuality implies possibility (not just conceivability)—and, in the same breath, that knowability implies intelligibility (not just conceivability). Possibility and intelligibility (at the constitutive level), like the world and its knowability (at the mundane), are two sides of one coin.

This essential connection between (real) possibility and understanding grounds and illuminates the otherwise puzzling (though so commonplace that the puzzle is seldom noticed) connection between laws and explanation. For laws are nothing other than true empirical universal claims with *modal* force: statements of what is and isn't possible among the phenomena. And, to explain is to make intelligible. Therefore, to show that, given the laws and the actual concrete circumstances, some actual phenomenon *had to* occur—or, in some cases, even just that it *could* occur—is to *explain* it.

Constitution, making sense of objects, is not free. It depends on an equilibrium among a number of constitutive and mundane skills—an equilibrium which, since it excludes the bulk of what it renders conceivable (testable), is empirically precarious. But, for the same reason, and for as long as it lasts, it is also an empirical achievement. The constituted objects participate in that achievement, deriving determinacy and normative status from it. But they also have an ability to resist that transcends that participation, because it is they, and they alone, upon which the equilibrium itself rests; by not cooperating, they have the power to bring it down. Even though in so doing they must annihilate themselves as what they are, nevertheless they can.

It is this potentially resistant yet normatively significant role for the objects themselves that Popper cannot accommodate and Kuhn cannot explain. Though it is more sophisticated than Davidson's coherentism, Popper's falsificationism fails ultimately for the same reason: it allows nothing but statements in the normative space of justifications. In particular, objects have no place at all. Yet scientific observations, theories, and explanations, like those in everyday life, are objective precisely because and to the extent that *objects* (objective phenomena) stand as accessible independent criteria for their correctness—*truth*—as made possible by an interdependent structure of constitutive and mundane *rule-following*.

NOTES:

1 A governing rule can be limited or inapplicable, for instance, if there is an excuse for not following it. Moreover, as Anscombe points out, this can sometimes even be counted a defect in the rule itself, such as when complying with the rule would be impossible, or contrary to some overriding rule.

2 To say that a scheme is general is to say that it affords the resources to express any number of different rules (by using tokens of different types). To say that the follower complies with an expression of a rule is to say not only that it responds to the token by complying with that rule, but also that, if the token had been different (expressing a different rule), then, *ceteris paribus*, the rule-follower would have responded by complying with that different rule instead.

3 The fact that the expression itself is complex—consisting of two words—is a separate point, and inessential in this case; the instructor could just as well ring a bell.

4 A relative of this regress argument is articulated by Kant in the Introduction to the Analytic of Principles (1781/1929, A132–133/ B172–173). Wittgenstein (1962) develops other relatives at *Investigations*, paragraphs 84–87 and 198–201. But the clearest antecedent occurs on the first page of Sellars (1954/63) "Some Reflections on Language Games".

5 This binds biological normality to typicality, but it does not equate the two, or even reduce the one to the other. What is abnormal for a species cannot be typical in the long run, but what is atypical can perfectly well be normal. Only some of what is typical for a species is required by its norms of proper functioning—namely, that which is invoked in a holistic functional account of how typical individuals succeed reproductively. To be atypical in ways irrelevant to that account is just to be odd, not defective.

6 Astonishingly, Fodor (1975) turns this argument on its head: since (he says) all learning must be understood as following explicit rules, some language or other—the "language of thought" (what Wittgenstein might scathe as the "last metalanguage")—must be innate.

7 Sellars (1954/63) introduces what he calls "pattern-governed" behavior in much this way. His aim is expressly to account for the possibility of learning a language—language understood as essentially "norm-conforming" behavior—while avoiding both the regress of explicit rules and a metaphysical appeal to meanings. John McDowell's (1984) exposition of Wittgenstein's treatment of rules has a similar structure. Wittgenstein is presented as steering a course between Charybdis, the idea that the basic level is not normative at all, and Scylla, a dilemma (rooted in the regress) between the "paradoxical" idea that anything whatever could be interpreted as according with a given norm, and a "mythological" (roughly metaphysical) idea of meanings as somehow super-rigid or unmistakable. In discussing how such a middle course is possible, McDowell talks about communal practices and initiation into customs; but, unlike Sellars, he does not mention conditioning.

8 These remarks are an allusion to the notion of "scorekeeping" (though not just for *language* games) as introduced by Lewis (1979/83) and much elaborated by Brandom (1994, especially chapter 3).

9 It goes without saying that the concrete training dispositions of elders and peers are themselves also socially instilled and norm-governed in essentially the same way as are first-order socialized dispositions. There is no reason to suppose that such normative dispositions can be specified in (or reduced to) nonnormative

terms. The suggestion that the effectiveness of at least some training might be attributable to nonnormative mechanisms (such as
conditioning or behavioral reinforcement) has no bearing on the
specifiability of what is taught or learned. It seems to me that
Brandom's discussion (1994, 34–46) of what he calls "social regularity accounts" is confused on this point.

10 The terms 'history' and 'tradition' are used here in thin senses. In
a fuller and more proper sense, a people has a history and a
tradition only when it sustains and preserves what I will go on to
describe as constitutive commitment and objectivity (not unre-
lated to what Heidegger calls an understanding of being).

11 To say that telling is a *responsive* rule-following is to say that it is a
means by which something about the teller (perhaps an internal
state, or how the teller performs something else) can be passively
contingent on the conditions told. The challenge is to explain
how some telling can be objective, in a way that the responsive
capacities of compass needles and birds—what Brandom (1994,
especially chapter 4) calls "reliable differential responsive dispositions"—are not. As will emerge, I maintain that telling can be
objective only insofar as it is not only responsive but also *responsible*—that is, as it essentially involves an active taking of responsibility both for the correctness of individual responses and for the
responsive capacities themselves. Thus, to this extent at least, the
account of objective telling will parallel what Kant says about the
essential unity of receptivity and spontaneity (passivity and activity) in objective intuition. (See also section 16 and note 26 below.)

12 Though arrived at by a different route, this is essentially the
complaint lodged against Crispin Wright's (1980) reading of
Wittgenstein by McDowell (1984). The example that follows in
the text distantly echoes one in McDowell's paper; but the treatment of the issue that I go on to offer has no counterpart there.

13 That's 'grock', not 'grok'. (Apologies nonetheless to Heinlein and
all strangers in strange lands.)

14 Rorty (1991, especially part 1) bites the pragmatist (or "antirepre-
sentationalist") bullet, declaring that a hankering after objective
truth—characteristic of a secularized culture in which the scientist replaces the priest (35)—is not something we should try to

satisfy, but rather try to eradicate (37). He recommends instead (13) a community that strives after intersubjective agreement and novelty (what Heidegger calls *Gerede* and *Neugier*)—a community in which, as it seems to me, the priest is replaced by the *couturier*.

Brandom says of his own account that it is built on the pragmatist idea that "[b]eing true is ... to be understood as being *properly* taken-true (believed)." (1994, 291) But, more subtle and more ambitious than Rorty, he wants also to reconstruct, within a social pragmatist framework, both representation and objective correctness; or, as he puts it, to show how we can in fact

> anchor our thought and talk in particular objects that it is about—the objects that must be consulted in order to assess the truth of our claims and the beliefs they express.
>
> (582)

He has, however, and can have no account of what it is to "consult" an object. Thus, in elaborating the idea later in the chapter, he writes:

> The social metaphysics of claim-making settles what it means for a claim to be true by settling what one is doing in *taking* it to be true. It does not settle which claims *are* true— that is, are *correctly* taken to be true.   (601)

Brandom may have, in his earlier chapters, an account of making *something* (in terms of what he calls "the game of giving and asking for reasons"); but to call it an account of *claim*-making, prior to an account of truth, would be (as Brandom well knows) to beg the question. Claim-making, as the quoted passage implies, just is taking something to be *true*; and that presupposes the notion of truth. (This can be seen as a variant of the point that McDowell makes against Davidson: "When Davidson argues that a body of beliefs is sure to be mostly true, he helps himself to the idea of a body of beliefs, a body of states that have content." (1994, 68)

Brandom does show (603–604) that his ingenious version of social pragmatism—what he calls an "*I-thou*" as opposed to an "*I-we*" social account—does not entail the thesis that, if everybody believes *p*, then *p* (helping himself to the term 'belief'). Following this proof (and three others closely related), he remarks:

> The demonstrations just presented define a robust sense in which the facts as construed in this work are independent of what anyone or everyone is committed to. The *claim-making* practices described here are accordingly properly understood as making possible genuine *fact-stating* discourse, for they incorporate practices of assessing claims and inferences according to their *objective* correctness—a kind of correctness that answers to how things actually are, rather than to how they are *taken* to be, by anyone (including oneself) or everyone.   (606–607)

But the second sentence, at least, is a non sequitur. What the proofs show is that there is no legal move, in Brandom's system, from 'Everybody believes *p*' (or: 'I believe *p*') to '*p*'. But they don't show anything at all about what *could* legitimate '*p*' instead; in particular, they don't begin to show how '*p*' could "answer to how things actually are"—which is just to say that they don't show how any of the moves could be *claim*-makings or *fact*-statings.

15 By "naturalism appropriately construed" I mean the thesis that people are, though distinctive, still naturally evolved creatures (somehow implemented in whatever physics tells us about).

16 Thus, 'co-constituted' is roughly a successor notion to Hanson's 'theory-laden'.

17 Autonomy is the counter-concept to phenomenalism (empirical idealism), whether individual or social.

18 A common misreading of Kant takes something like this to be the basic idea of the transcendental deduction.

19 The ability to recognize and produce phonemes in a natural language has something of this character; and I suspect the same is true for many professional skills.

20 The repetition of Heidegger's terminology, 'discovery' versus 'disclosure' (*Entdeckung* versus *Erschließung*) in this section, as well as 'resolute' and 'authentic' (*entschlossen* and *eigentlich*) later (in section 16) is deliberate.

21 It is conspicuous especially here that the present essay lacks any explicit treatment of judgement (or assertion); for, as Kant emphasizes (especially in section 19 of the B deduction), the function

of judgement is precisely to represent *combination in the object*. I have proceeded in the present uncommon manner in a double hope: first that the basic structure of objectivity might be delineable independently of any particular doctrine of judgement; and second that, on that basis, a more originalary account of the forms of judgement (categories) might eventually prove possible. (A companion lack of, and need for, discussion of spatio-temporal form will be notable in section 14, when I introduce the fundamental notion of a *"locus* of incompatibility".)

22 Note that the resources to recognize or identify are by no means limited to those of immediate perception. Depending on the domain, there can and in general will be mundane experimental, inferential, and theoretical skills that extend the recognizable (or observable or measurable) well beyond what is directly perceptible. As with all mundane skills, these too are "co-constituted" along with the phenomena they render accessible.

23 Much of the point of this section (and, indeed, much of the point of the present essay) was anticipated half a century ago in Sellars's (1948/80) "Concepts as Involving Laws and Inconceivable without Them". A restriction tantamount to my excluded zone is clearly described in the first paragraph of his section 5. In that same section, he also uses the term 'domain' more or less I do, and introduces his term 'material invariances' (which he later equates with laws of nature) to much the same effect as my constitutive standards. Finally, he contrasts possibility and conceivability in basically the same way as they are here, and for what is at least a closely related reason.

24 Note that this definition gives a very different sense to the term 'reliable' than it typically has in "reliabilist" epistemology.

25 To import Sellars's (1956/63) expression into somewhat different context, this is as much as to say that constituted objects must themselves have a place in "the space of reasons". And compare McDowell's invocation of the same phrase.

> The world itself must exert a rational constraint on our thinking. If we suppose that rational answerability lapses at some outermost point of the space of reasons, short of the world itself, our picture ceases to depict anything recogniz-

able as empirical judgement; we have obliterated empirical content altogether. (1994, 42–43)

26 In this and the preceding several paragraphs, I take myself to be elaborating on a theme sounded (but not elaborated) in both Kuhn and McDowell. Thus, Kuhn writes:

> Finally, at a still higher level, there is another set of commitments without which no man is a scientist. The scientist must, for example, be concerned to understand the world and to extend the precision and scope with which it has been ordered. That commitment must, in turn, lead him to scrutinize, either for himself or through colleagues, some aspect of nature in great empirical detail. And, if that scrutiny displays pockets of apparent disorder, then these must challenge him to a new refinement of his observational techniques or to a further articulation of his theories.
>
> (1962/70, 42)

And McDowell:

> … the faculty of spontaneity carries with it a standing obligation to reflect on the credentials of the putatively rational linkages that, at any time, one takes to govern the active business of adjusting one's world-view in response to experience. Ensuring that our empirical concepts and conceptions pass muster is ongoing and arduous work for the understanding. It requires patience and something like humility.
>
> (1994, 40; see also pages 12, 43, and 81)

27 Davidson (1986, 310); later in the same paragraph, he quotes Rorty with approval:

> … nothing counts as justification except by reference to what we already accept, and there is no way to get outside our beliefs and our language so as to find some test other than coherence. (Rorty 1979, 178.)

28 Weight can be considered a kind of pseudo-property in the following way: if the mass of the Earth is held constant, and the thing is restricted to the region near the Earth's surface, then the weight is a function of nothing aside from these constraints and the thing itself.

29 This list includes several traditional "secondary" properties, at least some of which might be thought to belong with weight in the category of "pseudo-property" (see preceding note). Thus, colors depend on certain accidents of human vision—for instance, the fact that a mixture of blue and yellow light can be the same color as green light. But that accident determines only what the colors are, and does not in the slightest affect the colors of any things, which are a function of them alone, hence proper to them.

30 It seems not to have occurred to Popper that the class of logically possible basic statements not ruled out by any theory will always be vast, simply because so many of them are irrelevant—framed, for instance, in a vocabulary that makes no logical contact with the theory at all. By contrast, as I define the "possible" (what, in his terms, a theory "permits"), it is relativized to what is conceivable (recognizable) with the resources of the domain in question, and includes only what is not ruled out *within that*.

31 Popper is, in effect, anticipating Davidson here (and is thus subject to the same criticisms). He realizes that events as such, psychological or otherwise, cannot justify any statements (because they are not in the space of reasons); yet he wants them to bear somehow on the empirical probity of certain statements by causing or motivating their acceptance.

32 Kant says that the understanding is the faculty of knowledge, both transcendental and empirical. It would better fit my uses of the terms—including construing faculties as abilities or skills— to distinguish a transcendental (that is, constitutive) faculty of understanding from an empirical (that is, mundane) faculty of knowledge. Of course, taking faculties to be interactive skills— something like abilities to apply concepts in the world—makes them overlap importantly with what Kant calls imagination, and even sensibility, as well. Roughly, I'm putting constituted domains and objects where Kant has sensibility, skillful exercises where he has imagination, and the responsive/responsible skills themselves where he has knowledge and understanding. (In other words, my structure is a lot like Heidegger's being-in-the-world.)

Note, by the way, that to associate my 'constitutive' with Kant's 'transcendental' is not to suggest that constitutive standards take the place of the categories.

Acknowledgments

The eleven previously published essays are reprinted here substantially unchanged. Formatting and citations have been rendered consistent; and, occasionally, wording has been adjusted in the interest of clarity. Section divisions and/or headings have be added to chapters 5, 6, 8, and 10. An explanatory note has been added to each of chapters 7, 8, 11, and 12, and a qualifying appendix to chapter 5, each clearly marked as added in 1997.

Though he is acknowledged many times below, I would like above all to thank Bert Dreyfus for first teaching me what philosophy is and much of what I will ever know about it.

THE NATURE AND PLAUSIBILITY OF COGNITIVISM was first published (along with thirty-one comments and an author's response) in *Behavioral and Brain Sciences* 1 (1981): 215–226; and reprinted that same year in the first edition of *Mind Design* (Haugeland 1981). Reprinted with the permission of Cambridge University Press.

For inspiration and constant guiding criticism, I owe more than I can properly express to Bert Dreyfus. I am also indebted to Bob Brandom, Dan Dennett, Jay Garfield, Allan Gibbard, Bill House, and Zenon Pylyshyn for helpful comments and corrections.

UNDERSTANDING NATURAL LANGUAGE was presented at the APA Eastern meetings in 1979 (where C. Wade Savage and James Moor commented) and at a Berkeley Cognitive Science colloquium, before appearing in *The Journal of Philosophy* 76 (1979): 619–632. It has been reprinted in *Foundations of Cognitive Science: The Essential Readings*, Jay Garfield, ed. (New York: Paragon House, 1990), 398–410; and *Mind and Cognition*, William Lycan, ed. (Cambridge, MA: Basil Blackwell, 1990), 660–670. Reprinted by permission of *The Journal of Philosophy*.

I am grateful for suggestions from Nuel Belnap, Bob Brandom, Bert Dreyfus, Jay Garfield, and Zenon Pylyshyn.

HUME ON PERSONAL IDENTITY grew out of a question I asked following a talk by David Pears to the Philosophy Department at Berkeley in the fall of 1973. Paul Grice reformulated the question and subsequently suggested that we jointly write a brief article based on the idea behind it. Later that fall, I wrote and presented a first draft to Barry Stroud's Hume seminar; early in the spring, I wrote a second draft and presented it to the Philosophy Department at the University of Pittsburgh; finally, sometime in 1977, I made a third revision, responding to some suggestions by Annette Baier and remarks in Stroud (1977). That draft is printed here essentially unchanged (only an ill-considered final sentence about Kant has been deleted); it has not previously been published.

Although Grice never actually worked on any of the drafts, he and I had several lengthy discussions about Hume, and about this idea in particular, during the course of which what he taught me about Hume and philosophy was limited only by my ability to learn.

ANALOG AND ANALOG first appeared in *Philosophical Topics* 12 (1981): 213–225. That volume of the journal was subsequently republished as *Mind, Brain, and Function*, J.I. Biro and Robert W. Shahan, eds. (Norman: University of Oklahoma Press, 1982). Reprinted by permission of *Philosophical Topics*.

WEAK SUPERVENIENCE was presented in various drafts at Western Ontario, Minnesota, Stanford, and Princeton from 1978 to 1980 before being published in *The American Philosophical Quarterly* 19 (1982): 93–103—by whose permission it is here reprinted.

ONTOLOGICAL SUPERVENIENCE was delivered at a Spindel Conference on Supervenience at Memphis State in 1983, and published in a special supplement to *The Southern Journal of Philosophy* 22 (1984): 1–12, devoted to the proceedings of that conference. Reprinted by permission of *The Southern Journal of Philosophy*.

THE INTENTIONALITY ALL-STARS was around for a long time before assuming its present form and making it into print. The first recognizable draft was patched together in 1981, largely out of chunks "borrowed" from other things I was working on at the time (1980, 1982, 1982a), and read at the University of British Columbia, Hampshire College, SUNY Buffalo, Memphis State, and Chicago. I revised it in 1984, and read the revised version at the Chapel Hill Colloquium, Tufts, Loyola (New Orleans), and Rochester. In 1988 I revised it yet again, producing a version more than twice as long as the earlier ones. That text was finally published in *Philosophical Perspectives 4: Action Theory and Philosophy of Mind*, James E. Tomberlin, ed. (copyright by Ridgeview Publishing Co., Atascadero, CA, 1990), 383–427, and then reprinted in *The Philosopher's Annual 1989, Volume 12*, Patrick Grim, Gary Mar, and Peter Williams, eds. (Atascadero: Ridgeview, 1991), 87–131. Reprinted by permission of Ridgeview Publishing Company.

In the long history of this essay I have incurred too many debts to recount (or even remember), but I am especially grateful for substantial comments and criticisms from Johnathan Bennett, Bob Brandom, Earl Conee, Dan Dennett, Bert Dreyfus, and Jerry Fodor.

REPRESENTATIONAL GENERA grew out of a talk entitled "Is There Distributed Representation?" given at the Cognitive Science Society Meetings in Montreal and at the University of Missouri, Saint Louis in academic year 1988/89; and the final version was one of two keynote addresses at the Fourth International Conference on Computers and Philosophy (Carnegie Mellon University, 1989). However (as previously promised) it was first published in *Philosophy and Connectionist Theory*, William Ramsey, Stephen Stich, and David Rumelhart, eds. (Hillsdale: Lawrence Erlbaum, 1991), 61–89; only later did it appear in the CMU conference proceedings, *Philosophy and the Computer*, Leslie Burkholder, ed. (Boulder: Westview Press, 1992), 105–134. Reprinted by permission of Lawrence Erlbaum Associates.

My consideration of the issues raised in this paper was inspired especially by discussions with Tim van Gelder and Sonia Sedivy.

MIND EMBODIED AND EMBEDDED grew out of discussions with Bill Clancey, Alison Gopnick, and especially Bert Dreyfus at a conference in Santa Fe in June 1992, where a preliminary version was then hastily composed and presented. Over the next two years, more developed versions were presented at Helsinki, Taipei (Academia Sinica), Berkeley (Cognitive Sciences Group), Pittsburgh (Center for Philosophy of Science), APA Pacific meetings, Prague (Center for Theoretical Studies), and at an NEH Summer Institute in Santa Cruz. It was first published in *Mind and Cognition: Philosophical Prespectives on Cognitive Science and Artificial Intelligence*, Leila Haaparanta and Sara Heinämaa, eds., *Acta Philosophica Fennica* 58 (1995): 233–267; and reprinted in *Mind and Cognition*, Yu-Houng Houng and Jih-Ching Ho, eds. (Taipei: Institute of European and American Studies, Academia Sinica, 1995), 3–37.

I am grateful for comments on earlier drafts from Lilli Alanen, Jim Conant, Fred Stoutland, Lisa Van Alstyne, Tim van Gelder, and G.H. von Wright.

OBJECTIVE PERCEPTION was presented, in academic year 1991/92, at Indiana, Simon Frazer, Lund (Sweden), Göteborg (Sweden), and Tampere (Finland). It was published in *Perception: Vancouver Studies in Cognitive Science, Volume V*, Kathleen Akins, ed. (New York: Oxford University Press, 1996), 268–289. Used by permission of Oxford University Press, Inc.

I am grateful for comments from Jim Conant, Dan Dennett, Fred Dretske, Chris Peacocke, and Tim van Gelder.

PATTERN AND BEING was written especially for the volume *Dennett and His Critics*, Bo Dahlbom, ed. (Cambridge, MA: Basil Blackwell, 1993), 53–69. Reprinted by permission of Basil Blackwell.

UNDERSTANDING: DENNETT AND SEARLE grew out of a talk entitled "Intentionality and Stance", given at an international symposium on consciousness in Turku (Finland) in 1992, and was published by the organizers of that symposium in *Consciousness in Philosophy and Cognitive Neuroscience*, Antti Revonsuo and Matti Kamppinen, eds., (Hillsdale, NJ: Lawrence Erlbaum, 1994), 115–128. Reprinted by permission of Lawrence Erlbaum Associates.

TRUTH AND RULE-FOLLOWING grew out of a short talk entitled "Can a Machine Follow a Rule?" given at the 16th International Wittgenstein Symposium in Kirchberg am Wechsel, Austria, in 1993, which was published as "Remarks on Machines and Rule-Following" in *Philosophy and The Cognitive Sciences: Proceedings of the 16th International Wittgenstein Symposium*, Roberto Casati, Barry Smith, and Graham White, eds. (Vienna: Hölder-Pichler-Tempsky, 1994). Intermediate versions were presented at an NEH Summer Institute in Santa Cruz and Rice University in 1994 and 1995. The present essay, about four times longer than its ancestor, is new in this volume.

For help along the way, I am grateful especially for advice from Bob Brandom, Jim Conant, John McDowell, and Joan Wellman. I have also profitted from discussions with and/or comments from Aryeh Frankfurter, Henry Jackman, Rebecca Kukla, Ken Manders, Ram Neta, Doug Patterson, Anna Pilatova, David Stern, and Jennifer Whiting.

Bibliography

Anderson, Alan Ross, ed. 1964. *Minds and Machines*. Englewood Cliffs, NJ: Prentice Hall. [1]

Alt, Franz L., ed. 1964. *Advances in Computers*, volume 1. New York: Academic Press. [2]

Anscombe, G.E.M. 1957. *Intention*. Oxford: Basil Blackwell. [13]

Bar-Hillel, Yehoshua. 1964. "The Present Status of Automatic Translation of Languages", in Alt 1964. [2]

Baron, Robert J. 1970. "A Model for Cortical Memory", *Journal of Mathematical Psychology*, 7: 37–59. [1]

Batali, John. "Trails as Archetypes of Intentionality" (unpublished). [9]

Black, Max, ed. 1965. *Philosophy in America*. Ithaca: Cornell University Press. [1]

Block, Ned, ed. 1980. *Readings in Philosophy of Psychology* (two volumes), Cambridge, MA: Harvard University Press. [7]
—— 1986. "Advertisement for a Semantics for Psychology", in French, Euhling, and Wettstein 1986. [7]

Block, Ned and Jerry Fodor. 1972. "What Psychological States Are Not", Philosophical Review, 81: 159–181; reprinted in Block 1980, volume 1 (with revisions), and in Fodor 1981. [7]

Bobrow, Daniel, and Allan Collins, eds. 1975. *Representation and Understanding*. New York: Academic Press. [2]

Bobrow, Daniel and Terry Winograd. 1977. "An Overview of KRL-0, a Knowledge Representation Language", *Cognitive Science*, 1: 3–46. [2]

Bogen, James, and James E. McGuire, eds. 1985. *How Things Are*. Dordrecht: Reidel. [8]

Brandom, Robert. 1979. "Freedom and Constraint by Norms", *American Philosophical Quarterly*, 16: 187–196. [7]

—— 1983. "Asserting", *Noûs*, XVII: 637–650. [7]

—— 1994. *Making it Explicit*. Cambridge, MA: Harvard University Press. [13]

Brentano, Franz. 1874/1973. *Psychologie vom empirischen Standpunct*. Leipzig: Duncker und Humblot. Translation, by Antos C. Rancurello, D.B. Terrell, and Linda L. McAlister): *Psychology from an Empirical Standpoint*. (London: Routledge & Kegan Paul, 1973.) (An earlier translation of a substantial exerpt is included in Chisholm 1960.) [7]

Brooks, Rod. 1990. "Elephants Don't Play Chess", *Robotics and Autonomous Systems* 6: 3–15. [9]

—— 1991. "Intelligence without Representation", *Artificial Intelligence* 47: 139–159; reprinted (revised and enlarged) in Haugeland 1997. [9]

Campbell, Fergus W. 1974. "The Transmission of Spatial Information through the Visual System", in Schmitt and Worden 1974. [1]

Castellan, John N., David B. Pisoni, and George R. Potts, eds. 1977. *Cognitive Theory II*. Hillsdale, NJ: Lawrence Erlbaum Associates. [1]

Cathey, W. Thomas. 1974. *Optical Information Processing and Holography*. New York: John Wiley and Sons. [1]

Cavanaugh, J.P. 1972. *Holographic Processes Realizable in the Neural Realm*. Unpublished PhD thesis, Carnegie Mellon University. [1]

Chisholm, Roderick. 1957. *Perceiving: A Philosophical Study*. Ithaca, NY: Cornell University Press. [7]

—— 1960. *Realism and the Background of Phenomenology*. New York: The Free Press; facsimile edition available from Ridgeview Publishing Company, Atascadero, CA. [7]

Churchland, Paul M. 1989. *A Neurocomputational Perspective: The Nature of Mind and the Structure of Science*. Cambridge, MA: Bradford/MIT Press. [8]

Cummins, Robert. 1975. "Functional Analysis", *Journal of Philosophy*, 72: 741–765; reprinted in Block 1980, volume 1. [1]

Davidson, Donald. 1963/80. "Actions, Reasons, and Causes", *Journal of Philosophy*, 60: 685–700; reprinted in Davidson 1980. [7]

—— 1970/80. "Mental Events", in Foster and Swanson 1970; reprinted in Davidson 1980 and Block 1980, volume 1. [1][5][7][10]

—— 1973/80. "The Material Mind", in Suppes, et al, 1973; reprinted in Davidson 1980 and Haugeland 1981. [1]

—— 1973/84. "Radical Interpretation", *Dialectica*, 27: 313–328; reprinted in Davidson 1984. [1]

—— 1974/84. "On the Very Idea of a Conceptual Scheme", *Proceedings and Addresses of the American Philosophical Association*, 47: 5–20; reprinted in Davidson 1984. [7][13]

—— 1980. *Essays on Actions and Events*. Oxford: Clarendon Press. [1][5][7][10]

—— 1984. *Inquiries into Truth and Interpretation*. Oxford: Clarendon Press. [1][13]

—— 1986. "A Coherence Theory of Truth and Knowledge", in LePore 1986. [13]

de Beaugrande, Robert, and Benjamin Colby. 1979. "Narrative Models of Action and Interaction", *Cognitive Science*, 3: 42–66. [2]

de Groot, Adriaan D. 1965. *Thought and Choice in Chess*. The Hague: Mouton. [1]

Dennett, Daniel. 1971/78. "Intentional Systems", *Journal of Philosophy*, 68: 87–106; reprinted in Dennett 1978 and Haugeland 1981. [1][7][11]

—— 1973/78. "Mechanism and Responsibility", in Honderich 1973; reprinted in Dennett 1978. [11]

—— 1975/78. "Why the Law of Effect Will Not Go Away", *Journal for the Theory of Social Behavior*, 5: 169–187; reprinted in Dennett 1978. [1]

—— 1977/78. "Critical Notice: *The Language of Thought* by Jerry Fodor", *Mind*, 86: 265–280; reprinted, under the title "A Cure for the Common Code?", in Dennett 1978 and Block 1980, volume 2. [7]

—— 1978. *Brainstorms: Philosophical Essays on Mind and Psychology*. Cambridge, MA: Bradford/MIT Press. [1][5][7][11]

—— 1978a/78. "Why You Can't Make a Computer that Feels Pain", *Synthese*, 38: 415–456; reprinted in Dennett, 1978. [1]

—— 1978b. "Two Approaches to Mental Images", in Dennett 1978. [1]

—— 1978c. "How to Change Your Mind", in Dennett 1978. [7]

—— 1981/87. "True Believers: The Intentional Strategy and Why It Works", in Heath 1981; reprinted in Dennett 1987 and Haugeland 1997. [7]

—— 1981/87b. Three Kinds of Intentional Psychology", in Healey 1981; reprinted in Dennett 1987. [12]

—— 1982/87. "Beyond Belief", in Woodfield 1982; reprinted in Dennett 1987. [7]

—— 1983/87. "Intentional Systems in Cognitive Ethology: The 'Panglossian Paradigm' Defended", *The Behavioral and Brain Sciences*, 6: 343–90; reprinted in Dennett 1987. [12]

—— 1984. *Elbow Room*. Cambridge, MA: Bradford/MIT Press. [7]

—— 1987. *The Intentional Stance*. Cambridge, MA: Bradford/MIT Press. [7][10][12]

—— 1987a/87. "Evolution, Error, and Intentionality", in Wilks and Partridge 1987; reprinted in Dennett 1987. [7]

—— 1991. "Real Patterns", *Journal of Philosophy*, 89: 27–51. [11][13]

Descartes, René. 1641/1984. *Meditationes de Prima Philosophiae*. Paris: Michel Soly. Translation (including the objections and replies) by John Cottingham, Robert Soothoff, and Dugald Murdoch: *The Philosophical Writings of Descartes, Volume 2*. (Cambridge: Cambridge University Press, 1984). [7]

—— 1644/1985. *Principia of Philosophiae,.* Amsterdam: Elzevir. Translation, by John Cottingham, Robert Soothoff, and Dugald Murdoch: *The Philosophical Writings of Descartes, Volume 1*. (Cambridge: Cambridge University Press, 1985). [11]

Dewey, John. 1925; second edition, 1929. *Experience and Nature*. La Salle, IL: Open Court. [7]

Dretske, Fred. 1981. *Knowledge and the Flow of Information*. Cambridge, MA: Bradford/MIT Press. [7][10]

Dreyfus, Hubert L. 1972/92. *What Computers Can't Do*. New York: Harper & Row; second edition, slightly revised and with a new introduction, 1979. Third edition, under the title *What Computers Still Can't Do*, and with yet a third introduction, Bradford/MIT Press, 1992. (Pagination in the second and third editions is the same, but differs from the first.) [1][5][7][9]

Erickson Robert P. 1974. "Parallel 'Population' Neural Coding in Feature Extraction", in Schmitt and Worden 1974. [1]

Feigl, Herbert, and Michael Scriven, eds. 1956. *Minnesota Studies in the Philosophy of Science, Volume I: The Foundations of Science and the Concepts of Psychology and Psychoanalysis*. Minneapolis: University of Minnesota Press. [13]

Field, Hartry. 1978. "Mental Representation", *Erkenntnis*, 13: 9–61; reprinted with an added postscript in Block 1980, volume 2. [7]

Firth, Ian Mason. 1972. *Holography and Computer Generated Holograms*. London: Mills and Boon. [1]

Fodor, Jerry A. 1965. "Explanation in Psychology", in Black 1965. [1]

—— 1974/81. "Special Sciences (or: The Disunity of Science as a Working Hypothesis)", *Synthese*, 28: 97–115; reprinted in Fodor 1981 and Block 1980, volume 1. [1][5]

—— 1975. *The Language of Thought*. New York: Thomas Y. Crowell. [7][13]

—— 1980/81. "Methodological Solipsism Considered as a Research Strategy in Cognitive Psychology" (including 25 commentaries and the author's responses), *Behavioral and Brain Sciences*, 3: 63–109; reprinted (without commentaries or responses) in Fodor 1981 and Haugeland 1981. [7]

—— 1981. *Representations*. Cambridge, MA: Bradford/MIT Press. [7]

—— 1983. *The Modularity of Mind*. Cambridge, MA: Bradford/MIT Press. [7]

Fodor, Jerry A., and Zenon W. Pylyshyn. 1988. "Connectionism and Cognitive Architecture: A Critical Analysis", *Cognition: International Journal of Cognitive Science*, 28: 3–71; reprinted in Pinker and Mehler 1988 and (abridged) in Haugeland 1997. [8]

Foster, Lawrence, and J.W. Swanson, eds. 1970. *Experience and Theory*. Amherst, MA: University of Massachusetts Press. [1][5][7][10]

French, P., T. Euhling, and H. Wettstein, eds. 1986. *Studies in the Philosophy of Mind: Midwest Studies in Philosophy, X*. Minneapolis: University of Minnesota Press. [7]

Gabor, D. 1969. "Associative Holographic Memories", *IBM Journal of Research and Development*, 13: 156–159. [1]

Gardner, Martin. 1979. "Mathematical Games", *Scientific American*, 240 (June 1979): 20–34. [2]

Gibson, James J. 1979. *The Ecological Approach to Visual Perception*. Boston: Houghton Mifflin. [9]

Goodman, Nelson. 1968. *Languages of Art*. Indianapolis: Bobbs-Merrill. [4]

Grandy, Richard. 1973. "Reference through Meaning and Belief", *Journal of Philosophy*, 70: 439–452. [1]

Greeno, James. 1977. "Process of Understanding in Problem Solving", in Castellan, Pisoni, and Potts 1977. [1]

Grice, H. Paul. 1957. "Meaning", *Philosophical Review*, 66: 377–88. [7]

Gunderson, Keith, ed. 1975. *Language, Mind and Knowledge: Minnesota Studies in the Philosophy of Science*, volume 7. Minneapolis: University of Minnesota Press. [7]

Hare, Richard M. 1952. *The Language of Morals*. Oxford: Clarendon Press. [5]

Harman, Gilbert. 1973. *Thought*. Princeton: Princeton University Press. [1]

Haugeland, John. 1980. "Programs, Causal Powers, and Intentionality", *Behavioral and Brain Sciences*, 3: 432–433. [7]
—— ed. 1981. *Mind Design*. Cambridge, MA: Bradford/MIT Press. [1][2][7][12]
—— 1982. "Heidegger on Being a Person", *Noûs*, 16: 15–26. [7]
—— 1982a. "The Mother of Intention", *Noûs*, 16: 613–19. [7]
—— 1983. "Weak Supervenience", *American Philosophical Quarterly*, 19: 93–103; included in this volume as chapter 6. [6][7]
—— 1985. *Artificial Intelligence: The Very Idea*. Cambridge, MA: Bradford/MIT Press. [7]
—— ed. 1997. *Mind Design II*. Cambridge, MA: Bradford/MIT Press. [2][7][8][12]

Healey, Richard. 1981. *Reduction, Time, and Reality: Studies in the Philosophy of the Natural Sciences*. Cambridge: Cambridge University Press. [12]

Hearst, Eliot. 1967. "Psychology across the Chessboard", *Psychology Today*, June 1967: 28–37. [1]

Heath, Anthony F., ed. 1981. *Scientific Explanation*. Oxford: Clarendon Press. [7]

Heidegger, Martin. 1927/62. *Sein und Zeit*. Tübingen: Max Niemeyer Verlag. Translation, by John Macquarrie and Edward Robinson: *Being and Time*. (New York: Harper & Row, 1962.) [7][13]

Hellman, Geoffrey, and Frank Thompson. 1975. "Physicalism: Ontology, Determinism, and Reduction", *Journal of Philosophy*, 72: 551–564. [6]
—— 1977. "Physicalist Materialism", *Noûs*, 11: 309–345. [6]

Hemple, Carl G. 1965. Aspects of Scientific Explanation. New York: Free Press. [1]

Hempel, Carl G., and Paul Oppenheim. 1948. "Studies in the Logic of Explanation", *Philosophy of Science*, 15: 135–175; reprinted, with a new postscript, in Hemple 1965. [1]

Herriot, D. R. 1968. "Applications of Laser Light", *Scientific American*, 218 (September 1968): 140–156. [1]

Hinton, Geoffrey E., Jay L. McClelland, and David E. Rumelhart. 1986. "Distributed Representations", in Rumelhart, et al, 1986. [8]

Honderich, Ted , ed. 1973. *Essays on Freedon and Action*. London: Routledge & Kegan Paul. [11]

Hook, Sydney, ed. 1960. *Dimensions of Mind: A Symposium*. New York: New York University Press. [1]

Horgan, Terrance, and John Tienson, eds. 1987. *Connectionism and the Philosophy of Mind*. Published as a special supplement to volume 26 of *The Southern Journal of Philosophy*. [8]

Hudson, Liam. 1972. *The Cult of the Fact*. London: Cape. [1]

Hume, David. 1739/1888. *A Treatise of Human Nature*. L.A. Selby-Bigge, ed. Oxford: Clarendon Press. [3]

Kabrisky, M. 1966. *A Proposed Model for Visual Information Processing in the Human Brain*. Urbana: University of Illinois Press. [1]

Kant, Immanuel. 1781/1929. *Critik der reinen Vernunft*. Riga: Harrknoch. Translation, by Norman Kemp Smith: *Critique of Pure Reason*. (New York: St. Martin's Press, 1929.) [10][13]

Kemp Smith, Norman. 1941. *The Philosophy of David Hume*. London: MacMillan. [3]

Kim, Jaegwon. 1978. "Supervenience and Nomological Incommensurables", *American Philosophical Quarterly*, 15: 149–56. [5]
——— 1979. "Causality, Identity, and Supervenience in the Mind-Body Problem", *Midwest Studies in Philosophy*, 4: 31–49. [5]

Kosslyn, Steven, and J. R. Pomerantz. 1977. "Imagery, Propositions and the Form of Internal Representations", *Cognitive Psychology*, 9: 52–76. [1]

Krantz, David H., Richard C. Atkinson, R. Duncan Luce, and Ptrick Suppes, eds. 1974. *Contemporary Developments in Mathematical Psychology, volume 2: Measurement, Psychophysics, and Neural Information Processing*. San Francisco: W. H. Freeman. [1]

Kuhn, Thomas S. 1962/70; second edition, with a new postscript, 1970. *The Structure of Scientific Revolutions*. Chicago: University of Chicago Press. [1][10][13]

Leith, Emmett N., and Juris Upatnieks. 1965. "Photography by Laser",
    Scientific American, 212 (June 1965): 24–35. [1]

LePore, Ernest, ed. 1986. *Truth and Interpretation: Perspectives on the
    Philosophy of Donald Davidson*. Oxford: Basil Blackwell. [13]

Lewis, David K. 1969. *Convention: A Philosophical Study*. Cambridge, MA:
    Harvard University Press. [7]
—— 1971. "Analog and Digital", *Nous*, 5: 321–27. [4]
—— 1974/83. "Radical Interpretation", *Synthese*, 27: 331–344; reprinted
    in Lewis 1983, volume 1. [1]
—— 1979/83. "Scorekeeping in a Language Game", *Journal of Philosophi-
    cal Logic*, 8: 339–359; reprinted in Lewis 1983, volume 1. [2][13]
—— 1983. *Philosophical Papers, volume 1*. New York: Oxford University
    Press. [2][13]

MacKay, Alfred, and Daniel Merrill, eds. 1976. *Issues in the Philosophy of
    Language*. New Haven: Yale University Press.

Marr, David. 1977. "Artificial Intelligence—A Personal View", *Artificial
    Intelligence*, 9: 37–48; reprinted in Haugeland 1981. [1]

McCarthy, John. 1979. "Ascribing Mental Qualities to Machines", in
    Ringle 1979. [1]

McClelland, Jay L., and David E. Rumelhart. 1986. "A Distributed
    Model of Human Learning and Memory", in McClelland, et al, 1986.
    [8]

McClelland, Jay L., David E. Rumelhart, and the PDP Research Group.
    1986. *Parallel Distributed Processing: Explorations in the Microstructure of
    Cognition. Volume 2: Psychological and Biological Models*. Cambridge,
    MA: Bradford/MIT Press. [8]

McDowell, John. 1984. "Wittgenstein on Following a Rule", *Synthese*, 58:
    325–363. [13]
—— 1994. *Mind and World*. Cambridge, MA: Harvard University Press.
    [13]

McNabb, D.G.C. 1966. *David Hume: His Theory of Knowledge and Morality*
    (second edition). Oxford: Basil Blackwell[3]

Minsky, Marvin. 1974. "A Framework for Representing Knowledge",
    MIT AI Lab Memo #306; exerpts reprinted in Winston 1975; other
    exerpts reprinted in Haugeland 1981 and 1997. [2]

Minsky, Marvin, and Seymour Papert. 1972. "Progress Report on
    Artificial Intelligence", MIT AI Lab Memo #252. [1]

Nagel, Thomas. 1974. "What Is It Like to Be a Bat?" *Philosophical Review*, 83: 435–451; reprinted in Block 1980, volume 1. [7]

Pavio, Allen. 1975. "Imagery and Synchronic Thinking", *Canadian Psychological Review*, 16: 147–163. [1]

Penelhum, Terrence. 1955/65. "Hume on Personal Identity", *Philosophical Review*, 64: 571–589; reprinted in Sesonske and Fleming 1965. [3]

Pinker, Steven, and Jacques Mehler, eds. 1988. *Connections and Symbols*. Cambridge, MA: Bradford/MIT Press. Reprint of a special issue of *Cognition: International Journal of Cognitive Science*, volume 28. [8]

Pollen, Daniel A., and Joseph H. Taylor. 1974. "The Striate Cortex and the Spatial Analysis of Visual Space", in Schmitt and Worden 1974. [1]

Popper, Karl R. 1935/68. *Logik der Forschung*. Vienna: Julius Springer Verlag. Translation, by the author (with new appendices and footnotes): *The Logic of Scientific Discovery*. (New York: Harper & Row, 1959, slightly revised 1968.) [13]

Pribram, Karl H. 1971. *Languages of the Brain*. Englewood Cliffs, NJ: Prentice Hall. [1]
—— 1974. "How is it that Sensing so Much we can do so Little?" in Schmitt and Worden 1974. [1]

Pribram, Karl H., Marc Nuwer, and Robert J. Baron. 1974. "The Holographic Hypothesis of Memory Structure in Brain Function and Perception", in Krantz, et al, 1974. [1]

Price, H.H. 1940/65. "The Permanent Significance of Hume's Philosophy", *Philosophy*, 15: 10–36; reprinted in Sesonske and Fleming 1965. [3]

Putnam, Hilary. 1960/75. "Minds and Machines", in Hook 1960; reprinted in Anderson 1964 and Putnam 1975a. [1]
—— 1973. "Reductionism and the Nature of Psychology", *Cognition*, 2: 131–146; reprinted in Haugeland 1981. [1]
—— 1975. "The Meaning of 'Meaning'", in Gunderson 1975; reprinted in Putnam 1975a. [2][7]
—— 1975a. *Mind, Language, and Reality: Philosophical Papers, volume 2*. Cambridge: Cambridge University Press. [1][2][7]

Pylyshyn, Zenon W. 1973. "What the Mind's Eye Tells the Mind's Brain: A Critique of Mental Imagery", *Psychological Bulletin*, 80: 1–24. [1]

—— 1978. "Imagery and Artificial Intelligence", in Savage 1978; reprinted in Block 1980, volume 2. [1]

—— 1984. *Computation and Cognition: Toward a Foundation for Cognitive Science.* Cambridge, MA: Bradford/MIT Press. [7]

Quine, Willard Van Orman. 1960. *Word and Object.* Cambridge, MA: MIT Press. [1][7]

—— 1978. "Facts of the Matter", *Southwestern Journal of Philosophy*, 9 (number 2): 155–169. [6]

Rawls, John. 1955. "Two Concepts of Rules", *Philosophical Review*, 64: 3–32. [13]

Ringle, Martin. ed. 1979. *Philosophical Perspectives in Artificial Intelligence.* Atlantic Highlands, NJ: Humanities Press. [1]

Rorty, Richard. 1979. *Philosophy and the Mirror of Nature.* Princeton: Princeton University Press. [13]

—— 1991. *Objectivity, Relativism, and Truth.* Cambridge: Cambridge University Press. [13]

Rumelhart, David E. 1975. "Notes on a Schema for Stories", in Bobrow and Collins 1975. [2]

Rumelhart, David E., Jay L. McClelland, and the PDP Research Group. 1986. *Parallel Distributed Processing: Explorations in the Microstructure of Cognition. Volume 1: Foundations.* Cambridge, MA: Bradford/MIT Press. [7][8]

Savage, Wade C., ed. 1978. *Perception and Cognition: Issues in the Foundations of Psychology. Minnesota Studies in the Philosophy of Science*, volume 9. Minneapolis: University of Minnesota Press. [1]

Schank, Roger and Robert Abelson. 1975. "Scripts, Plans, and Knowledge", *International Joint Conference on Artificial Intelligence*, IV. Cambridge, MA: The MIT AI Lab. [2]

Schmitt, Francis O., and Frederick G. Worden, eds. 1974. *The Neurosciences: Third Study Program.* Cambridge, MA: MIT Press. [1]

Searle, John R. 1969. *Speech Acts: An Essay in the Philosophy of Language.* Cambridge: Cambridge University Press. [13]

—— 1979. "A Taxonomy of Illocutionary Acts", in Searle 1979a. [13]

—— 1979a. *Expression and Meaning.* Cambridge: Cambridge University Press. [13]

—— 1980. "Minds, Brains, and Programs" (including 27 commentaries and the author's responses), *Behavioral and Brain Sciences*, 3: 417–457;

reprinted (without commentaries or responses) in Haugeland 1981 and 1997. [7][12]

—— 1983. *Intentionality*. Cambridge: Cambridge University Press. [7]

—— 1992. *The Rediscovery of the Mind*. Cambridge: MIT Press. [12]

Sellars, Wilfrid. 1948/80. "Concepts as Involving Laws and Inconceivable without Them." *Philosophy of Science*, 15: 287–315; reprinted in Sellars 1980. [13]

—— 1954/63. "Some Reflections on Language Games", *Philosophy of Science*, 21: 204–228; reprinted with revisions in Sellars 1963. [7][13]

—— 1956/63. "Empiricism and the Philosophy of Mind", in Feigl and Scriven 1956; reprinted in Sellars 1963. [13]

—— 1963. *Science, Perception and Reality*. London: Routledge & Kegan Paul. [1][7][13]

—— 1963/67. "Abstract Entities", *Review of Metaphysics*, 16: 627–671; reprinted in Sellars 1967. [8]

—— 1967. *Philosophical Perspectives, Volume II: Metaphysics and Epistemology*. Reseda, CA: Ridgeview. [8]

—— 1969. "Language as Thought and as Communication", *Philosophy and Phenomenological Research*, 29: 506–527. [7]

—— 1980. *Pure Pragmatics and Possible Worlds: The Early Essays of Wilfrid Sellars*, edited by Jeffrey F. Sicha. Reseda, CA: Ridgeview Publishing. [13]

—— 1985. "Toward a Theory of Predication", in Bogen and McGuire 1985. [8]

Sesonske, Alexander, and Noel Fleming, eds. 1965. *Human Understanding: Studies in the Philosophy of David Hume*. Belmont, CA: Wadsworth. [3]

Shepard, Roger, and J. Metzler. 1971. "Mental Rotation of Three-Dimensional Objects", *Science*, 171: 701–703. [1]

Shoemaker, Sydney. 1975. "Functionalism and Qualia", *Philosophical Studies*, 27: 291–315. [1]

Simon, Herbert A. 1969/81 (second edition revised and enlarged). *The Sciences of the Artificial*. Cambridge, MA: MIT Press. [1][9].

Stalnaker, Robert. 1976. "Propositions", in MacKay and Merrill 1976. [7]

—— 1984. *Inquiry*, Cambridge, MA: Bradford/MIT Press. [7]

Stroud, Barry. 1977. *Hume*. London: Routledge & Kegan Paul. [3]

Suppes, Patrick, et al., eds. 1973. *Logic, Methodology, and Philosophy of Science* (proceedings of the fourth International Congress for Logic,

Methodology, and Philosophy of Science, 1971). Amsterdam: North-Holland. [1]

Taylor, Charles. 1971. "Interpretation and the Sciences of Man", *Review of Metaphysics*, 15: 3–51. [2]

van Gelder, Timothy. 1989. *Distributed Representation*. Unpublished PhD dissertation, Department of Philosophy, University of Pittsburgh. [8]

van Heerden, Pieter J. 1963. "A New Method of Storing and Retrieving Information", *Applied Optics*, 2: 387–392. [1]

Waltz, David. 1972. *Generating Semantic Descriptions from Drawings of Scenes with Shadows*. MIT Ph.D. thesis; published in Winston 1975. [1]

Wilensky, Robert. 1978. "Why John Married Mary: Understanding Stories Involving Recurring Goals", *Cognitive Science*, 2: 235–266. [2]

Wilks, Yorick. 1974. "Natural Language Understanding Systems within the AI Paradigm", Stanford AI Memo #237. [2]

Wilks, Yorick, and D. Partridge, eds. 1987. *Sourcebook on the Foundations of Artificial Intelligence*. Cambridge: Cambridge University Press. [7]

Wilson, Neil L. 1959. "Substances without Substrata", *Review of Metaphysics*, 12: 521–539. [1]

Winograd, Terry. 1971. "Understanding Natural Language", *Cognitive Psychology*, 1: 1–191; reprinted by Academic Press, New York, 1972. [1]

Winston, Patrick H., ed. 1975. *The Psychology of Computer Vision*. New York: McGraw Hill. [1]

Wittgenstein, Ludwig. 1921/74. "*Logisch-philosophische Abhandlung*", *Annalen der Naturphilosophie*, 14: 185–262. Translation, by David F. Pears and Brian F. McGuinness (German and English on facing pages, with Bertrand Russell's introduction): *Tractatus Logico-Philosophicus*. (London: Routledge & Kegan Paul, 1961, revised 1974.) [8]
—— 1962. *Philosophical Investigations*. (German and English on facing pages; translation by G.E.M. Anscombe.) New York: Macmillan. [13]

Woodfield, Andrew, ed. 1982. *Thought and Object*. Oxford: Clarendon Press. [7]

Wright, Crispin. 1980. *Wittgenstein on the Foundations of Mathematics*. London: Duckworth. [13]

Yevick, Meriam L. 1975. "Holographic or Fourier Logic", *Pattern Recognition*, 7: 197–213. [1]

Index

accountability, unit of 160
achievement
    constitution as 253, 279, 293, 298,
        353
    disclosure as 331, 333
    science as 259
Aesop 57
affordance 221–223
agents
    community members 312
    competent 142
    rational 159
    rule-followers 306
analog
    definition of 84
    devices 82–87
    images as ? 173
    not second-order digital 86–87
    second-order digital 84–86
animals
    as perceivers 241, 247
    don't understand 2, 254, 286,
        301–304
    have ersatz intentionality
        303–304
    supermonkeys 249–253, 255
anomalous monism 89–91
anomaly 135, 297
Anscombe, G.E.M. 305
ant, Simon's 209–211, 216, 218

approximation 83, 85–86
artificial intelligence 40, 47, 49–50,
    59–60, 138, 140, 157, 219
    See also GOFAI
ascription
    constraints on 139, 144, 146
    intentional 138–145
    principle of 142, 158
aspects (aspectual shape) 295, 298
Austin, J.L. 146
authenticity 342
autonomy (of objects) 280, 325, 330

background, the 61, 164, 180, 185,
    187, 194
Bailey's razor 113, 116, 119, 123
bandwidth (of coupling) 220–229,
    234–237
Bar-Hillel, Yehoshua 48, 51
baseball
    as constituted 320–321
    intentionality metaphor 127–162
behaviorism 42
    neo- versus paleo- 138
beholdenness
    theory of truth 346–348
    to objects 254, 278, 348
    to satisfaction conditions 299
being 269, 282–284, 318, 356

being-in-the-world 361

biography 58, 141

black box 18
   intentional (IBB) 21–28, 138, 142

Block, Ned 88, 163

Brandom, Robert 4, 147, 169, 317,
   355, 356, 357–358

Brooks, Rodney 217–221, 232

calculus of individuals 110

care/caring 2, 55
   See also commitment *and* involvement

causality
   and Humean identity 67–70
   and normativity 128, 136, 141, 151,
     152, 158, 345–346
   and strict laws 90–92
   robust versus mathematical 93,
     106

censoriousness 147–149

charismatic florist 316–317, 351

chess
   as constituted 277–279, 321–324,
     327–329, 331–332
   as instituted 151
   automatic 321–322
   compared to science 257–258
   empirical 329–331
   esoteric 327–329
   illegal moves paradoxical 332
   illegal moves unacceptable 251,
     278, 342
   in the Life world 276
   perception 247–251, 295–297
   pieces aren't things 247–248,
     280–282, 329
   players of 18–19, 22, 32, 36, 47–48,
     55–56, 139, 278–279
   stance 297

supervenience example 104
   trying to win 55–56, 139, 250, 340
   without language 249–250,
     254–257

chicken-sexers 327

cogency conditions 22–23, 25,
   37–40

cognition, verbal 146–147

cognitive processes 26

cognitivism 9–43

coherence
   and interpretation 133
   internal versus external 133,
     345–346
   situational 54
   theory of truth 344–348

coin, two sides of 6, 353

commitment
   as transcendental ground 304
   constitutive 252, 257–259,
     340–343
   deontic 320, 341–342
   existential 2, 340–343
   scientific 257–259, 343, 360
   to rules or standards 252, 278,
     284, 297–301, 340

common sense, holism of 48–52

competence 142

complexity 76

compliance and inertness clause 321,
   329, 330

components
   of a pattern 207, 267–268, 271
   of a system 13, 29–30, 212–214

computers
   definition of 137
   don't give a damn 47, 60
   don't understand 286, 301–304

conceivable (versus possible)
332–333

concepts
having/applying 247, 256, 361
structured 50

concreteness 121, 349

conditioning 147, 311

conditions of possibility 254, 341

conformism 147–151, 311–313

connectionism 195–199, 301
See also distributed representation

consciousness 159, 294, 300

constitution
definition of (letting be) 325
versus institution 318, 337–338

constitutive
commitment 252, 257–259,
340–343
regulations 320
rules 318–320
skills 323–325, 334–336
standards 252, 257–262, 279, 286,
293, 320–326, 332–333
definition of 320

content
elements of
absolute 191
associative 201
relative 193
non-standard usage 203
piggyback 187
skeletal versus fleshed-out
185–189

contingent, the 112, 114, 121–122, 128

convention 150, 320

copyability, perfect 75–76, 78

correctness
and objectivity 338
objects as criteria for 276, 279,
314, 337–338, 343

of perception 253–254
of recognitions 273
versus propriety 309–310,
313–317, 337–338

counting as 269, 326

coupling
with the world 220, 223–228, 234
within/among components 159,
215, 218

criteria, objects as 276, 279, 314,
337–338, 343

Cummins, Robert 12

custom/practice, social 4, 147–152,
207, 235, 311–313

dasein 167, 170, 287

Davidson, Donald 17, 23, 48, 89–96,
105, 106, 161, 258–260, 269,
345, 352, 357, 360

de Groot, Adriaan D. 36

default assignments 50

definition 50, 75

Dennett, Daniel C. 59, 104, 138, 147,
161, 249, 260, 267–287,
291–304, 348

Derrida, Jacques 131

Descartes, René 112, 127, 131, 207,
223, 233, 288

describability 89–91

design stance 283, 303
See also "how it works"

determination (by physics) 109–111,
114–120

determinism (lack of) 99

Dewey, John 153, 233

digital
definition of 78
devices 75–82

language as ? 173
second-order 84–86
simulation 85–87
why language is 168–169
dimensions
of analog devices 83–86
of iconic contents 192–193
of instantiation 28
direction of fit 305–306, 311, 313
disclosure 331, 333, 351–352
dispositions 12, 140, 147–151, 356
second-order or meta 147, 311
distributed representation 140, 157,
174, 195, 198–203, 232
dog (would bark) 262
domain 96–98, 101
constituted 260, 298, 352
double checking 252, 279
Dretske, Fred 242–246, 253
Dreyfus, Hubert L. 36, 52, 105, 147,
224–225, 229–233

eliminative materialism 107
embodiment 223–228
emergence 151
empirical testability 333–336
engineering 80, 169
environment. See world
equilibrium, precarious 333–336,
344–345
equipment/tools 152–154, 232–237
error 145, 260, 273, 334–336
eternal, the 112, 120–121
events
mental versus physical 89–91
robust versus mathematical
91–94, 101, 106

evolution
biological 151, 308
cultural/social 151, 312
excluded zone 331–333, 337, 347, 353
exhaustion (by physics) 109–111,
114–123
existential
commitment 2, 340–343
holism 55–60
explanation
and encapsulation 29–30
and understanding 10, 113, 260,
286, 353
deductive-nomological 10, 260
derivational-nomological 11, 38
morphological 12
multiple 117
systematic 13–14, 24, 26, 41, 308
explicit
rules 39, 149, 248, 306–307, 311
versus implicit 186

falsifiability 290, 351
feedback 226, 250
fiber-optics bundle 11–12
Field, Hartry 132
finitude 295
Fodor, Jerry A. 17, 88, 91, 132, 161,
269, 355
Frege, Gottlob 317
functional components 13, 29–30,
212–214

games
as self-contained 256
formal 82
perils of, as examples 320, 327,
329–330, 343
versus language 155, 256
versus science 257–258, 343

Gibson, James J. 221–223

giving up the game 252, 259, 279, 284, 297, 301, 342

GOFAI 202, 301–304
See also artificial intelligence

Goodman, Nelson 78–81, 84, 293

Grice, H. Paul 63, 145–146

grocking 315–316

Hare, Richard 107

Heidegger, Martin 2, 4, 147, 167, 170, 233, 317, 356, 357, 358, 361

Hellman, Geoffrey 109–111, 118, 120–121

Hempel, Carl G. 10

hermeneutics 54–55

Hobbes, Thomas 127

holism
 and patterns 130–132, 135, 208
 and systematicity 134–136, 139
 common-sense 48–52
 existential 55–60
 not in Hume 69
 of biological function 308
 of interpretation 47–48, 134–135, 268
 of representation 173
 prior versus real-time 49–50
 situation 52–54
 vapid 130–132, 138, 147

holograms 31–33, 36, 176, 182

"how it works" 13, 38, 283

Hume, David 63–71, 317

Husserl, Edmund 71

hylomorphism 120–121

identity theory
 token 91, 96–100, 109–111, 114–123, 132, 140, 346
  counterexample to (chess) 281–282
 versus implementation 247–248, 289, 329
 type 91, 109, 132

identity, personal (Hume) 63–71

implicit
 versus explicit 186
 versus tacit 142

incommensurability 352

incompatibility
 among mundane results 333–335
 objects as loci of 337, 348

independent
 objects as 314, 330, 344–345
 versus alien (constraint) 345–348

individuals, calculus of 110

information
 carrying 242–245, 309, 313
 processing system (IPS) 24–28, 210

insight 37–40

insistence 252, 254, 256, 259–261, 286, 341

instantiation (physical and intentional) 26–28

institution
 (process) 151, 157–158, 207, 310–311
 (product) 112, 147, 151, 235, 311–313, 314–317
 versus constitution 318, 337–338

integrity (of things) 261–262, 348–349

intelligence and meaning 18, 230–237

intelligibility 37–40, 113, 116, 215–217, 298, 353
intentional
  ascription 138–145
  black box (IBB) 21–28, 138, 142
  instantiation 27
  interpretation 17–28, 47–48, 133–138, 207, 275
  stance 268, 283, 286–287, 292–293
  states 21, 267
  systems theory 249
intentionality 127–162
  as normative 128, 157–158, 294–295
  as-if 301–302
  ersatz 301–304
  intrinsic versus observer-relative 163, 164, 294, 299
  mental 129
  original versus derivative 129, 136–137, 145, 156, 163, 232
interaction
  among tokens 136–138
  intrasystematic 13, 24, 30, 211–215
  with environment 138–145, 218–219
interfaces 30, 213–215
interpretation
  and making sense 19–23, 48, 55, 133–135
  constraints on 27, 37, 134–135
  de-/re-interpretation 24, 26–28
  holism of 47–48, 134, 135, 268
  intentional 17–28, 47–48, 133–138, 207, 275
  principle of 134, 158
  radical 268, 339
  scheme of 18, 49, 277
  textual 54
interrelationism 207–208
intimacy 207–209, 217, 223, 237

involvement, subjective/personal 56–60, 339–340
  See also commitment
isomorphism 174

Kant, Immanuel 112, 254, 298, 317, 354, 356, 358, 361
Kemp Smith, Norman 65
Kim, Jaegwon 95–96
know-how. See skills/know-how
knowledge (versus understanding) 286, 353
Kuhn, Thomas S. 2, 42, 258–259, 352, 360

language
  and ascription 145–147
  as constituted 256, 344
  as social practice 153–156
  natural 47–60
  objectivity without 249–250, 254–257
  of thought 138, 140, 163, 355
  versus games 155, 256
laws
  and explanation 10–11, 353
  physical 90, 99
  psycho-physical 17, 95
  strict 90–91, 114
  versus norms 317
learning 35, 37, 147, 197, 255–256, 309–311
letting be 286, 325–327, 329, 337, 352
Lettvin, Jerrold 104
levels (within systems) 16, 212
Lewis, David 80–81, 84, 150, 161, 355
Life world (game of Life) 270–271
  chess in 276
love and faith 2, 341

MacNabb, D.G.C. 66

making sense
  and intentionality 292
  and interpretation 19–23, 48, 55,
      133, 135
  as mark of the mental 1
  behavior as 139
  definition of 353
  disclosure as 331, 352
  of chess pieces 329
  of the world 37–40
  phenomena as 318
  understanding speech 181

Marr, David 30

materialism 3–4, 15, 291
  eliminative 107, 115
  physicalist 109–123
  vapid 128–131, 151

mattering (to someone) 55–56, 250
  See also commitment and involve-
      ment

McDowell, John 355, 357, 360

meaning 17–26, 59
  See also intentionality and repre-
      sentation

meaningful, intelligence abides in
      the world as 230–237

measurement. See observation

medium independence 76, 82

mental
  events 89–91
  intentionality 129
  the mark of 1

Merleau-Ponty, Maurice 233

Mill, John Stuart 317

monism, anomalous 89–91

moods 33–35

moral (of a story) 58

mousetrap psychology 143–145

mundane skills 323–325, 334–336

muscular gestalts 224–226

Nagel, Thomas 162

naturalism 317

network, connectionist 195–199

neurons 29–30, 202

Newell, Allen 217

normative
  and causal both 345–346
  biological functions as 158, 303,
      308–310
  constraints on interpretation
      134–135
  effect (versus force) 306
  ersatz 303
  force/authority 149, 252, 306,
      308, 311, 320, 333, 341, 343
  institutions as 148–150, 311–313
  intentionality as 128, 157–158,
      294–295
  perception as 253–254, 296
  recognition as 272, 276–278
  representation as 172
  status 154–156, 314, 325, 353
  the meaningful as 232
  versus causal/regular 150, 317
  versus factual (rules) 306

objectivity
  and correctness 314, 317, 338
  and truth 316, 317, 343
  everyday 260–262
  of perception 253–254
  scientific 257–259, 351–354
  without language 249–250,
      254–257, 359

objects
  as accessible/resistant 325, 338,
      342, 347, 353

as authoritative/criterial 276, 279,
    325, 343
as autonomous/independent 314,
    325, 330, 344–345
as constituted 284, 286, 325, 329,
    337
as loci of incompatibility 337, 348
combination in 261, 332, 333, 359
definition of 325
in a formal sense 241, 325, 348
of perception 242, 246, 250–251,
    253–254, 262, 298
recognized 272–273
    See also thing
observation 48, 257–259, 334, 338,
    359, 360
Ockham's razor 113
    See also Bailey's razor
ontology 113, 267, 280, 297
    regional 298
Oppenheim, Paul 10

Papert, Seymour 59
paradigm 42, 259–260, 298
    imposter 42
patterns
    among Humean ideas 68–70
    and holism 130–132, 135, 208
    and subpatterns 68, 248, 271,
        276–277
    and their elements 267–268
    association of 32, 196
    gestalts 247
    in PDP networks 196–200
    of behavior 275, 292–293
    of interaction with environment
        4, 138–145, 218
    of interpretable tokens 19–23, 31,
        37, 132–138
    of intrasystematic interaction
        13–14

orderly arrangements 273–278
    recognition of 32, 36, 197–201,
        271–278
    versus randomness 272–273
    ways of life as 147, 151
perception 22, 138, 219–223, 295–297
    and understanding 242, 247
    animal 241, 247
    objective correctness of 253–254
perfection 77–78, 83
person: first/third 162, 339
personal identity (Hume) 63–71
phenomena
    and interpretation 21
    constituted as objective 284, 325
    recognition of 252
physical
    definition of 258
    determination 109–111, 114–120
    events 89–91
    exhaustion 109–111, 114–123
    instantiation 27
    primacy of 94, 99
    two senses of 93
physicalism 94, 103, 109–123
physics
    and digital simulation 87
    and ordinary events 92
    reduction to 17
pineal gland 223, 228
Popper, Karl R. 290, 351–352, 361
positive procedure 77–82, 85
possibility
    actuality implies 353
    and possible worlds 100, 191
    and reality 262
    and understanding 286, 353
    conditions of 254, 341
    versus conceivability 332–333

practice/custom, social 4, 147–152, 207, 235, 311–313

pragmatics 60

pragmatism 170, 317, 356–358, 358
  neo 147–156

precarious equilibrium 333–336, 344–345

present and manifest, not 172, 230–231, 324

primitive magnitudes 84

principle of charity 48, 165, 207

problem solving 25–26, 219

procedure
  approximation 83, 86
  positive 77–82, 85
  reliable 77

progress, scientific 42, 112

property
  definition of 261, 349–350
  intrinsic 23, 129, 261, 280, 349

propriety (versus correctness) 309–310, 313–317, 337–338

psychologism 317

psychology
  cognitive 9–43, 132
  mousetrap 143–145
  scientific 26, 40–43

Putnam, Hilary 12, 17

Pylyshyn, Zenon W. 132

Quine, W.V.O. 18, 44, 48, 123, 138, 288

randomness (versus pattern) 272–273

rationality 18, 133–134, 141, 156, 260, 284, 293

Rawls, John 318–320

realism 280

reasoning 25, 33, 219

recognition
  and distributed representation 197–203
  as a mundane skill 331–333
  normativity of 272, 276–278
  of objects 272–273
  of patterns 32, 36, 197–201, 271–278
  of phenomena 252
  outer versus inner 285–286
  versus differential response 272, 276

reduction
  and type identity 109, 116, 132
  intentional 26–28
  nomological 16, 94
  systematic 16–17
  vapid 132, 134

regularity (versus norm) 150, 317

reliability
  of chess as achievement 298
  of digital procedures 77
  of skills 322, 334
    definition of 334

representation 171–203
  as normative 172
  as standing in for 172, 230
  distributed 140, 157, 174, 195, 198–203, 232
  iconic or image-like 174, 192–194
  internal or mental 188, 230
  logical or language-like 4, 174, 190–191, 193
  quasilinguistic 18–21, 35
  scheme of 172–173, 188, 200, 231
  symbolic 219–221
  versus recording 177–185

resemblance
  and Humean identity 67

and representation 133, 174
   See also similarity
resilience
   of commitment 341
   of digital devices 86
   of skills or abilities 322, 334
      definition of 322
resistance (of objects) 338, 342, 347,
   353
resoluteness 252, 341
responsibility
   deontic versus existential 342
   for one's skills and concepts 343,
      356
revolution
   conceptual 336
   scientific 259
roles (instituted) 147, 152–153, 160,
   312–313
Rorty, Richard 131, 317, 356, 360
rule-following 149, 305–308, 313,
   341, 354
rules
   basic (governing) 307, 309, 311, 313
   constitutive 318–320
   exhibited versus governing
      305–307, 341
   explicit 39, 149, 248, 306–307, 311
   expressed versus articulated 307
   made to be broken 135
   normative versus factual 306
   of thumb 90, 318
   regress of 307, 344
   regulative 319
Rumelhart, David 61

San Jose, the way to 234
satisfaction conditions 156,
   294–296, 299

scheme
   conceptual 298, 352
   for expressing rules 149, 306–307
   of interpretation 18, 49, 277
   representational 172–173, 188,
      200, 231
science
   and constitutive standards
      258–260, 343
   as achievement 259
   as worldly 236
   cognitive psychology as 40–43
   not a game 257–258, 343
   unexplained explainers 15, 17, 70
   unity of 15, 17, 111, 228
scientist (being one) 259, 360
Searle, John R. 131, 146, 163, 164,
   291–304, 305, 318–320
segregation strategy 34–36
self. *See* subject/self
Sellars, Wilfrid 147, 167, 176, 345,
   354, 355, 359
semantic
   activity versus inertness 137
   articulation 137, 146
   compositionality 20, 137, 174
   intrigue 144–146
similarity 32, 196–198, 201
Simon, Herbert A. 16, 30, 209–211,
   215–220
   ant example 209–211, 216, 218
simulation (digital) 85–87
situated
   action 201
   cognition 209
   tokens 134
situation, holism of 52–54
skills/know-how
   and distributed representation
      198–201

as co-constituted 279, 324, 346
as reliable and resilient 322, 334
Brooks's robots 218
chess 36, 257, 323, 328
constitutive 323–325, 334–336
coupling with world 220,
    223–228, 234
definition of 322
different from thought 35–36, 159
mundane 323–325, 334–336
not witless 180
recognition as 279, 286, 331–333
revision or repair of 334–336, 342
Skinner, B.F. 131
social practices 4, 147–152, 207, 235,
    311–313
solipsism 207
Stalnaker, Robert 138, 147
stance (à la Dennett) 282–284, 287,
    297, 300, 341
    See also intentional: stance
standards
    constitutive 252, 257–262, 279,
        286, 293, 320–326, 332–333
    holding things to 254, 261
status, normative 154–156, 314, 325,
    353
Stroud, Barry 70
subject/self
    and beliefs/desires 294
    as constituted 299–300
    identity of (Hume) 63–71
    involvement of 56–60, 339–340
    rational agent 159
    thinking thing 159
    unit of social accountability 160
substance. *See* thing
subsumption (and the physical) 90,
    258
success (and ascription) 142

super-monkeys 249–253, 255
Supertrap 144
supervenience
    and token identities 94–98
    nomological 99
    ontological 109–120
    weak 96–105, 109–120
syntax 81, 137, 168–169
synthetic a priori 259
system 299
    and subsystems 211–214
    definition of 13–14, 213
    information processing (IPS)
        24–28, 210
    intentional (unity of) 299
    levels within 16, 212
    mind-body-world 209
    nervous 29–30
systematicity (lest holism be trivial)
    134–136, 139

tacit (versus implicit) 142
teleology, ersatz 303
tell, ability to
    and conformism 151
    and constitutive standards 285
    and information 242
    as a skill 229
    definition of 313
    in chess play 251, 278–279, 323,
        328
    properly versus correctly 313–317
    properties (of things) 349
    recognition as 272
    what makes sense 37
    what's in a scene 189, 194
    whether objects comply 347
temporal, the 112, 114, 121–122
theory-laden-ness 358

thing (*res*)
  chess pieces are not 247–248,
    280–282, 329
  definition of 261, 348–350
  sense of 'physical' 93
  standards for 261, 264, 350
Thompson, Frank 109–111, 118,
  120–121
tokens and types 20–21, 76–79, 91,
  132–137
  See also identity theory
  type identity of tokens 78–79
tools/equipment 152–154, 232–237
transduction 146, 203, 220, 223–225
translation
  and understanding 49, 56
  indeterminacy of 44
  mechanical 41
  radical 18, 48, 133, 268
transubstantiation 82, 131
truth 142, 156
  and objectivity 316, 317, 317, 343
  as normative constraint 134
  beholdenness theory 346–348
  coherence theory 344–348
  not just consensus 316
  See also correctness
Turing machine 270
Turing test 294
Turing's piano 178–179

understanding
  and cognitivism 36–40
  and constitution 254, 353
  and explanation/laws/science 10,
    113, 260, 286, 353
  and perception 242, 247
  and possibility 286, 353
  animals and computers lack 254,
    286, 301–304

as mark of the mental 1
of natural language 41, 47–60
versus knowledge 286, 353, 361

vapid
  holism 130–132, 138, 147
  materialism 128–131, 151
  reduction 132, 134
vicarious coping 230–231, 302
vigilance 251–252, 259, 335

wave hits (on corks) 101–103
way of life 147, 151, 341
What else could it be? 31–33
Wilks, Yorick 51
witless (recording) 180
Wittgenstein, Ludwig 147, 176, 233,
  354
world/environment, the
  as meaningful 231–237
  coupling with 220, 223–228, 234
  interaction with 138–145, 218–219
  interpretation and 133
  its own best model 219, 232
  making sense of 37–40